新TOEIC® テストスコア別攻略シリーズ 5

新TOEIC® テスト 990点攻略

濵﨑潤之輔・著

JN238496

旺文社

はじめに

900点の壁を超えられずにもがき続けていた頃，1年間に数十冊のTOEIC対策本を使って勉強に明け暮れた。だが，どんなに頑張ってみてもスコアは全く伸びなかった。学習法を根本から見直し，1冊の本から徹底的に学び尽くすやり方に変更。半年後の公開テストでは，100点以上のスコアアップを実現し，970点を取ることができた。

その後は990点取得を目指して学習を継続，コンスタントに990点近くを取ることができるようになった。しかし，990点満点を目指すのであれば，今のやり方では実現するはずがない。さまざまな教材と学習法を実践して成果を検証，同時に「いかに自分の努力が足りていないのか」を再認識することにより，自らを律し鼓舞し続けてきた。その結果，僕がつかんだこと。それは，「諦めずに挑戦し続けようとする気持ちさえあれば，990点は誰にでも手が届く世界にあり，あり得ないような努力や能力は必要ない」ということである。

本書は990点を狙う学習者の盲点となる問題を集約し，効果的に訓練を積めるように仕上げた。無駄な問題は1問たりとも収録しておらず，選択肢に登場する難語も過去の公開テストに登場したものを入れるようにした。

900点取得に必要な訓練と，990点取得に必要な訓練の間にある「差」。990点取得者と，取得していない学習者の間にある「小さな差」をカバーする訓練を，是非，本書で徹底的に積んでほしい。この本が990点という「高嶺の花」をつかむことにこだわり続けるあなたのお役に立てるよう，心から願っている。

濵﨑潤之輔

もくじ

編集：岩村明子，山田弘美
編集協力：株式会社メディアビーコン，鹿島由紀子，Michael Joyce，Sarah Matsumoto
装丁デザイン：内津剛（及川真咲デザイン事務所）装丁写真：荒川潤
本文デザイン：尾引美代　本文イラスト：村林タカノブ
録音：有限会社スタジオユニバーサル（Chris Koprowski，Julia Yermakov（以上，米），
Michael Rhys（英），Guy Perryman（豪），Carolyn Miller（加））

本書の使い方

本書は以下の要素で構成されています。特長をしっかり把握して，より効果的に本書をご活用ください。

▶990点獲得のポイントと攻略法

990点を獲得するためのポイントを確認します。例題を解いた後，「これがHUMMER式アプローチ！」を読み，それぞれのポイントを押さえましょう。

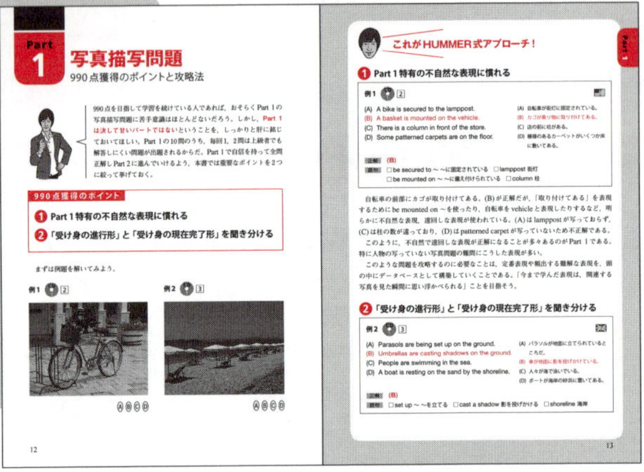

Part 1 写真描写問題
990点獲得のポイントと攻略法

990点を目指して学習を続けている人であれば，おそらくPart 1の写真描写問題に苦手意識はほとんどないだろう。しかし，Part 1は決して甘いパートではないということを，しっかりと肝に銘じておいてほしい。Part 1の10問のうち，毎回1，2問は上級者でも解答しにくい問題が出題されるからだ。Part 1で自信を持って全問正解しPart 2に進んでいけるよう，本書では重要なポイントを2つに絞って挙げておく。

990点獲得のポイント
1 Part 1特有の不自然な表現に慣れる
2 「受け身の進行形」と「受け身の現在完了形」を聞き分ける

まずは例題を解いてみよう。

例1 2
例2 3

Ⓐ Ⓑ Ⓒ Ⓓ　Ⓐ Ⓑ Ⓒ Ⓓ

12

これがHUMMER式アプローチ！

1 Part 1特有の不自然な表現に慣れる

例1 2
(A) A bike is secured to the lamppost. (A) 自転車が街灯に固定されている。
(B) A basket is mounted on the vehicle. (B) カゴが乗り物に取り付けてある。
(C) There is a column in front of the store. (C) 店の前に柱がある。
(D) Some patterned carpets are on the floor. (D) 模様のあるカーペットがいくつか床に敷いてある。

正解 (B)
語句 □be secured to ～ ～に固定されている □lamppost 街灯
□be mounted on ～ ～に備え付けられている □column 柱

自転車の前部にカゴが取り付けてある。(B)が正解だが，「取り付けてある」を表現するためにbe mounted on ～を使ったり，自転車をvehicleと表現したりするなど，明らかに不自然な表現，遠回しな表現が使われている。(A)はlamppostが写っておらず，(C)は柱の数が違っており，(D)はpatterned carpetが写っていないため不正解である。
このように，不自然で遠回しな表現が正解になることが多々あるのがPart 1である。特に人物の写っていない写真問題の難問にこうした表現が多い。
このような問題を攻略するのに必要なことは，定番表現や頻出する難解な表現を，頭の中にデータベースとして構築していくことである。「今まで学んだ表現は，関連する写真を見た瞬間に思い浮かべられる」ことを目指そう。

2 「受け身の進行形」と「受け身の現在完了形」を聞き分ける

例2 3
(A) Parasols are being set up on the ground. (A) パラソルが地面に立てられているところだ。
(B) Umbrellas are casting shadows on the ground. (B) 傘が地面に影を投げかけている。
(C) People are swimming in the sea. (C) 人々が海で泳いでいる。
(D) A boat is resting on the sand by the shoreline. (D) ボートが海岸の砂浜に置いてある。

正解 (B)
語句 □set up ～ ～を立てる □cast a shadow 影を投げかける □shoreline 海岸

13

▶Training

Partごとに考えられたトレーニングで，990点獲得のために必要な力をつけるページです。問題形式はTOEICとは異なります。

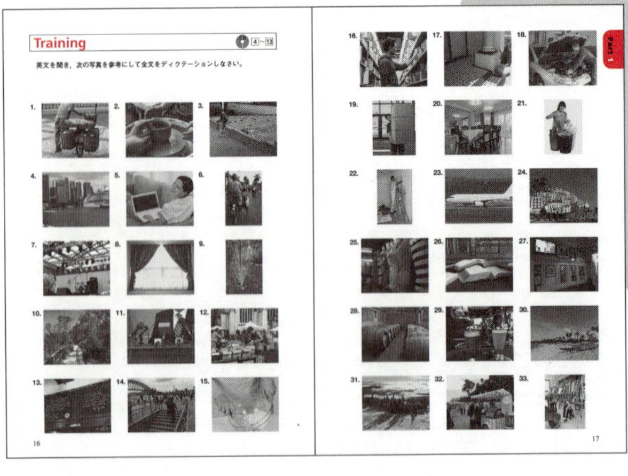

Training 4～13

英文を聞き，次の写真を参考にして全文をディクテーションしなさい。

1. 2. 3. 4. 5. 6. 7. 8. 9. 10. 11. 12. 13. 14. 15.

16

16. 17. 18. 19. 20. 21. 22. 23. 24. 25. 26. 27. 28. 29. 30. 31. 32. 33.

17

▶Practice Test

「990点獲得のポイントと攻略法」と「Training」で学んだ内容がしっかりと身に付いているか，問題を解いて確かめましょう。

Practice Test 29～34

最初の発言と続く3つの選択肢を聞き，最も適切な答えを(A) (B) (C)の中から1つ選びなさい（マークシートは別冊p.158にあります）。

1. Mark your answer on your answer sheet.
2. Mark your answer on your answer sheet.
3. Mark your answer on your answer sheet.
4. Mark your answer on your answer sheet.
5. Mark your answer on your answer sheet.
6. Mark your answer on your answer sheet.
7. Mark your answer on your answer sheet.
8. Mark your answer on your answer sheet.
9. Mark your answer on your answer sheet.
10. Mark your answer on your answer sheet.
11. Mark your answer on your answer sheet.
12. Mark your answer on your answer sheet.
13. Mark your answer on your answer sheet.
14. Mark your answer on your answer sheet.
15. Mark your answer on your answer sheet.

46

16. Mark your answer on your answer sheet.
17. Mark your answer on your answer sheet.
18. Mark your answer on your answer sheet.
19. Mark your answer on your answer sheet.
20. Mark your answer on your answer sheet.
21. Mark your answer on your answer sheet.
22. Mark your answer on your answer sheet.
23. Mark your answer on your answer sheet.
24. Mark your answer on your answer sheet.
25. Mark your answer on your answer sheet.
26. Mark your answer on your answer sheet.
27. Mark your answer on your answer sheet.
28. Mark your answer on your answer sheet.
29. Mark your answer on your answer sheet.
30. Mark your answer on your answer sheet.

Part 2

47

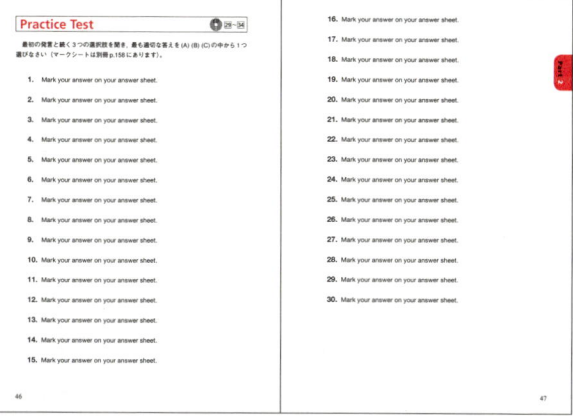

▶Final Test（模擬テスト）

本冊での全ての学習が終わったら，別冊のFinal Testを解いてみましょう。問題は実際のTOEICテストよりやや難しめに作ってあります。予想スコア換算表が付いていますので，本番での予想スコアを出すこともできます。

READING TEST

In the Reading test, you will read a variety of texts and answer several different types of reading comprehension questions. The entire Reading test will last 75 minutes. There are three parts, and directions are given for each part. You are encouraged to answer as many questions as possible within the time allowed.

You must mark your answers on the separate answer sheet. Do not write your answers in your test book.

PART 5

Directions: A word or phrase is missing in each of the sentences below. Four answer choices are given below each sentence. Select the best answer to complete the sentence. Then mark the letter (A), (B), (C), or (D) on your answer sheet.

101. A restructuring of the major divisions will end up taking place after SO & T ------- Supersoft next month.
(A) foresees
(B) acquires
(C) rests
(D) merges

102. The annual shareholders' meeting will be held in the Hamptons in ------- with company tradition.
(A) connecting
(B) keeping
(C) realizing
(D) concluding

103. For being a senior partner at Berizon and Rukoil Law Firm, frequent travel to other countries is one of the -------.
(A) recoupment
(B) requirements
(C) reflections
(D) refurbishment

104. Mr. Moskovitz reviewed the latest proposal and ------- it to the manager for approval.
(A) continued
(B) extinguished
(C) forwarded
(D) converted

18

105. Von Vai Industry's new fall line of siding for houses is guaranteed to ------- the look of your house.
(A) quicken
(B) depict
(C) exemplify
(D) enhance

106. Please print your address on the label in the space provided and ------- it to the top of the bottle.
(A) abide
(B) affix
(C) detach
(D) confine

107. Donations to the Takashi Tanaka & Family Home will be greatly appreciated, yet are only -------.
(A) optional
(B) usable
(C) individual
(D) candid

108. The new attorneys and counselors must be under the supervision of a senior manager for several months before they are ------- any clients.
(A) garnered
(B) assumed
(C) incurred
(D) assigned

109. This will be the ------- biggest merger in the history of our company.
(A) one
(B) any
(C) single
(D) most

110. Due to the ------- of a self-development training program at Ballmer Company, staff absenteeism has been reduced to 10 percent.
(A) implementation
(B) temptation
(C) independency
(D) indemnity

111. Follow the ------- of steps to unlock the emergency exit door, or you will not be able to open it again.
(A) orbit
(B) sequence
(C) instruction
(D) expertness

112. The mayor said that ------- should be placed on public health and security, rather than on the preservation of local traditions.
(A) tenseness
(B) priority
(C) routine
(D) measurement

Final Test・問題

GO ON TO THE NEXT PAGE →

19

ほかにも！

コラム

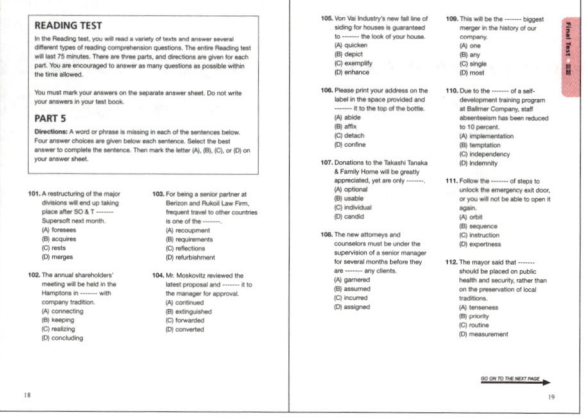

本編では書ききれなかったリスニング力向上のためのポイントや，990点を獲得した先輩の学習法などをまとめています。学習の合間に読んで，今後に役立てましょう。

TOEICテストとは？

アメリカで作成されている世界共通のテスト

TOEIC（Test of English for International Communication）とは，英語によるコミュニケーション能力を測定する世界共通のテスト。このテストは，アメリカにある非営利のテスト開発機関である ETS（Educational Testing Service）によって開発・制作されています。

10～990点までのスコアで評価

受験者の能力は合格・不合格ではなく，10～990点の5点刻みのスコアで評価されるのが特長です。

解答はマークシート方式

解答方法は，正解だと思う選択肢番号を塗りつぶすマークシート方式。解答を記述させる問題はありません。

TOEICテストの構成

Listening セクション，Reading セクションをあわせて全200問

TOEICテストは以下のように，Listening と Reading の2つのセクションで構成されています。2時間で200問に解答し，途中休憩はありません。

Listening 45分・100問	Part 1	写真描写問題・・・**10**問
	Part 2	応答問題・・・**30**問
	Part 3	会話問題・・・**30**問
	Part 4	説明文問題・・・**30**問
Reading 75分・100問	Part 5	短文穴埋め問題・・・**40**問
	Part 6	長文穴埋め問題・・・**12**問
	Part 7	読解問題　1つの文書・・・**28**問
		2つの文書・・・**20**問

実施スケジュール

年10回の実施

公開テストは，原則として年10回（1月，3月，4月，5月，6月，7月，9月，10月，11月，12月の日曜日）実施されます。ただし，受験地によって異なるので，事前に確認が必要です。

受験料 5,725円(消費税含む)。

受験申込

携帯電話やコンビニでも申し込みできる

公開テストは以下の方法で申し込みができます。申込方法によって申込期間が異なるので注意してください。

❶インターネット

TOEICの公式ホームページから申し込みができます。受験料は，クレジットカードやコンビニエンスストア店頭などで支払い可能です。携帯電話やスマートフォンでも申し込みできます。

❷コンビニ端末

セブンイレブンやローソンなどの店頭に設置されている情報端末を操作し，ガイダンスに従って申込手続を行います。受験料は印刷された払込票などをレジに提出して支払います。

? 問い合わせ先

一般財団法人 国際ビジネスコミュニケーション協会

●IIBC試験運営センター
〒100-0014　東京都千代田区永田町2-14-2　山王グランドビル
電話：03-5521-6033／FAX：03-3581-4783
（土・日・祝日・年末年始を除く10:00～17:00）

●名古屋事業所
〒460-0003　名古屋市中区錦2-4-3　錦パークビル
電話：052-220-0286（土・日・祝日・年末年始を除く10:00～17:00）

●大阪事業所
〒541-0059　大阪府大阪市中央区博労町3-6-1　御堂筋エスジービル
電話：06-6258-0224（土・日・祝日・年末年始を除く10:00～17:00）

●TOEIC公式ホームページ
http://www.toeic.or.jp/

※このページの情報は2014年6月現在のものです。詳細や変更は実施団体のホームページなどでご確認ください。

付属CDについて

付属のCDには [2] で示された個所の音声が収録されています。以下の収録内容一覧とともに，CD番号・トラック番号を確認の上，音声をご利用ください。

CD 1（収録時間約62分）

本冊のリスニング問題の音声が収録されています。

Unit	トラック番号
Part 1	2～16
Part 2	17～34
Part 3&4	35～54
Part 2正解	55～60

CD 2（収録時間約48分）

別冊（Final Test）のリスニング問題の音声が収録されています。

Part	トラック番号
Part 1	2～12
Part 2	13～43
Part 3	44～54
Part 4	55～65

注意：ディスクの裏面には，指紋，汚れ，傷などがつかないよう，お取り扱いにご注意ください。一部の再生機器（パソコン，ゲーム機など）では再生に不具合が生じることがありますので，ご承知おきください。

また，CDプレーヤーで正常に再生できるCDをパソコン等に取り込む際に不具合が生じた場合は，そのソフトウェアの製造元にお問い合わせください。

Part

1

写真描写問題

Part 1

写真描写問題

990点獲得のポイントと攻略法

990点を目指して学習を続けている人であれば，おそらくPart 1の写真描写問題に苦手意識はほとんどないだろう。しかし，**Part 1は決して甘いパートではない**ということを，しっかりと肝に銘じておいてほしい。Part 1の10問のうち，毎回1，2問は上級者でも解答しにくい問題が出題されるからだ。Part 1で自信を持って全問正解しPart 2に進んでいけるよう，本書では重要なポイントを2つに絞って挙げておく。

990点獲得のポイント

1. **Part 1特有の不自然な表現に慣れる**
2. **「受け身の進行形」と「受け身の現在完了形」を聞き分ける**

まずは例題を解いてみよう。

例1 2

Ⓐ Ⓑ Ⓒ Ⓓ

例2 3

Ⓐ Ⓑ Ⓒ Ⓓ

これがHUMMER式アプローチ！

1 Part 1特有の不自然な表現に慣れる

例1 CD 1 2

(A) A bike is secured to the lamppost.
(B) A basket is mounted on the vehicle.
(C) There is a column in front of the store.
(D) Some patterned carpets are on the floor.

(A) 自転車が街灯に固定されている。
(B) カゴが乗り物に取り付けてある。
(C) 店の前に柱がある。
(D) 模様のあるカーペットがいくつか床に敷いてある。

正解 **(B)**

語句 □be secured to ～ ～に固定されている □lamppost 街灯
□be mounted on ～ ～に備え付けられている □column 柱

自転車の前部にカゴが取り付けてある。(B)が正解だが，「取り付けてある」を表現するためにbe mounted on ～を使ったり，自転車をvehicleと表現したりするなど，明らかに不自然な表現，遠回しな表現が使われている。(A)はlamppostが写っておらず，(C)は柱の数が違っており，(D)はpatterned carpetが写っていないため不正解である。

このように，不自然で遠回しな表現が正解になることが多々あるのがPart 1である。特に人物の写っていない写真問題の難問にこうした表現が多い。

このような問題を攻略するのに必要なことは，定番表現や頻出する難解な表現を，頭の中にデータベースとして構築していくことである。「今まで学んだ表現は，関連する写真を見た瞬間に思い浮かべられる」ことを目指そう。

2 「受け身の進行形」と「受け身の現在完了形」を聞き分ける

例2 CD 1 3

(A) Parasols are being set up on the ground.
(B) Umbrellas are casting shadows on the ground.
(C) People are swimming in the sea.
(D) A boat is resting on the sand by the shoreline.

(A) パラソルが地面に立てられているところだ。
(B) 傘が地面に影を投げかけている。
(C) 人々が海で泳いでいる。
(D) ボートが海岸の砂浜に置いてある。

正解 **(B)**

語句 □set up ～ ～を立てる □cast a shadow 影を投げかける □shoreline 海岸

傘がいくつか立っていて，地面にその影を投げかけている。この問題のポイントはcasting shadowsという表現を知っているかどうかである。正解は(B)だ。(C)は海が見えているだけで，泳いでいる人は写真のどこにも見当たらない。(D)のshorelineは問題ないが，ボートはどこにも登場していないため不正解である。

この問題で注目したいのは(A)だ。これは受け身の進行形で，「今この瞬間に誰かによってパラソルが立てられている」という動作の進行を表しており，この問題では当然，不正解である。だが，これがParasols have been set up on the ground. だったらどうだろうか。これは,「立てられる」という動作が「完了」していることを表しているので，正解になり得る。

受け身の進行形の部分（are being set up）と，受け身の現在完了形の部分（have been set up）は非常に聞き分けにくいが，この部分を完璧に聞き分けることがPart 1で満点を目指す学習者にとっては重要だ。ここを正確に聞き取って，100％内容を理解できるようになるための訓練を積む必要がある。

超上級の技術

受け身の進行形と受け身の現在完了形について，もう少し見てみよう。次の例文のうち，写真を正しく描写しているのはどちらだろうか。

(1) Pottery is being exhibited on the shelves.
（陶器が棚に展示されている）

(2) Pottery has been set up on the shelves.
（陶器が棚に設置されている）

受け身の現在完了形である(2)が正しいことはすぐ分かるだろうが，実は(1)も正解である。

物が主語の受け身の進行形を聞くと「人が物に対して何か動作をしている最中である」と思ってしまいがちである。だが,(1)は何かの「動作」が継続していることを示しているのではなく,「展示される」という受け身の「状態」が今まさに継続中であることを示している。したがって受け身の進行形の場合，必ずしも人が何かの動作をしている最中とは限らないのである。be being exhibited「展示されている」, be being displayed「陳列されている」, be being reflected「映し出されている」などがこれに該当する表現だ。以下に例文を挙げておく。

(3) Some merchandise is being displayed in front of the store.
（いくつかの商品が店の前に展示されている）

(4) Some buildings are being reflected in the water.
（いくつかの建物が水面に映っている）

990点獲得への道

例2 (B)のcasting shadowsは，それほど難しい言い回しではない。だが，この英文が正解となるような写真を見て「これはcasting shadowsが来るかもしれない」と予想して音声を待ち構えることができれば，すでにTOEIC学習者として上級レベルにいると言っても差し支えないだろう。

毎回1～2問出題される難易度の高い問題は，他のパートにはあまり出現しない，なじみの薄い表現を含んでいることが多い。そのため，Part 1で出題される可能性のある表現をできる限りたくさんマスターしておく必要がある。**正解になり得る定番表現と，やや難解な表現をデータベースとして構築するための方法**として，本書では**ディクテーション**を推奨する。音を正確に認識し，文字として書き出すことにより，本当にその表現が身に付いているかどうかが一目瞭然となるからだ。

次ページ以降に，今後出題される可能性のある例文を50個用意した。Part 1特有の不自然な表現を中心に，受け身の進行形や受け身の現在完了形を含むものを多めに精選して掲載してある。

Part 1はシンプルなトレーニングを徹底的に繰り返すことが肝要であり，それによって確実に実力を養成していくことができる。ディクテーション以外にも，**オーバーラッピング，リピーティング，シャドーイング**を何回も繰り返して行うようにし，50個の例文を完璧にマスターしてほしい。

これらの表現をマスターすれば，Part 1に出題される難問に対応する力が飛躍的に伸びたことを実感できるはずである。

まとめ

Part 1は，ディクテーションで正解データベースを構築しよう！

Training

CD 1 4 ～ 13

英文を聞き，次の写真を参考にして全文をディクテーションしなさい。

1. 

2. 

3. 

4. 

5. 

6. 

7. 

8. 

9. 

10. 

11. 

12. 

13. 

14. 

15. 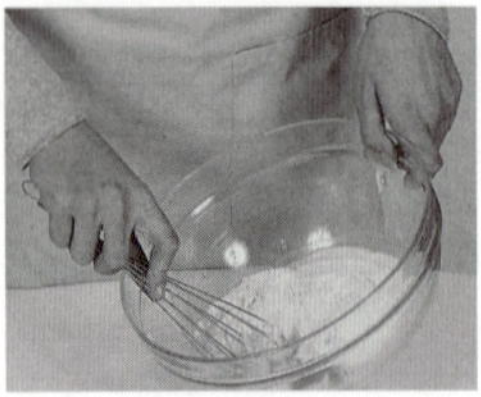

16.

17.

18.

19.

20.

21.

22.
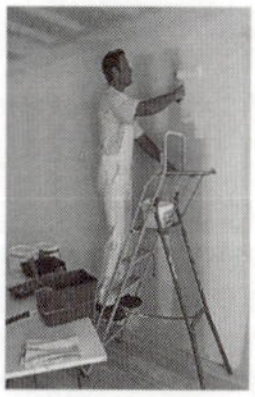

23.

24.

25.

26.

27.

28.

29.

30.

31.

32.

33.

34.

35.

36.

37.

38.

39.

40.

41.

42.

43.

44.

45.

46.

47.

48.

49.

50.

Training 英文と訳

CD 1 4～13

4

1. Some baskets are mounted on a bicycle.
(いくつかのカゴが自転車の上に取り付けてある)

2. Some people are molding some clay.
(何人かの人たちが粘土を形作っている)

□ mold ～を形作る
□ clay 粘土

3. Some stones have been used to create a wall.
(壁を作るために石が使われている)

4. Some high-rise buildings overlook the water.
(いくつかの高層ビルが水辺を見下ろしている)

□ high-rise building 高層ビル
□ overlook ～を見下ろす

5. The woman has turned away from her computer.
(女性がパソコンから顔を背けている)

□ turn away from ～
～から（顔・目などを）背ける

5

6. A man's head is sheltered by his hat.
(男性の頭が帽子によって隠されている)

□ be sheltered by ～
～に隠されている

7. Some equipment is suspended over the stage.
(いくつかの装置が舞台の上の方にぶら下がっている)

□ be suspended
ぶら下がっている

8. Some drapes are partially covering the window panes.
(カーテンが部分的に窓ガラスを覆っている)

□ drape カーテン
□ window pane 窓ガラス

9. Water is being sprayed from equipment.
(水が器具からまかれている)

□ be sprayed from ～
～からまかれる

10. A walkway is bordered by a low fence in the park.
(公園にある歩道が低いフェンスで仕切られている)

□ be bordered by ～
～で仕切られている

6

11. Some microphones are attached to the podium.
(いくつかのマイクが演台に取り付けてある)

□ be attached to ～
～に取り付けられている

12. Some things are being stored in boxes outside.
(物が屋外で箱の中に入れられている)

□ be stored in ～
～に収納される

13. A chalkboard is displaying menu items.
(黒板にメニューの品目が表示されている)

□ chalkboard 黒板

14. The staircase has railings on both sides.
(階段の両側に手すりがある)

□ staircase 階段

15. A man is stirring ingredients with a utensil.
(男性が器具で材料をかき混ぜている)

□ stir ～をかき混ぜる
□ utensil 器具

7

16. A man is browsing some books in the store.
（男性が店内で本を見て回っている）

□ browse ～を見て回る

17. There are patterned floor tiles on the porch.
（玄関に模様のある床タイルが敷いてある）

□ patterned 模様のある
□ porch 玄関

18. A mechanic is carrying out an inspection in the workshop.
（整備士が作業場で検査を行っている）

□ carry out ～ ～を実施する
□ inspection 検査
□ workshop 作業場，研修会

19. A stack of boxes is being transported by the man.
（積み重ねられた箱が男性によって運ばれている）

□ transport ～を運ぶ

20. A tablecloth has been draped on the table.
（テーブルクロスがテーブルに掛けられている）

□ drape ～を掛ける

8

21. A woman is sorting things into containers.
（女性が物を容器に仕分けしている）

□ sort ～を仕分けする
□ container 容器，コンテナー

22. A man standing on a ladder is applying paint to the wall.
（はしごの上に立っている男性が壁にペンキを塗っている）

□ apply A to B AをBに塗る，適用する

23. An aircraft is taxiing on the ground.
（飛行機が地面を滑走している）

□ taxi（航空機が）ゆっくり滑走する
□ ground 地面，着陸する

24. Houses are crowded together on the hillside.
（丘の斜面に家が密集している）

□ be crowded 密集している

25. Many clothes have been displayed inside the shop.
（たくさんの衣類が店の中に陳列されている）

9

26. Several reading materials have been piled on the desk.
（数冊の読み物が机の上に重ねられている）

27. Some artwork has been hung from a wall.
（いくつかの芸術作品が壁に掛けられている）

□ artwork 芸術作品
□ hang ～を掛ける

28. Some barrels have been laid in the warehouse.
（いくつかのたるが倉庫に置かれている）

□ barrel たる
□ warehouse 倉庫

29. Some beverages have been set on the counter.
（いくつかの飲み物がカウンターの上に置かれている）

30. Some boats have been resting on the beach.
(いくつかのボートが砂浜に置いてある)

□rest もたれかかっている，～を休ませる

10

31. Some trees are casting shadows on the land.
(いくつかの木が地面に影を投げかけている)

32. Some customers are being served at the food cart.
(何人かの客が食べ物を売っているカートで接客されている)

□be served 接客される

33. Some easels have been set up in the studio.
(いくつかのイーゼルがスタジオの中に立てられている)

□easel イーゼル
□be set up 立てられる

34. Some fish are being chilled on ice.
(何匹かの魚が氷の上で冷蔵されている)

□be chilled 冷やされる

35. An item has been taken out of the display case.
(商品が陳列ケースの外に出されている)

11

36. Some plates have been set next to the sink.
(いくつかの皿が流しの横に置かれている)

37. Some protective gear is worn by the women.
(防具が女性たちによって身に着けられている)

□protective gear 防具

38. Some sacks have been stacked in a warehouse.
(いくつかの袋が倉庫に積まれている)

39. Some foods are being displayed in a glass case.
(いくつかの食べ物がガラスケースの中に陳列されている)

40. Some vehicles have been left unattended on the street.
(何台かの車が通りに放置されている)

□be left unattended 放置される

12

41. The car's trunk has been opened.
(車のトランクが開けられている)

42. Heavy machinery is in use at a construction site.
(重機が建設現場で使われている)

□be in use 使用中である

43. The man is feeding a board into the machinery.
(男性が板を機械に押し込んでいる)

□feed (機械などに)～を押し込む，～に餌をやる

44. The women are examining an item.
(女性たちが商品を詳しく見ている)

□examine ～を詳しく見る

45. Some people are wearing gardening gloves.
（何人かの人たちがガーデニング用の手袋を着用している）

□gardening gloves ガーデニング用の手袋

13

46. A vehicle has been raised in the air in the workshop.
（乗り物が作業場で空中に持ち上げられている）

□be raised in the air 空中に持ち上げられる

47. The woman is crouching on the ground.
（女性が地面にかがんでいる）

□crouch かがむ

48. The women are holding different types of clothes.
（女性たちは違う種類の衣類を手にしている）

49. They are wearing headphones on their heads.
（彼らは頭にヘッドホンをしている）

□wear（ヘッドホン）を身に着けている

50. There are multiple levels of shelves in the library.
（図書館には複数の段のある棚がある）

□multiple levels 複数の段

Practice Test

CD 1 14～16

4つの英文を聞き，写真の状況を最も適切に説明しているものを (A) (B) (C) (D) の中から 1つ選びなさい（マークシートは別冊 p.158 にあります）。

1.

2.

3.

4.

5.

6.

7.

8.

9.

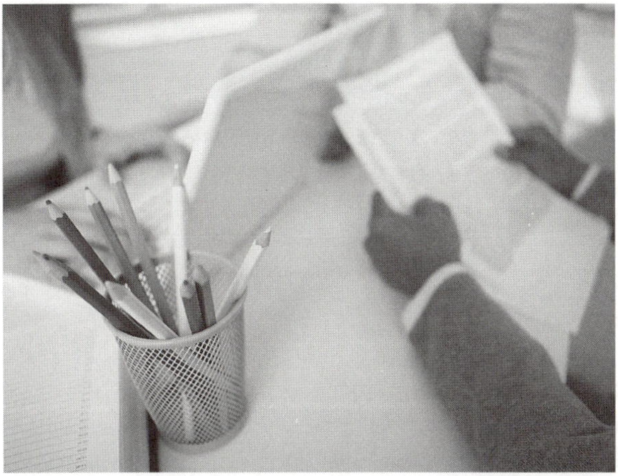

10.

1.

14

(A) A man is decorating the windowsill with pottery.
(B) A man is viewing some artwork in an exhibition.
(C) A man is washing the dirt from his hands.
(D) A man is molding some clay in a workshop.

(A) 男性が窓台を陶器で飾っている。
(B) 男性が展覧会で作品を見ている。
(C) 男性が手の汚れを洗い流している。
(D) 男性が作業場で粘土を形作っている。

正解 **(D)**

解説 (D)のmolding some clayという表現がポイントである。(A)はwindowsillが写真には写っておらず，(B)はviewという動作もexhibitionという場所も，写真からは確認することができない。(C)は，手は確かに汚れてはいるが，洗い流している最中ではない。

語句 □windowsill 窓台 □dirt 汚れ，土

2.

(A) A man is sweeping the carriage porch.
(B) A man is stacking boxes into piles.
(C) A man is doing chores in a storehouse.
(D) A man is organizing some brushes.

(A) 男性が車寄せを掃き掃除している。
(B) 男性が箱を積み重ねている。
(C) 男性が倉庫で雑用をしている。
(D) 男性がブラシを整理している。

正解 **(C)**

解説 正解の(C)は男性の動作をdo a chore「雑用をする」という表現で抽象的に表している。(A)の動作は正しいが，場所がcarriage porchではない。(B)はboxesが写っておらず，(D)はbrushを整理しているわけではないため不正解だ。

語句 □carriage porch 車寄せ □storehouse 倉庫 □organize ～を整理する

3.

(A) Some luggage is being unloaded out of an airplane.
(B) An aircraft is taxiing on the runway.
(C) The airport terminal has been closed.
(D) A ramp has been connected to the aircraft.

(A) 荷物が飛行機から降ろされている。
(B) 飛行機が滑走路をゆっくり滑走している。
(C) 空港のターミナルは閉鎖されている。
(D) タラップが飛行機に接続されている。

正解 **(D)**

解説 (D)のrampに「タラップ」という意味があることを知っているかどうかがポイントである。だが，知らなかったとしても他の選択肢が明らかに写真の状況と異なるので(D)を選べるだろう。(A)は荷物が写っていないので不正解。(B)も不正解だが，動詞のtaxi「(飛行機が) ゆっくり進む」は押さえておこう。(C)のターミナルの閉鎖は，写真からは判断できない。

語句 □runway 滑走路　□ramp タラップ，斜面，(高速道路への) 出入道路

4.

(A) An alley runs toward an archway.
(B) A path leads to the porch.
(C) Pedestrians are walking along the street.
(D) The ground is shaded by a lamppost.

(A) 小道がアーチに向かっている。
(B) 小道が玄関先につながっている。
(C) 歩行者が通りを歩いている。
(D) 地面が街灯に影を投げかけられている。

正解 **(A)**

解説 (A)のalleyと(B)のpathは両方とも「小道」だが，小道は扇状の部分がある建築物につながっているため(A)が正解だ。(B)のporch「玄関先」も時々登場する表現である。(C)はpedestriansが写っていないため不正解，(D)は街灯が写っていないため不正解。

語句 □archway (上にアーチがかかっている) 道　□pedestrian 歩行者

5.

15

(A) The doorway has been cleaned by the brush.
(B) The porch is being cleaned with the brush.
(C) A chair has been set next to the door.
(D) A chair is being set by the brush.

(A) 戸口がブラシで掃除されたところだ。
(B) 玄関先がブラシで掃除されているところだ。
(C) 椅子がドアの横に置かれている。
(D) 椅子がブラシのそばに置かれているところだ。

正解 **(C)**

解説 受け身の進行形と現在完了形が混在しており，不正解の選択肢も紛らわしいものが多い難問である。それでも(C)のhas been setをしっかりと聞き取れれば問題あるまい。掃除が完了しているかどうかは写真から判断できず，あるいはその最中でもないため，(A)，(B)は不正解。椅子が今まさに置かれている場面ではないため(D)も不正解だ。

語句 □doorway 戸口，玄関先

6.

(A) Some documents are being passed.
(B) Some documents are being examined by the women.
(C) Some documents are being scattered on the desk.
(D) Some documents are being written at the desk.
(A) いくつかの書類が手渡されているところだ。
(B) いくつかの書類が女性たちによって調べられているところだ。
(C) いくつかの書類が机の上にばらまかれているところだ。
(D) いくつかの書類が机で書かれているところだ。

正解 **(B)**

解説 (B)に出てくるexamineは書類やメニューを見ている写真の正解になることが多い。(A)のbeing passed, (C)の being scattered, (D)の being written はいずれも写真の状況とは一致しない。

語句 □scatter ～をまき散らす

7.

(A) Some flowers are being arranged by the doorway.
(B) Some people are using tap water by the window.
(C) Some people are decorating the windowsill with flowers.
(D) Some flowers have been arranged on the windowsill.
(A) いくつかの花が戸口のそばに並べられているところだ。
(B) 何人かの人たちが窓のそばで水道水を使っている。
(C) 何人かの人たちが窓台を花で飾っている。
(D) いくつかの花が窓台に並べられている。

正解 **(D)**

解説 花が窓台に並べられている状態を表している(D)が正解。(A)は, 花が並べられているところではなく, doorwayも写真に写っていないので不正解。(B)は人物が登場していない時点で不正解である。また, tap「蛇口」も写っていない。(C)はこの写真の状況を成立させる前の段階で人々が行ったはずの動作であり, 現在進行中の動作ではない。

語句 □tap water 水道水

8.

(A) The woman is pulling off her jacket.
(B) Some people are working on a sewing project together.
(C) The woman is putting on some clothes.
(D) Some people are purchasing a sewing machine.
(A) 女性が上着を脱いでいる。
(B) 何人かの人たちが縫い仕事を一緒に行っている。
(C) 女性が衣類を身に着けている。
(D) 何人かの人たちがミシンを購入している。

正解 **(B)**

解説 写真には2人の女性が何かを一緒に縫っている様子が写っている。(B)はその様子をworking on

a sewing project と，やや遠回しに表現している。(A) の pull off ～「～を脱ぐ」，(C) の put on ～「～を身に着ける」という動作は写真に登場しておらず，(D) は sewing machine を購入している場面ではないので不正解だ。

語句 □work on ～ ～に取り組む

9.

16

(A) Some writing tools have been collected in a cup.
(B) Some office supplies are scattered on the desk.
(C) Some people are putting mugs on the desk.
(D) Some writing materials have been in use at the desk.

(A) いくつかの筆記用具がカップの中にまとめられている。
(B) いくつかの事務用品が机の上に散らばっている。
(C) 何人かの人たちが机の上にマグカップを置いている。
(D) いくつかの筆記用具が机で使われている。

正解 **(A)**

解説 (A) は写真の状況を have been collected と受け身の現在完了形で的確に表している。(B) は scattered が写真の状況とは違っており，(C) は people が写っていない。(D) の be in use「使われている」かどうかは，この写真では判断できないので選択できない。

語句 □writing tools 筆記用具　□office supplies 事務用品（常に複数形）
□writing materials 筆記用具

10.

(A) The man is checking out some reading materials in the library.
(B) Some people are examining some library books.
(C) A librarian has been staffed at the counter.
(D) The man is returning some library books at the counter.

(A) 男性が図書館で読み物を借りている。
(B) 何人かの人たちが図書館の本を読んでいる。
(C) カウンターに図書館員が配置されている。
(D) 男性がカウンターで図書館の本を返却している。

正解 **(C)**

解説 (C) に登場する staff「職員を配置する」という動詞を覚えておこう。通例 be staffed で「(人が) 配置されている」という意味である。(A) の checking out は写真からは判断できないため不正解。(B) は examining some library books という動作が写っておらず，(D) の returning は写真からは判断できないため不正解である。想像で選ばないことが重要だ。

語句 □check out ～ ～を借りる

Column 1

本気で挑戦を続ければ，必ず結果は手に入る。

リスニング力向上のために

リスニング力を向上させる練習法としては，リピーティング（リプロダクション），リテンション，シャドーイング，ディクテーションなどがある。その中でも，僕がスコアアップに最も効果があったと感じるのは**シャドーイング**と，その前段階として行った**スラッシュリーディング**である。

スラッシュリーディングと「やまと言葉落とし」

練習開始当時（リスニングスコア400点前後），僕はまず，スラッシュリーディングから取り組むことにした。文章の内容を「読んで」理解することを，リスニングの下準備として行ったのだ。事前に意味の分からない単語やセンテンスがない状態にしておき，英文を前から順に理解していく。その際は**「やまと言葉落とし」という，英語のカタマリを簡潔な日本語に置き換えて理解する方法**を取り入れた。例えば，What time of day is this announcement being made? であれば「いつのアナウンス？」と置き換えるのだ。この訓練を続けることにより，英文を瞬時に理解できるようになった。また，英文の内容を語順通り理解し記憶にとどめておく力も鍛えられ，特にPart 3 & 4で「質問と選択肢を先読みして記憶に残す」のに役立った。

隙間時間を活用してシャドーイング！

上記の訓練を繰り返すうちに，日本語という「補助輪」がいつの間にか外れ，**英語を英語のまま理解できるようになった。**そこで僕は，**模試1セット分のシャドーイングを行うことを日課とし，家事を行う時間や自宅と駅への往復などの隙間時間に行うようにした。**すると耳が英語に慣れ，TOEICの音声はもちろんのこと，CNNなどのニュース英語の聞き取りの精度も格段に向上したのだ。

本書の問題を一通り解き終えた後は，付属のCDを使って毎日シャドーイングをやってみてほしい。**2枚のCDを日替わりで交互に使用し，休まず毎日行うのだ。**3カ月後，自身のリスニング力が明らかに向上していることをあなたは実感するはずだ。

Part

2

応答問題

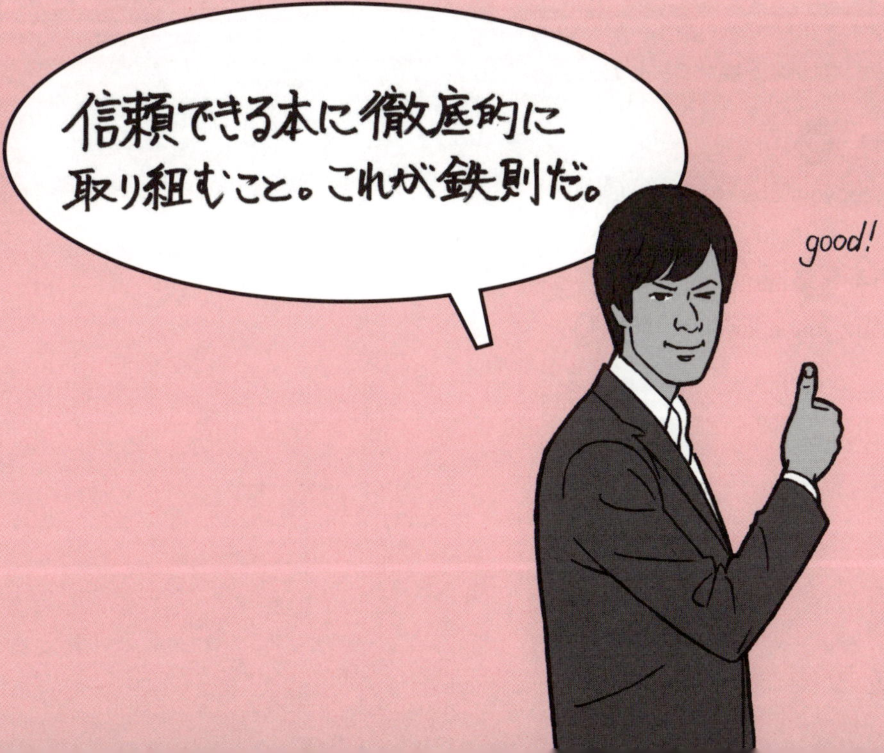
信頼できる本に徹底的に
取り組むこと。これが鉄則だ。
good!

Part 2 応答問題

990点獲得のポイントと攻略法

リスニングパートで満点を取っている人でも，Part 2に絶対の自信を持っている人はそう多くはないはずである。他のパートに比べて集中力が必要な上，上級者でも解きにくい「変化球」が飛んでくるからだ。このパートをパーフェクトにクリアするために必要な力，それは**変化球に対する瞬発力**だ。Part 1に引き続きディクテーションを行い，正解データベースの構築を図ろう。

990点獲得のポイント

1. **「素直ではない応答」に慣れる**
2. **「疑問形ではない発言に対する応答」に慣れる**

まずは例題を解いてみよう。

例1 CD 1 17

Mark your answer.　Ⓐ Ⓑ Ⓒ

例2 CD 1 18

Mark your answer.　Ⓐ Ⓑ Ⓒ

これがHUMMER式アプローチ！

❶「素直ではない応答」に慣れる

例1 CD 1 17

How was your flight from Toronto?
(A) I will arrive there this evening.
(B) No, it's from Vancouver.
(C) Actually, I was asleep for most of it.

トロントからのフライトはいかがでしたか。
(A) 今日の夕方，そこに到着する予定です。
(B) いいえ，それはバンクーバーからです。
(C) 実は，ほとんどの間寝ていました。

正解 **(C)**

問いかけではフライトの感想を尋ねている。(C)はフライトに対するストレートな応答ではないが，フライト中にしていたことを述べており，自然な会話を成立させているので正解である。(A)は自分の到着予定時間を述べており，問いかけに対する応答として成立しない。(B)はNoの時点でHowで始まる問いかけの応答にならず，内容もフライトの感想ではないので不正解である。

How was your flight?という質問に対しては「快適だった」などの感想を期待するのが普通だろう。しかし，Part 2ではこのように**「素直ではない応答」が正解として出題される**ことがあるので注意が必要である。このような問題に柔軟に対応できるよう，**最初の発言を瞬時に100％理解する**訓練を日頃の問題演習時から意識して行うようにしていこう。

❷「疑問形ではない発言に対する応答」に慣れる

例2 CD 1 18

Look, these are our latest sweaters.
(A) What other colors do you have?
(B) From a dependable supplier.
(C) I bought it at the grocery store.

見てください，こちらが当社の最新のセーターです。
(A) 他にどんな色がありますか。
(B) 信頼できる納入業者からです。
(C) 私はそれを食料雑貨品店で購入しました。

正解 **(A)**
語句 □dependable 信頼できる　□grocery store 食料雑貨品店

セーターを見せられた後，それに関する質問で応答している(A)が正解である。(B)は納入業者がどこなのかを質問された場合の応答であり，(C)はthe grocery storeがセーターを購入する場所としてふさわしくない。

疑問形ではない発言に対する応答は，予想することが非常に難しい。この問題のように，疑問文が正解となる場合もある。最初の発言と応答の両方を完璧に聞き取って理解し**「発言と応答の自然な流れ」となるペアを作る**ことに注力しよう。

超上級の技術

Part 2を全問正解するには，最初の発言と各選択肢が会話として成立しているかどうかを確実にチェックしていかなければならない。そこで，990点を目指す学習者には，ぜひ以下の流れで解答に当たってみてほしい。

① 最初の発言を聞き取り，完全に覚えて英語のままリピート
② (A)の選択肢を聞く　→　会話が成立するか判断
③ もう一度最初の発言を英語のままリピート
④ (B)の選択肢を聞く　→　会話が成立するか判断
⑤ もう一度最初の発言を英語のままリピート
⑥ (C)の選択肢を聞く　→　会話が成立するか判断

ハードルは高いが，こうすれば「最初の発言は何だったか？」と不安になることもなく，最初の発言と選択肢との関係を確実にチェックしていくことができる。

では，次のように最初の発言が長い選択疑問文の場合はどうしたらよいだろうか。

Has your notice of resignation been acknowledged yet, or haven't you submitted it yet?
（あなたの退職届はもう受理されましたか，それともまだ提出していないのですか）

このような場合は，最低限必要な情報を抽出してリピートすることをお勧めする。この問題の場合はresignation acknowledged, or haven't submittedという感じである。

最初のうちは，英語を一度日本語に置き換えてもよい。慣れてくるとその作業が自然と不要になり，英語を英語のまま理解し，しっかり記憶できるようになる。990点獲得を目指すのであれば，ぜひそのレベルまで到達してほしい。

990点獲得への道

Part 2は**瞬発力**が要求されるパートである。特に，例題で取り上げたような「変化球」の場合，放送文の内容を理解し，会話の場面や発言の意図までを瞬時に理解する力が必要だ。

次ページからのディクテーショントレーニングによって，Part 1と同様に，正解データベースを構築していこう。データベース強化により**「数多くの変化球」の存在を知っておくことが，会話を瞬時に理解するための最高の対策**となり得る。もちろん「球種」を知った後は，実戦をより多く積んで「瞬時にそれを打ち返す練習」を継続するのみだ。模試や練習問題でトレーニングを重ねよう。CD 1の最後には，Part 2 Practice Testの正解の会話を収録してある。こちらも活用して正解データベースをしっかり構築してほしい。

また，問題も選択肢も全て音声のみのPart 2では，他のパート以上に**集中力**が要求される。**呼吸を整え，落ち着いて解答する**ようにしたい。1問ごとに気持ちをリセットし，自信を持って解答できなかったときは後に引きずらないようにする。リスニングパート全体で**97問以上**正解できれば**495点**は手に入るので，割り切って気持ちを切り替え，次の1問に全力で集中するようにしよう。

まとめ

ディクテーションで正解データベースを構築し，「変化球」に対する「瞬発力」を高めよう。
1問ごとに気持ちをリセットし，「集中力」を維持することも大切だ！

Training

CD 1 19～28

英文を聞き，全文をディクテーションしなさい。

Training　英文と訳

CD 1 19～28

19

1. Could you replace the ink cartridge in this copier?
（このコピー機のインクカートリッジを交換してくださいますか）
▼ Would you wait until this afternoon?
（午後までお待ちいただけますか）

2. The company outing is for all the staff, right?
（会社のピクニックは全スタッフが対象ですよね）
▼ I heard everyone's invited.
（全員が招待されていると聞いています）

3. Why don't I ask for the vice president's ideas?
（副社長の意見を伺ってきましょうか）
▼ Could you tell me what he says later?
（彼が何と言っているかを，後で教えていただけますか）

4. Our company has lost a lot of essential employees.
（当社は極めて重要な従業員をたくさん失いました）
▼ We have to recruit immediately.
（私たちはすぐに新入社員を募集しなければなりません）

5. When do you expect the copier to be delivered?
（いつコピー機が届くと思いますか）
▼ I heard it left the warehouse yesterday.
（昨日倉庫を出たと聞いています）

20

6. Would you like me to move my suitcase?
（スーツケースを移動させましょうか）
▼ No, it's not in the way.
（いいえ，邪魔ではありません）

7. I'd like to know who has the documents from the meeting.
（誰が会議の書類を持っているかを知りたいのです）
▼ Mr. Takeuchi may have the leftover ones.
（Takeuchi さんが残りの分を持っているかもしれません）

HUMMERのココがポイント》 1.のような発言には，通常「はい，やります」や「いいえ，できません」などの応答を予測しがちだが，「保留」という回答もあることを覚えておこう。7. leftover「残りの」は覚えておきたい表現。このTrainingやp.46からのPractice Test，また実際の試験などで知らない表現が出てきたら，それをまとめてオリジナルの単語帳を作り，覚えていくようにしよう。

8. Excuse me, on which floor is Mr. Kei's legal office?
（すみません，Keiさんの法律事務所はどの階にありますか）
▼ Oh, it's above us.
（ああ，私たちの上の階です）

9. I'm worried renting this device may cause a problem.
（この装置を借りて問題が起きないか心配です）
▼ I don't think you should be worried about that.
（あなたがそのことを心配する必要はないと思います）

10. Is this the finalized list of attendees, or will more people come?
（これは参加者リストの最終版ですか，それとももっとたくさんの人が来ますか）
▼ This is the list of the attendees who've responded so far.
（これはこれまでに返事をくれた参加者のリストです）

21

11. Which means of transportation should I use to get there fastest?
（最も早くそこに到着するにはどの交通手段を使うべきですか）
▼ You're in a rush, right?
（お急ぎなのですね）

12. When will we receive the commission checks?
（いつ手数料の小切手を受け取れますか）
▼ Mr. Taka said on the same day as our payday.
（給料日と同じ日だとTakaさんが言っていました）

13. I can't believe how crowded this restaurant is.
（このレストランがこんなに混んでいるなんて信じられません）
▼ That's because it received a great review in the newspaper yesterday.
（昨日，新聞で高く評価されたからです）

14. Please tell me how long you've been an attorney.
（あなたがどれくらいの間，弁護士をしているのか教えてください）
▼ It'll be two years next February.
（今度の2月で2年になります）

15. Your business cards can be picked up at the HR department.
（名刺は人事部でもらってくることができます）
▼ Oh, they're ready?
（ああ，もう準備ができたのですね）

HUMMERのココがポイント 10.は少し長い発言だが，finalized list of attendees，more people comeと短くしてリピートしよう。11.や15.のように，最初の発言の内容を簡潔に要約して確認している応答が正解になる場合も多々ある。こうした応答は，短いからこそ，特に集中力が必要だ。

22

16. We are likely to see price raises for many everyday items.
(多くの日用品が値上げされそうですね)
▼ That's what I think too.
(私もそう思います)

17. Which route would you take to get to the top?
(どの道を通って頂上まで行きますか)
▼ We'll go past the small park.
(小さな公園の横を通って行くつもりです)

18. Do you know who was absent from the meeting this morning?
(今朝の会議を欠席したのは誰か分かりますか)
▼ I have no idea, but I'll go find out.
(分かりませんが，調べてきます)

19. This copier still isn't fixed, is it?
(このコピー機はまだ修理されていないのですね)
▼ I thought it was.
(修理済みだと思っていました)

20. There was heavy traffic last night.
(昨晩は渋滞していました)
▼ I think it was even worse this morning.
(今朝の方がさらにひどかったと思います)

23

21. Should I leave the document on your desk or hers?
(その書類はあなたの机に置けばいいですか，それとも彼女の机にですか)
▼ Could you file it in the cabinet in the corner?
(それは隅の戸棚のファイルに保管してくれますか)

22. Aren't Mr. Iwanaga and Mr. Hisamitsu coming to the party?
(Iwanaga さんと Hisamitsu さんはパーティに来ないのですか)
▼ I think they'll be in Gombe State then.
(彼らはその頃，Gombe 州にいると思います)

23. Do you know when your fitness club membership expires?
(あなたのフィットネスクラブの会員権がいつ切れるか知っていますか)
▼ Actually, I renewed it last week.
(実は，先週更新しました)

HUMMERのココがポイント》 17. の応答にある go past ～は「～を通過する，通り過ぎる」という意味である。19. の応答の was の後には，問いかけにある fixed が省略されている。 20. の応答にある it は，最初の発言の「交通渋滞」を受けたものだ。

24. What did Mr. Yoshi talk about at the meeting?
（Yoshiさんは会議で何について話しましたか）
▼ Oh, nothing special.
（ああ，特別なことは何も）

25. Would you like some coffee?
（コーヒーはいかがですか）
▼ Do you know whether they serve decaf or not?
（カフェイン抜きで出してもらえるかどうか知っていますか）

24

26. You have to use a swipe card to enter the room.
（その部屋に入るには磁気カードを使わなければなりません）
▼ I have to get the card from the management office, don't I?
（管理室からカードを手に入れなければなりませんね）

27. I'll call you when your consultant is ready.
（あなたの相談員の準備ができましたらお呼びいたします）
▼ Thank you so much. I'll take a seat.
（ありがとうございます。座っています）

28. Do you want to eat lunch at your place or mine?
（お昼ご飯を食べるのは，あなたの所にしますか，私の所にしますか）
▼ Actually, I'd prefer to eat out today.
（実は，今日は外で食べたいのです）

29. I'd like to move this copier over to the corner.
（このコピー機を向こうの隅に移動させたいのです）
▼ Actually, I prefer it by the window.
（実は，私はそれを窓のそばに置きたいのです）

30. We should hold an annual celebration for all our employees.
（全従業員のために，祝賀会を毎年開くべきです）
▼ Oh, that'd be a nice gesture, I think.
（ああ，それは良いことだと思います）

25

31. Can I please use this copier?
（このコピー機を使ってもいいですか）
▼ Unfortunately, it's not working.
（残念ながら，それは動きません）

HUMMERのココがポイント 24.のように肩透かしに思える応答が正解となる場合もあり，会話として「あり得る」選択肢かどうかが重要である。25.のdecaf「カフェイン抜きのコーヒー」や26.のswipe card「磁気カード」のような表現も押さえておくこと。27.のI'll call youや30.のa nice gestureなど，どのような意味で使われるのか判断に迷うようなものにもすぐに反応できるようにしておこう。

32. Did sales increase in Canada last year?
(昨年，カナダでの売上は増加しましたか)
▼ To tell the truth, the figures aren't in yet.
(実は，数字がまだ出ていません)

33. If you have many things to do, you could ask Ms. Matsuda for some help.
(することがたくさんあるのなら，Matsudaさんに手伝いをお願いできます)
▼ Oh, thank you for letting me know.
(ああ，教えてくれてありがとう)

34. Tommy, would you rather work alone or as a team?
(Tommy，１人で仕事をしたいですか，それともチームがいいですか)
▼ It doesn't make any difference to me.
(どちらでも構いません)

35. We've met at the annual conference, haven't we?
(年次会議でお会いしましたよね)
▼ Hmm, I don't believe so.
(うーん，会っていないと思いますけど)

26

36. Did you bring the receipt with you?
(レシートは持ってきましたか)
▼ It's in my wallet.
(財布に入っています)

37. I'd like to purchase three tickets for the performance.
(その公演のチケットを３枚買いたいのですが)
▼ For what time?
(何時のでしょうか)

38. I heard the orchestra performance will be outdoors.
(そのオーケストラの公演は野外で行われると聞いています)
▼ Oh, hopefully, it won't rain tonight.
(ああ，できれば今晩は雨が降りませんように)

39. There is a spill on one of the tables.
(テーブルの１つに何かがこぼれています)
▼ Could you tell me which table it is?
(どのテーブルか教えていただけますか)

HUMMERのココがポイント 34. のような選択疑問文に対し「どちらでもよい」という応答としては，他に Either is fine. / I don't care. / It doesn't matter to me. なども押さえておこう。

40. More toner cartridges will be delivered next Monday.
(来週の月曜日にもっと多くのトナーカートリッジが届きます)
▼ Good, we're running low.
(いいですね，残り少なくなっているので)

27

41. Let's not tell the instructors about the issue until Friday.
(金曜日までその問題のことはインストラクターたちには言わないでおきましょう)
▼ OK, let's wait.
(分かりました，待ちましょう)

42. Rachel went to the event last week.
(Rachelは先週そのイベントに行きました)
▼ I wish I could have joined her.
(私も彼女と一緒に行ければよかったのですが)

43. I tried the new restaurant across from our building.
(私たちの建物の向かいにある新しいレストランに行ってきました)
▼ Oh, what did you think?
(ああ，いかがでしたか)

44. I need to have these pants dry-cleaned immediately.
(このズボンをすぐにドライクリーニングに出さなくてはいけないのですが)
▼ Would you like me to drop them off for you?
(代わりに私が出してきてあげましょうか)

45. You should get Finn's input on this important issue.
(この重要な問題について，Finnの意見を聞いてみるべきです)
▼ I'll call him after lunch.
(昼食後に彼に電話してみます)

28

46. This vending machine won't take my bill at all.
(この自動販売機には全然お札が入っていきません)
▼ Let me insert it for you if you don't mind.
(もしよかったら，私にやらせてみてください)

47. I was impressed by your wonderful painting.
(あなたの素晴らしい絵画作品に感銘を受けました)
▼ Actually, I think it still needs a few changes.
(実は，それにはまだ数カ所修正が必要だと思っているんです)

HUMMERのココがポイント》 40.のbe running low「残り少なくなっている」はrun short of ～「～が足りなくなる」と一緒に覚えておきたい。42.のI wish I could have joined her.のような仮定法過去完了がリスニングで出題されても反応できるようにしておこう。文法事項に少しでも疑問が生じた場合には，その都度，文法書で確認をすることが大切である。

48. My back feels good since we started using new chairs.
（新しい椅子を使い始めてから，背中の調子が良いです）
▼ They seem to be more comfortable than the old ones.
（前の椅子よりも快適なようですね）

49. Mr. Morrison will give us a cost estimate for the event.
（Morrison さんがそのイベントの費用の見積もりをくれます）
▼ I think it'll probably cost a lot.
（おそらくかなり費用がかかると思います）

50. You're getting a raise next month, right?
（来月昇給するのですよね）
▼ According to my boss.
（私の上司によるとね）

Practice Test

CD 1 29～34

最初の発言と続く3つの選択肢を聞き，最も適切な答えを(A) (B) (C)の中から1つ選びなさい（マークシートは別冊p.158にあります）。

1. Mark your answer on your answer sheet.

2. Mark your answer on your answer sheet.

3. Mark your answer on your answer sheet.

4. Mark your answer on your answer sheet.

5. Mark your answer on your answer sheet.

6. Mark your answer on your answer sheet.

7. Mark your answer on your answer sheet.

8. Mark your answer on your answer sheet.

9. Mark your answer on your answer sheet.

10. Mark your answer on your answer sheet.

11. Mark your answer on your answer sheet.

12. Mark your answer on your answer sheet.

13. Mark your answer on your answer sheet.

14. Mark your answer on your answer sheet.

15. Mark your answer on your answer sheet.

16. Mark your answer on your answer sheet.

17. Mark your answer on your answer sheet.

18. Mark your answer on your answer sheet.

19. Mark your answer on your answer sheet.

20. Mark your answer on your answer sheet.

21. Mark your answer on your answer sheet.

22. Mark your answer on your answer sheet.

23. Mark your answer on your answer sheet.

24. Mark your answer on your answer sheet.

25. Mark your answer on your answer sheet.

26. Mark your answer on your answer sheet.

27. Mark your answer on your answer sheet.

28. Mark your answer on your answer sheet.

29. Mark your answer on your answer sheet.

30. Mark your answer on your answer sheet.

Practice Test 正解と解説

1.

29

Could you replace the fluorescent lights now?	蛍光灯を今すぐ交換していただけますか。
(A) Actually, it's not that heavy.	(A) 実は，それはそんなに重くはありません。
(B) I didn't place an order for a dress.	(B) 洋服の注文はしませんでした。
(C) I'm sorry, they don't arrive until Monday.	(C) 申し訳ありません，それは月曜日まで届きません。

正解 **(C)**

解説 the fluorescent lights を今すぐ交換してほしいという発言に対し，「月曜日まで届きません（＝今は交換できません）」と応答している (C) が正解だ。(A) は会話が成立していないため不正解。(B) は for a dress がなければ適切な応答になる。

語句 □fluorescent light 蛍光灯　□place an order for～ ～の注文をする

2.

Isn't Mr. Kato in charge of cleaning the windows today?	Kato さんは今日，窓の清掃担当ではありませんか。
(A) Let's clean the floor immediately.	(A) すぐに床を清掃しましょう。
(B) I really appreciate that.	(B) 本当に感謝しています。
(C) Actually, I've been doing it since last week.	(C) 実は，先週から私がそれをしています。

正解 **(C)**

解説 否定疑問文（Isn't Mr. Kato ～？）は，Is Mr. Kato ～？と同じだと考えて対応すれば問題ない。「Kato さんが窓の清掃担当ですよね」という問いかけに対して「実は，先週から私がしています」と応答している (C) が正解だ。

語句 □immediately すぐに

3.

I was just wondering if you could move these books for us.	私たちのためにこれらの本を移動していただけないでしょうか。
(A) Yes, I'd like to go to that movie.	(A) はい，その映画を見に行きたいです。
(B) By when?	(B) いつまでにやればいいですか。
(C) This book was filmed this year.	(C) この本は今年，映画化されました。

正解 **(B)**

解説 最初の発言は I was just wondering if ～を使った丁寧な依頼の表現だ。(B) は短すぎるので正確に聞き取るのが難しい。聞き取れなかった場合は一度保留にして，次の選択肢を聞こう。(A) は move と音の似ている movie を使ったひっかけ。(C) は book という語は登場するが，会話が全く成立していない。

語句 □I was just wondering if you could do ～していただけませんか
□be filmed 映画化される

4.

Do you think I should follow Mr. Takatori's advice about this problem?	この問題についてTakatoriさんの助言に従うべきだと思いますか。
(A) Would you tell me what he said?	(A) 彼が何と言ったか教えていただけますか。
(B) No, I don't take his class.	(B) いいえ，彼の講義は受けていません。
(C) By the end of this month.	(C) 今月末までに。

正解 **(A)**

解説 (A)は，そもそもTakatoriさんの助言を知らないのでその内容を尋ねるという流れである。(A)だけを聞いてそれを正解だと確信するのは難しいが，(B)，(C)ではいずれも会話が成立しない。正解かどうかをすぐに判断しにくい選択肢も中にはあるが，TOEICでは不正解の選択肢は明らかに不正解となるように作られている。他の選択肢を聞いた上で，消去法で判断しよう。

5.

Our company has lost a lot of excellent employees over the past ten months.	当社は過去10カ月に多くの優秀な従業員を失ってきました。
(A) Unfortunately, that's true.	(A) 残念ながら，それは事実です。
(B) That's a consistently excellent company.	(B) それは一貫して素晴らしい会社です。
(C) Would you like me to hire you?	(C) あなたを雇ってほしいのですか。

正解 **(A)**

解説 最初の発言に「同意」している(A)が正解。他に考えられる応答例としては「補足（これは当社始まって以来のことです）」「提案（求人広告を出してはどうでしょうか）」「感謝（ご報告ありがとうございます）」「否定（そんなはずはありません）」など。疑問形ではない発言に対する応答はこのように何通りも考えられるため，難易度が高くなる傾向がある。

語句 □consistently 一貫して

6.

30

How was your holiday in your home town?	故郷での休暇はいかがでしたか。
(A) Yes, it was the first time for me.	(A) はい，それは私にとって初めてでした。
(B) Actually, my vacation was canceled.	(B) 実は，休暇は取りやめになったのです。
(C) You'll be allowed to take a leave of absence.	(C) あなたは休暇を取ることを認めてもらえるでしょう。

正解 **(B)**

解説 感想を求められているため「良い」「悪い」や，具体的に何をしたかを答えるはず，と考えがちである。ところが(B)のように「休暇が取りやめになった」という意表を突いた応答も正解になるということを押さえておこう。(A)はHowに対してYesで答えている時点で不適切であり，(C)は会話が成立していない。

語句 □take a leave of absence 休暇を取る

7.

They're our latest shoes.
(A) I bought it last night.
(B) This is the latest news on the issue.
(C) How are they selling?

それらは当社の最新の靴です。
(A) それを昨晩買いました。
(B) これはその問題についての最新ニュースです。
(C) 売れ行きはいかがですか。

正解 (C)

解説 会話の状況を瞬時にイメージできるよう，日々の訓練で想像力を鍛えておこう。特に最初の発言が平叙文の場合は注意が必要だ。靴を紹介している最初の発言への応答としては，(C)が自然な内容である。(A)はitがthemであれば最初の発言のshoesを受けているので，文法上は正解になり得る。(B)は最初の発言にあるlatestと，shoesに音の似ているissueという語を含んでいるが，会話が成立していない。

語句 □latest 最新の　□issue 問題

8.

When will the guests arrive here?
(A) Yes, they have enough time to do so.
(B) I heard they left the station just now.
(C) No, we should phone for a taxi.

いつゲストはここに到着しますか。
(A) はい，彼らはそうする時間が十分にあります。
(B) 彼らはたった今駅を出たと聞きました。
(C) いいえ，電話でタクシーを呼ぶべきです。

正解 (B)

解説 whenに対して具体的な時刻を答えている選択肢はないが，到着時刻が推測できる情報を与えている(B)が正解だ。(A)，(C)はwhenに対してYes / Noで応答している時点で不正解である。

語句 □phone for a taxi 電話でタクシーを呼ぶ

9.

Will the company provide software training for all new employees?
(A) That's what I heard.
(B) At the company's outing.
(C) I'd like to use the training room.

その会社は全ての新人従業員にソフトウェアに関する研修を行いますか。
(A) そう聞いています。
(B) 会社のピクニックで。
(C) トレーニングルームを使いたいです。

正解 (A)

解説 最初の発言に同意している(A)が正解である。(B)はwhen，もしくはwhereに対する応答だ。(C)は最初の発言にある単語trainingを使っているが，会話が成立していない。

語句 □outing ピクニック，外出

10.

Do you know who has the device I'd like to use today?
(A) The device is very simple to use.
(B) I saw Mr. Sherrick using it.
(C) You can put them on the shelf.

今日私が使いたい機器を誰が持っているか知っていますか。
(A) その機器は非常に使いやすいです。
(B) Sherrickさんがそれを使っているのを見ました。
(C) それらをその棚に置いてもよいです。

正解 **(B)**

解説 発言者が知りたいのは「誰が機器を持っているか」である。「使っている人を見た」という情報で間接的に応答している(B)が正解。(A)は機器の使いやすさを述べているだけであり，適切な応答にはならない。(C)は質問とは無関係な応答である。

語句 □device 機器　□simple to use 使いやすい

11. 31

The dentist is on this floor, isn't it?	歯医者はこの階ですよね。
(A) Oh, it's one flight up.	(A) ああ，1階上です。
(B) Sorry, this is my floor.	(B) すみません，この階で降ります。
(C) You should consult a dentist immediately.	(C) すぐに歯医者に診てもらうべきです。

正解 **(A)**

解説 歯医者のある階を確認する問いかけに対する応答なので，階数を答えるか「知らない」などの応答がくると予想できる。1つ上の階にあると答えている(A)が正解。one flight upで「1つ上の階」という意味になることを押さえておこう。(B)はエレベーターから降りたい人のセリフであり，(C)にはdentistが出てくるが会話として成立しない。

語句 □This is my floor. この階で降ります。

12.

Showing this handout to a third party may cause a problem.	この資料を第三者に見せるのは問題があるかもしれません。
(A) The show will include a live musical performance.	(A) そのショーには音楽の生演奏があります。
(B) It'll be fine.	(B) きっと問題ないでしょう。
(C) I'll give you some handouts soon.	(C) すぐに資料を差し上げます。

正解 **(B)**

解説 発言者の「懸念」に対し，「問題ありません」と「否定」している(B)が正解。この他に「同意(そうですね)」や「提案（～さんに確認します)」なども正解として考えられる。(A)はshowが最初の発言と同じだが，発言に対応していない。(C)もhandoutという語は出てくるが，適切な応答ではない。

語句 □handout 資料，パンフレット　□third party 第三者

13.

This is the latest catalog, isn't it?
(A) They're the latest best sellers.
(B) No, I think we have enough time.
(C) Yes, could you send it to the client?

これが最新版のカタログですよね。
(A) それらは最新のベストセラーです。
(B) いいえ，私たちには十分な時間があると思います。
(C) はい，それをクライアントに送っていただけますか。

正解 **(C)**

解説 latest catalog を it で受け，それを client に送ってほしいと依頼している (C) が正解。(A) は問いかけにある the latest という表現を含んではいるが，ベストセラーの話にすり替わっているため不正解。(B) は No まではよいが，I 以下が不適切。これは「締め切りに間に合うでしょうか」などの問いかけに対する応答である。

14.

Have you got the packet for the event yet?
(A) I haven't checked my post today.
(B) I had trouble getting a bucket yesterday.
(C) I waited in line at the event.

イベント用の荷物はもう届きましたか。
(A) 今日は郵便物を確認していません。
(B) 昨日はバケツを手に入れるのに苦労しました。
(C) イベントで列に並んで待ちました。

正解 **(A)**

解説 発言者は荷物がすでに届いているかを知りたいようだ。(A) は「郵便物を確認していない」と答えており，適切な応答である。(B) は packet に音の似ている bucket を話題に挙げているだけで，質問に対する答えにはなっていない。(C) にも event が出てくるが，packet の状況には何ら関係がなく，会話が成立していない。

語句 □have trouble doing　～するのに苦労する

15.

Do you know when we get repaid for transportation and accommodation costs?
(A) I got an airline ticket yesterday.
(B) I had a great time.
(C) Maybe you should ask Ms. Motegi later.

交通費と宿泊費をいつ返金してもらえるか知っていますか。
(A) 昨日，航空券を手に入れました。
(B) 素晴らしい時間を過ごしました。
(C) 後で Motegi さんに聞くべきかもしれません。

正解 **(C)**

解説 発言者は交通費と宿泊費をいつ返金してもらえるのかを知りたいようだ。(C) は「他の人に聞いた方がよい（＝自分は知らない）」と言っており，会話が成立する。(A) も (B) も質問に全く答えていないので不正解である。

16.

32

This store is busy even on weekdays.
(A) Do you believe he is busy?
(B) I have every Thursday off.
(C) I believe so.

このお店は平日でさえにぎわっています。
(A) あなたは彼が忙しいと思いますか。
(B) 私は毎週木曜日がお休みです。
(C) 私もそう思います。

正解 (C)

解説 最初の発言から，この店が普段から人気があって混み合っていることを理解しよう。これに同意している(C)が正解である。(A)と(B)はbusyやThursdayなど，最初の発言に出てくる語と関連した語を含んでいるが，全く応答になっていない。

17.

How long have you been in our company?
(A) This company was established five years ago.
(B) He's been here for two years.
(C) I have only just joined.

あなたは当社でどのくらいの間，働いていますか。
(A) この会社は5年前に設立されました。
(B) 彼はここに2年間います。
(C) 最近入ったばかりです。

正解 (C)

解説 勤務している期間を尋ねているのに対し，「最近入ったばかり」と応答している(C)が正解。応答に具体的な期間がくるとは限らないことに注意しよう。(A), (B)は具体的な年数を含んでいるが，(A)は会社の設立された時期，(B)は第三者の勤務期間を答えているので不正解。選択肢の主語や時制，数は常に意識して聞く必要がある。

語句 □establish ～を設立する

18.

I have a package for you.
(A) We'll pack fragile items.
(B) Mr. Shimizu is going to come pick it up.
(C) That'll save the trip to the bank.

あなた宛ての荷物を預かっています。
(A) 壊れ物を梱包します。
(B) Shimizuさんがそれを取りに行きます。
(C) 銀行に行く手間が省けます。

正解 (B)

解説 「荷物を預かっています」という発言に対し，誰が取りに行くかを答えている(B)が正解。この他に応答として考えられるのは「取りに行きます」「そのまま預かっていてください」「持ってきてください」などである。(A)はpackageの関連語であるpackが含まれているが，応答になっていない。(C)は最初の発言に関係のない内容である。

語句 □pack ～を梱包する　□fragile 壊れやすい　□save the trip to ～ ～に行く手間を省く

19.

I'm surprised to see many prices have increased.	多くの商品の価格が上がっているのを知って驚いています。
(A) I am, too.	(A) 私もです。
(B) What will be the prize?	(B) 賞品は何ですか。
(C) Yes, between Monday and Wednesday.	(C) はい，月曜日から水曜日までの間です。

正解 **(A)**

解説 物価の高騰に驚いている発言に対し，I am (surprised), too. と「同意」している (A) が正解。(B) は最初の発言の surprised や prices に発音が似ている prize を使ったひっかけの選択肢である。(C) は最初の発言とは全く関係のない内容である。

20.

You'll choose the fastest route, right?	あなたは最も早く行ける道を選びますよね。
(A) Ms. Mori did the job fastest.	(A) Moriさんが一番早くその仕事をしました。
(B) I didn't choose the class, actually.	(B) 実は，そのクラスを選びませんでした。
(C) I'm thinking about taking the expressway.	(C) 高速道路を利用することを考えています。

正解 **(C)**

解説 発言者はどの route で行くのかを確認している。考えられる応答は，Yes / No，具体的な route の提示，もしくは「まだ決めていない」などになりそうだと予測することができる。ここでは，選んだ route を具体的に説明している (C) が正解。(A) は問いかけにもある fastest を使ったひっかけ，(B) は choose が共通しているだけで，会話が成立しない。

21.

33

Do you know who isn't coming to the banquet tonight?	今晩，誰が宴会に来ないのかを知っていますか。
(A) I was invited to the celebration.	(A) 祝賀会に招待されました。
(B) No, let me go check.	(B) いいえ，調べに行かせてください。
(C) I'll be waiting, so please get ready.	(C) 待っているので，支度をしてきてください。

正解 **(B)**

解説 「誰が来ないか知っていますか」という質問に対し，「知らないので調べてくる」と応答している (B) が正解だ。(A) は banquet「宴会」と近い意味の celebration「祝賀会」という語を含んでいるが，質問に対する答えにはなっていない。(C) は出掛ける準備のできていない相手に対する言葉である。

22.

That escalator hasn't been fixed yet, has it?
(A) I'd like to use the elevator.
(B) Mr. Taya said it was.
(C) By taking the escalator.

あのエスカレーターは，まだ修理されていないですよね。
(A) エレベーターを使いたいです。
(B) 修理されたとTayaさんが言っていました。
(C) エスカレーターを利用することによって。

正解 **(B)**

解説 escalatorがすでに修理されたかどうかの確認に対し，伝聞の形でit（＝escalator）が修理されたと述べている(B)が正解。(A)は「（代わりに/それなら）エレベーターを使いましょう」などであれば会話として成立するが，「エレベーターを使いたい」と言うだけでは不十分。(C)は問いかけと同じくescalatorが出てくるが，応答になっていない。

23.

I'll teleconference with Mr. Kono this evening.
(A) The conference was held in room 201.
(B) Please tell me when you're done.
(C) Yes, it was too long.

今晩，Konoさんとテレビ会議を行います。
(A) 会議は201号室で行われました。
(B) 終わったら教えてください。
(C) はい，それは長すぎました。

正解 **(B)**

解説 応答を予測しにくい問題だが，会議が終わったら教えてほしいと答えている(B)を聞いた時点で，正解だと判断できるよう最初の発言を正確に聞き取り，しっかりと記憶しよう。(A)は時制が最初の発言と対応しておらず，was heldがwill be heldであれば正解になり得る。(C)は過去に行われた何かに対する感想を述べているため，会話が成立していない。

語句 □teleconference with ～ ～とテレビ会議を行う

24.

Our client will arrive on an overnight flight from Chicago, right?
(A) Unfortunately, it was canceled.
(B) At this time, it's engaged in repairs.
(C) Are we almost there?

当社のクライアントはシカゴからの深夜便でやってきますよね。
(A) 残念ながら，キャンセルになりました。
(B) 現時点で，それは修理中です。
(C) 私たちはもうすぐそこに着きますか。

正解 **(A)**

解説 発言者はクライアントの到着手段を確認している。キャンセルになったという新たな情報を提供して応答している(A)が正解。(B)は質問の答えになっていないため不正解。(C)は一緒に目的地に向かっている人に向けた発言であり，ここでは不適切である。

語句 □overnight flight 深夜便　□be engaged in repairs 修理中である

25.

You have to be in the hotel lobby at five o'clock.
(A) At the reception desk.
(B) The banquet has been canceled.
(C) OK, I'll be there without fail.

あなたは5時にホテルのロビーにいなくてはいけません。
(A) 受付の所です。
(B) 宴会はキャンセルになりました。
(C) 分かりました，必ずそこにいます。

正解 **(C)**

解説 「5時にロビーにいてください」という発言に「必ずいます」と答えている(C)が正解。(A)は場所を聞かれた場合の応答であり不正解。(B)は最初の発言にあるhotelから連想されるbanquetを使ったひっかけの選択肢である。

語句 □reception desk 受付　□without fail 必ず，確実に

26.

34

I didn't have time to check the bulletin board today.
(A) I can see you're busy.
(B) He's on the board of directors.
(C) That's nice of you to say.

今日は掲示板を見る時間がありませんでした。
(A) あなたが忙しいことは分かります。
(B) 彼は取締役会に出席しています。
(C) そう言ってくれてありがとう。

正解 **(A)**

解説 応答を予測しにくい問題だが，(A)は発言者の気持ちを酌んだ自然な応答となるので正解である。(B)はboardという単語が登場しているが，最初の発言では「掲示板」，(B)では「取締役会」の意味で，会話が成立していない。(C)は相手の言葉に感謝するときのせりふである。

27.

I'd like you to stop by Shinsuk's office to pick up your new ID card.
(A) I'll do it immediately.
(B) OK, I'll pick you up at the train station.
(C) You need the credit card information.

Shinsukさんのオフィスへ立ち寄って，あなたの新しいIDカードを取ってきてほしいのですが。
(A) すぐにそうします。
(B) 分かりました，駅まで迎えに行きます。
(C) あなたはクレジットカードの情報が必要です。

正解 **(A)**

解説 発言者はIDカードを取りに行くよう頼んでいる。「すぐにそうします」(do it＝pick up my new ID card) と答えている(A)が正解だ。(B)はIDカードではなく，相手を迎えに行くと言っているので応答になっていない。(C)も質問に全く関係のない内容なので不正解である。

語句 □stop by ～ ～に立ち寄る　□pick up ～ ～を取ってくる　□pick＋人＋up 人を迎えに行く

28.

The conference room is too hot, isn't it?	会議室が暑すぎませんか。
(A) I'll call for an urgent meeting with them tonight.	(A) 彼らに今晩，緊急会議を要請する予定です。
(B) We have a mild climate here.	(B) こちらの気候は穏やかです。
(C) Could you lower the temperature?	(C) 温度を下げていただけますか。

正解 **(C)**

解説 「会議室が暑すぎる（ので何とかしませんか？）」という発言に対しては，「そうでもない」「窓を開けよう」「冷房を入れよう」などの応答が考えられる。温度を下げるよう頼んでいる(C)が正解。(A)はconferenceの関連語であるmeetingが使われているが，会話が成立していない。(B)は土地の気候を答えており，質問には関係ない内容である。

29.

This restaurant has wireless Internet access, doesn't it?	このレストランでは無線のインターネット接続が使えますよね。
(A) It was so good to eat.	(A) おいしい食事でした。
(B) No, this location doesn't have it.	(B) いいえ，ここにはそれがありません。
(C) I spend a few hours a day on the Internet.	(C) 1日に数時間をインターネットに費やしています。

正解 **(B)**

解説 Internetが使えるかという質問に対し，ここにはそれ（it = wireless Internet access）がない，つまり使えないと述べている(B)が正解だ。(A)はrestaurantから連想される内容ではあるが，応答になっていない。(C)はInternet利用に関する内容だが，問いかけに対する答えになっていない。

語句 □spend A on B　AをBに費やす

30.

Did you go to the performance with Ms. Albright yesterday?	Albrightさんと一緒に，昨日その公演に行きましたか。
(A) I wanted to go, but I couldn't leave work.	(A) 行きたかったのですが，仕事を離れられませんでした。
(B) She brought him to the park.	(B) 彼女は彼を公園に連れて行きました。
(C) Her performance is always flawless.	(C) 彼女のパフォーマンスはいつも完璧です。

正解 **(A)**

解説 「公演に行ったか」という問いかけに対する応答を選択する。(A)は「行きたかったが仕事で行けなかった」という内容で会話が成立するので正解。(B)は最初の発言と関係のない内容であり，(C)はHerが誰を指すのか不明であるため，正解として選択するべきではない。

語句 □flawless 欠点のない，完璧な

Column 2

990点獲得の先輩に聞く！ **学習の秘訣①**

高木恭子さん　（英語教材制作会社勤務・40代）

■990点を獲得したのは… 2013年1月

■990点を獲得するまでの期間… 900点を超えてから990点までかかったのは2年10ヶ月

Q 990点を目指したきっかけは何ですか？

2008年ごろに濱﨑さんのブログ『独学でTOEIC990点を目指す！』がきっかけでTOEICの学習を開始。スコアが900点を超えた後TOEIC教材作成などの英語を使う仕事に従事。英語を職業として生きていくための資格証明として，絶対に990点が欲しいと思いました。

Q どのように壁を乗り越えましたか？

2010年3月に925点を取得後，なかなか950点が越えられず，「自分にはもうこれが限界か？」と自問自答していました。そこで試しにPart 7を解く順番を変えてみたのです。これまではQ.153から解いていたのを，Q.176のシングルパッセージ中，最も長い英文から解くようにしてみました。すると，まだ時間に余裕があるうちに長い英文を読むことで取りこぼしが減り，2012年9月に初めて950点を突破できました。このように，**受験のたびに自ら設定した課題を改善することで，越えられない壁を打破できた**と思います。

Q 最も効果的だった学習法を教えてください！

私は特に，**Part 5とPart 2を集中して勉強**しました。どちらのパートも瞬間的に解けなければいくら考えても終わりのため，苦手意識が特に強かったからです。具体的には，Part 5については，**問題集を何度も解くことで，その問題を見れば正解と解説の内容を思い出せるように**しました。Part 2については，**最初の発言を聞いて，自分で正解の応答を言えるまで『TOEICテスト 新公式問題集』全冊分を繰り返し聞きました。**Part 2を集中的に学習すると，Part 3・Part 4の「木」問題（注：本冊p.64）に対する苦手意識も段々少なくなり，リスニングで高得点を取れるようになりました。それが，全体のスコアアップにもつながったと思います。

Q 英語学習において，今後の目標は何ですか？

990点を取得した経験を活かし，TOEIC教材の作成や編集を通じて，英語学習に取り組む方の役に立てればと思います。

Q 読者へのメッセージをお願いします！

育児や介護，病気療養など，自分では制御できない事情で学習時間が限られている方も多いと思います。育児中の私もその1人です。よく「スキマ時間を使え」と言いますが，「どこにもスキマなんてない…」という時期は人生上避けられないものです。ただし，**「スキマ」はなくても，「スキあらば」どこでも学習はできます。**例えば私は，子どもが泣きやまず抱っこをしている数分を利用してPart 7を解くことすらあります。台所では冷蔵庫に貼った単語を覚え，町内会の清掃活動中もリスニングの音声を聞く，といった具合です。朝は4時台に起きて家事，その後TOEICの学習をして出勤します。このように，**まとまった時間は取れなくても気持ちで負ける必要はありません。**頑張っていきましょう。読者の皆さまが本書でHUMMER式の解法を体得され，一問一問解く喜びを感じることを，そして990点を獲得されることを心より願っております。

Part

3&4

会話問題＆説明文問題

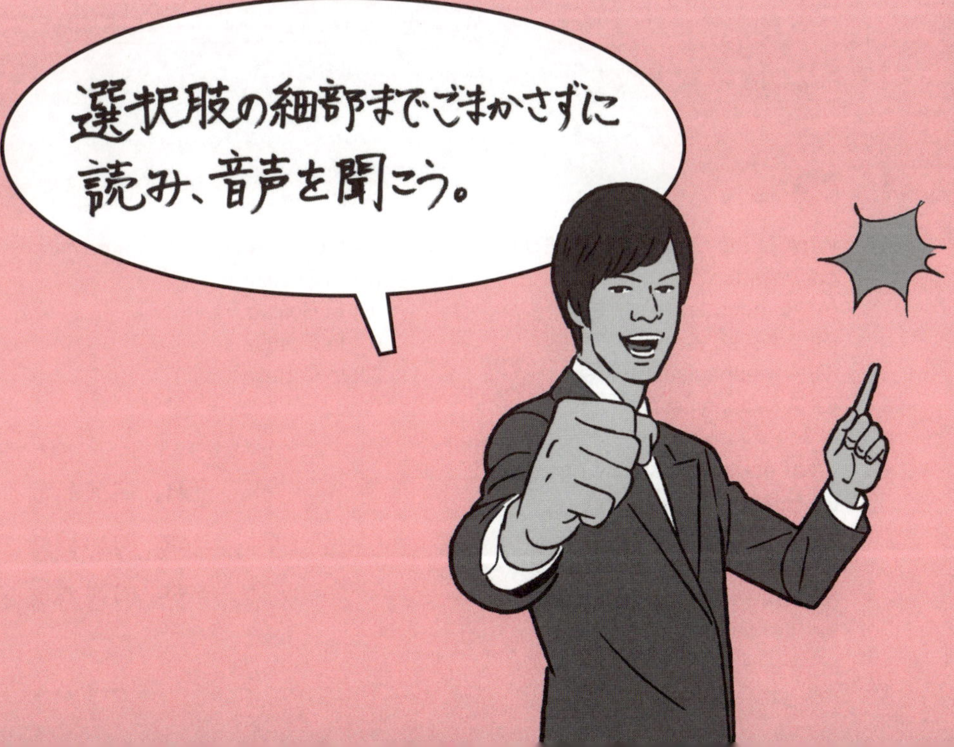
選択肢の細部までごまかさずに
読み、音声を聞こう。

Part
3&4 会話問題&説明文問題
990点獲得のポイントと攻略法

Part 3 & 4の攻め方は基本的に同じだ。990点を目指すレベルにいる学習者はすでに，Part 3の会話やPart 4のトークの内容をほぼ100%聞き取って理解できるだろう。しかし，990点を獲得するには，単に「聞いて内容を理解する」のでは不十分だ。**音声が流れる前に質問と選択肢を読み**，これから流れる音声の**ポイントをできる限り絞り込んだ上で音声を聞こう**。この**能動的リスニング**を身に付ければ，Part 3 & 4の全問正解も決して夢ではない。

990点獲得のポイント

1 設問を先読みし，ポイントを絞り込んで音声を聞く

2 「木」問題※を攻略する

※「木」問題・・・正解の根拠が一度しか登場しない問題

まずは例題を解いてみよう。どちらも，設問を先読みした上で解いてみてほしい。

例1 CD 1 35

41. What is the reason for the flight cancellation?
(A) An accident
(B) Adverse weather
(C) A mechanical problem
(D) A security issue

42. What does Matt say he can do?
(A) Reserve a bus ticket
(B) Contact a travel agent
(C) Check alternative airports
(D) Write an inspection report

43. Where is the factory located?
(A) In Tianjin
(B) In Beijing
(C) In Florida
(D) In Ottawa

41. Ⓐ Ⓑ Ⓒ Ⓓ
42. Ⓐ Ⓑ Ⓒ Ⓓ
43. Ⓐ Ⓑ Ⓒ Ⓓ

例2 CD 1 36

71. When does the event start?
(A) On March 4
(B) On March 5
(C) On March 6
(D) On March 10

72. According to the speaker, what can listeners do online?
(A) Fill a registration form
(B) Get travel assistance
(C) Check the event schedule
(D) See a list of exhibitors

73. What is cheaper online?
(A) Shipping charges
(B) Customized products
(C) Entrance fee
(D) Product catalog

71. Ⓐ Ⓑ Ⓒ Ⓓ
72. Ⓐ Ⓑ Ⓒ Ⓓ
73. Ⓐ Ⓑ Ⓒ Ⓓ

これがHUMMER式アプローチ！

❶ 設問を先読みし，ポイントを絞り込んで音声を聞く

リスニングパートは基本的には「受け身」のパートだが，Part 3 & 4は「攻め」のパートだ。質問と選択肢が問題冊子に書かれているので，これを先に読んでおくことで，音声が流れる前にある程度まで**会話やトークのポイントを絞り込んでおく**ことができる。**そのために必要なリーディング力を鍛え上げる**ことも，リスニングパートで満点を取るためのカギとなる。

先読みは，内容を無理に頭にたたき込もうとせず，読む回数を増やすことにより**自然に頭に残す**つもりで行うとよい。意味が取りづらい表現が登場した場合は理解を優先して丁寧に読む。練習を積み重ねることにより，緩急の付け方も体得できるだろう。

音声が流れている間にほぼ解答を終えると，与えられている1セット分の解答時間（8秒×3問分＝24秒間）を次の設問の先読みに使うことができる。まずは次の手順で練習してみよう。

（例）設問**41.**～**43.**の場合。
①**41.**～**43.**の質問だけを読む。
②**41.**の質問＋選択肢を読む。
③**42.**の質問＋選択肢を読む。
④**43.**の質問＋選択肢を読む。
⑤**41.**～**43.**の質問だけを読む。
⑥以下音声が流れ始めるまで⑤を繰り返す。

余裕ができたら，①の段階から選択肢の先読みも加えよう。最終的には，**24秒間で1セット分の質問と選択肢の全てを3回以上先読みできる**ことを目指したい。各質問と選択肢をきちんと意味をとった上で3回以上先読みすることができれば，それらの内容が確実に頭に残っていることを実感できるはずだ。その域に達すれば，**音声に99％集中しつつ質問と選択肢を眺めているだけで，音声を聞きながら正解を選ぶことができる**ようになる。

では，質問と選択肢から聞き取るべきポイントをどのように絞り込んでいくか，**例1**で解説していこう。

例1

41. What is the reason for the flight cancellation?	欠航の理由は何か。
(A) An accident	(A) 事故
(B) Adverse weather	(B) 悪天候
(C) A mechanical problem	(C) 機械的な問題
(D) A security issue	(D) セキュリティーの問題
42. What does Matt say he can do?	Mattは何ができると言っているか。
(A) Reserve a bus ticket	(A) バスの乗車券を予約する
(B) Contact a travel agent	(B) 旅行代理店に連絡する
(C) Check alternative airports	(C) 代わりの空港を確認する
(D) Write an inspection report	(D) 検査報告書を書く
43. Where is the factory located?	工場はどこにあるか。
(A) In Tianjin	(A) 天津
(B) In Beijing	(B) 北京
(C) In Florida	(C) フロリダ
(D) In Ottawa	(D) オタワ

先読みを終えた段階で，僕は以下のことを頭の中に巡らせている。

41.「フライトなぜキャンセル？　事故，天候，機械，セキュリティー？」
42.「Matt何できる？　旅行業界の関係者？」
43.「工場，どこ？　天津，北京，フロリダ，オタワ？」

このように設問を先読みして集中して聞くべき部分を絞り込んだ上で，能動的に音声を聞いていく。それでは，実際にこの問題の音声を聞いてみよう。

例1 CD1 35

Questions 41 through 43 refer to the following conversation.
設問41-43は次の会話に関するものである。

M1: This is Matt Ali from Ottawa Travels. I have unfortunate news. I'm afraid your flight to Beijing for tomorrow has been canceled Q41 due to an approaching snowstorm.

M2: I was afraid this might happen. But I really need to get to Beijing tomorrow. Is there any way you can help me?

M1: Q42 I can check the flight conditions at other airports. If any of them have flights leaving for Beijing tomorrow, maybe you can leave from there.

M2: I would appreciate that. Our client is most insistent that they receive the inspection report on time, and in order to do so, Q43 I must reach their factory in Tianjin tomorrow.

M1: こちらはOttawa TravelsのMatt Aliです。残念なお知らせです。吹雪が迫っているため，明日ご搭乗予定の北京行きの便が欠航となりました。

M2: そうなるのではないかと心配していました。でも，どうしても明日北京に行く必要があるのです。助けていただく方法は何かありませんか。

M1: 他の空港の飛行状況を確認できます。もし明日北京に到着する便があれば，お客さまはそちらから出発できるかもしれません。

M2: それは助かります。取引先が検査報告書を時間通りに受け取ることに非常にこだわっていまして，そのために，私は明日，天津にある取引先の工場に行かなければならないのです。

正解 **41.** (B)　**42.** (C)　**43.** (A)

語句 □unfortunate 残念な　□insistent 強要する，断固たる

41.「フライトなぜキャンセル？　事故，天候，機械，セキュリティー？」と記憶して聞いていく。due to an approaching snowstorm. から，天候が理由だと分かる。

42.「Matt何できる？　旅行業界の関係者？」と記憶して聞いていく。I can check the flight conditions at other airports. から(C) Check alternative airportsが正解。other airportsがalternative airportsと言い換えられている点に注意したい。

43.「工場，どこ？　天津，北京，フロリダ，オタワ？」と記憶して聞いていく。 your flight to Beijing, need to get to Beijing, flights leaving for BeijingとBeijingが3回も登場するが，正解はfactory in Tianjinから(A)の天津。会話の最後まで集中して聞くようにしよう。

❷「木」問題を攻略する

「木」問題とは，会話やトークに**正解の根拠が一度しか登場しない問題**のことである（反対に，Where does this conversation most likely take place? のように，会話の随所に正解のヒントとなる内容が登場する問題を「森」問題と呼ぶ）。

「木」問題は内容が難しいわけではない。集中力が途切れた一瞬に，一度しか登場しない**正解の根拠を聞き逃してしまう**ことが問題なのだ。**例2**で具体的に見てみよう。

例2 CD 1 36

Questions 71 through 73 refer to the following advertisement.
設問71-73は次の宣伝に関するものである。

If your business uses office paper and printing products, you must visit the 4th Birmingham Stationery Show, Q71 held March 6 through 10 at the Birmingham Convention Center. The convention center is easily accessible by bus or car and is fifteen minutes' walk from the nearest train station. Products showcased at the event include greeting cards, invitations, personalized stationery, decorative home office products, writing instruments and much much more. Q72 Go to Birmingham Stationery Show Online to see a list of suppliers exhibiting at the show. Q73 You can also purchase admission tickets from our Web site and save 5 dollars.

会社で事務用紙や印刷機器をお使いでしたら，3月6日から10日までBirminghamコンベンションセンターで開催される第4回Birmingham 文房具フェアにぜひご参加ください。コンベンションセンターはバスや車で行きやすく，最寄りの駅からは徒歩15分です。イベントで展示される製品には，挨拶状，招待状，名前入りの便箋，装飾的なホームオフィス向け製品，筆記用具など，さらにたくさんのものがあります。フェアで展示予定の供給業者のリストについては，Birmingham 文房具フェアのウェブサイトをご覧ください。ウェブサイトでは入場券を購入することもでき，その場合は5ドルの割引となります。

語句 □showcase ～を展示する □decorative 装飾的な

71. When does the event start?
(A) On March 4
(B) On March 5
(C) On March 6
(D) On March 10

イベントはいつ始まるか。
(A) 3月4日
(B) 3月5日
(C) 3月6日
(D) 3月10日

72. According to the speaker, what can listeners do online?
(A) Fill a registration form
(B) Get travel assistance
(C) Check the event schedule
(D) See a list of exhibitors

話し手によると，聞き手はインターネットで何ができるか。
(A) 登録用紙に記入する
(B) 移動の支援を受ける
(C) イベントスケジュールを確認する
(D) 出展者のリストを参照する

73. What is cheaper online?	インターネットだと安くなるものは何か。
(A) Shipping charges	(A) 送料
(B) Customized products	(B) 特別注文の製品
(C) Entrance fee	(C) 入場料
(D) Product catalog	(D) 製品カタログ

正解 **71. (C)** **72. (D)** **73. (C)**

設問を先読みするときに，**72.** と **73.** はどちらも質問に online という語が登場していることを意識する。これは，立て続けに**2問分の正解の根拠が登場する可能性**があるということだ。online に関する内容が聞こえ始めたら，集中力のギアを一段階上げよう。

71. 先読みの際に「いつ始まるのか」をポイントとして絞り込む。トークでは held March 6 through 10 と 2 つの日付けが登場するが，開始は6日なので(C)が正解だ。簡単な問題だが，こうした問題を甘く見ず，丁寧に解答しよう。

72. 先読みの際に意識した online がトークの終盤で出てくる。a list of suppliers exhibiting at the show「フェアで展示予定の供給業者のリスト」を a list of exhibitors と言い換えた(D)が正解だ。

73. トークの最後に admission tickets を購入すると save 5 dollars「5 ドルの割引となる」と述べられているため，正解は(C)だ。**72.** と **73.** の正解の根拠が連続しているので，聞き逃さないよう気を付けたい。

990 点獲得への道

Part 3 & 4は，1セット分の質問と選択肢を，音声が流れるまでに何度も読み，内容を頭に残しておく。最終的には，24 秒間に1セット分の質問と選択肢を**3回先読み**できるレベルを目指そう。**「先読み力」の養成が，Part 3 & 4の完全制覇につながる**。

この先の Training では，先読みをして会話やトークのポイントを絞る訓練を行うと同時に，正解の根拠となる部分をリテンションしてアウトプットする訓練を積む。これにより，音声を聞く際の集中力と，選択肢で音声の内容がパラフレーズされていても正解を選び取るためのリテンション力を確実に身に付けることができる。

まとめ

Part 3 & 4 では設問を先読みして，ポイントを絞り込む。「木」問題に必要な集中力も高めよう。

Part 3 Training

CD 1 37

(1) 以下の質問と選択肢を読み，会話のポイントを予測しなさい。

1. What has one of the speakers been preparing?
(A) A conference agenda
(B) A participant list
(C) A travel itinerary
(D) A seating plan

2. Who most likely is Dr. Jackson?
(A) A secretary
(B) A surgeon
(C) An author
(D) A professor

3. What will happen next week?
(A) A conference will be held at the office.
(B) A class will take place at headquarters.
(C) Transportation tickets will be arranged.
(D) A promotion will be announced.

(2) 2人の短い会話を聞き，上の質問に対して最も適切な答えを(A) (B) (C) (D)の中から1つ選びなさい（マークシートは別冊p.157にあります）。

(3) 正解の根拠となる部分をできる限り正確に書きなさい。

HUMMERのココがポイント

1. 質問のone of は無視して「（話者）何用意？」と考えて差し支えない。選択肢から，「人が集まる」ことに関する話題だと予測できる。
2. (C)のauthorは文脈によってはDr.と呼ばれる可能性があるので，正解の候補から外してしまわないようにしよう。
3. next weekがポイントだ。(A)と(B)はconferenceとclassを，(C)と(D)はticketとpromotionを頭に入れておこう。

これらを踏まえ，再度質問にある「1. preparing，2. Jackson，3. next week」を特に意識して音声を待とう。

Questions 1 through 3 refer to the following conversation.

設問 1-3 は次の会話に関するものである。

W1: Ms. Knowles, has Dr. Jackson confirmed his participation in the upcoming conference? Q1 The list of participants I've been working on is almost ready, but I need his confirmation before I can finish it.

W2: Actually, I tried to call him earlier about another matter, but Q2 his secretary said he's on a book signing tour right now and won't be back for two weeks.

W1: Oh no. I was hoping to get it done before Q3 I travel to the head office next week to attend the Conflict Management Course, so Brenda can start working on the seating arrangements. I guess that will have to wait, then.

W1: Knowlesさん，Jackson先生は今度の会議の出欠を決めたのかしら。私が作っている出席者リストはほとんどできているんだけど，完成させるには先生の出欠確認が必要なのよ。

W2: 実は別件で先ほど先生に電話をしようとしたんだけど，秘書が言うには，先生は今，書籍のサイン会のツアーに出ていて，2週間戻らないそうなのよ。

W1: まあ。私はコンフリクト・マネジメント講座に出席するために来週本社に出張するから，その前に完成させて，Brendaが座席の用意を始められるようにしたかったのに。じゃあ，まだ待たなければならないようね。

語句 □work on ～ ～に取り組む

1. 話し手の1人は何を準備しているか。

(A) 会議の議題一覧　(B) 出席者のリスト　(C) 出張の日程表　(D) 座席の配置図

正解 **(B)**

解説 下線部から(B)が正解となる。The list of participantsが，選択肢ではA participant listと少しだけ言い換えられている。

2. Jackson先生は誰だと考えられるか。

(A) 秘書　(B) 外科医　(C) 作家　(D) 教授

正解 **(C)**

解説 下線部からJackson先生は書籍のサイン会のツアーに出ている最中であることが分かる。この問題に正解するための根拠はここにしか登場しないので，絶対に聞き逃すことのないようにしたい。Dr.という呼称はprofessorやsurgeonを連想させるが，引っかからないように。

語句 □surgeon 外科医

3. 来週何が起こるか。

(A) オフィスで会議が開催される。

(B) 本社で講座が開講される。

(C) 交通チケットが手配される。

(D) 昇進が発表される。

正解 **(B)**

解説 下線部から(B)が正解だ。conferenceやofficeに引っぱられて(A)を正解に選ばないように注意しよう。先読みをする段階で，全ての選択肢を正確に把握しておくことが大切だ。

Training

CD 1 38

(1) 以下の質問と選択肢を読み，会話のポイントを予測しなさい。

4. Why has Natalie stopped getting coffee at work?
(A) She doesn't like coffee.
(B) She thinks it's too expensive.
(C) She prefers mild coffee.
(D) She wants to cut down on caffeine.

5. What is suggested about the new machine?
(A) It is affordable.
(B) It makes other beverages.
(C) It is customizable.
(D) It takes less time.

6. What does Natalie say she may do?
(A) Purchase the product herself
(B) Tell others about the product
(C) Test the product tomorrow
(D) Start bringing her own mug

(2) 2人の短い会話を聞き，上の質問に対して最も適切な答えを (A) (B) (C) (D) の中から１つ選びなさい（マークシートは別冊 p.157 にあります）。

(3) 正解の根拠となる部分をできる限り正確に書きなさい。

HUMMERのココがポイント

4. 質問から stopped getting coffee という動作を意識し，選択肢にその理由が並んでいることを押さえる。
5. 質問に new machine が登場する。TOEIC の会話で扱われるテーマは基本的に１つなので，4. と合わせて考えると，「飲み物」に関する機械ではないかと予想できる。
6. 登場人物が次にとる行動を解答する。次の行動は会話の後半で言われることが多い。

Questions 4 through 6 refer to the following conversation.

設問 4-6 は次の会話に関するものである。

W1: Natalie, have you tried the new coffee machine in the employee lounge?

W2: No, Q4 I stopped getting coffee at work because it was too strong for me. Why?

W1: You should try it. Q5 The new machine brews coffee individually, so you can adjust the strength and temperature to suit your taste, unlike the old one where you had to share a pot with all the other workers.

W2: Nice. I'll definitely try it out during lunch break and if it's good, Q6 I'll recommend it to my friends for their workplaces too.

W1: Natalie，従業員休憩室の新しいコーヒーメーカーをもう試した？

W2: いいえ，職場のコーヒーは私には濃過ぎるから，飲むのをやめたの。どうして？

W1: 試した方がいいわよ。他の従業員全員とポットを共有しなければならなかった古いコーヒーメーカーと違って，新しいのは個別にコーヒーを入れるから，好みに合わせて濃さや温度を調節できるのよ。

W2: それはいいわね。昼休みに絶対に試してみるわ。もし気に入ったら，友人たちにも彼らの職場用に薦めてみるわ。

語句 □strong（お茶，コーヒーなどが）濃い　□brew（お茶，コーヒーなど）を入れる

Part 3

4. Natalieはなぜ職場でコーヒーを飲むのをやめたのか。

(A) コーヒーが好きではないから。
(B) 値段が高過ぎると思っているから。
(C) マイルドなコーヒーの方が好きだから。
(D) カフェインを減らしたいから。

正解 **(C)**

解説 下線部から(C)が正解だ。it was too strong for me.「私には濃過ぎる」を，prefers mild coffee「マイルドなコーヒーの方が好きだ」と言い換えている。

語句 □cut down on ～ ～を減らす

5. 新しいコーヒーメーカーについてどんなことが分かるか。

(A) 値段が手頃である。
(B) 他の飲み物を作る。
(C) 好みに合わせて調整できる。
(D) より短い時間でできる。

正解 **(C)**

解説 最初に登場する女性の2回目の発言から，(C)が正解。brewの意味が取りづらいかもしれないが，直後の「（コーヒーの）濃さと温度を調節できる」と述べている部分をきちんと聞き取ることができれば大丈夫だ。

語句 □customizable カスタマイズ可能な

6. Natalieは何をするかもしれないと言っているか。

(A) その製品を自分で購入する
(B) その製品について他の人に話す
(C) その製品を明日試す
(D) 自分のマグカップを持参し始める

正解 **(B)**

解説 2人目の女性であるNatalieが2回目の発言で，I'll recommend it to my friends for their workplaces too. と言っている。「友人たちに薦める」が(B)の内容と一致するので正解だ。

Training

CD 1 39

(1) 以下の質問と選択肢を読み，会話のポイントを予測しなさい。

7. What event are the speakers going to attend after work?
(A) A retirement party
(B) A promotional event
(C) An opening ceremony
(D) A congratulatory gathering

8. How many people probably went for the interview?
(A) 2
(B) 6
(C) 10
(D) 12

9. What does one of the speakers wish to do?
(A) Inspect an educational certificate
(B) Visit a construction site
(C) Study a scale drawing of a building
(D) Discuss the importance of a project

(2) 2人の短い会話を聞き，上の質問に対して最も適切な答えを (A) (B) (C) (D) の中から1つ選びなさい（マークシートは別冊p.157にあります）。

(3) 正解の根拠となる部分をできる限り正確に書きなさい。

HUMMERのココがポイント

7. (B) の promotional event は「販売促進イベント」であり，「昇進祝い」ではないので勘違いしないようにしよう。会話がお祝いごとであれば (D) が正解と意識しておく。

8. 質問は interview に行った人数だ。12 が dozen で言い換えられるのは TOEIC の定番なので，注意して音声を聞こう。

9. (A) の educational certificate「教育修了証書」と (C) の scale drawing「縮尺図」の意味を推測できる余裕を持ちたい。scale の意味が分からない場合は無視して，a drawing of a building と考えておけばよい。

Questions 7 through 9 refer to the following conversation.

設問 7-9 は次の会話に関するものである。

M1: Hi, Ted. Q7 We're organizing a small get-together after work to celebrate Lucas' promotion to Head Architect. We'll meet at six at Bistro Emanuel. Are you in?	M1: Ted，こんにちは。Lucasの主任建築士への昇進を祝って，仕事の後にささやかなパーティーを企画しているんだ。Bistro Emanuelに6時に集合なんだけど，参加できる？
M2: Sure, I'll be there. I was wondering who would replace Mr. Hoffman after he retires. Q8 I heard they interviewed a dozen candidates for the position, but I'm so glad Lucas got it. I worked with him on the Laramie Primary School Project and he was brilliant.	M2: もちろん参加するよ。Hoffmanさんの退職後，誰が後任になるんだろうって思っていたんだ。そのポジションを巡って12人の候補者が面接を受けたと聞いたけど，Lucasが勝ち取ったのはうれしいよ。彼とはLaramie小学校のプロジェクトで一緒に仕事をしたんだ。彼は優秀だったな。
M1: I feel the same way. By the way, Q9 I'm working on a new public school design. Could I take a look at the architectural plan of Laramie Primary School?	M1: 同感だよ。ところで，私は今，新しいパブリックスクールの設計に取り組んでいるんだ。Laramie小学校の建築図面を見せてもらってもいいかな。

語句 □get-together パーティー　□Are you in? 参加できますか。　□brilliant 優秀な
□architectural 建築上の

7. 2人は仕事の後に何のイベントに出席する予定か。

(A) 退職パーティー　(B) 販売促進イベント　(C) 開会式　(D) 祝いの会合

正解 **(D)**

解説 下線部のget-together after work to celebrate Lucas' promotionが(D)と合致する。2人目の男性の発言に出てくるhe retiresから正解を(A)と勘違いしないように気を付けたい。

語句 □promotional event 販売促進イベント　□congratulatory gathering 祝いの会合

8. 何人の人が面接を受けに行ったと考えられるか。

(A) 2人　(B) 6人　(C) 10人　(D) 12人

正解 **(D)**

解説 2人目の男性の発言にa dozen candidatesとあるので(D)が正解だ。dozenを12に言い換えたり，decadeを10 yearsに言い換えたりするのが，TOEICでは頻出のパターンだ。質問や選択肢に12や10 yearsが登場した瞬間に「dozenやdecadeが来るな」と想定しておこう。

9. 話し手の1人は何をしたいと思っているか。

(A) 教育修了証書を検査する　(B) 建設現場を訪れる
(C) 建物の縮尺図を研究する　(D) プロジェクトの重要性を話し合う

正解 **(C)**

解説 1人目の男性の2回目の発言に，I'm working on a new public school design. Could I take a look at the architectural plan of Laramie Primary School? とあるため，(C)が正解だと判断できる。scale drawing「縮尺図」という表現を押さえておこう。

語句 □educational certificate 教育修了証書

Training

CD 1 40

(1) 以下の質問と選択肢を読み，会話のポイントを予測しなさい。

10. What time are the speakers supposed to be at the destination?
(A) In 10 minutes
(B) In 15 minutes
(C) In 20 minutes
(D) In 30 minutes

11. How will the speakers get to the destination?
(A) On foot
(B) By car
(C) By bus
(D) By train

12. What will one of the speakers do next?
(A) Call the supervisor
(B) Report the situation
(C) Mail the handouts
(D) Present at a conference

(2) 2人の短い会話を聞き，上の質問に対して最も適切な答えを (A) (B) (C) (D) の中から1つ選びなさい（マークシートは別冊 p.157 にあります）。

(3) 正解の根拠となる部分をできる限り正確に書きなさい。

HUMMERのココがポイント

10. 選択肢から，数字の言い換えを意識する。15分なら a quarter of an hour，30分であれば half an hour だ。
11. 交通手段に関する問い。おそらく複数の交通手段がトークの中に登場し，実際に利用したものがどれなのかを解答することになりそうだと心得ておこう。
12. 選択肢はどれもあり得そうなことばかりだ。do next 系の問題は，トークの終盤に正解の根拠が述べられることが多い。最後まで集中力を保とう。(D) の present には「～を贈る，表す，提示する」などの意味があるが，ここでは「conference でプレゼンを行う」という意味の自動詞だ。

このセットは「時間 ⇒ 交通手段 ⇒ 次にすること」という流れの TOEIC 頻出パターンである。会話の内容を推測しやすいかもしれないが，推測に頼らず，常に「音声中心」で解答にあたり，「細部まで一言一句聞き逃さない」という姿勢を崩してはならない。

Questions 10 through 12 refer to the following conversation.

設問 10-12 は次の会話に関するものである。

M1: Bad news, Jim. There's a long queue at the taxi stand and we'll have to wait at least half an hour to get one.

M2: But Q10 we're supposed to be at the conference hall in twenty minutes! What if we take the number 10? The bus stop's right there.

M1: With these road conditions, I doubt the bus will be any faster. I don't know what they will do without the handouts if we don't get there on time, though ... I'll tell you what. Q11 If we take the subway, we can make it in fifteen, if we're lucky.

M2: OK. Q12 I'll text the manager to let him know what's going on.

M1: 悪い知らせだよ，Jim。タクシー乗り場には長い列ができていて，乗れるまでには最低でも30分待たなければならない。

M2: でも僕らは20分後には会議場にいなければならないよ！ 10番のバスに乗るのはどうだろう。バス停がすぐそこだ。

M1: この道路状況でバスの方が速いとは思えない。でももし僕たちが間に合わなかったら，配布資料なしで彼らがどうするのかは分からないけれどね…。そうだ。地下鉄を使えば，運が良ければ15分後に到着できるよ。

M2: 分かった。部長に携帯メールを送って，現状を伝えるよ。

語句 □queue 列 □What if ～ ～したらどうか □doubt (that 節を伴って) ～ではないと思う □make it たどり着く □text 携帯メールを送る □what's going on 何が起こっているのか

10. 2人は目的地に何分後にいなければならないか。

(A) 10分後 (B) 15分後 (C) 20分後 (D) 30分後

正解 **(C)**

解説 2人目の男性の最初の発言に，we're supposed to be at the conference hall in twenty minutes! とある。2人は会議場に20分後には到着していないといけないため，正解は(C)だ。この発言の直前にat least half an hour「少なくとも30分」とあるが，これはタクシーの予想待ち時間である。混同しないよう，出来事と時間を一対一対応で結び付けておこう。

語句 □destination 目的地

11. 2人は目的地にどうやって到着する予定か。

(A) 徒歩で (B) 車で (C) バスで (D) 電車で

正解 **(D)**

解説 会話には，タクシー，バス，そして地下鉄が登場する。1人目の男性の2回目の発言にIf we take the subway, we can make it in fifteenとあり，直後に2人目の男性がOK.と返答しているので，正解は(D)だ。(A)に関しては会話の中で言及されていない。

12. 話し手の1人は次に何をするか。

(A) 管理者に電話をする (B) 状況を報告する

(C) 配布資料を郵送する (D) 会議で発表する

正解 **(B)**

解説 2人目の男性が，2回目の発言でI'll text the manager to let him know what's going on. と述べているため，「携帯メールで」部長に状況を知らせることが分かる。よって正解は(B)だ。

Part 3 Practice Test

CD 1 41～45

2人の短い会話を聞き，質問に対して最も適切な答えを(A) (B) (C) (D)の中から1つ選びなさい（マークシートは別冊p.158にあります）。

1. What does the customer ask about?
(A) Store location
(B) Discount amount
(C) Coupon validity
(D) Delivery costs

2. What kind of product did the customer purchase last year?
(A) Eye glasses
(B) Trousers
(C) Footwear
(D) Jewelry

3. What is the customer advised to do?
(A) Subscribe to a fan club
(B) Check out new products
(C) Set up a Web site
(D) Request a catalog

---

4. What does the man ask the woman to do?
(A) Search the Internet
(B) Terminate a contract
(C) Make a formal complaint
(D) Fix a computer

5. What does the man wish to obtain?
(A) A free trial
(B) User feedback
(C) A cost comparison
(D) An e-mail address

6. What will the man do next?
(A) Check the cables
(B) Call a specialist
(C) Visit a client
(D) Go out to eat

---

7. What is the man unable to find?
(A) An optical instrument
(B) A hand tool
(C) A protective device
(D) Cleaning gear

8. What did the man do last weekend?
(A) Purchase a small vehicle
(B) Visit an art gallery
(C) Obtain an old object
(D) Work in the garden

9. Why most likely is the woman surprised?
(A) She has met the man before.
(B) She thought the item was too heavy.
(C) She was not aware of the announcement.
(D) She discovered that they live near each other.

---

10. What most likely is the problem?
(A) A class is fully occupied.
(B) A locker cannot be opened.
(C) An item is missing from a locker.
(D) A hallway is blocked.

11. What does the customer want to do?
(A) Get a physical examination
(B) Maximize exercise efficiency
(C) Become a professional trainer
(D) Shorten her workout time

12. What is suggested about the ProTrain Program?
(A) It is offered every day.
(B) It includes motivational tips.
(C) It requires enrollment.
(D) It is free of charge.

---

13. What does the man specify about the product?
(A) It must be able to print high resolution documents.
(B) It needs to be able to adapt to different paper sizes.
(C) It must be able to make copies fast.
(D) It must have an additional function.

14. What probably happened last month?
(A) A piece of equipment was purchased.
(B) A product was released.
(C) A company was founded.
(D) An item was leased.

15. When can the man upgrade the product?
(A) In ten months
(B) In a year
(C) In two years
(D) At any time

Part 3 Practice Test 正解と解説

CD 1 41

Questions 1 through 3 refer to the following conversation.
設問 1-3 は次の会話に関するものである。

W1: Hello. Q1 Could you tell me if I can still use the discount coupon I have? The coupon ID code is 26789.	W1: もしもし。私が持っている割引券がまだ使えるかどうか教えてくださいますか。割引券のIDコードは26789です。
W2: Let me check that for you. Please hold ... Yes, you can use it at any of our outlets in Los Angeles for a 20 percent discount.	W2: 確認させていただきます。少々お待ちを…，はい，ご利用になれます。ロサンゼルス市内のどの店舗でも2割引きとなります。
W1: Great. Q2 I bought a pair of boots from your store last year and they are so comfortable, I wanted to buy a second pair.	W1: それはよかったわ。昨年そちらのお店でブーツを買ったのですが，とても履き心地が良いので，2足目を買いたいと思っていたのです。
W2: I'm happy to hear that. Q3 May I also suggest that you browse our new Web site where you can see our latest collection?	W2: そうおっしゃっていただけて光栄です。よろしければ，弊社の新しいウェブサイトもご覧ください。そこで，最新のコレクションをご覧いただけます。

語句 □outlet 直販店，店舗

1. What does the customer ask about?
(A) Store location
(B) Discount amount
(C) Coupon validity
(D) Delivery costs

顧客は何について尋ねているか。
(A) 店舗の場所
(B) 割引額
(C) 割引券の有効性
(D) 配送費

正解 **(C)**

解説 (B)～(D)は全て「費用」に関わる内容になっている。先読みをする段階で，きっちりと各選択肢の意味の違いを認識しておく必要がある。また，冒頭のあいさつ後，すぐにCould you tell me if I can still use the discount coupon I have? と，正解の根拠が流れてくるため，会話の開始時から最大限に集中力を高めておく必要がある。ここを聞き逃すと，後に出てくるa 20 percent discountを正解の根拠だと勘違いして(B)のDiscount amountを誤って選んでしまう恐れがあるのだ。

語句 □validity 有効性

2. What kind of product did the customer purchase last year?
(A) Eye glasses
(B) Trousers
(C) Footwear
(D) Jewelry

顧客は昨年どのような商品を購入したか。
(A) 眼鏡
(B) ズボン
(C) 履物
(D) 宝石類

正解 **(C)**

解説 1人目の女性が2回目の発言でI bought a pair of boots from your store last yearと言っているため，ブーツを買ったことが分かる。bootsを聞き逃した場合，すぐ後に出てくるI wanted to buy a second pair.から連想される(A)のEye glassesを選んでしまう恐れがある。比較的易しめの「木」問題ではあるが，甘く見ずに毎回「きちんと細部まで100%聞き取ってやるぞ」という心意気で臨んでほしい。

語句 □trousers ズボン

3. What is the customer advised to do?
(A) Subscribe to a fan club
(B) Check out new products
(C) Set up a Web site
(D) Request a catalog

顧客は何をするよう勧められているか。
(A) ファンクラブの会費を払う
(B) 新製品を確認する
(C) ウェブサイトを開設する
(D) カタログを請求する

正解 **(B)**

解説 May I also suggest that you browse our new Web siteという発言が会話の最後の方に出てくる。最新のコレクションを見られるウェブサイトの閲覧を勧めるのは，新製品をチェックするためと考えるのが自然。この文の前半を聞き逃した場合には新製品から連想して(D) Request a catalogを選んでしまう可能性もある。

語句 □subscribe to ～ ～の会費［予約金］を払う，～を予約購読する
□check out ～ ～を見てみる

CD 1 42

Questions 4 through 6 refer to the following conversation.

設問4-6 は次の会話に関するものである。

M: I can't believe our Internet is down again! I think it's time we switched providers. Q4 Can you call OWL Networks and tell them we won't be requiring their services anymore?

W: Sure, Mr. Brockman. However, we will need a new service provider first. How about Catville Communications? Their customer representatives are very friendly.

M: Hmm... Q5 I'd like to compare the expenses before I pick a new provider. Anyway, Q6 I'm going to get a bite to eat now. Hopefully it will be up and running when I return. If Mr. Feldman from Bart Global drops by, please tell him I'll be back within an hour.

M: 信じられない，インターネットがまたダウンした！　プロバイダーを変える時期だと思うよ。OWL Networksに電話して，もうサービスは不要だと言ってくれる？

W: 分かりました，Brockmanさん。ですけど，まず新しいサービスプロバイダーが必要ですよね。Catville Communicationsはどうでしょう。そこの顧客担当者はとても親切です。

M: うーん…新しいプロバイダーを選ぶ前に，費用を比較したいところだな。いずれにせよ，今ちょっと食事に行ってくる。できれば，帰ったときには直っているといいけど。もしBart　GlobalのFeldmanさんが立ち寄ったら，私は1時間以内に戻ると伝えておいて。

語句　□switch ～を変える，交換する　□get a bite to eat 軽く食事をする
□hopefully 願わくは（～だといいのだが）
□up and running（コンピューターなどが）正常に作動して　□drop by 立ち寄る

4. What does the man ask the woman to do?
(A) Search the Internet
(B) Terminate a contract
(C) Make a formal complaint
(D) Fix a computer

男性は女性に何をするように頼んでいるか。
(A) インターネットで検索する
(B) 契約を打ち切る
(C) 正式に苦情を申し立てる
(D) コンピューターを修理する

正解　**(B)**

解説　質問の主語が男性なので，何かを依頼するのは男性のはずである。男性の最初の発言の下線部より，(B)が正解だ。インターネットがたびたびダウンすることに対し苦情を申し立てるのは当たり前の流れのようだが，冒頭のI can't believe our Internet is down again!を聞いただけで(C)を選択することのないようにしたい。

語句　□terminate ～を終結させる　□formal complaint 正式な苦情

5. What does the man wish to obtain?
(A) A free trial
(B) User feedback
(C) A cost comparison
(D) An e-mail address

男性は何を入手したがっているか。
(A) 無料の試用
(B) ユーザーからのフィードバック
(C) 費用の比較
(D) Eメールアドレス

正解 **(C)**

解説 男性の2回目の発言の下線部より，費用の比較をしたいということが分かる。compare the expensesをcost comparisonと言い換えた(C)が正解だ。他の選択肢の内容は，いずれも会話に登場していない。

語句 □free trial 無料の試用

6. What will the man do next?
(A) Check the cables
(B) Call a specialist
(C) Visit a client
(D) Go out to eat

男性は次に何をするか。
(A) ケーブルを確認する
(B) 専門家に電話をする
(C) 取引先を訪れる
(D) 食事に出掛ける

正解 **(D)**

解説 「次に何をするか」を示す情報は，会話の後半に登場することが多い。男性の2回目の発言に，I'm going to get a bite to eat now.とあるため，男性は今から食事に出掛けるということが分かる。よって，正解は(D)だ。男性の次の行動に関する手掛かりはここからしか得られないので，かなり難しいが，選択肢にまで事前に目を通しておくと解きやすい。質問の主語がthe manやthe womanの問題，つまり会話をしている2人のうちのどちらかに関する質問は非常に多く，主語となっている人物自身が正解の根拠を述べることがほとんどである。

CD 1 43

Questions 7 through 9 refer to the following conversation.

設問7-9は次の会話に関するものである。

M: Hi. Q7 I'm looking for a claw hammer but I can't find one. Aren't they in the gardening section?	M: こんにちは。くぎ抜きの付いた金づちを探しているのですが，見つかりません。園芸コーナーにはないのですか。
W: No, they're over there in aisle 5. If you follow me, I'll show you exactly where they are. Are you doing a little handiwork?	W: ありません。向こうの5番売り場です。ついてきてくだされば，置いてある場所までご案内しますよ。ちょっとした手仕事をされるのですか。
M: Well, Q8 last weekend I picked up a beautiful antique mirror at a garage sale and now I need to hang it up. It's big and heavy so it's quite challenging. I had a hard time carrying it to my house in a wheelbarrow, even though it was only two blocks away.	M: ええと，先週末にガレージセールで年代物の美しい鏡を手に入れたので，今すぐにそれを掛けなければならないのです。大きくて重いのでかなり大変です。たった2ブロックの距離でしたが，自宅まで手押し車で運ぶのに苦労しました。
W: Q9 You're kidding! Do you mean the garage sale on Elm Street? We live right next to that house!	W: まさか！ Elm Streetのガレージセールのことですか。私たちはその家のすぐ隣に住んでいるのです！

語句 □claw hammer くぎ抜きの付いた金づち □handiwork 手仕事, 手細工 □antique 年代物の □wheelbarrow 手押し車

7. What is the man unable to find?
男性が見つけられないものは何か。

(A) An optical instrument　光学機器
(B) A hand tool　手工具
(C) A protective device　保護装置
(D) Cleaning gear　清掃用具

正解 **(B)**

解説 質問から，男性が何かを探しており，それを見つけられずにいるということが分かる。男性の最初の発言にあるclaw hammerをhand toolと言い換えている(B)が正解。他の選択肢が明らかに違うので，消去法でも判断できるだろう。

語句 □optical instrument 光学機器 □hand tool 手工具 □gear 道具，備品

8. What did the man do last weekend?
(A) Purchase a small vehicle
(B) Visit an art gallery
(C) Obtain an old object
(D) Work in the garden

男性は先週末に何をしたか。
(A) 小型の乗り物を購入した
(B) 画廊を訪れた
(C) 古い物を入手した
(D) 庭仕事をした

正解 **(C)**

解説 7.に引き続き，主語が男性なので男性の発言にヒントがあると考えて音声を聞こう。last weekendが正解につながるキーワードとなる。男性は2回目の発言でlast weekend I picked up a beautiful antique mirror at a garage saleと述べている。antique mirrorをold objectと抽象的に言い換えた(C)が正解である。

9. Why most likely is the woman surprised?
(A) She has met the man before.
(B) She thought the item was too heavy.
(C) She was not aware of the announcement.
(D) She discovered that they live near each other.

女性はなぜ驚いていると考えられるか。
(A) 以前に男性に会ったことがあるから。
(B) 品物が重すぎると思ったから。
(C) 告知を知らなかったから。
(D) 互いに近所に住んでいることが分かったから。

正解 **(D)**

解説 女性は2回目の発言でYou're kidding! Do you mean the garage sale on Elm Street? We live right next to that house! と言っている。that houseは，直前の男性の発言にあるa garage saleが開催された場所を指しており，男性がそこからわずか2ブロックの距離に住んでいることが分かっている。正解は(D)だ。男性の2回目の発言後半の内容は(B)に近いが，女性は鏡の重さに対して驚いているわけではない。

CD 1 44

Questions 10 through 12 refer to the following conversation.

設問 10-12 は次の会話に関するものである。

W1: Welcome to Whitesand Gym. How may I help you?

W2: Q10 Actually, this locker key doesn't seem to work so I'd like another one. Also, I would like to sign up for personal training. I have a very busy schedule, so Q11 I want to make sure I'm getting the most out of my workouts.

W1: That's a great idea. We offer a free quarterly consultation to all our members, but if you would like a more extensive personal coaching experience, Q12 we recommend you join the ProTrain Program. Once you are enrolled, you receive 1-on-1 training with one of our certified trainers, an hour a day up to 3 times a week, as well as effective nutrition advice.

W1: Whitesand Gymへようこそ。どうなさいましたか。

W2: 実はこのロッカーの鍵が作動しないようなので，別の鍵が欲しいのです。また，個別トレーニングの申し込みもしたいのですが。私はとても忙しいので，確実にトレーニングを最大限活用できるようにしたいのです。

W1: 素晴らしいお考えです。当ジムでは全てのメンバーのために3カ月ごとの無料相談を行っておりますが，もしもっと広範囲にわたる個別指導体験をお望みでしたら，ProTrain Programへのご入会をお勧めします。ご入会されますと，当ジムの公認トレーナーによるマンツーマンのトレーニングを1日に1時間，週3回まで受けられます。また，栄養面での効果的なアドバイスも受けられます。

語句 □work 作動する，機能する　□get the most out of ～ ～を最大限に活用する　□workout トレーニング　□enroll ～を登録させる，入会させる　□1-on-1 マンツーマンの　□certified 公認の，資格のある　□up to ～ 最大で～まで

10. What most likely is the problem?

(A) A class is fully occupied.
(B) A locker cannot be opened.
(C) An item is missing from a locker.
(D) A hallway is blocked.

何が問題だと考えられるか。

(A) クラスが完全に埋まっている。
(B) ロッカーが開かない。
(C) ロッカーから物が紛失している。
(D) 廊下が封鎖されている。

正解 **(B)**

解説 会話の登場人物が困っている内容を問う設問は，Part 3と4に頻繁に登場する。2人目の女性の最初の発言の「ロッカーの鍵が作動しない」ということが，(B)の選択肢では「ロッカーが開かない」と言い換えられている。他の選択肢の内容は，会話では全く触れられていない。

語句 □hallway 廊下

11. What does the customer want to do?
(A) Get a physical examination
(B) Maximize exercise efficiency
(C) Become a professional trainer
(D) Shorten her workout time

顧客がしたいことは何か。
(A) 身体検査を受ける
(B) トレーニングの効率を最大化する
(C) プロのトレーナーになる
(D) トレーニングの時間を短縮する

正解 **(B)**

解説 10.と同じく，この設問に対する正解の根拠も2人目の女性の最初の発言にある。下線部を言い換えた，(B)のMaximize exercise efficiencyが正解だ。1回の発言に2つの設問に対する正解の根拠があることも常に想定し，設問を1つ解き終えても気を抜かないようにしよう。

語句 □physical examination 身体検査

12. What is suggested about the ProTrain Program?
(A) It is offered every day.
(B) It includes motivational tips.
(C) It requires enrollment.
(D) It is free of charge.

ProTrain Programについてどんなことが分かるか。
(A) 毎日行われている。
(B) やる気を起こさせる助言が含まれている。
(C) 入会が必要である。
(D) 無料である。

正解 **(C)**

解説 ProTrain Programは，1人目の女性の2回目の発言に登場する。女性はProTrain Programを勧めた後，このプログラムに入会するとマンツーマンのトレーニングと栄養に関するアドバイスをもらえると説明している。マンツーマントレーニングと栄養に関するアドバイスに関しては選択肢にないため，(C)が正解だと判断できる。

語句 □motivational tip やる気を起こさせる助言

CD 1 45

Questions 13 through 15 refer to the following conversation.

設問 13-15 は次の会話に関するものである。

M: Hello. This is Mark Cohen from DIY Technologies. We're looking to lease a black and white copier for our office. Could you provide me with a quote? Oh, and Q13 we need one with high speed since we produce several thousand copies per month.

W: Hello, Mr. Cohen. In that case, Q14 I'd like to suggest the new Horax-2000 monochrome copier from Gotland Electronics, which came out just last month. How long are you planning to lease the item?

M: Around two years. After that, we'll probably want to upgrade.

W: Q15 Actually, you can upgrade whenever you want during your lease. We are happy to provide you with the newest technology to support your business.

M: こんにちは。DIY TechnologiesのMark Cohenと申します。オフィス用にモノクロのコピー機のリースを考えています。見積もりをしていただけないでしょうか。ああ，それと，弊社では毎月数千枚ものコピーをするので，高速のコピー機が必要です。

W: こんにちは，Cohenさん。その場合でしたら，Gotland Electronicsから先月出たばかりの新製品，Horax-2000モノクロコピー機をお薦めいたします。どのくらいの期間，リースを予定されていますか。

M: およそ2年ほどです。その後，恐らくアップグレードをしたいと思います。

W: 実際のところ，リース期間中であればいつでもアップグレードができます。最新のテクノロジーをご提供することでお客さまのビジネスをサポートできますことを，光栄に思います。

語句 □look to do ～することを計画する □in that case もしそうなら，その場合 □monochrome モノクロの

13. What does the man specify about the product?

(A) It must be able to print high resolution documents.
(B) It needs to be able to adapt to different paper sizes.
(C) It must be able to make copies fast.
(D) It must have an additional function.

男性は製品について何を指定しているか。

(A) 高解像度の文書を印刷できなければならない。
(B) さまざまな用紙サイズに対応できなければならない。
(C) 高速でコピーできなければならない。
(D) 付加機能がなければならない。

正解 **(C)**

解説 男性は最初の発言でコピー機のリースの見積もりを依頼しており，質問のproductとはこのコピー機のことを指している。下線部の内容をIt must be able to make copies fast.と言い表している(C)が正解だ。他の選択肢のキーワードは，(A) high resolution「高解像度」，(B) different paper sizes「さまざまな用紙サイズ」，そして(D) additional function「付加機能」だが，いずれも会話内では言及されていない。

語句 □high resolution 高解像度 □adapt to ～ ～に適合する

14. What probably happened last month?

(A) A piece of equipment was purchased.
(B) A product was released.
(C) A company was founded.
(D) An item was leased.

先月何が起こったと考えられるか。

(A) 装置が1台購入された。
(B) 製品が発売された。
(C) 会社が設立された。
(D) 商品がリースされた。

正解 **(B)**

解説 女性の最初の発言に，I'd like to suggest the new Horax-2000 monochrome copier from Gotland Electronics, which came out just last month. とあり，came out を was released と言い換えている (B) が正解だ。キーワードとなる last month が文末にあるため，きちんと集中してそこまでの内容を聞き取り，理解する必要がある。

15. When can the man upgrade the product?

(A) In ten months
(B) In a year
(C) In two years
(D) At any time

男性は製品をいつアップグレードできるか。

(A) 10カ月後
(B) 1年後
(C) 2年後
(D) いつでも

正解 **(D)**

解説 男性は2回目の発言で「2年ほどしたらアップグレードしたい」と言っており，これに対して女性は直後に Actually, you can upgrade whenever you want during your lease. と述べている。つまり，リース期間中ならアップグレードはいつでもできるので，正解は (D)。事前にきっちり質問と選択肢を読み，正確に理解して音声を待ち構えることが求められる問題だ。

Part 4 Training

CD 1 46

(1) 以下の質問と選択肢を読み，トークのポイントを予測しなさい。

1. What is the next stop?
(A) North Point Ferry Piers
(B) Hong Kong International Airport
(C) Kowloon Station
(D) Fortress Hill

2. According to the speaker, what has been changed?
(A) Storage space
(B) Bus destination
(C) Time of arrival
(D) Driving route

3. What are passengers asked to do?
(A) Have their tickets ready
(B) Leave the aisle clear
(C) Check the timetable
(D) Use the safety equipment

(2) 英文を聞き，上の質問に対して最も適切な答えを (A) (B) (C) (D) の中から1つ選びなさい（マークシートは別冊 p.157 にあります）。

(3) 正解の根拠となる部分をできる限り正確に書きなさい。

HUMMERのココがポイント

1. 質問のnext stopを特に意識してリテンションしておくこと。この語から，トークはバスか電車に関するアナウンスだと予想できる。選択肢の各駅名もきちんと頭の中で音読し，音声が流れてきたときに瞬時に一致させられるようにしておこう。
2. 質問のchangedがポイントだ。選択肢からは(A) storage，(B) destination，(C) time，(D) routeを特に押さえておこう。
3. 聞き手である乗客が求められることが問われているが，これはdo next系の問題と同様に，トークの終盤に正解の根拠が述べられる可能性が高いと意識しておこう。(C)のtimetableはトーク中ではscheduleやtimelineなどの語で登場する可能性もある。

Questions 1 through 3 refer to the following announcement.

設問 1-3 は次のアナウンスに関するものである。

Welcome on board the Swan Bus Service to North Point Ferry Piers. Q1 The next stop is Fortress Hill. Due to road construction, Q2 the estimated arrival time at North Point Ferry Piers has been changed from twelve o'clock to twelve-fifteen. Passengers to Hong Kong International Airport should change buses at Kowloon Station, where your connecting bus will be waiting. While on board, we advise you to store your luggage in the overhead compartments and Q3 keep your seat belt fastened at all times.

North Point Ferry Piers 行きの Swan Bus Serviceにご乗車ありがとうございます。次の停留所はFortress Hillです。道路工事が行われているため，North Point Ferry Piersへの到着予定時刻は12時から12時15分に変更となりました。香港国際空港に向かわれるお客さまはKowloon駅でバスを乗り換えてください。乗り換えのバスがそこで待っている予定です。ご乗車中はお荷物を頭上の荷物入れに収納し，シートベルトを常に着用したままにしてください。

Part 4

1. 次の停留所はどこか。

(A) North Point Ferry Piers
(B) 香港国際空港
(C) Kowloon駅
(D) Fortress Hill

正解 **(D)**

解説 選択肢にある地名は，一通りトークの中に登場するのが普通である。ここでは「次の」を表すnextがそのまま出てくると想定し，意識を集中して待ち構えよう。冒頭から2文目にThe next stop is Fortress Hill. とあるため，(D)が正解となる。nextは言い換えづらい言葉なので，ほとんどの場合そのままトークにも出てくる。

2. 話し手によると，何が変更されたか。

(A) 収納スペース　(B) バスの目的地　(C) 到着時刻　(D) 運行経路

正解 **(C)**

解説 トークの前半にthe estimated arrival time at North Point Ferry Piers has been changed from twelve o'clock to twelve-fifteen. とあるため，正解は(C)だ。時間や場所などの変更前と後の情報はfrom A to Bで表されることが多い。

語句 □storage space 収納スペース

3. 乗客は何をするように求められているか。

(A) 乗車券を用意する
(B) 通路を空けたままにする
(C) 時刻表を確認する
(D) 安全装備を使用する

正解 **(D)**

解説 聞き手が何をするべきなのかは，トークの後半で述べられることがほとんどである。トークの最後にkeep your seat belt fastened at all times. とあるので，これをUse the safety equipmentと言い換えている(D)が正解だ。他の選択肢は状況的に十分あり得る内容ではあるが，トークの中では言及されていないので不正解である。

語句 □safety equipment 安全装備

Training

CD 1 47

(1) 以下の質問と選択肢を読み，トークのポイントを予測しなさい。

4. How long will the event last?
(A) A month
(B) Two months
(C) Ten months
(D) A year

5. Who is Eleanor De Marco?
(A) A swimming coach
(B) A gym receptionist
(C) A movie star
(D) A yoga teacher

6. What are participants advised to do?
(A) Put on sunblock
(B) Book a place in advance
(C) Check the activities calendar
(D) Bring a towel and sandals

(2) 英文を聞き，上の質問に対して最も適切な答えを (A) (B) (C) (D) の中から1つ選びなさい（マークシートは別冊 p.157 にあります）。

(3) 正解の根拠となる部分をできる限り正確に書きなさい。

HUMMERのココがポイント

4. How long ～? から期間を問う問題であることをつかむ。選択肢にある期間を表す数字は，トークの中では他の言い方をされる可能性があるということを頭の片隅に入れておく。
5. Eleanor De Marco が何者であるかに注意。(C) 以外はフィットネスクラブに関する仕事なので，それぞれの職種の違いを意識してリテンションする。
6. 質問は聞き手である参加者が求められていることだが，これも do next 系とほぼ同じパターンの問題なので，トークの終盤に集中力を再度意識的に上げるようにすること。

Questions 4 through 6 refer to the following advertisement.

設問 4-6 は次の宣伝に関するものである。

With luxurious guest rooms and impeccable guest services, Northman Hotel is where you want to be. This summer, Northman Hotel will collaborate with Hilary's Gym to make sure guests get the most out of the summer months. Every Saturday from 8 A.M. to 10 A.M. Q4 during July and August, hotel guests and also those not staying at the hotel can participate in Q5 a free group yoga lesson instructed by gym instructor and professional dancer, Eleanor De Marco. Q6 Remember to bring your own mat and wear sunscreen as the lessons will take place outside in the garden beside the swimming pool.

豪華な客室と申し分のないお客さまサービスを備えたNorthman Hotelこそ，皆さまが行きたくなる場所です。この夏，Northman HotelはHilary's Gymと提携し，お客さまが夏の数カ月間，確実にご満足いただけるようにします。7月と8月の間，毎週土曜日の午前8時から10時まで，宿泊されているお客さまと，さらに宿泊されていないお客さまも，ジムのインストラクターでプロダンサーのEleanor De Marcoによるヨガの無料グループレッスンにご参加いただけます。レッスンは屋外のスイミングプールのそばにある庭園で行われるため，各自マットのご持参と，日焼け止めを塗ることを忘れないようお願いします。

語句 □impeccable 申し分のない □wear sunscreen 日焼け止めを塗る

4. イベントはどのくらいの期間続くか。

(A) 1カ月 (B) 2カ月 (C) 10カ月 (D) 1年

正解 **(B)**

解説 トーク中盤でイベントの期間をduring July and Augustと述べている。数字を使って言い換えている(B)が正解だ。ここより前の部分でget the most out of the summer months.と話してはいるが，具体的な期間を述べているのはこの部分だけなので聞き逃すわけにはいかない。

5. Eleanor De Marcoとは誰か。

(A) 水泳のコーチ (B) ジムの受付係 (C) 映画スター (D) ヨガの先生

正解 **(D)**

解説 Eleanor De Marcoはトークの後半でa free group yoga lesson instructed by gym instructor and professional dancer, Eleanor De Marco.と紹介されているため(D)が正解だ。この人物はprofessional dancerでもあるが，選択肢には一致するものがない。

6. 参加者は何をするように勧められているか。

(A) 日焼け止めを塗る (B) 事前に場所を予約する

(C) アクティビティーの予定表を確認する (D) タオルとサンダルを持参する

正解 **(A)**

解説 聞き手が「何をするか」「何をするよう求められているか」に関する設問は，Part 4に頻出である。トークの終盤にwear sunscreenとあるが，正解の根拠はこの一瞬しか登場しないのでやや難易度が高い。wear sunscreenは「日焼け止めを塗る」という意味であり，それが選択肢ではPut on sunblockと言い換えられている。正解は(A)だ。

語句 □put on sunblock 日焼け止めを塗る

Training

CD 1 48

(1) 以下の質問と選択肢を読み，トークのポイントを予測しなさい。

7. What kind of establishment is Blue Birds?
(A) A career counseling firm
(B) A human resource agency
(C) A charity organization
(D) A medical institution

8. How long will the course take?
(A) A day
(B) Two days
(C) A month
(D) A fortnight

9. Who is Naomi Grant?
(A) A high school student
(B) A college instructor
(C) A healthcare professional
(D) A hospital surgeon

(2) 英文を聞き，上の質問に対して最も適切な答えを (A) (B) (C) (D) の中から 1 つ選びなさい（マークシートは別冊 p.157 にあります）。

(3) 正解の根拠となる部分をできる限り正確に書きなさい。

HUMMERのココがポイント

7. Blue Birds という固有名詞に留意しつつ，(A) の career counseling firm と (B) の human resource agency を混同しないよう意識して音声を待つこと。
8. 期間に関する質問なので「言い換え表現が来るのでは」と意識しておく。
9. Naomi Grant という名前に注意して音声を聞く。(C) の healthcare professional と (D) の hospital surgeon は意味が近いので混同しないように。

Questions 7 through 9 refer to the following news broadcast.

設問7-9は次のニュース放送に関するものである。

And now for local news. This fall, Q7 Blue Birds, a charity organization based in Jackson Town is hosting a course for those interested in working as a childcare provider. Q8 The one-day course is divided into two parts. The first part is designed to teach the participants how to care for children and infants, and the second part to provide safety tips such as what to do in case of an emergency. Many people, including local high school students, have already reserved a place in the course. Q9 Naomi Grant, a nurse from Jackson Hospital who will be teaching the course, commented that it's a good idea to be aware of possible accidents small children often get involved in, so you don't have to panic when something goes wrong.

それでは地域のニュースの時間です。この秋，Jackson Townを本拠地とした慈善団体，Blue Birdsが，保育士として働くことに興味を持っている方を対象とした講座を開講します。1日講座は2部に分かれています。第1部の目的は，参加者に子どもや乳児の面倒を見る方法を教えることです。第2部では，緊急時の対処法などの安全の秘訣を教えます。地元の高校生を含む多くの方が，すでにこの講座に申し込んでいます。講座で指導を行うJackson病院の看護師，Naomi Grantさんは，問題発生時に慌ててしまわないように，小さな子どもがしばしば巻き込まれる可能性のある事故について意識しておくことは得策であると述べています。

語句 □now for ～ さて次は～です　□based in ～ ～を本拠としている
□childcare provider 保育士　□infant 乳児　□panic 慌てる，うろたえる

7. Blue Birdsとはどのような種類の組織か。

(A) 職業相談会社　(B) 人材バンク　(C) 慈善団体　(D) 医療機関

正解 **(C)**

解説 Blue Birdsに関してはトークの冒頭で紹介されている。Blue Birds, a charity organizationと説明されているため，(C)が正解だ。

8. 講座はどのくらいの期間かかるか。

(A) 1日　(B) 2日　(C) 1カ月　(D) 2週間

正解 **(A)**

解説 The one-day courseと説明されているので，正解は(A)だ。他の選択肢にある期間に関しては，トーク中に全く述べられていない。

9. Naomi Grantとは誰か。

(A) 高校生　(B) 大学の講師　(C) 医療従事者　(D) 病院の外科医

正解 **(C)**

解説 Naomi Grantはトークの後半に登場し，Naomi Grant, a nurse from Jackson Hospitalと紹介されている。nurseをhealthcare professionalと上位語に言い換えた(C)が正解だ。上位語とは，dogやcatをanimalと言い換えるような，共通項をまとめた抽象的なものを指す。TOEICでは，このような抽象化を使った言い換えが多用されている。

Training

CD 1 49

(1) 以下の質問と選択肢を読み，トークのポイントを予測しなさい。

10. Where does the speaker probably work?
(A) At a human resource agency
(B) At a pharmaceutical company
(C) At an electronics manufacturer
(D) At a telecommunications provider

11. What does the speaker say about Coral-2000?
(A) It just came out on the market.
(B) It weighs less than the BG-3000.
(C) It is more expensive than the BG-3000.
(D) It has functions not available on the BG-3000.

12. Who most likely is the listener?
(A) A veteran employee
(B) A job candidate
(C) A new recruit
(D) A mobile phone salesperson

(2) 英文を聞き，上の質問に対して最も適切な答えを (A) (B) (C) (D) の中から1つ選びなさい（マークシートは別冊p.157にあります）。

(3) 正解の根拠となる部分をできる限り正確に書きなさい。

HUMMERのココがポイント

10. 出題頻度が非常に高い，場所に関する問題だ。選択肢には似通った内容のものはないが，甘く見ず，確実に正解したい。
11. Coral-2000という特定の機種を，BG-3000という他の機種と比較した内容の選択肢が3つある。「重さ」「価格」「機能」に注意して内容を聞き取ろう。
12. 3つ目の設問にWho most likely is the listener?とあることに，違和感を覚える上級学習者もいるだろう。通常この手の設問は最初にくることが多く，正解の根拠もトークの早い段階で登場することが多い。しかしながら今回，最後にこの設問があるということは，やはりトークの後半に正解の根拠が出てくるのではないかと想像して音声を聞こう。ひねりのある良問だ。最後まで，確実に細部を聞き取って理解してほしい。(B)のjob candidateと(C)のnew recruitを混同しないようにしよう。

Questions 10 through 12 refer to the following telephone message.

設問 10-12 は次の電話のメッセージに関するものである。

Hello. Q10 This is Sam Houser from the human resources department of Clark-Myers Pharmaceuticals with a message for Ms. Teresa Fisher. Ms. Fisher, I received your e-mail about your choice of company-issued mobile phones. Unfortunately, we ran out of the model of your choice. So you have two options: you can wait for us to restock and receive the phone a little later, or you can choose another model. Personally, Q11 I recommend the Coral-2000 since it is similar to the BG-3000 that you chose, but is newer and lighter. If you choose the latter option, you will receive the phone Q12 on your first day at Clark-Myers.	もしもし。こちらはClark-Myers製薬人事部のSam Houserですが，Teresa Fisherさんにご伝言があります。Fisherさんが選ばれた会社支給の携帯電話についてのEメールを受け取りました。残念ながら，お選びのモデルは在庫切れです。そのため，選択肢は次の2つがあります。在庫が補充されるのを待ってから少し遅れて受け取るか，または他のモデルを選ぶかです。個人的にはCoral-2000をお薦めします。理由はお選びになったBG-3000と似ているからですが，こちらの方がより新しく，より軽いです。後者をお選びの場合は，Clark-Myersでの初出勤日に電話を受け取ることになります。

語句 □company-issued 会社支給の □restock ～を補充する，新たに仕入れる

10. 話し手はどこで働いていると思われるか。

(A) 人材バンク (B) 製薬会社 (C) 電機メーカー (D) 通信接続業者

正解 **(B)**

解説 話し手が勤務している会社を問うタイプの問題は頻出だ。このタイプの設問はトークの前半に正解の根拠が述べられることが多い。冒頭のThis is Sam Houser from the human resources department of Clark-Myers Pharmaceuticalsを聞き取ることができれば(B)を選ぶことができる。

語句 □telecommunications provider 通信接続業者

11. 話し手はCoral-2000について何と言っているか。

(A) 市場に出たばかりである。
(B) BG-3000よりも軽い。
(C) BG-3000よりも値段が高い。
(D) BG-3000にはない機能がある。

正解 **(B)**

解説 Coral-2000に関することはトークの後半に述べられている。I recommend the Coral-2000 since it is similar to the BG-3000 that you chose, but is newer and lighter. とあるため，(B)が正解だ。Coral-2000はBG-3000よりもnewerではあるが，市場に出たばかりとはどこにも述べられていないため，(A)は不正解である。

語句 □come out on the market 市場に出る

12. 聞き手は誰だと考えられるか。

(A) 熟練の従業員 (B) 就職希望者 (C) 新入社員 (D) 携帯電話の販売員

正解 **(C)**

解説 冒頭で話し手は人事部の者だと名乗っているが，聞き手が誰なのかを特定する情報はなかなか登場しない。決め手は後半に登場するon your first day at Clark-Myers.だ。この部分から聞き手は話し手の会社で働き始めると判断できるので，(C)が正解だ。

Part 4

Part 4 Practice Test

CD 1 50～54

さまざまな英文を聞き，質問に対して最も適切な答えを(A) (B) (C) (D) の中から1つ選びなさい（マークシートは別冊p.158にあります）。

1. What does the speaker say about the last few months?
(A) They have been lowering prices of goods.
(B) They have not been selling many products.
(C) They have been using a new strategy.
(D) They have been developing a new product.

2. What will happen at the launch party?
(A) Books will be signed by Susan Derkins.
(B) Free gift bags will be distributed to clients.
(C) A store gift card will be given to attendees.
(D) A coupon may be used to purchase drinks.

3. When will the report be given?
(A) Today
(B) On Friday
(C) At the end of the month
(D) In a few months

---

4. What will most likely be discussed at the workshop?
(A) New developments in medicinal science
(B) Measures to fight adult illiteracy
(C) Environmentally-conscious nature tours
(D) Management of special dietary needs

5. What will be distributed tomorrow morning?
(A) Workshop agendas
(B) Tour catalogs
(C) Nametags
(D) Invitation letters

6. What does the speaker say she will do?
(A) Contact the restaurant
(B) Cancel a prior reservation
(C) Send a dinner menu
(D) Update the participant list

---

7. What will Josephine do?
(A) Announce an employee trip
(B) Talk about a past event
(C) Install a computer program
(D) Distribute a marketing survey

8. What is Pete Hamilton scheduled to do?
(A) Work on the wiring of computers
(B) Prepare equipment for donation
(C) Save sensitive information to disks
(D) Answer questions listeners may have

9. Who most likely is Kelly Young?
(A) An employee of an electronics recycling company
(B) The head of the Marketing Department
(C) A specialist in computer engineering
(D) A staff member at a nonprofit organization

---

10. Why did the caller purchase the item?
(A) He read positive reviews about the item.
(B) He previously owned the same item.
(C) His friends recommended the item.
(D) He wanted to make it a gift for someone.

11. What did the caller do last week?
(A) Try to repair a vehicle
(B) Participate in a cycling race
(C) Purchase a product from a store
(D) Call the customer service department

12. What is the listener asked to do?
(A) Refund the cost to the caller's credit card
(B) Fix the product and send it back to the caller
(C) Exchange the product for another item
(D) Replace the product with the same model

---

13. What is the reason for the change?
(A) The office is getting too crowded.
(B) The management has changed.
(C) The business is failing.
(D) The company is expanding.

14. What did Mordica traditionally produce?
(A) Computer supplies
(B) Electronic equipment
(C) Cleaning products
(D) Athletic clothing

15. What does the speaker say about the company?
(A) Its products are exceptional.
(B) Its e-mail system stopped working.
(C) It will reopen its business next year.
(D) Some of its services will be discontinued.

Part 4 Practice Test 正解と解説

CD 1 50

Questions 1 through 3 refer to the following excerpt from a meeting.

設問 1-3 は次の会議の一部に関するものである。

Good afternoon, everyone. As you know, Q1 sales have been slow during the last few months, so we need something that will turn the tides. After much discussion, the marketing team has decided to use a new promotional strategy. Instead of spending $1,000 on paper advertising, the team believes it would be more effective to give out a $10 store gift card to 100 customers. To test this, Q2 the gift cards will be given away to customers who attend the launch party of the new novel by Susan Derkins this Friday. The effectiveness will then be measured by how many people return to the store. Q3 Lena Gaul will report on the results at the end of the month.

皆さん，こんにちは。ご存じの通り，ここ数カ月間は売り上げが低迷していますので，形勢を変えるような何かが必要です。議論を重ねた結果，マーケティングチームでは新たな販売促進戦略を採ることに決めました。紙面での広告に1,000ドル費やす代わりに，店の商品券10ドル分を100人の顧客に配る方が効果的であるとチームでは確信しています。これを検証するために，今週の金曜日，Susan Derkinsの新しい小説の出版記念パーティーに参加する顧客に商品券を配ります。その後，どれだけの人が店に戻ってくるかによって，その効果を測定します。結果については，Lena Gaulが月末に報告します。

語句 □slow（売り上げが）低迷している □turn the tides 形勢を変える □give out～ ～を配る □give away～ ～をただで与える □launch party 新商品発売の記念パーティー

1. What does the speaker say about the last few months?

(A) They have been lowering prices of goods.
(B) They have not been selling many products.
(C) They have been using a new strategy.
(D) They have been developing a new product.

話し手はここ数カ月間について何と言っているか。

(A) 商品の価格を下げている。
(B) 多くの製品が売れているわけではない。
(C) 新たな戦略を採っている。
(D) 新製品を開発している。

正解 **(B)**

解説 下線部より正解は(B)だ。ここでのslowは「（売り上げが）低迷している」という意味の形容詞である。下線部の内容が，正解の選択肢では否定文で表されていることに注意。他の選択肢については，(A)は下がったのはpricesではなくsalesなので不正解。(C)のnew strategyについては，これから取り組むことなので不正解。(D)については，トークの中にそのような話題は登場しない。

語句 □lower ～を下げる

2. What will happen at the launch party?
(A) Books will be signed by Susan Derkins.
(B) Free gift bags will be distributed to clients.
(C) A store gift card will be given to attendees.
(D) A coupon may be used to purchase drinks.

出版記念パーティーでは何が起こるか。
(A) Susan Derkinsが本にサインをする。
(B) 無料のギフトバッグが顧客に配られる。
(C) 店の商品券が参加者に与えられる。
(D) 飲み物の購入にクーポンを使用できる。

正解 **(C)**

解説 the launch partyとはここでは「出版記念パーティー」のことである。下線部からパーティーの出席者に商品券が配布されることが分かる。よって正解は(C)。他の選択肢については，(A)は出版記念パーティーだがサイン会があるとは述べられていないため不適切。(B)と(D)の内容に関してはトーク内に言及がない。あくまでもトークの中できちんと言及されていることを根拠に正解を選ぶようにしなくてはならない。

3. When will the report be given?
(A) Today
(B) On Friday
(C) At the end of the month
(D) In a few months

調査報告はいつ行われるか。
(A) 今日
(B) 金曜日
(C) 月末
(D) 数カ月後

正解 **(C)**

解説 調査報告が行われる時期が問われている。下線部から(C)が正解となる。他の選択肢については，(B)にあるFridayのみがトーク内で言及されているが，この日はSusan Derkinsの新しい小説の出版記念パーティーの開催日である。

CD 1 51

Questions 4 through 6 refer to the following voice-mail message.

設問 4-6 は次の音声メッセージに関するものである。

Good morning, Mr. Yu. This is Joan from the office. I'm calling to tell you that the nametags for Q4 the workshop on eco tourism are ready. I will personally bring them to the workshop venue, and Q5 they will be distributed to invited participants at the reception desk tomorrow morning. Also, I received your memo about arranging a vegetarian meal for the delegate from India. I called the restaurant and they said they will e-mail me the revised menu for the reception dinner as soon as possible. Q6 I'll forward it to you after I receive it.

おはようございます，Yuさん。こちらはオフィスのJoanです。エコツーリズムについての講習会用の名札が準備できたことをお伝えするために電話しました。名札は，私が講習会場に直接持参して，明日の朝，受付で招待された参加者に配布されます。また，インドの代表者のためにベジタリアン用の食事を手配することについて，あなたのメモを受け取りました。レストランに電話したところ，歓迎ディナーのメニューを修正して私にEメールで大至急送ってくれるそうです。受信したら，そちらに転送します。

語句 □nametag 名札　□delegate 代表者

4. What will most likely be discussed at the workshop?

(A) New developments in medicinal science
(B) Measures to fight adult illiteracy
(C) Environmentally-conscious nature tours
(D) Management of special dietary needs

講習会では何について議論されると考えられるか。

(A) 医薬科学における新たな開発
(B) 成人の非識字と闘うための手段
(C) 環境意識の高い人向けの自然ツアー
(D) 特別な規定食の必要性の管理

正解 **(C)**

解説 the workshop on eco tourismと冒頭で述べられているため，これが正解の根拠となる。eco tourismを言い換えた，(C)のEnvironmentally-conscious nature toursが正解だ。他の3つの選択肢は明らかに異なるので100%の確信を持って消去できる。

語句 □medicinal 医薬の　□illiteracy 非識字　□dietary 規定食

5. What will be distributed tomorrow morning?
(A) Workshop agendas
(B) Tour catalogs
(C) Nametags
(D) Invitation letters

明日の朝には何が配布されるか。
(A) 講習会の議題
(B) ツアーのカタログ
(C) 名札
(D) 招待状

正解 **(C)**

解説 トークの中盤でthey will be distributed to invited participants at the reception desk tomorrow morning.と述べられており，theyは前に出ているnametagsを指すので正解は(C)だ。(A)と(B)に関してはトークの中で触れられていない。(D)はinvitedから連想されるInvitationを使った選択肢だが，招待状の配布が行われる予定はない。

6. What does the speaker say she will do?
(A) Contact the restaurant
(B) Cancel a prior reservation
(C) Send a dinner menu
(D) Update the participant list

話し手は何をすると言っているか。
(A) レストランに連絡する
(B) 前の予約を取り消す
(C) ディナーのメニューを送る
(D) 参加者のリストを更新する

正解 **(C)**

解説 トークの最後にI'll forward it to you after I receive it.とあり，itは直前に出てくるrevised menuを指しているため，正解は(C)だ。設問の先読みをした時点で，「話し手がこれからすること」がトークの後半に登場すると予想しておきたい。

CD 1 52

Questions 7 through 9 refer to the following excerpt from a meeting.

設問 7-9 は次の会議の一部に関するものである。

Q7 Before Josephine reports on last week's conference in London, I'd like to announce that all the computers in the Marketing Department will be replaced with newer models at the end of this month. The old computers will be donated to Q9 Youth Starts, a nonprofit organization that works with local schools to provide better educational opportunities for children. Please make sure you save all the data you need to a memory device. Q8 Pete Hamilton will be coming around the office to clear all data from the computers in case there is sensitive information left on them. Q9 Kelly Young from Youth Starts will pick up the old computers after the new ones are installed.

Josephineが先週のロンドンでの会議について報告する前に，私からお知らせしたいことがあります。それは，今月末に，マーケティング部のコンピューターを全て新型のものに取り換えるということです。古いコンピューターは，子どもたちにより良い教育の機会を提供するために地元の学校と連携している，非営利組織のYouth Startsに寄贈します。必要なデータは全て，記憶装置に必ず保存するようにしてください。万が一，コンピューターに機密情報が残っている場合に備えて，Pete Hamiltonがオフィスを回って，全てのデータを消去します。新しいコンピューターが設置されたら，Youth StartsのKelly Youngが古いコンピューターを引き取りに来ます。

語句 □nonprofit organization 非営利組織（＝NPO） □sensitive 機密の

7. What will Josephine do?
(A) Announce an employee trip
(B) Talk about a past event
(C) Install a computer program
(D) Distribute a marketing survey

Josephineは何をする予定か。
(A) 社員旅行について告知する
(B) 過去のイベントについて話す
(C) コンピュータープログラムをインストールする
(D) マーケティングの調査書を配布する

正解 **(B)**

解説 冒頭でいきなり，Before Josephine reports on last week's conference in LondonとJosephineが行うことについて述べている。このようにトークの出だしが正解の根拠になることもあるので，最初から最後まで全ての内容を聞き逃さないよう音声に集中しよう。reports on last week's conferenceをTalk about a past eventと言い換えた(B)が正解だ。

8. What is Pete Hamilton scheduled to do?
(A) Work on the wiring of computers
(B) Prepare equipment for donation
(C) Save sensitive information to disks
(D) Answer questions listeners may have

Pete Hamiltonは何をする予定か。
(A) コンピューターの配線に取り掛かる
(B) 寄贈用の機器を準備する
(C) 機密情報をディスクに保存する
(D) 聞き手が持っているかもしれない質問に答える

正解 **(B)**

解説 質問の主語であるPete Hamiltonはトークの後半に登場する。下線部に「彼はコンピューターの全てのデータを消去するためオフィスを回る」とあるが，これをそのまま言い換えた選択肢が存在しないので難しい。データを消去するのは，古いコンピューターを寄贈する準備のためだと考えられるので，(B)が正解となる。(C)は聞き手がすべきことである。

語句 □wiring 配線

Part 4

9. Who most likely is Kelly Young?
(A) An employee of an electronics recycling company
(B) The head of the Marketing Department
(C) A specialist in computer engineering
(D) A staff member at a nonprofit organization

Kelly Youngは誰だと考えられるか。
(A) 電子機器のリサイクル会社の従業員
(B) マーケティング部の部長
(C) コンピューターエンジニアリングの専門家
(D) 非営利組織のスタッフ

正解 **(D)**

解説 Kelly Young from Youth Startsという情報がトークの最後に登場する。Youth Startsがどのような組織であるかについては，すでに中盤でa nonprofit organizationだと述べられている。以上の情報から，(D)が正解だ。この問題のように，正解の根拠が複数となる例もあるので，3問全てのマークをし終えるまで，トークの内容はできる限り覚えておくようにしたい。

CD 1 53

Questions 10 through 12 refer to the following telephone message.

設問 10-12 は次の電話のメッセージに関するものである。

Hello. My name is Daniel Weaver and I purchased the Lockman XT-65 Multi-tool two weeks ago from your Web store. Q10 I bought the product since so many people wrote good things about it in the review section. However, Q11 when I used it for the first time last week to repair my bicycle, one of the blades snapped in two. I am appalled by the low quality of the item, and would like to return it. If possible, Q12 I would like it replaced with a multi-tool from a different maker, namely the HG-3000 from Tendon International. Since they are both the same price, I believe this should not be a problem. Please call me back to confirm. Thank you.

もしもし。私はDaniel Weaverと申しまして，2週間前にそちらのオンラインストアでLockman XT-65 Multi-toolを購入した者です。レビュー欄で大変多くの方が製品を褒めていたので購入しました。ところが先週，自転車を修理するために初めて使用したところ，ブレードの1つが2つにぽきっと折れてしまいました。商品の質の低さにあぜんとしてしまい，返品させていただきたいと思います。可能であれば，他のメーカーの万能工具，具体的に言えばTendon InternationalのHG-3000と交換していただきたいと思います。どちらも同じ値段ですので，問題はないかと思います。確認のために折り返しお電話をください。よろしくお願いします。

語句 □multi-tool 万能工具　□blade ブレード，刃　□snap ぽきっと折れる
□be appalled by ～ ～にあぜんとする　□namely 具体的に言えば，すなわち

10. Why did the caller purchase the item?
(A) He read positive reviews about the item.
(B) He previously owned the same item.
(C) His friends recommended the item.
(D) He wanted to make it a gift for someone.

電話をかけている人はなぜ商品を購入したか。
(A) 商品についての肯定的なレビューを読んだから。
(B) 以前にも同じ商品を持っていたから。
(C) 友人たちが商品を薦めたから。
(D) 誰かに贈るプレゼントにしたかったから。

正解 **(A)**

解説 トークの最初の方でI bought the product since so many people wrote good things about it in the review section.と言っている。since以下が製品を購入した理由であり「大変多くの人が製品を褒めていた」と述べている。これに該当するのは(A)だ。

11. What did the caller do last week?
(A) Try to repair a vehicle
(B) Participate in a cycling race
(C) Purchase a product from a store
(D) Call the customer service department

電話をかけている人は先週何をしたか。
(A) 乗り物を修理しようとした
(B) 自転車レースに参加した
(C) 店から商品を購入した
(D) 顧客サービス部に電話をした

正解 **(A)**

解説 前半でwhen I used it for the first time last week to repair my bicycleと話しており，itは話題として最初に出したLockman XT-65 Multi-toolのことを指している。これに合致する(A)が正解だ。bicycleがvehicleに言い換えられていることに注意。(C)は2週間前のことであり，(B)と(D)に関する言及はない。

12. What is the listener asked to do?
(A) Refund the cost to the caller's credit card
(B) Fix the product and send it back to the caller
(C) Exchange the product for another item
(D) Replace the product with the same model

聞き手は何をするように頼まれているか。
(A) 電話をかけている人のクレジットカードに費用を返金する
(B) 商品を修理して，電話をかけている人に送り返す
(C) 商品を他のものと交換する
(D) 同じ型の商品と交換する

正解 **(C)**

解説 先読みの段階で(C)と(D)の選択肢の違いをはっきりと認識して，(C)「他の商品」か(D)「同型の商品」かを区別して待ち構えよう。トークの後半でI would like it replaced with a multi-tool from a different makerと述べられている。交換を希望している製品はdifferent makerのものなので，正解はanother itemの(C)。

CD 1 54

Questions 13 through 15 refer to the following announcement.

設問 13-15 は次のお知らせに関するものである。

We are proud to announce that Mordica is changing its name to MD Services. Q13 The name change is due to the significant improvements in our business activities. Today, Q14 our services stretch far beyond the production of traditional Mordica cleaning sprays and detergents. But don't be alarmed, our current structure and contacts will remain the same. Most of our services will also continue to operate as usual, but Q15 a small portion will be discontinued. At the same time, all e-mail addresses will be changed to lastname@MD.com. The old e-mail addresses will be operational until the end of this year. We look forward to growing side by side with our valued customers under the new company name.

Mordicaの社名がMD Servicesに変更となることをご案内申し上げます。この社名変更の理由は，弊社の事業活動が著しく向上したためです。現在，弊社の事業内容は，従来のMordica掃除用スプレーおよび洗剤の生産にとどまらず，はるかに拡充しています。ただし，心配はご無用です。現行の体制と連絡担当は変更ありません。事業に関しても，ほとんどのものは従来通りの運用を継続しますが，ごく一部が停止となります。同時に，Eメールアドレスは全て，名字@MD.comに変更となります。従来のEメールアドレスは年末まで使用できます。新たな社名のもと，大切なお客さまと共に歩んで成長していけることを心待ちにしております。

語句 □stretch 伸びる □far beyond ～ ～をはるかに超えて □detergent 洗浄剤
□don't be alarmed 心配は無用です □structure 体制 □as usual 従来通り
□operational 使用可能な

13. What is the reason for the change?
(A) The office is getting too crowded.
(B) The management has changed.
(C) The business is failing.
(D) The company is expanding.

変更の理由は何か。
(A) オフィスの人が多くなり過ぎているから。
(B) 経営陣が変わったから。
(C) 会社の業績が悪化しているから。
(D) 会社が発展しているから。

正解 **(D)**

解説 変更になるのは社名であることがトークの冒頭で分かる。直後に，変更の理由はThe name change is due to the significant improvements in our business activities.であると述べている。「事業活動が著しく向上した」ことをThe company is expanding.と言い換えた(D)が正解だ。

語句 □fail 失敗する，うまくいかない

14. What did Mordica traditionally produce?
(A) Computer supplies
(B) Electronic equipment
(C) Cleaning products
(D) Athletic clothing

Mordicaは昔から何を生産したか。
(A) コンピューターの供給品
(B) 電子装置
(C) 清掃用品
(D) スポーツウエア

正解 **(C)**

解説 Mordicaの生産品に関する質問であるため，その説明を待ち構えながら音声を聞く。トーク前半でour services stretch far beyond the production of traditional Mordica cleaning sprays and detergents.と述べられており，Mordicaは元々掃除用スプレーや洗剤を製造していたということが分かる。よって正解は(C)だ。

15. What does the speaker say about the company?
(A) Its products are exceptional.
(B) Its e-mail system stopped working.
(C) It will reopen its business next year.
(D) Some of its services will be discontinued.

話し手は会社について何と言っているか。
(A) 製品が非常に優れている。
(B) Eメールシステムが停止した。
(C) 営業を来年再開する予定である。
(D) 一部の事業が停止予定である。

正解 **(D)**

解説 トークの後半でa small portion will be discontinued.と言っているため，会社は現在の業務の一部を停止することが分かる。これに合致する(D)が正解となる。(A)と(C)に関してはトーク内に言及がない。(B)のEメールシステムについては，アドレスの変更はあるものの，従来のアドレスは今年いっぱい使用できるため不正解だ。

語句 □exceptional 非常に優れている

Column ③

990点獲得の先輩に聞く！ 学習の秘訣②

竹田直次郎さん （アスク出版 英語書籍編集・36才）

■**990点を獲得したのは**… 2011年9月
■**990点を獲得するまでの期間**… 半年

Q 990点を目指したきっかけは何ですか？

私は，TOEICの参考書を作っています。でも，出す本，出す本，ことごとく売れない。チクショーと思いました。学習者の役に立つ本を作りたい想いは人一倍あるのに……。悩みに悩んで，思い至ったのが，**読者と同じように，勉強して，受験して，失敗してみよう。そこにきっと，ヒントがあるに違いない**ということでした。そして，やるからには990点。そこを目指そうと思ったのです。

Q 英語学習において，今後の目標は何ですか？

990点＝「英語ペラペラ」というわけではありません（残念ながら）。**話す＆書く力を身に付けるには，プラスアルファのトレーニングが必要**です。次は，そっちの力も鍛えていきたいですね。

Q 読者へのメッセージをお願いします！

純粋に英語力を鍛えるという意味では，TOEICで満点を取る必要はありません。とてもマニアックな世界です……。**しかし！それでも990点獲りたいですよね。その想いは大切なんじゃないかなと思います。そう思うからこそ，勉強を続けられますし。**「TOEICなんて意味ない」「990点でもしゃべれない」などなど，外野からはいろんな声が聞こえてくると思いますが，そんなの無視です。無視，無視。頑張りましょう！

Q 最も効果的だった学習法を教えてください！

満点獲得に足りないのは，**大量の英文を早く，的確に処理する力**だと自己分析しました。特にPart 7。そこで力を入れたのが，**良質な模試をたくさん解くこと**でした。もちろん，時間をキッチリ計って，本番同様に解いていきます。10セット以上は解いたでしょうか。読解速度がアップしただけでなく，全問解き終えるために，Part 5，6，7，**それぞれの問題をどのくらいのスピードで解けばよいのか，タイムマネジメント力が身に付きました。**これが大きかったと思います。

Q どのように壁を乗り越えましたか？

スコアアップという点で壁を感じることはありませんでした。ただ，この2年ほど公開テストを連続受験しているのですが，ほぼ毎月，試験を受けるというのは，ちょっとしんどかったりもします。貴重な日曜日を潰してしまいますからね。それでも，続けられているのは，**同じように頑張っている受験仲間を見つけられた**から。SNS上，あるいは，著名な先生のセミナーに参加するなどして，多くの方と交流しています。皆さん，驚くほど熱心です。自分も頑張らなければ，と刺激を受けています。

Part

5

短文穴埋め問題

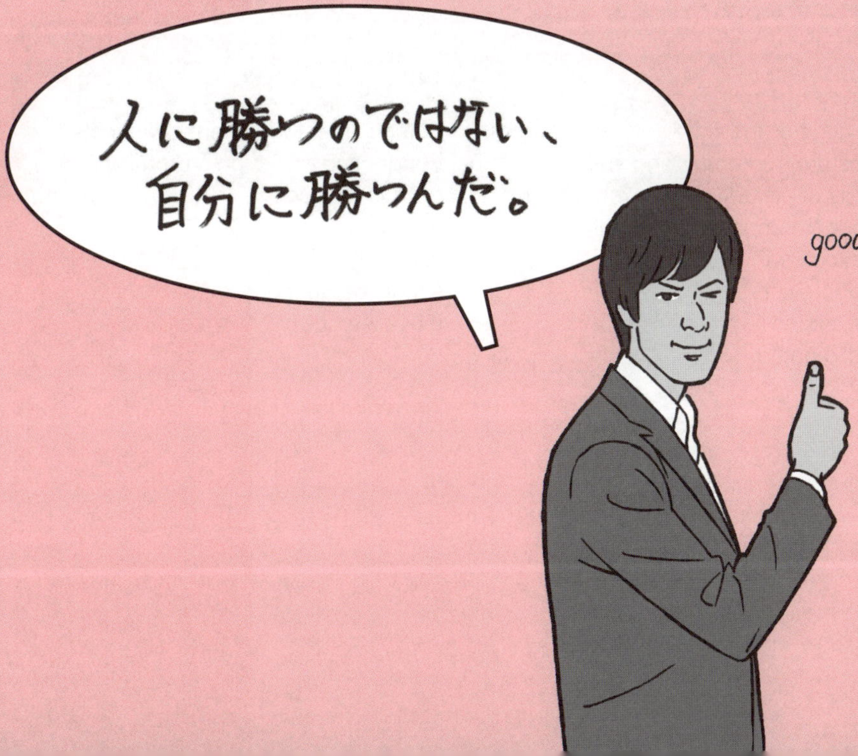
人に勝つのではない、
自分に勝つんだ。
good!

Part 5

短文穴埋め問題

990点獲得のポイントと攻略法

990点にあとわずかで手が届こうかという学習者が，最後の最後までツメに時間を要するパート，それがPart 5である。公開テストでは毎回1〜2問程度の難問が登場し，それらのほとんどが語彙問題・語法問題である。難問に対応できる力をこの章で身に付けよう。

990点獲得のポイント

上級者でも落としやすい語彙問題・語法問題を攻略

まずは例題を解いてみよう。

例1

The head of the ward ------- resources to restore the proper and stable supply of electricity after the heavy typhoon had passed the region.

(A) allocated
(B) abbreviated
(C) asserted
(D) delegated

Ⓐ Ⓑ Ⓒ Ⓓ

例2

Scientists at MLJ Pharmaceuticals are conducting ------- on a promising new drug for cancer.

(A) survey
(B) study
(C) deliberation
(D) research

Ⓐ Ⓑ Ⓒ Ⓓ

これがHUMMER式アプローチ！

上級者でも落としやすい語彙問題・語法問題を攻略

例1

The head of the ward ------- resources to restore the proper and stable supply of electricity after the heavy typhoon had passed the region.

(A) allocated　　(B) abbreviated
(C) asserted　　(D) delegated

大型台風がその地域を通過した後，電気の適切で安定した供給を復旧させるため，区長は資金を割り当てた。

正解 **(A)**

語句 □the head of the ward 区長　□resource（通例 -s で）資金　□restore ～を修復する　□proper 適切な　□stable 安定した　□supply 供給　□electricity 電気　□allocate ～を割り当てる　□abbreviate ～を省略する　□assert ～を断言する，強く主張する　□delegate ～を代表として派遣する，委任する

まず，選択肢に目をやって，語彙・語法・時制・態・主述の一致・数・品詞のどれが問われているのかを判断する。ただし，どのタイプの問題であろうと**文頭から全文を読んだ上で解答しよう**。

例1は，選択肢に同じ品詞（動詞の過去形 or 過去分詞形）が並んでいることを確認し，文頭から最後まで読み進める。restore や had passed などの動詞はあるものの，この文全体の動詞に当たる語がないことから，選択肢は全て動詞であると判断する。The head が restore the proper and stable supply of electricity するために，resources「資金」にどのような行動を取るべきなのか。resources を allocate「分配」すればよいので，(A) が正解となる。

abbreviate という単語を知らない場合，「もしかしたらこちらの方がより適切なのでは」と迷うかもしれない。だが，allocate の意味と用法をきちんとマスターしていれば，(B) を正解として選択することはあり得ない。また，このように知らない語が問題文や選択肢に出てきたら意味や用法を調べ，**確実に語彙力を身に付けていこう**。

990点を取るためには，リーディングパートで495点満点を取る必要がある。全問を解くスピードを意識しつつも，ミスはご法度だ。もちろん1～2問ミスしても495点を取れることもあるが，**妥協なく全問正解できる地力**を付けていくことに専念するのが王道である。

例2

Scientists at MLJ Pharmaceuticals are conducting ------- on a promising new drug for cancer.

(A) survey　　(B) study
(C) deliberation　　(D) research

MLJ製薬の科学者たちは，がんの有望な新薬の調査を行っている。

正解 (D)

語句 □promising 有望な　□survey 調査　□study 調査，研究　□deliberation 熟考，熟慮　□conduct research 調査を行う

選択肢には，似たような意味の単語が並んでいることを確認し，問題文を読み進めていく。空所前のconductから「調査を行う」という意味を作れば文意が通ると判断し，選択肢に進む。すると「調査」を意味する単語が3つ存在するので，視点を切り替えて**語法からの切り口**で考え直してみる。(A)のsurveyと(B)のstudyは「調査」という意味では可算名詞なので直前にaが必要である。よって，正解は不可算名詞の(D) researchだ。

超上級の技術

訓練をある程度積んだ後は，空所前後の情報と選択肢からいきなり正解を選ぶ練習をしてみよう。ただし，その場合も空所を埋めた後は問題文を最後まで読み，全文の内容を確認する必要がある。全文の確認が必要な理由は，次のような問題にひっかからないようにするためである。

The ------- of the road will be much more convenient for the people living in the region.

(A) widens
(B) width
(C) widen
(D) widening

theとofの間にある空所には名詞が入るので答えは(B)という学習者は少なくないはずだ。ところが，この問題にはもう1つ名詞がある。(D) wideningだ。width「道路の幅」が付近の住民にとってよりいっそう便利なことになり得るはずはなく，widening「道路の拡張」が彼らの生活を便利なものにするのだ。よって，正解は(D)。

この問題では不正解の(B) widthが正解の(D) wideningより上に置かれているが，事前に選択肢を見て(D)が動名詞であることを意識しておけば，名詞だからと(B)に飛び付くことは防げる。事前に選択肢に目を通すことと，完成したセンテンスの文意を取ることを怠らないことが肝要だ。

990点獲得への道

例1は文脈から主語と目的語を適切につなぐ動詞を選ぶ語彙問題であり，**例2**は単に文脈から判断するだけでは解けない語法問題であった。後者のような問題も毎回1～2問ではあるが出題される。文脈から解けない場合は，文法，語法など他の切り口から考えてみるなど，**瞬時に問題の見方を切り替える柔軟性を持とう**。

次ページ以降のTrainingでは，本番で出題される上限いっぱいの難易度の練習問題40問に挑戦してもらう。そして，Trainingの問題を，正解と選択肢を変えて学習するReview of Trainingのコーナーを設けることにより，**解いた問題の隅々までをデータベースとして蓄積**できるよう配慮した。「TOEICに出題される問題の最高峰」を体感し，それらをしっかりと自分のものにしてほしい。

まとめ

Part 5は完成させたセンテンスの文意を必ず確認し，文脈と文法，語法全ての面から問題に対峙しよう。

Training

空所に入る最も適切なものを(A) (B) (C) (D) の中から1つ選びなさい（マークシートは別冊p.157にあります）。

1. That Yurika Kubo picked up the award for New Salesperson of the Year ------- no surprise to her department.
(A) gets into
(B) makes for
(C) goes through
(D) comes as

2. HM Electronics Corporation is the ------- largest manufacturer of farm machine parts in the country.
(A) every
(B) each
(C) single
(D) all

3. A few days after receipt of the payment, the ------- will appear on your online banking statement.
(A) substitute
(B) service
(C) transaction
(D) coincidence

4. Our company and J.K. Airport Terminal Co., Ltd. agreed to work ------- one another to construct a big mall at the airport.
(A) overtime
(B) below
(C) alongside
(D) together

5. All workers are encouraged to ------- with the interns who will be joining us for the summer period.
(A) interact
(B) attend
(C) familiarize
(D) activate

6. The board of directors has been ------- since last month about expanding into Canada's big market next year.
(A) deliberating
(B) marketing
(C) approving
(D) transforming

7. We are planning a music festival to ------- with the peace conference taking place in the area next summer.
(A) adapt
(B) tally
(C) adjust
(D) coincide

8. The president said to the product manager that Bob Smith's attention to detail made him a very capable and ------- worker.
(A) industrious
(B) comprehensive
(C) uttermost
(D) residuary

9. Mr. Robinson was ------- responsible for the great success of this product without relying on his staff.
(A) intimately
(B) intensely
(C) principally
(D) solely

10. We ask that all staff wear suits in order to foster an atmosphere of ------- in the office.
(A) professionalism
(B) instance
(C) morale
(D) controversy

11. A ------- in product quality would produce great dissatisfaction followed by a drop in consumer confidence.
(A) plummet
(B) lapse
(C) novice
(D) development

12. If we want to compete in this tough industry, we need to implement a ------- training program as soon as possible.
(A) remediable
(B) hectic
(C) rigorous
(D) various

13. We can hardly afford to pay our present staff's wages at this time, ------- take on new workers.
(A) more or less
(B) no less than
(C) much less
(D) more than

14. The new manufacturing equipment which was introduced last year has greatly enhanced the ------- of factory operations.
(A) qualification
(B) remedy
(C) effect
(D) efficiency

15. Exact ------- is required when paying the fare for the airport bus.
(A) number
(B) quantity
(C) change
(D) coin

16. The city council was dedicated to ------- the course of the river to reduce the risk of flooding.
(A) forwarding
(B) diverting
(C) reversing
(D) widening

17. The new business venture proved to be only ------- profitable and was deemed unworthy of further financial support by the backers.
(A) newly
(B) summarily
(C) marginally
(D) implausibly

18. I have no ------- in recommending Charles Laine for the position of CFO of the company.
(A) malfunction
(B) abrasion
(C) residue
(D) hesitation

19. The chairperson spoke ------- to the rest of the commission, and persuaded them to endorse his plan at the last minute.
(A) apprehensively
(B) delicately
(C) outstandingly
(D) convincingly

20. As is the ------- with using your laptop computer, you need to pay attention to the battery life when you use this portable device.
(A) way
(B) action
(C) portal
(D) case

21. Though the doctors' salaries are low and the work is tough, they are devoted to curing the disease ------- long the process may take.
(A) as far as
(B) whereas
(C) no matter how
(D) no wonder

22. The anti-asthmatic drug Theophylline-Z has yet to be approved for use in ------- with pharmaceuticals that treat kidney disease.
(A) conjunction
(B) compliance
(C) accordance
(D) alliance

23. Our company has hired several experts to determine whether the company's growth is -------.
(A) sustainable
(B) suspensive
(C) susceptible
(D) suspensory

24. A person from the architecture firm measured the ------- of the second floor and made a price quote yesterday.
(A) dividers
(B) expenses
(C) styles
(D) dimensions

25. The flight was ------- delayed due to a mechanical problem on the aircraft.
(A) immediately
(B) soon
(C) briefly
(D) shortly

26. The committee members voted in favor of the suggestion which Ms. Green submitted because the head of the department ------- them to do so.
(A) assembled
(B) urged
(C) proceeded
(D) processed

27. Last night, Mr. Anderson ------- left a list of important clients in a taxi, but the driver delivered it this morning.
(A) nervously
(B) inadvertently
(C) previously
(D) accordingly

28. It is expected to take a few years, ------- a decade, to repair the historical building which was damaged by the storm last night.

(A) nevertheless
(B) if not
(C) while
(D) after all

29. You can attend over 20 different events ------- the renowned author's intriguing workshop.

(A) in addition
(B) above all
(C) even though
(D) aside from

30. To achieve ------- performance, Precision Machine 3200 must be kept within a temperature range of 10 to 20 degrees centigrade.

(A) comparative
(B) consecutive
(C) optimal
(D) optimistic

31. Our stock has already been -------, so we need you to ship as many smartphones as possible immediately.

(A) inspired
(B) increased
(C) depleted
(D) completed

32. The recipient ------- her appreciation to her colleagues and bowed deeply to the audience.

(A) congratulated
(B) thanked
(C) expressed
(D) talked

33. Executing tasks for teams in each of the 12 departments, Ms. McKechnie has proven herself to be quite -------.

(A) insignificant
(B) lively
(C) general
(D) versatile

34. There were complaints that the manufacturer's directions were too ------- and did not provide enough product assembly information for the average consumer.

(A) elaborate
(B) surrealistic
(C) vague
(D) exhaustive

35. This scholarship is designed for students who may ------- not be able to get an education.

(A) rarely
(B) otherwise
(C) seldom
(D) scarcely

36. Ms. Morgan was modestly attired at the celebration yesterday, but she ------- wears flashy clothes.
(A) customarily
(B) amazingly
(C) literally
(D) immensely

37. Please contact our retailing shop immediately if the device is ------- when you receive it.
(A) fragile
(B) immovable
(C) considerable
(D) defective

38. The City Council decided to take under consideration the case which was ------- by a representative from a civic group.
(A) let in
(B) brought up
(C) given off
(D) shown up

39. ------- in the costs of building materials have made it almost impossible for construction companies to forecast their spending.
(A) Tolerances
(B) Fluctuations
(C) Vulnerabilities
(D) Proposals

40. The institute has announced the increasing number of part-time workers may have an ------- effect on our economy.
(A) adventive
(B) advanced
(C) adventitious
(D) adverse

Training 正解と解説

1.

That Yurika Kubo picked up the award for New Salesperson of the Year ------- no surprise to her department.

(A) gets into (B) makes for
(C) goes through (D) comes as

Yurika Kubo が年間最優秀新人販売員に選ばれた事実は，彼女の部署の人たちにとって驚くべきことではない。

正解 (D)

解説 文頭のThatからYearまでのカタマリが，この問題全体の主部である。「Yurika Kuboが賞に選ばれたこと」は彼女の部署にとっては驚くべきことではないという文脈に当てはまるのは，(D) come as ～「～という結果になる」である。(A) get into ～「～に参加する，興味を持つ」，(B) make for ～「～に役立つ，貢献する」，(C) go through ～「～を経験する」。

語句 □pick up ～ ～を獲得する

2.

HM Electronics Corporation is the ------- largest manufacturer of farm machine parts in the country.

(A) every (B) each
(C) single (D) all

HM Electronics社は，国内の農業機械部品に関する製造業者のうち，単独で最大の業者だ。

正解 (C)

解説 (C) single「単独の」を入れて，the single largest manufacturer「単独で最大の製造業者」とすれば文脈に合う。形容詞(A) every「全ての」や(B) each「それぞれの」はmanufacturerを修飾することはできるが，いずれも文意が通らない。(D)のall「全ての」も同様に不適切だ。

語句 □manufacturer 製造業者，メーカー

3.

A few days after receipt of the payment, the ------- will appear on your online banking statement.

(A) substitute (B) service
(C) transaction (D) coincidence

支払いを受領した数日後に，取引はオンライン上の銀行取引明細書に反映されるだろう。

正解 (C)

解説 まず空所以外を一通り読むと，空所には「オンライン上に現れる」ものが入ることが分かる。「支払いを受領した後」に反映されるものは何かと考えた場合，(C)のtransaction「取引」を入れると文意が通じる。(A) substitute「代用品，～を代用する」，(B) service「サービス」，(D) coincidence「偶然の一致」。

4.

Our company and J.K. Airport Terminal Co., Ltd. agreed to work ------- one another to construct a big mall at the airport.

(A) overtime (B) below
(C) alongside (D) together

当社と J.K. Airport Terminal社は，空港に大型のショッピングモールを協力して建設することに合意した。

正解 **(C)**

解説 これはなかなかの難問である。「2つの会社が-------建設することに合意した」という文脈から，(C) alongside「～と一緒に」と(D) together「一緒に」に絞る。空所直後に代名詞one anotherがあることから，前置詞の(C)が正解。(D)は副詞なので不適切である。(A) overtime「時間外に」，(B) below「～より下に」。

5.

All workers are encouraged to ------- with the interns who will be joining us for the summer period.

(A) interact (B) attend
(C) familiarize (D) activate

全ての従業員は，夏期に加わる予定のインターンとお互いにやりとりをするよう奨励されている。

正解 **(A)**

解説 interact with the interns「インターンと交流する」とすれば文意が通じるので，(A)が正解だ。(B) attend「～に出席する」や (D) activate「～を動かす，～に活気を与える」は，直後に対象となる名詞が必要。(C)はfamiliarize A with B「AをBに慣れ親しませる」のように使う。

語句 □be encouraged to do ～することが推奨される
□interact with ～ ～と交わる，～と相互に作用する

6.

The board of directors has been ------- since last month about expanding into Canada's big market next year.

(A) deliberating (B) marketing
(C) approving (D) transforming

役員会は，カナダの大規模な市場に来年進出することについて，先月からずっと議論してきている。

正解 **(A)**

解説 問題文は現在完了進行形〈have been＋現在分詞〉の文であり，sinceがあるので動詞は過去から継続されていることである。選択肢の中で後ろにaboutをとる自動詞は(A) deliberate「協議する，熟考する」のみだ。deliberateは形容詞として「故意の，慎重な」という意味があることも覚えておこう。(B) market「～を市場に出す」，(C) approve「賛成する」，(D) transform「変形する」。

7.

We are planning a music festival to ------- with the peace conference taking place in the area next summer.

(A) adapt (B) tally
(C) adjust (D) coincide

我々は，その地域で来夏に行われる平和会議に合わせて音楽祭を開催することを計画している。

正解 **(D)**

解説 (D)のcoincideを空欄に入れると，「平和会議と同時に起こるように音楽祭を計画している」と

なるため文意が通る。coincide with ～「～と同時に起こる，～と一致する」を覚えておこう。(A) adapt「適合する」，(B) tally「一致する，符合する」，(C) adjust「順応する」。

8.

The president said to the product manager that Bob Smith's attention to detail made him a very capable and ------- worker.

(A) industrious　(B) comprehensive
(C) uttermost　(D) residuary

社長は生産部長に，Bob Smithは細部にわたる注意力があるので，非常に有能で勤勉な労働者だと話した。

正解 **(A)**

解説 a very capable and ------- workerから，空所には，andの前にあるcapable「有能な」と同様プラスの意味を持ち，なおかつworkerを修飾するのにふさわしい形容詞が入る。(A)のindustrious「勤勉な」がこの条件を満たすので正解だ。(B) comprehensive「包括的な」，(C) uttermost「最も遠く離れた，極度の（＝utmost)」，(D) residuary「残りの，残余の」。

9.

Mr. Robinson was ------- responsible for the great success of this product without relying on his staff.

(A) intimately　(B) intensely
(C) principally　(D) solely

Robinsonさんはスタッフに頼ることなくこの製品を大いに成功させたことに対して，単独で責任を負っていた。

正解 **(D)**

解説 後半のwithout relying on his staffが解答の根拠となる。この部分がなければ，(C) principally「主に」と(D) solely「1人で」が正解になり得るが，Robinsonさんは「スタッフに頼らなかった」ことから「1人でこの製品の成功に責任を負った」と判断することができるため，正解は(D)だ。(A) intimately「親密に」，(B) intensely「激しく，強烈に」。

語句 □be solely responsible for ～ ～に対して単独で責任を負っている

10.

We ask that all staff wear suits in order to foster an atmosphere of ------- in the office.

(A) professionalism　(B) instance
(C) morale　(D) controversy

私たちは，オフィス内でプロ意識のある雰囲気を育むために，全てのスタッフにスーツの着用を求めている。

正解 **(A)**

解説 スーツ着用の理由はan atmosphere of professionalism「プロ意識のある雰囲気」のためである。(C) morale「士気」はimprove [boost, raise] morale「士気を高める」の形で用いることも押さえておこう。(B) instance「例，場合」，(D) controversy「論争」。

語句 □foster an atmosphere 雰囲気を育む

Part 5

11.

A ------- in product quality would produce great dissatisfaction followed by a drop in consumer confidence.

(A) plummet　　(B) lapse
(C) novice　　(D) development

製品の質における欠陥は大きな不満を生み出し，消費者の信頼を失うだろう。

正解 **(B)**

解説 「製品の質における -------」によって「大きな不満を生み出し，消費者の信頼を失う」ので，マイナスの意味を持ち，文意が通るものを選択する必要がある。(B) lapse「過失，ミス，欠陥」が適切。併せて「（時の）経過」という意味も押さえておこう。不正解の選択肢も，どれもTOEIC頻出の重要語である。(A) plummet「急落」，(C) novice「初心者，未経験者」，(D) development「発展，開発」。

12.

If we want to compete in this tough industry, we need to implement a ------- training program as soon as possible.

(A) remediable　　(B) hectic
(C) rigorous　　(D) various

この厳しい業界で張り合っていきたいなら，私たちは厳しいトレーニングプログラムをできるだけ早く実施すべきだ。

正解 **(C)**

解説 どんな「トレーニングプログラム」を実施すべきなのか。「厳しい業界で張り合うために」という文脈から，「厳しい，ハードな」という意味を持つ語が入ると想像できる。正解は (C) rigorousだ。「（規則が）厳しい」という意味ではstringentが頻出だということを併せて覚えておこう。(D) various「さまざまな」は，programが単数形なので不適切。(A) remediable「治療できる，治せる」，(B) hectic「非常に忙しい」。

13.

We can hardly afford to pay our present staff's wages at this time, ------- take on new workers.

(A) more or less　　(B) no less than
(C) much less　　(D) more than

現時点で我々は現在いるスタッフの賃金を支払う余裕がなく，まして新しい従業員を雇う余裕などあるはずもない。

正解 **(C)**

解説 前半にcan hardly afford to pay「支払う余裕がない」とあり，our present staff's wages「現在いるスタッフの賃金」すら支払う余裕がないことが分かる。その状況で新たに従業員を雇うことはできない，と続ければ文意が通るため，正解は(C)のmuch less ～「まして～ない」だ。この種の比較級を用いた定型表現についてしっかりと整理しておこう。(A) more or less「多かれ少なかれ」，(B) no less than ～「～ほども多くの」，(D) more than ～「～を超える，～より大きい」。

語句 □afford to do ～する余裕がある　□take on ～ ～を雇う

14.

The new manufacturing equipment which was introduced last year has greatly enhanced the ------- of factory operations.

(A) qualification　　(B) remedy
(C) effect　　(D) efficiency

昨年導入された新しい製造設備は工場の操業効率を大いに高めた。

正解 (D)

解説 「新しい製造設備が工場の操業の ------- を高めた」という内容だ。新しい設備がもたらすであろうことは，操業の「効率」を高めることである。正解は (D) の efficiency。(A) qualification「資格」や (B) remedy「救済」を高めることはできないし, (C) effect を選んで工場の操業の「効果」としても文意が通らない。

語句 □enhance ～を高める

15.

Exact ------- is required when paying the fare for the airport bus. (A) number (B) quantity (C) change (D) coin	空港バスの運賃の支払い時には，（お釣りの要らない）ぴったりの小銭が必要となる。

正解 (C)

解説 支払いの場面で「正確な, ちょうどの」何かを考える。(C) change「小銭」を空所に入れ, exact change で「お釣りの要らないちょうどの小銭」という意味になる。(A) number「数」, (B) quantity「量」, (D) coin「硬貨」。

16.

The city council was dedicated to ------- the course of the river to reduce the risk of flooding. (A) forwarding (B) diverting (C) reversing (D) widening	洪水の危険性を減らすため, 市議会は川の流れを変更することに尽力した。

正解 (B)

解説 「洪水の危険を減らすために」the course に何をすればよいのかを考える。(B) diverting の原形 divert は「～をそらす, 迂回させる」という意味で, the course に対する動詞として適切である。他の3つは，いずれも the course を目的語にとろうとすると文意が通らない。(A) forward「～を転送する」, (C) reverse「～を逆転する，反転する」, (D) widen「～を広くする」。

語句 □city council 市議会 □flooding 洪水

17.

The new business venture proved to be only ------- profitable and was deemed unworthy of further financial support by the backers. (A) newly (B) summarily (C) marginally (D) implausibly	その新たな投機的事業はわずかな利益しか出ないことが分かり, 後援者たちによるさらなる財政的支援の対象としてふさわしくないと見なされた。

正解 (C)

解説 was deemed unworthy of further financial support から，この新規の投機的事業は利益があまり出ていないと判断できる。よって,「わずかに」という意味を持つ (C) marginally が正解だ。(A) newly「最近，新たに」, (B) summarily「即座に，かいつまんで」, (D) implausibly「信じがたく，もっともらしくなく」。

語句 □business venture 投機的事業 □prove to be ～ ～であることが判明する
□deem ～と見なす，判断する □unworthy of ～ ～に値しない □backer 後援者

18.

I have no ------- in recommending Charles Laine for the position of CFO of the company.

(A) malfunction　(B) abrasion
(C) residue　(D) hesitation

私は，Charles Laineを会社のCFOの職に推薦することに何のためらいもない。

正解 (D)

解説 正解は(D)で，have no hesitation in doingで「躊躇せずに～する」という意味である。(B) abrasionは「すり減り，摩耗」という意味で，実際の試験でも出題されやすいので要注意。(C)のresidue「残り，残余」はremainder「残り，余り」の同義語として押さえておくこと。(A) malfunction「故障」。

語句 □CFO (= Chief Financial Officer) 最高財務責任者

19.

The chairperson spoke ------- to the rest of the commission, and persuaded them to endorse his plan at the last minute.

(A) apprehensively　(B) delicately
(C) outstandingly　(D) convincingly

議長は委員会の残りのメンバーが納得のいくように話をし，土壇場で彼の計画が承認されるよう説得した。

正解 (D)

解説 後半のpersuaded them to endorse his plan at the last minuteから，議長は委員会の残りのメンバーを説得したことが分かるため，正解は (D) convincingly「納得のいくように」だ。(A) apprehensively「不安げに，おずおずと」は形容詞のapprehensive「懸念して」も押さえておこう。(B) delicately「繊細に，上品に」，(C) outstandingly「目立って，非常に素晴らしく」。

語句 □persuade ＋人＋ to do 人に～するよう説得する　□endorse ～を承認する，裏書きする

20.

As is the ------- with using your laptop computer, you need to pay attention to the battery life when you use this portable device.

(A) way　(B) action
(C) portal　(D) case

ノートパソコンを使う場合と同じように，この携帯機器を使うときはバッテリーの寿命に気を付ける必要がある。

正解 (D)

解説 正解は(D)で，as is the case with ～は「～(の場合) と同じように」という意味。as is often the case with ～「～の場合にはよくあることだが」も押さえておこう。(A) way「方法」，(B) action「行動」，(C) portal「門」。

語句 □laptop computer ノートパソコン

21.

Though the doctors' salaries are low and the work is tough, they are devoted to curing the disease ------- long the process may take.

(A) as far as　(B) whereas
(C) no matter how　(D) no wonder

医者の給料は安く仕事は大変だが，彼らはどんなにその過程に時間がかかってもよいと考えつつ，その病気を治すことに献身的な努力を注いでいる。

正解 (C)

解説 正解は(C)で，〈no matter how ＋形容詞 or 副詞〉で「どんなに～であろうとも」という意味だ。

be devoted [committed] to doing「～に献身する」も頻出表現なので押さえておこう。前置詞toの目的語として -ing形を使う。(A) as far as ～「～に関する限り」, (B) whereas ～「～である一方で」, (D) no wonder ～「～も不思議ではない」。

22.

The anti-asthmatic drug Theophylline-Z has yet to be approved for use in ------- with pharmaceuticals that treat kidney disease.

(A) conjunction　(B) compliance
(C) accordance　(D) alliance

抗ぜんそく薬Theophylline-Zは，腎臓病を治療する薬と一緒に使用することがまだ認められていない。

正解 **(A)**

解説 選択肢の単語は全てin ～ withの形をとるものばかりなので，文意から判断する。「Theophylline-Zは腎臓病の治療薬と -------に使用することがまだ認められていない」という意味なので，in conjunction with ～「～と併せて」を入れると文意が通る。正解は(A)だ。(B) compliance「従うこと，服従」，(C) accordance「合致，一致」，(D) alliance「同盟，提携」。

語句 □anti-asthmatic drug 抗ぜんそく薬　□have yet to do まだ～していない
□pharmaceuticals 薬剤　□kidney disease 腎臓病

23.

Our company has hired several experts to determine whether the company's growth is -------.

(A) sustainable　(B) suspensive
(C) susceptible　(D) suspensory

我が社は会社の成長が維持できるものなのかどうかを見極めるために，数人の専門家を雇った。

正解 **(A)**

解説「我が社が数人の専門家を雇った」理由は，「会社の成長が -------なのかどうかを見極める」ためである。growthを説明できる選択肢は，(A)のsustainable「維持できる」か(C)のsusceptible「影響を受けやすい」かであるが，専門家が見極める対象としてふさわしいのは「成長が維持できるかどうか」である。(B) suspensive「中止の」，(D) suspensory「懸垂の，中止の」。

24.

A person from the architecture firm measured the ------- of the second floor and made a price quote yesterday.

(A) dividers　(B) expenses
(C) styles　(D) dimensions

昨日建築会社からやって来た人が2階の広さを測り，見積書を作成した。

正解 **(D)**

解説「2階の -------を測った」とあり，選択肢の中で測定できるのは(D)のdimensions「広さ，面積」だけだ。(A) divider「間仕切り」はリスニングでも狙われやすい単語なので押さえておこう。(B) expense「費用」，(C) style「様式」。

語句 □price quote 見積書

Part 5

25.

The flight was ------- delayed due to a mechanical problem on the aircraft.
(A) immediately (B) soon
(C) briefly (D) shortly

機体の機械系統の故障により，そのフライトは少しの時間遅れた。

正解 (C)

解説 「機体の機械系統の故障によりフライトは ------- 遅れた」のであり，delayed を修飾する副詞の(C) briefly「少しの間」が正解となる。(A) immediately, (B) soon, (D) shortly は，どれも「すぐに，間もなく」という意味であり，これから行われる動作を主に修飾するので不正解。

語句 □be delayed 遅れる

26.

The committee members voted in favor of the suggestion which Ms. Green submitted because the head of the department ------- them to do so.
(A) assembled (B) urged
(C) proceeded (D) processed

部長がそうするよう促したため，委員会のメンバーはGreenさんが提出した案に賛成票を投じた。

正解 (B)

解説 空所の後が〈人＋to 不定詞〉となっている。この形で使うことができる動詞は (B) urge「～を促す」だ。urged them to do so で「彼らにそうするよう促した」となり，do so = vote in favor of the suggestion である。(A) assemble「～を組み立てる」，(C) proceed「着手する，先に進む」，(D) process「～を処理する」。

語句 □vote in favor of ～ ～に賛成票を投じる

27.

Last night, Mr. Anderson ------- left a list of important clients in a taxi, but the driver delivered it this morning.
(A) nervously (B) inadvertently
(C) previously (D) accordingly

昨晩，Anderson さんはタクシーにうっかり重要な顧客のリストを忘れてきてしまったが，運転手が今朝それを届けてくれた。

正解 (B)

解説 まず問題文全体を読み進めてみると，「Anderson さんはリストをタクシーに置き忘れたが，運転手が届けてくれた」という内容であることが分かる。空所には left「置き忘れた」を修飾する副詞が入るが，文脈から (B) の inadvertently「不注意にも」を入れるのが適切だ。(A) nervously「神経質に」，(C) previously「以前」，(D) accordingly「それに応じて」。

28.

It is expected to take a few years, ------- a decade, to repair the historical building which was damaged by the storm last night.
(A) nevertheless (B) if not
(C) while (D) after all

昨晩の嵐によって損害を受けたその歴史的な建物を修理するには，10年もかかりはしないが，数年はかかるだろうと予測されている。

正解 (B)

解説 「10年は -------，その歴史的な建物を修理するのに数年はかかる」という内容だ。(B) の if not ～「～ではないにしろ」を入れて if not a decade にすれば「10年とは言わないまでも」となり，a few years をより際立たせることになる。decade = ten years の言い換えも TOEIC 頻出なので押さえておこう。(A) nevertheless「それにもかかわらず」, (C) while「～する間に」, (D) after all「結局」。

語句 □decade 10年

29.

You can attend over 20 different events ------- the renowned author's intriguing workshop. (A) in addition (B) above all (C) even though (D) aside from	あなたは有名な著者の魅力的なワークショップ以外にも，20種類以上のさまざまなイベントに参加することができます。

正解 (D)

解説 問題文の内容は「有名な著者のワークショップ-------20以上のイベントに参加できる」である。(D) の aside from ～ は besides と同じように使い「～以外に」という意味であり，これが正解。(A) in addition「その上」, (B) above all「とりわけ」, (C) even though ～「～にもかかわらず」。

語句 □renowned 有名な □intriguing 魅力的な，興味をそそる

30.

To achieve ------- performance, Precision Machine 3200 must be kept within a temperature range of 10 to 20 degrees centigrade. (A) comparative (B) consecutive (C) optimal (D) optimistic	最適性能を引き出すために，Precision Machine 3200は摂氏10度から20度以内の温度に保ってください。

正解 (C)

解説 正解は (C) で，optimal performance「最適性能」という意味になる。(B) の consecutive「連続した」は TOEIC 頻出で，third consecutive day / three consecutive days「3日連続で」のように使う。(A) comparative「比較の，相対的な」, (D) optimistic「楽観的な」。

31.

Our stock has already been -------, so we need you to ship as many smartphones as possible immediately. (A) inspired (B) increased (C) depleted (D) completed	私たちの在庫はすでになくなってしまっているため，できるだけたくさんのスマートフォンをすぐに出荷いただくようお願いいたします。

正解 (C)

解説 「在庫がなくなったのですぐに出荷してほしい」というのが大意である。在庫がなくなったことは，deplete「～を使い果たす」を使って表現することができるので，(C) が正解。(A) inspire「～を奮い立たせる」, (B) increase「～を増やす」, (D) complete「～を完成させる」。

32.

The recipient ------- her appreciation to her colleagues and bowed deeply to the audience.

(A) congratulated　　(B) thanked
(C) expressed　　(D) talked

受賞者は同僚に感謝の意を表し，聴衆に深くお辞儀をした。

正解 **(C)**

解説 「感謝の意を表す」はexpress one's appreciationと表現するので，正解は(C)。(A)のcongratulateは，主に人を目的語にとって「～を祝う」という意味であり，(B)のthankも人を目的語にとるためいずれも不適切。(D)のtalkは自動詞だと目的語をとれず，他動詞だと目的語について論じるニュアンスになるためここでは不適切。

語句 □recipient 受賞者，受取人　□appreciation 感謝　□bow お辞儀をする

33.

Executing tasks for teams in each of the 12 departments, Ms. McKechnie has proven herself to be quite -------.

(A) insignificant　　(B) lively
(C) general　　(D) versatile

12の部署それぞれのチームのために仕事をこなすことで，McKechnieさんは自身が非常に多才であるということを知らしめている。

正解 **(D)**

解説 Executing tasks for teams in each of the 12 departmentsから，McKechnieさんは12の部署にある各チームの仕事を一手に引き受けていることが分かる。彼女が有能であることを示す言葉を選べばよいので，正解は(D) versatile「万能の，多才な」だ。(A) insignificant「重要ではない，大したことがない」，(B) lively「精力的な，陽気な」，(C) general「全般的な」。

語句 □execute ～を実行する　□prove oneself to be ～ 自分が～だということを証明する

34.

There were complaints that the manufacturer's directions were too ------- and did not provide enough product assembly information for the average consumer.

(A) elaborate　　(B) surrealistic
(C) vague　　(D) exhaustive

製造業者の指示が曖昧すぎて，平均的な消費者にとって十分な製品組み立て情報が提供されていないというクレームがあった。

正解 **(C)**

解説 the manufacturer's directions were too ------- はクレームの内容であり，この文脈でdirections「指示」の補語となるのは(C) vague「曖昧な，ぼんやりとした」である。(D)のexhaustiveはexhaust「～を使い果たす，疲れ果てさせる」の派生語で，「徹底的な，包括的な」という意味。他にexhausting「疲労させる，骨の折れる」も覚えておこう。(A) elaborate「精巧な，入念な」，(B) surrealistic「超現実的な」。

語句 □assembly 組み立て

35.

This scholarship is designed for students who may ------- not be able to get an education.

(A) rarely　　(B) otherwise
(C) seldom　　(D) scarcely

この奨学金は，受け取らないと教育を受けることができないかもしれない生徒のためのものである。

正解　**(B)**

解説　空所を除いて考えると「この奨学金は教育を受けることができない生徒のために作られている」という内容だ。つまり，奨学金を受け取らなければ（＝そうしなければ），生徒は教育が受けられないという文脈から，(B) の otherwise「そうしなければ」が適切だ。他の選択肢は全て not の意味が含まれた語で，文脈上不適切。(A) rarely「まれにしか～しない」，(C) seldom「めったに～しない」，(D) scarcely「ほとんど～ない」。

語句　□scholarship 奨学金

36.

Ms. Morgan was modestly attired at the celebration yesterday, but she ------- wears flashy clothes.

(A) customarily　　(B) amazingly
(C) literally　　(D) immensely

Morgan さんは昨日の祝賀会では地味な服装をしていたが，普段は派手な服を着ている。

正解　**(A)**

解説　逆接の but で 2 つの節がつながっている。「昨日の祝賀会では，Morgan さんは地味な服装であった」が，「派手な服を着ている」のはいつなのか。(A) の customarily「習慣的に」を空所に入れれば，後半の節は「習慣的に派手な服を着ている＝いつも派手な格好をしている」となるため文意が通る。(B) amazingly「驚くほどに」，(C) literally「文字通り」，(D) immensely「非常に」。

語句　□be modestly attired 地味な服装をしている　□flashy clothes 派手な服

37.

Please contact our retailing shop immediately if the device is ------- when you receive it.

(A) fragile　　(B) immovable
(C) considerable　　(D) defective

受け取り時に機器が不良品であった場合には，すぐに私どもの小売店までご連絡ください。

正解　**(D)**

解説　「機器が ------- である場合には，すぐにご連絡ください」という内容だ。文脈から (D) の defective「欠陥がある」が正解となる。(A) fragile は，割れやすいものなど，商品の性質として「壊れやすい」という意味なので，それを理由に小売店への連絡はしないはずだ。(B) immovable「動かせない」は，壊れていて動かないのではなく「動かせない＝固定の」という意味であり不正解。(C) considerable「かなりの」。

38.

The City Council decided to take under consideration the case which was ------- by a representative from a civic group.

(A) let in　　(B) brought up
(C) given off　　(D) shown up

市議会は，市民団体の代表が提出した案件を考慮することを決定した。

正解　**(B)**

解説　「市議会は，市民団体の代表によって ------- された案件を検討する」が問題文の内容だ。ここから (B) の bring up ～「～を提出する」が正解となる。(A) let in ～「～を中に入れる」，(C) give off ～「～を発する」，(D) show up「現れる」。

語句　□take ～ under consideration ～を考慮に入れる　□representative 代表者

39.

------- in the costs of building materials have made it almost impossible for construction companies to forecast their spending.

(A) Tolerances　(B) Fluctuations
(C) Vulnerabilities　(D) Proposals

建設資材のコスト変動のため，建設会社が費用を予測することはほとんど不可能な状態になっている。

正解　**(B)**

解説　建設会社が費用を予測する際の妨げになっているものは何か考える。正解は (B) の fluctuation「変動」だ。コストにおける (A) tolerance「我慢」，(C) vulnerability「脆弱性」では文意が通らない。(D) proposal「提案」は前置詞に in ではなく on を用い，proposal on ～「～に関する提案」とする必要がある。

語句　□forecast ～を予想する，予測する

40.

The institute has announced the increasing number of part-time workers may have an ------- effect on our economy.

(A) adventive　(B) advanced
(C) adventitious　(D) adverse

その機関は，非常勤労働者の数が増えることは私たちの経済に悪影響を及ぼすかもしれないと発表している。

正解　**(D)**

解説　正解は (D) adverse「逆の，不利な」。adverse は adverse effect「悪影響」，adversely affect ～「～に悪影響を与える」の形で出題されることがあるので覚えておこう。(A) adventive「外来の」，(B) advanced「進歩した」，(C) adventitious「外来の，偶然の」。

語句　□institute 機関，協会

Review of Training

空所に入る最も適切なものを (A) (B) (C) (D) の中から 1 つ選びなさい（マークシートは別冊 p.157 にあります）。

1. That Yurika Kubo ------- the award for New Salesperson of the Year comes as no surprise to her department.
(A) put up
(B) picked up
(C) signed up
(D) tidied up

2. HM Electronics Corporation is the single largest manufacturer of ------- machine parts in the country.
(A) phase
(B) farm
(C) pharmacy
(D) farmhand

3. A few days after ------- of the payment, the transaction will appear on your online banking statement.
(A) reference
(B) remainder
(C) release
(D) receipt

4. Our company and J.K. Airport Terminal Co., Ltd. agreed to work alongside ------- to construct a big mall at the airport.
(A) each
(B) another
(C) one another
(D) others

5. All workers are encouraged to interact with the interns who will be ------- us for the summer period.
(A) joining
(B) applying
(C) registering
(D) adding

6. The board of directors has been deliberating since last month about ------- into Canada's big market next year.
(A) expanding
(B) extending
(C) ensuring
(D) expiring

7. We are planning a music festival to coincide with the peace conference ------- in the area next summer.
(A) having held
(B) hosting
(C) having organized
(D) taking place

8. The president said to the product manager that Bob Smith's attention to detail made him a very ------- and industrious worker.
(A) affordable
(B) possible
(C) capable
(D) undependable

9. Mr. Robinson was solely ------- for the great success of this product without relying on his staff.
(A) charged
(B) unaccountable
(C) obligated
(D) responsible

10. We ask that all staff wear suits in order to ------- an atmosphere of professionalism in the office.
(A) raise
(B) foster
(C) bring
(D) rear

11. A lapse in product quality would produce great ------- followed by a drop in consumer confidence.
(A) dissatisfactory
(B) dissatisfaction
(C) satisfaction
(D) satisfactory

12. If we want to compete in this tough industry, we need to ------- a rigorous training program as soon as possible.
(A) implore
(B) imply
(C) implement
(D) impress

13. We can hardly afford to pay our present staff's wages at this time, much less take ------- new workers.
(A) on
(B) after
(C) up
(D) along

14. The new manufacturing equipment which was introduced last year has greatly ------- the efficiency of factory operations.
(A) ascended
(B) enhanced
(C) enriched
(D) exalted

15. Exact change is ------- when paying the fare for the airport bus.
(A) resolved
(B) required
(C) restored
(D) revitalized

16. The city council was ------- to diverting the course of the river to reduce the risk of flooding.
(A) decided
(B) diluted
(C) dedicated
(D) declined

17. The new business venture proved to be only marginally profitable and was ------- unworthy of further financial support by the backers.
(A) remained
(B) compounded
(C) dazzled
(D) deemed

18. I have no hesitation in ------- Charles Laine for the position of CFO of the company.
(A) restructuring
(B) commenting
(C) cooperating
(D) recommending

19. The chairperson spoke convincingly to the rest of the commission, and persuaded them to ------- his plan at the last minute.
(A) endorse
(B) enlarge
(C) extract
(D) encourage

20. As is the case with using your laptop computer, you need to pay attention to the battery life when you use this portable -------.
(A) drapery
(B) device
(C) directory
(D) donation

21. Though the doctors' salaries are low and the work is tough, they are devoted to curing the disease no matter how long the ------- may take.
(A) process
(B) proceeds
(C) proximity
(D) productivity

22. The anti-asthmatic drug Theophylline-Z has yet to be approved for use in conjunction with pharmaceuticals that ------- kidney disease.
(A) deal
(B) handle
(C) address
(D) treat

23. Our company has hired several experts to ------- whether the company's growth is sustainable.
(A) determine
(B) designate
(C) deplete
(D) deserve

24. A person from the ------- firm measured the dimensions of the second floor and made a price quote yesterday.
(A) archway
(B) architect
(C) architecture
(D) archive

25. The flight was briefly delayed ------- a mechanical problem on the aircraft.
(A) thanks for
(B) due to
(C) in addition to
(D) hence

26. The committee members voted in ------- the suggestion which Ms. Green submitted because the head of the department urged them to do so.
(A) the presence of
(B) relation to
(C) the direction of
(D) favor of

27. Last night, Mr. Anderson inadvertently left a list of important clients in a taxi, but the driver ------- it this morning.
(A) delighted
(B) demolished
(C) delivered
(D) deteriorated

28. It is expected to take a few years, if not a -------, to repair the historical building which was damaged by the storm last night.
(A) demeanor
(B) detergent
(C) decade
(D) diagnosis

29. You can attend over 20 different events aside from the renowned author's ------- workshop.
(A) inaccurate
(B) intriguing
(C) intact
(D) inactive

30. To ------- optimal performance, Precision Machine 3200 must be kept within a temperature range of 10 to 20 degrees centigrade.
(A) achieve
(B) affect
(C) decrease
(D) focus

31. Our stock has already been depleted, so we need you to ship as ------- smartphones as possible immediately.
(A) soon
(B) much
(C) many
(D) far

32. The recipient expressed her ------- to her colleagues and bowed deeply to the audience.
(A) appreciation
(B) appearance
(C) adjustment
(D) advocate

33. Executing tasks for teams in each of the 12 departments, Ms. McKechnie has ------- herself to be quite versatile.
(A) attested
(B) illustrated
(C) established
(D) proven

34. There were complaints that the manufacturer's directions were too vague and did not provide enough product ------- information for the average consumer.
(A) assembled
(B) assembly
(C) assembler
(D) assemble

35. This scholarship is ------- for students who may otherwise not be able to get an education.
(A) delighted
(B) depleted
(C) designed
(D) dedicated

36. Ms. Morgan was ------- attired at the celebration yesterday, but she customarily wears flashy clothes.
(A) consistently
(B) voluntarily
(C) respectively
(D) modestly

37. Please contact our ------- shop immediately if the device is defective when you receive it.
(A) retailing
(B) misleading
(C) embarrassing
(D) accounting

38. The City Council decided to take under consideration the case which was brought up by a representative from a ------- group.
(A) city
(B) civilize
(C) civilization
(D) civic

39. Fluctuations in the costs of building materials have made it almost impossible for construction companies to ------- their spending.
(A) foreclose
(B) forerun
(C) forecast
(D) forestall

40. The institute has announced the increasing number of part-time workers may have an adverse ------- on our economy.
(A) affect
(B) effect
(C) effector
(D) affection

Review of Training 正解と解説

1. Yurika Kubo が年間最優秀新人販売員に選ばれた事実は，彼女の部署の人たちにとって驚くべきことではない。

正解 **(B)**

解説 (B) の pick up ～「(賞など) を獲得する」だけは文意が通る。(A) put up ～「～を建てる，用意する」，(C) sign up「(署名して) 参加する」，(D) tidy up ～「～をきれいに片付ける」。

2. HM Electronics 社は，国内の農業機械部品に関する製造業者のうち，単独で最大の業者だ。

正解 **(B)**

解説 farm machine parts で「農業機械用の部品」という意味になる。(A) phase「段階」，(C) pharmacy「薬局」，(D) farmhand「農場労働者」。

3. 支払いを受領した数日後に，取引はオンライン上の銀行取引明細書に反映されるだろう。

正解 **(D)**

解説 receipt of the payment で「支払いの受領」という意味になる。(A) reference「参照，推薦」，(B) remainder「残り，余り」，(C) release「公開」。

4. 当社と J.K. Airport Terminal 社は，空港に大型のショッピングモールを協力して建設することに合意した。

正解 **(C)**

解説 work alongside one another で「一緒に働く」である。work alongside ～「～と並んで働く，行動を共にする」を覚えておこう。(A) each「めいめい」，(B) another「もう 1 つ」，(D) others「他のもの」は不適切。

5. 全ての従業員は，夏期に加わる予定のインターンとお互いにやりとりをするよう奨励されている。

正解 **(A)**

解説 us を目的語にとり「夏の間に私たちに加わるインターン」となる (A) の join が正解だ。(B) apply「申し込む」，(C) register「登録する」，(D) add「～を加える」。

6. 役員会は，カナダの大規模な市場に来年進出することについて，先月からずっと議論してきている。

正解 **(A)**

解説 (A) expand，(B) extend はどちらも「拡大する」という意味を持つが，expand は 3 次元の方向に広がるイメージ, extend は 2 次元方向に伸びるイメージの動詞だ。自動詞で into を伴って「市場への進出，業務の拡大」を表すには (A) expand を使う。(C) ensure「～を保証する」，(D) expire「有効期限が切れる」。

7. 我々は，その地域で来夏に行われる平和会議に合わせて音楽祭を開催することを計画している。

正解 **(D)**

解説 主語に conference や meeting などがきて「行われる」の意味になる動詞は (D) の take place

だ。(A) hold「～を開催する」,(B) host「～を主催する」,(C) organize「組織する」。

8. 社長は生産部長に，Bob Smithは細部にわたる注意力があるので，非常に有能で勤勉な労働者だと話した。

正解 **(C)**

解説 文脈に合い，かつ人を修飾できる形容詞は(C)のcapable「有能な」だ。(A) affordable「余裕のある」,(B) possible「可能な」,(D) undependable「頼りにできない」。

9. Robinsonさんはスタッフに頼ることなくこの製品を大いに成功させたことに対して，単独で責任を負っていた。

正解 **(D)**

解説 文脈から(D)を入れればbe responsible for ～「～に責任がある」となり正解。(A) charged「感情の高ぶった」,(B) unaccountable「責任がない」,(C) obligated「～する義務がある」。

10. 私たちは，オフィス内でプロ意識のある雰囲気を育むために，全てのスタッフにスーツの着用を求めている。

正解 **(B)**

解説 an atmosphere「雰囲気」を目的語にとって意味が通るのは(B)のfoster「～を育てる，促進する」だ。他の選択肢にも「育てる」という意味はあるが，目的語にatmosphereをとることはできない。

Part 5

11. 製品の質における欠陥は大きな不満を生み出し，消費者の信頼を失うだろう。

正解 **(B)**

解説 空所にはgreatが修飾し，lapse「欠陥」が生み出すマイナスの内容を表す名詞が入る。(B)のdissatisfaction「不満」が正解だ。(A) dissatisfactory「不満足な」,(C) satisfaction「満足」,(D) satisfactory「満足な」。

12. この厳しい業界で張り合っていきたいなら，私たちは厳しいトレーニングプログラムをできるだけ早く実施すべきだ。

正解 **(C)**

解説 厳しいトレーニングプログラムを「実施する」とすれば適切な内容になる。(A) implore「～を請う」,(B) imply「～をほのめかす」,(D) impress「～を感動させる」。

13. 現時点で我々は現在いるスタッフの賃金を支払う余裕がなく，まして新しい従業員を雇う余裕などあるはずもない。

正解 **(A)**

解説 空所の前のtakeと組み合わせて「～を雇う」という意味になるものを選べば文意が通る。正解は(A)のtake on ～だ。(B) take after ～「～に似ている」,(C) take up ～「～を取り上げる」,(D) take along ～「～を持って行く，連れて行く」。

14. 昨年導入された新しい製造設備は工場の操業効率を大いに高めた。

正解 **(B)**

解説 the efficiency を目的語にとり「効率を高める」という意味になる (B) enhance が正解。(A) ascend「～を登る」, (C) enrich「～を豊かにする」, (D) exalt「～を昇進させる」。

15. 空港バスの運賃の支払い時には,（お釣りの要らない）ぴったりの小銭が必要となる。

正解 **(B)**

解説 支払い時にお釣りのないように「要求した」となる (B) require が正解。(A) resolve「～を解決する，決心する」, (C) restore「～を修復する」, (D) revitalize「～に再び活力を与える」。

16. 洪水の危険性を減らすため，市議会は川の流れを変更することに尽力した。

正解 **(C)**

解説 be ～ to doing の形をとれるのは (C) の dedicated で，be dedicated to doing で「～することに専念する」だ。(A) decide「～を決める」, (B) dilute「～を薄める」, (D) decline「～を断る」。

17. その新たな投機的事業はわずかな利益しか出ないことが分かり，後援者たちによるさらなる財政的支援の対象としてふさわしくないと見なされた。

正解 **(D)**

解説 正解は (D) で，deem A B で「A を B と見なす」という意味だ。A にあたる The new business venture が主語になった受動態の文である。(A) remain「～のままである」, (B) compound「～を悪化させる，混ぜる」, (C) dazzle「～の目をくらませる」。

18. 私は，Charles Laine を会社の CFO の職に推薦することに何のためらいもない。

正解 **(D)**

解説 recommend A for B で「A を B に推薦する」で，正解は (D) だ。他の選択肢では文意が通らない。(A) restructure「～を再編成する」, (B) comment「～と批評する」, (C) cooperate「協力する」。

19. 議長は委員会の残りのメンバーが納得のいくように話をし，土壇場で彼の計画が承認されるよう説得した。

正解 **(A)**

解説 his plan を目的語にとって文意が通るのは (A) の endorse「～を承認する」だ。(B) enlarge「～を拡大する」, (C) extract「～を抽出する」, (D) encourage「～を勇気づける」。

20. ノートパソコンを使う場合と同じように，この携帯機器を使うときはバッテリーの寿命に気を付ける必要がある。

正解 **(B)**

解説 battery life「バッテリーの寿命」に気を付ける必要があるものは (B) の device「機器」。portable device で「携帯機器」の意味になる。(A) drapery「カーテン」, (C) directory「名簿」, (D) donation「寄付」。

21. 医者の給料は安く仕事は大変だが，彼らはどんなにその過程に時間がかかってもよいと考えつつ，その病気を治すことに献身的な努力を注いでいる。

正解 **(A)**

解説 文脈から, may takeの主語は(A)のprocess「過程」であると判断することができる。(B) proceeds「収益」, (C) proximity「近いこと」, (D) productivity「生産性」。

22. 抗ぜんそく薬Theophylline-Zは，腎臓病を治療する薬と一緒に使用することがまだ認められていない。

正解 **(D)**

解説 空所前後にあるpharmaceuticals「薬」とkidney disease「腎臓病」の関係から，「～を治療する」という意味を持つ(D)のtreatが正解だ。(A) deal「扱う」, (B) handle「～を取り扱う」, (C) address「～に対処する，話し掛ける」。

23. 我が社は会社の成長が維持できるものなのかどうかを見極めるために，数人の専門家を雇った。

正解 **(A)**

解説 文脈から「～かを正確に知る，突きとめる」という意味の (A) determineが空所に入る。(B) designate「～を指定する」, (C) deplete「～を使い果たす」, (D) deserve「～に値する」。

24. 昨日建築会社からやって来た人が2階の広さを測り，見積書を作成した。

正解 **(C)**

解説 「建築会社」はarchitecture firmである。(A) archway「アーチのある道」, (B) architect「建築家」, (D) archive「記録文書」。

25. 機体の機械系統の故障により，そのフライトは少しの時間遅れた。

正解 **(B)**

解説 空所の後にはフライトが遅れた理由が説明されている。理由を表すのは(B)のdue toだ。(A) thanks for ～「～に感謝する」, (C) in addition to ～「～に加えて」, (D) hence「したがって」。

26. 部長がそうするよう促したため，委員会のメンバーはGreenさんが提出した案に賛成票を投じた。

正解 **(D)**

解説 vote in favor of ～で「～に賛成票を投じる」となる。(A) in the presence of ～「～の面前で」, (B) in relation to ～「～に関して」, (C) in the direction of ～「～の方向に」。

27. 昨晩，Andersonさんはタクシーにうっかり重要な顧客のリストを忘れてきてしまったが，運転手が今朝それを届けてくれた。

正解 **(C)**

解説 運転手は, Andersonさんがうっかりタクシーに置き忘れてきてしまったit（＝list）を「届けた」，とすれば意味を成す。(C) deliverが正解。(A) delight「～を喜ばせる」, (B) demolish「～を破壊する」, (D) deteriorate「～を悪化させる」。

28. 昨晩の嵐によって損害を受けたその歴史的な建物を修理するには，10年もかかりはしないが，数年はかかるだろうと予測されている。

正解 **(C)**

解説 a few yearsの比較対象となるのは，a decade（＝a period of 10 years）である。(A) demeanor「振る舞い，態度」，(B) detergent「洗剤」，(D) diagnosis「診断」。

29. あなたは有名な著者の魅力的なワークショップ以外にも，20種類以上のさまざまなイベントに参加することができます。

正解 **(B)**

解説 「有名な著者のワークショップ」を修飾する形容詞を選ぶ。intrigue「～の興味を引き付ける」の形容詞形，intriguing「魅力的な」が空所には適切だ。(A) inaccurate「不正確な」，(C) intact「無傷の」，(D) inactive「活動していない」。

30. 最適性能を引き出すために，Precision Machine 3200は摂氏10度から20度以内の温度に保ってください。

正解 **(A)**

解説 文脈から「～を達成する，得る」という意味の(A) achieveが正解。(B) affect「～に影響を与える」，(C) decrease「減少する」，(D) focus「焦点を合わせる」。

31. 私たちの在庫はすでになくなってしまっているため，できるだけたくさんのスマートフォンをすぐに出荷いただくようお願いいたします。

正解 **(C)**

解説 as ------- as possibleだからと言って，安易にsoonを選ばないように注意したい。immediatelyがあるのでsoonを選ぶと意味が重複してしまう。文脈からas many smartphones as possibleとすれば「できるだけたくさんのスマートフォン」となり，意味が通じる。smartphoneは可算名詞なので，(B) muchは不適切。

32. 受賞者は同僚に感謝の意を表し，聴衆に深くお辞儀をした。

正解 **(A)**

解説 express「～を表現する」ことができるのは，(A)のappreciation「感謝の気持ち」だ。(B) appearance「出現，登場」，(C) adjustment「調節」，(D) advocate「擁護者，提唱者」。

33. 12の部署それぞれのチームのために仕事をこなすことで，McKechnieさんは自身が非常に多才であるということを知らしめている。

正解 **(D)**

解説 prove oneself to be ～で「自分が～ということを証明する」という意味。(A) attest「～を証明する」，(B) illustrate「～を説明する」，(C) establish「～を設立する」。

34. 製造業者の指示が曖昧すぎて，平均的な消費者にとって十分な製品組み立て情報が提供されていないというクレームがあった。

正解 **(B)**

解説 文脈から「製品組み立ての情報」となる(B) assembly「組み立て」が正解だ。(A) assembled「組み立てられた」，(C) assembler「組立作業員」，(D) assemble「～を組み立てる」。

35. この奨学金は，受け取らないと教育を受けることができないかもしれない生徒のためのものである。

正解 **(C)**

解説 be designed for ～で「～のために考案されている」だ。(A) delight「～を喜ばせる」, (B) deplete「～を使い果たす」, (D) dedicate「～を捧げる，献身する」。

36. Morgan さんは昨日の祝賀会では地味な服装をしていたが，普段は派手な服を着ている。

正解 **(D)**

解説 2つの節が but で結ばれており，後半の節が普段は「派手である」と述べているため，前半は「派手ではない」とすればよい。(D) の modestly「控えめに」が正解。(A) consistently「一貫して」, (B) voluntarily「自発的に」, (C) respectively「それぞれ」。

37. 受け取り時に機器が不良品であった場合には，すぐに私どもの小売店までご連絡ください。

正解 **(A)**

解説 空所直後の shop を修飾する語は (A) の retailing「小売業」のみだ。(B) misleading「誤解を招く恐れのある」, (C) embarrassing「当惑させるような」, (D) accounting「会計，経理」。

38. 市議会は，市民団体の代表が提出した案件を考慮することを決定した。

正解 **(D)**

解説 「市民団体」は civic group だ。派生語はまとめて覚えていくようにしよう。(A) city「市」, (B) civilize「～を文明化する，洗練させる」, (C) civilization「文明，洗練」。

39. 建設資材のコスト変動のため，建設会社が費用を予測することはほとんど不可能な状態になっている。

正解 **(C)**

解説 価格の変動が，建設会社にとって費用をどうすることを難しくしているのか考える。正解は (C) の forecast「～を予想する」だ。(A) foreclose「～を妨げる」, (B) forerun「～を追い抜く，～の前を走る」, (D) forestall「～を未然に防ぐ」。

40. その機関は，非常勤労働者の数が増えることは私たちの経済に悪影響を及ぼすかもしれないと発表している。

正解 **(B)**

解説 adverse effect で「悪影響」という意味。(A) affect「～に影響を与える」, (C) effector「作動する人」, (D) affection「愛情」。

Practice Test

空所に入る最も適切なものを(A) (B) (C) (D) の中から1つ選びなさい（マークシートは別冊p.158にあります）。

1. The fact that the Canadian real estate sector has grown ------- in the last two decades is amazing for us.
(A) exemplarily
(B) exponentially
(C) candidly
(D) meticulously

2. Ms. Kaoruteen says that the most important attribute that the interviewers look for in job candidates is -------.
(A) reliable
(B) relying
(C) reliably
(D) reliability

3. The doctors have warned ------- activities in this weather can cause heat exhaustion or heat stroke in healthy individuals.
(A) strenuous
(B) versatile
(C) feasible
(D) stranded

4. Miracle Co., Ltd. has introduced steam mopping as an alternative to ------- customers who are accustomed to the conventional mop and bucket.
(A) lucrative
(B) integral
(C) commensurate
(D) janitorial

5. The Singapore retail giant might be famous for its cheap designer furniture, but it's almost as well-known as a ------- of pineapple juice.
(A) demeanor
(B) drapery
(C) splendor
(D) purveyor

6. We heard there were ------- in the unemployment statistics between the government figures and those of the private agencies.
(A) jargon
(B) affiliations
(C) outages
(D) discrepancies

7. All the club members enjoyed ------- meal at the restaurant which opened last month near our office.
(A) a vague
(B) an empty
(C) an eloquent
(D) a superb

8. ------- that all goes well, the installer will display a message to show you that both packages are successfully installed.
(A) Assuming
(B) Including
(C) Attaching
(D) Nevertheless

9. The mug fell off the ------- of the table when she accidentally bumped it with her hand.
(A) direction
(B) boundary
(C) diameter
(D) brink

10. People are eating dinner at a ------- pace as the view at night is so amazing.
(A) rapidly
(B) leisurely
(C) strategically
(D) slowly

11. Reportedly, the U.S. government is going to implement ------- laws to regulate pharmacy profession.
(A) avid
(B) abrupt
(C) stringent
(D) exquisite

12. The managing editor always says the real mission of journalists is to report events ------- as well as to work publicly.
(A) mistakenly
(B) provisionally
(C) impartially
(D) cursorily

13. The manager opted to ask workers to stay late, questioning the ------- of convincing the board to hire part-timers.
(A) continuity
(B) likelihood
(C) approximation
(D) admittance

14. The sales representative informed him that he had to pay off all of the credit card ------- before he can apply for a car loan.
(A) deviated
(B) debt
(C) debited
(D) deviancy

15. Though Mr. Osato's title is just "consultant," he is ------- the most respected advisor in the company.
(A) recently
(B) basically
(C) significantly
(D) respectively

16. ------- the three résumés the human resources department received, they have already narrowed their search down to one qualified candidate.
(A) Through
(B) Along
(C) Without
(D) Between

17. The Taiwanese government said that it was dedicated to increasing the number of tourist arrivals in the country in this fiscal year by ------- the visa process.
(A) invigorating
(B) depleting
(C) expediting
(D) demolishing

18. The foreman estimated it would take a week to dig the hole on the site and ------- the concrete before we could start framing the building.
(A) pour
(B) purvey
(C) prove
(D) prompt

19. Throughout her 20-year -------, Katie inspired numerous graduate students to pursue work in the academic areas that fascinated them most.
(A) turnout
(B) norm
(C) momentum
(D) tenure

20. The forecast showed hot weather, but in fact, we actually experienced a severe cold ------- last week.
(A) ventilation
(B) gala
(C) proximity
(D) spell

21. It is still ------- at local small shops that customers make their purchases on weekends in this region.
(A) predominantly
(B) inadvertently
(C) radically
(D) hourly

22. You may return the product to our store anytime you like ------- that you have the purchase receipt.
(A) supplied
(B) demanded
(C) granted
(D) provided

23. The tourist center to which we are heading is ------- indicated on the brochures we have so that we can easily find it.
(A) unanimously
(B) enthusiastically
(C) prominently
(D) proficiently

24. The weekly magazine that I am reading says stretching before and after exercise can ------- improve your health.
(A) exclusively
(B) concisely
(C) markedly
(D) unfavorably

25. Yesterday, a tentative agreement was reached between Nakano Motors and its ------- employees.
(A) abiding
(B) deteriorating
(C) striking
(D) consolidating

26. My doctor said to me that eating too much salt could ------- to high blood pressure in the near future.
(A) commit
(B) support
(C) devote
(D) contribute

27. The deadline for the project is next Monday so if you need an ------- you should request permission from your supervisor immediately.
(A) extinction
(B) excursion
(C) expansion
(D) extension

28. A lot of parents around me ------- their children to daycare centers to get them cared for during the day.
(A) impart
(B) entrust
(C) relegate
(D) assign

29. A lot of observers participated in the viewing even though the meteor shower was ------- less intense than specialists had anticipated.
(A) predictably
(B) preferably
(C) extremely
(D) somewhat

30. The property that got an estimate last week was ------- five times more than its initial price.
(A) worthy
(B) worthwhile
(C) worthless
(D) worth

31. According to today's newspaper, the oldest ------- in that competition was 68 years old.
(A) contestability
(B) contest
(C) contestation
(D) contestant

32. The guest house in the seminar house has three rooms, six beds and a ------- kitchen.
(A) common
(B) retrieved
(C) neglected
(D) prohibited

33. In the eastward sky, the group of clouds remained ------- for half an hour.
(A) stationery
(B) station
(C) stationary
(D) stationer

34. The old computer in this room has been ------- for two years, so it will be disposed of at the end of this month.
(A) null
(B) idle
(C) void
(D) invalid

35. This old apartment is now vacant and can be ------- for sale or lease as of next month.
(A) arranged
(B) lined
(C) listed
(D) pretended

36. Would you check with Mr. Yoshida or one of his ------- to see if they have any extra paper for printing flyers?
(A) submissions
(B) subordinates
(C) subjects
(D) subscriptions

37. The supplier packages every item very carefully to ------- nothing is damaged in transit.
(A) assure
(B) ensure
(C) censure
(D) unsure

38. The factory director ------- his assistants to inspect the factory thoroughly because some inspectors were coming the next day.
(A) commenced
(B) commented
(C) commanded
(D) commended

39. It is important to give the person in charge a clear ------- for choosing equipment when you make a presentation at an unfamiliar place.
(A) rationale
(B) fraction
(C) outfit
(D) inception

40. Everyone in our company knows that Ms. Shirakawa is the ------- behind the company's marketing strategy.
(A) masterstroke
(B) mastery
(C) masterpiece
(D) mastermind

Practice Test　正解と解説

1.

The fact that the Canadian real estate sector has grown ------- in the last two decades is amazing for us.
(A) exemplarily　(B) exponentially
(C) candidly　(D) meticulously

カナダの不動産業界が過去20年間で飛躍的に成長したという事実は，我々にとって驚くべきことである。

正解　(B)

解説　the Canadian real estate sector has grown ------- がamazingな内容となるように，has grownを適切に修飾できるのは，(B)のexponentially「急激に」である。他の選択肢の単語もTOEICで出題される可能性の高いものばかりなので，それぞれの形容詞形（exemplary, candid, meticulous）も一緒に覚えておこう。(A) exemplarily「模範となるように」，(C) candidly「率直に」，(D) meticulously「細心の注意を払って，慎重に」。

2.

Ms. Kaoruteen says that the most important attribute that the interviewers look for in job candidates is -------.
(A) reliable　(B) relying
(C) reliably　(D) reliability

面接官が志願者に対して求めている最も大切な資質は，信頼できることだとKaoruteenさんは言っている。

正解　(D)

解説　空所はbe動詞の後なので，副詞の(C) reliably「信頼すべき筋から」は不正解。文脈から，空所にはthe most important attribute「最も大切な資質」が何なのかを表す単語が入るため，(D)のreliability「信頼できること」を選ぶと意味を成す。形容詞の(A) reliable「信頼できる」，動名詞の(B) relying「頼ること」は文法的には入り得るが，意味が通らないので不正解。常に文法・語法と文脈の2つの切り口から考えて解答していこう。

語句　□attribute 特性，資質　□look for ～ ～を求める

3.

The doctors have warned ------- activities in this weather can cause heat exhaustion or heat stroke in healthy individuals.
(A) strenuous　(B) versatile
(C) feasible　(D) stranded

医者はこの天候の中での激しい運動によって，健康な人でも熱疲労や熱射病になる可能性があると警告している。

正解　(A)

解説　どんなactivitiesを行うとin this weatherでは熱疲労や熱射病につながるのかを考える。(A) strenuous「激しい」を空所に入れ，strenuous activities「激しい運動」とすれば文意が通る。その他の選択肢は(B) versatile「多目的な，多才な」，(C) feasible「実現可能な」，(D) stranded「動けなくなった，立ち往生した」で，それぞれversatile device「多目的な装置」，feasible design「実現可能な設計」，be stranded at the station「駅で足止めされる」などの形で使われる。

語句　□heat exhaustion 熱疲労　□heat stroke 熱射病

4.

Miracle Co., Ltd. has introduced steam mopping as an alternative to ------- customers who are accustomed to the conventional mop and bucket. (A) lucrative (B) integral (C) commensurate (D) janitorial	Miracle社は従来のモップとバケツに慣れている清掃員の顧客向けの代替案として，蒸気を使ったモップがけを紹介している。

正解 **(D)**

解説 who以下から，customersは普段モップやバケツを使っている人たちだと分かる。それがどんなcustomersなのかを説明する形容詞として，(D)のjanitorial「清掃員の」を選ぶと文意が通じる。名詞形のjanitor「管理人」も覚えておこう。(A) lucrative「もうかる」，(B) integral「不可欠の」，(C) commensurate「釣り合った，比例した」。

語句 □steam mopping 蒸気を使ったモップがけ　□alternative to ～ ～に代わるもの
□conventional 従来の

5.

The Singapore retail giant might be famous for its cheap designer furniture, but it's almost as well-known as a ------- of pineapple juice. (A) demeanor (B) drapery (C) splendor (D) purveyor	そのシンガポールの大手小売店は，廉価のデザイナー家具で有名かもしれないが，パイナップルジュースの供給業者としても同様に有名である。

正解 **(D)**

解説 巨大小売店が家具を扱っているのと同時に，ジュースの何として有名なのかを考える。(D)のpurveyor「供給業者」を空所に入れれば「パイナップルジュースの供給業者」となり文意が通じる。(A)のdemeanor「振る舞い，態度」はmanner「態度，振る舞い」の関連語として覚えておこう。(B) drapery「カーテン」，(C) splendor「豪華，壮大」。

語句 □retail giant 大手小売店　□well-known 有名な

6.

We heard there were ------- in the unemployment statistics between the government figures and those of the private agencies. (A) jargon (B) affiliations (C) outages (D) discrepancies	失業に関する統計について，政府と民間機関との間で数字に食い違いがあったと聞いている。

正解 **(D)**

解説 between the government figures and those of the private agenciesから，政府と民間機関の数字の間に生じる「何か」を空所に入れればよいということが分かる。(D)のdiscrepancyを入れると双方の公表した数字に「食い違い」があったとなり，文意が通じる。(A) jargon「専門用語」，(B) affiliation「加入，提携」，(C) outage「停止，停電」。

7.

All the club members enjoyed ------- meal at the restaurant which opened last month near our office. (A) a vague (B) an empty (C) an eloquent (D) a superb	クラブのメンバー全員が，オフィスの近くに先月開店したレストランの素晴らしい食事を楽しんだ。

正解 **(D)**

解説 mealを修飾できる唯一の選択肢が(D)のsuperb「素晴らしい」だ。(A)のvague「曖昧な」, (B)のempty「空の」, (C)のeloquent「雄弁な」はmealを修飾する形容詞としては不適切。

8.

------- that all goes well, the installer will display a message to show you that both packages are successfully installed.

(A) Assuming　(B) Including
(C) Attaching　(D) Nevertheless

全てがうまくいくと，インストーラーは両方のパッケージが無事にインストールされたことを知らせるメッセージを表示する。

正解 **(A)**

解説 問題文にある2つの節をつなぐことができる選択肢は，接続詞の(A) assuming「～と仮定すれば」だけである。(B)のincluding「～を含めて」は前置詞なので不適切。また，(B)，(C)はそれぞれ動詞include「～を含む」とattach「～を取り付ける」の現在分詞と見て，分詞構文の可能性も考えられるが，これらは節をとることができず，文脈上も意味を成さないので不適切。(D)のnevertheless「それにもかかわらず」は副詞で，2つの節をつなぐことはできない。

9.

The mug fell off the ------- of the table when she accidentally bumped it with her hand.

(A) direction　(B) boundary
(C) diameter　(D) brink

彼女の腕が偶然テーブルに当たってしまって，マグカップがテーブルの端から落ちた。

正解 **(D)**

解説 「マグカップがテーブルの -------から落ちた」というのが主節の内容だ。(D)のbrinkは「ふち」という意味なので，空所にはこれが適切である。(A) direction「方向，指示」，(B) boundary「境界」，(C) diameter「直径」。

語句 □fall off ～ ～から落ちる　□accidentally 偶然に　□ bump ～にぶつかる

10.

People are eating dinner at a ------- pace as the view at night is so amazing.

(A) rapidly　(B) leisurely
(C) strategically　(D) slowly

夜景がとても素晴らしいので，人々はのんびりしたペースでディナーを食べている。

正解 **(B)**

解説 これは難問である。名詞paceを修飾するのは基本的に形容詞だが，選択肢の語尾は全て-lyで終わっているため，副詞に見えるかもしれない。正解は(B)のleisurelyで，これは「のんびりと」という意味の副詞であると同時に,「のんびりした」という意味の形容詞である。(A) rapidly「急速に」，(C) strategically「戦略的に」，(D) slowly「ゆっくりと」は副詞なのでpaceを修飾できない。

11.

Reportedly, the U.S. government is going to implement ------- laws to regulate pharmacy profession.

(A) avid　(B) abrupt
(C) stringent　(D) exquisite

伝えられるところによれば，アメリカ政府は薬剤師の仕事を制限する厳しい法律を施行する方向に動いている。

正解 (C)

解説 regulate pharmacy profession「薬剤師の仕事を制限する」ためにimplement「施行する」予定のlawなので，(C)のstringent「厳しい」を空所に入れると文意が通る。他の選択肢は(A) avid「熱心な」，(B) abrupt「突然の」，(D) exquisite「この上なく素晴らしい，精緻な」でlawを修飾する語として不適切。それぞれの単語は，avid reader「熱心な読者」，abrupt change「突然の変更」，exquisite meal「最高の食事」のように，よく一緒に使われる組み合わせで覚えておこう。

語句 □reportedly 伝えられるところによれば　□regulate ～を規制する
□pharmacy profession 薬剤師業

12.

The managing editor always says the real mission of journalists is to report events ------- as well as to work publicly.

(A) mistakenly　(B) provisionally
(C) impartially　(D) cursorily

ジャーナリストの真の使命は，出来事を公平に報告し，公然と仕事をすることだと編集長はいつも言っている。

正解 (C)

解説 「ジャーナリストの真の使命は出来事を ------- 報告することだ」という内容から，空所には(C)のimpartially「公平に」を入れるのが適切である。関連語のpartiallyには「部分的に」という意味があるので一緒に覚えておくとよいだろう。(A) mistakenly「誤って」，(B) provisionally「一時的に」，(D) cursorily「ぞんざいに」。

語句 □publicly 公開で，公然と

13.

The manager opted to ask workers to stay late, questioning the ------- of convincing the board to hire part-timers.

(A) continuity　(B) likelihood
(C) approximation　(D) admittance

部長は，非常勤の従業員を雇うよう役員会を説得する見込みに疑問を抱いていたので，従業員に残業を頼むことにした。

正解 (B)

解説 分詞構文を使った問題で，questionの主語はthe managerである。カンマの前後の文脈から，空所にlikelihoodを入れて「役員会を説得する見込みに疑問を抱いていたので」とすれば意味が通じる。(C) approximation「接近」の関連語approximate「およその」，approximately「およそ」，(D) admittance「入場」の関連語admission「入学，入会」を押さえておこう。(A) continuity「連続性」。

語句 □opt to do ～することを選ぶ　□question ～を疑問に思う，質問する
□convince＋人＋to do 人を説得して～させる

14.

The sales representative informed him that he had to pay off all of the credit card ------- before he can apply for a car loan.

(A) deviated (B) debt
(C) debited (D) deviancy

その営業担当者は，車のローンに申し込む前に，クレジットカードによる借金を完済しなければならないと彼に知らせた。

正解 (B)

解説 「クレジットカードの利用による借金」は credit card debt と表現する。charge ～ to one's credit card「（利用料金）をクレジットカードに付ける」も押さえておこう。(A) deviate「逸脱する」，(C) debit「（お金を）引き落とす」，(D) deviancy「逸脱」。

語句 □sales representative 営業担当者 □pay off ～ ～を完済する □apply for ～ ～を申し込む

15.

Though Mr. Osato's title is just "consultant," he is ------- the most respected advisor in the company.

(A) recently (B) basically
(C) significantly (D) respectively

Osatoさんの肩書は単に「相談役」だが，基本的に彼は社内で最も尊敬されているアドバイザーである。

正解 (B)

解説 空所に入れて意味が通るのは(B)のbasically「基本的に」のみである。(A)のrecently「最近」は過去形や現在完了形で用いる。(C) significantly「かなり」，(D) respectively「それぞれ」。

語句 □title 肩書

16.

------- the three résumés the human resources department received, they have already narrowed their search down to one qualified candidate.

(A) Through (B) Along
(C) Without (D) Between

人事部が受け取った3通の履歴書の中で，彼らはすでに，審査を1人の適任の候補者に絞り込んでいる。

正解 (D)

解説 「人事部が受け取った3通の履歴書のうち，すでに彼らは1人に候補者を絞り込んでいる」という内容だ。「3通の履歴書」という「個々がハッキリしている」ものの「中で，間で」を表す前置詞は(D)のbetweenである。

語句 □narrow ～ down ～を絞り込む □qualified candidate 適任の志願者

17.

The Taiwanese government said that it was dedicated to increasing the number of tourist arrivals in the country in this fiscal year by ------- the visa process.

(A) invigorating (B) depleting
(C) expediting (D) demolishing

ビザの発給を早めることで，本会計年度内の国内への旅行者数を増やすことに尽力していると，台湾政府は述べた。

正解 (C)

解説 ビザの発給をどうすることで旅行者数を増やそうとしているのか考える。by expediting the visa process「ビザの発給を早めることによって」とすれば文意が通るので，正解は(C)だ。(B)のdeplete「～を激減させる，使い果たす」は，deplete customer confidence「顧客の信用を失う」のような使い方をすることを押さえておこう。(A) invigorate「～を生き生きとさせる」，(D) demolish「～を破壊する」。

Part 5

18.

The foreman estimated it would take a week to dig the hole on the site and ------- the concrete before we could start framing the building.

(A) pour (B) purvey
(C) prove (D) prompt

現場監督は，建物の骨組みを作り始める前段階として，現場に穴を掘ってコンクリートを注ぎ込む作業に1週間かかるだろうと見積った。

正解 (A)

解説 「建物の骨組みを作る前に穴を掘り，コンクリートを ------- する」という内容なので，掘ってできた穴にコンクリートを「流し込む」とすれば文意が通る。(A) の pour「～を注ぎ込む」が空所には適切だ。問題文中の動詞 frame「～の骨組みを作る」も覚えておこう。(B) purvey「～を供給する」，(C) prove「～を証明する」，(D) prompt「～を駆り立てる，促す」。

語句 □estimate ～を見積もる　□dig ～を掘る

19.

Throughout her 20-year -------, Katie inspired numerous graduate students to pursue work in the academic areas that fascinated them most.

(A) turnout (B) norm
(C) momentum (D) tenure

Katie は20年間の在職期間中ずっと，自分の心を最もとらえた学問分野で働くよう，多くの大学院生たちを鼓舞し続けた。

正解 (D)

解説 選択肢の単語の中で，20-year の後に置いて意味を成すものは (D) の tenure「在職期間」だ。他の選択肢の語は，(A) turnout「（催しの）人出」，(B) norm「規範，基準」，(C) momentum「勢い」で，それぞれ a large turnout「たくさんの人出」，an accepted social norm「一般的な社会規範」，add momentum to ～「～に拍車を掛ける」のように使う。

語句 □throughout ～の間中，ずっと　□inspire ～を元気づける，～に刺激を与える
□numerous 多数の　□fascinate ～を魅惑する

20.

The forecast showed hot weather, but in fact, we actually experienced a severe cold ------- last week.

(A) ventilation (B) gala
(C) proximity (D) spell

天気予報では暑くなるということだったが，実際は，厳しい寒さの期間を先週経験することになった。

正解 (D)

解説 (D) の spell はある特定の一続きの期間を表すということを押さえておこう。(A) ventilation「換気」，(B) gala「祭り」，(C) proximity「近いこと，近接」。

21.

It is still ------- at local small shops that customers make their purchases on weekends in this region.

(A) predominantly (B) inadvertently
(C) radically (D) hourly

この地域では，客が週末に買い物をするのは，まだ主に地元の小さな店である。

正解 (A)

解説 問題文は強調構文で still ～ shops が前に出ている。空所後の at local small shops「地元の小さな店で」を修飾する副詞を選ぶ問題だ。前置詞の at から始まる形容詞句を文脈上修飾することが

できるのは，(A) の predominantly「主に」だ。(B) の inadvertently「うっかり」は動作を表す動詞を修飾する。(C) radically「徹底的に，根本的に」，(D) hourly「1 時間ごとに」。

22.

You may return the product to our store anytime you like ------- that you have the purchase receipt.

(A) supplied　(B) demanded
(C) granted　(D) provided

購入時のレシートがあれば，いつでも好きなときに商品を返品することができます。

正解 **(D)**

解説 文脈と空所後にある that から provided that ～「もし～ならば」ではないかと判断し，再度全文の意味が通っているかを確認してみる。(A) supply「～を供給する」と (B) demand「～を要求する」は，TOEIC では超頻出単語だ。(C) grant「～を与える，許可する」は，名詞で「助成金」という意味があることも確認しておきたい。

23.

The tourist center to which we are heading is ------- indicated on the brochures we have so that we can easily find it.

(A) unanimously　(B) enthusiastically
(C) prominently　(D) proficiently

私たちが向かっている観光案内所は，簡単に見つけることができるよう，持参している小冊子にはっきりと掲載されている。

正解 **(C)**

解説 tourist center は brochures にどのように書かれているのかと考える。(C) prominently「目立つように」示されているので簡単に見つけることができる，とすれば文意が通る。(A) unanimously「満場一致で」，(B) enthusiastically「熱狂的に」，(D) proficiently「うまく，上手に」。

24.

The weekly magazine that I am reading says stretching before and after exercise can ------- improve your health.

(A) exclusively　(B) concisely
(C) markedly　(D) unfavorably

私が読んでいる週刊誌に，運動の前後にストレッチをすることは大いに健康を増進すると書いてある。

正解 **(C)**

解説 空所後の動詞 improve を修飾する副詞を選択する。(A) の exclusively「独占的に」，(B) の concisely「簡潔に」，そして (D) の unfavorably「好ましくなく」は，improve と一緒に使うには不適切。正解は (C) で，markedly improve で「～を非常に良くする」という意味になる。

25.

Yesterday, a tentative agreement was reached between Nakano Motors and its ------- employees.

(A) abiding (B) deteriorating
(C) striking (D) consolidating

Nakano Motorsとストライキ中の従業員が，昨日，一応の合意に達した。

正解 **(C)**

解説 会社と社員の間で一応の合意に対したという内容から，employeesの状況を考える。(C)のstrikingであれば，「ストライキ中の従業員」となり文意が通じる。(A)はabide by ～「～に従う」の形で覚えよう。(B) deteriorate「悪化する，～を悪化させる」と(D) consolidate「（～を）合併する」は自動詞としても他動詞としても使えることを押さえておこう。

語句 □tentative 仮の，一時的な

26.

My doctor said to me that eating too much salt could ------- to high blood pressure in the near future.

(A) commit (B) support
(C) devote (D) contribute

食塩を摂取し過ぎると近い将来高血圧になる，と主治医は私に言った。

正解 **(D)**

解説 contribute to ～ を「～に貢献する」とだけ覚えていると正解を選びにくい問題だ。Smoking contributes to deterioration of health.「喫煙は健康悪化の一因になる」のように，「～の一因となる」というネガティブな意味があることも覚えておこう。(A)はcommit oneself to ～「～すると約束する，～に献身する」を押さえておくこと。(B) support「～を支援する」，(C) devote「～を専念させる，捧げる」。

27.

The deadline for the project is next Monday so if you need an ------- you should request permission from your supervisor immediately.

(A) extinction (B) excursion
(C) expansion (D) extension

そのプロジェクトの締め切りは来週の月曜日なので，締め切りを延ばしてほしいのであれば，すぐに上司に許可を求めるべきだ。

正解 **(D)**

解説 「締め切りが近い」ので，「-------が必要なら上司に許可を求めるべきだ」という内容から，空所には「延期」を意味する(D)のextensionが入る。extensionは，TOEICでは「内線」という意味で使われることも多い。(A) extinction「消灯，絶滅」，(B) excursion「小旅行」，(C) expansion「拡大」。

28.

A lot of parents around me ------- their children to daycare centers to get them cared for during the day.

(A) impart (B) entrust
(C) relegate (D) assign

私の周囲の多くの親たちは，日中面倒を見てもらうため託児所に子どもを預けている。

正解 **(B)**

解説 entrust A to Bで「AをBに預ける」という意味だ。(A)はimpart A to Bで「AをBに分け与える」，(C)はrelegate A to Bで「AをBに降格させる」のように使う。(D)はThe manager assigned me to give a presentation.「部長は私にプレゼンをするよう任命した」のように使うと覚えておこう。

語句 □care for ～ ～の世話をする

29.

A lot of observers participated in the viewing even though the meteor shower was ------- less intense than specialists had anticipated.

(A) predictably (B) preferably

(C) extremely (D) somewhat

流星群は専門家が予想していたよりもいくぶん強烈さに欠けたが，たくさんの観測者たちが観測会に参加した。

正解 **(D)**

解説 less intense を修飾し，なおかつ文意が通るのは，(D) の副詞 somewhat だ。somewhat less intense とすれば「いくぶん強烈さに欠ける」となり，「専門家たちの予測よりもインパクトは弱い流星群ではあったが，大勢の人たちが集まった」という自然な文が完成する。(A) predictably「予想通り」，(B) preferably「できれば」，(C) extremely「極端に」。

語句 □observer 観測者 □viewing 鑑賞，観測 □meteor shower 流星群
□intense 強烈な，激しい

30.

The property that got an estimate last week was ------- five times more than its initial price.

(A) worthy (B) worthwhile

(C) worthless (D) worth

先週見積もりをしてもらった不動産は，元値よりも5倍の価値があった。

正解 **(D)**

解説 worth ～ times で「～倍の価値がある」だ。(A) worthy は基本的に名詞の前に置いてその名詞を修飾し，また be worthy of ～ で「～に値する」という意味になる。(B) worthwhile「価値のある」は It is worthwhile to do [doing] の形でも使うことを押さえておこう。(C) worthless「価値のない」。

31.

According to today's newspaper, the oldest ------- in that competition was 68 years old.

(A) contestability (B) contest

(C) contestation (D) contestant

今日の新聞によると，その競技会の最年長の出場者は68歳であった。

正解 **(D)**

解説 前後関係から，空所には「人」を表す単語が入ると判断できる。選択肢の中で人を表すものは，(D) の contestant「出場者」だ。語尾が -(t)ant の人を表す単語は，他に assistant「助手」，attendant「接客係」，participant「参加者」などがある。(A) contestability「議論の余地」，(B) contest「競技会，争い」，(C) contestation「論争」。

Part 5

32.

The guest house in the seminar house has three rooms, six beds and a ------- kitchen.

(A) common　(B) retrieved
(C) neglected　(D) prohibited

セミナーハウスにあるゲストハウスには，3つの部屋と6つのベッド，そして共同の台所がある。

正解　(A)

解説　空所直後のkitchenを修飾し，なおかつ文脈に合うものを選ぶ問題だ。common kitchenで「共同のキッチン，厨房」という意味である。(B)のretrieveはretrieve a document from a disk「ディスクから文書を読み出す」のように使い，「～を検索する，回収する」という意味で使われることが多い。(C) neglect「～を無視する」，(D) prohibit「～を禁止する」。

33.

In the eastward sky, the group of clouds remained ------- for half an hour.

(A) stationery　(B) station
(C) stationary　(D) stationer

東側の空には，30分の間，雲の一群が動かずにある。

正解　(C)

解説　文脈から，雲の一群が「動かない」という意味の選択肢を選べばよいということが分かる。(C)のstationaryが「動かない」という意味の形容詞なので正解だ。方角を表すeastward「東の」と一緒に，westward，northward，そしてsouthwardも押さえておきたい。(A) stationery「文房具，事務用品」，(B) station「駅」，(D) stationer「文房具店（の店主）」。

34.

The old computer in this room has been ------- for two years, so it will be disposed of at the end of this month.

(A) null　(B) idle
(C) void　(D) invalid

この部屋にある古いコンピューターは2年間使われていないため，今月末に処分される。

正解　(B)

解説　The old computerの状態を表し「今月末にそのパソコンが処分されてしまう」という文脈に合う形容詞を選択する。正解は(B)のidle「動いていない，使われていない」だ。(A) null「無効な」，(C) void「無効の」，(D) invalid「無効な」。null and void「無効の」という表現も押さえておこう。

語句　□dispose of ～ ～を捨てる

35.

This old apartment is now vacant and can be ------- for sale or lease as of next month.

(A) arranged　(B) lined
(C) listed　(D) pretended

この古いアパートは現在空いており，来月から売りに出すことも貸すことも可能だ。

正解　(C)

解説　be listed for saleで「売りに出されている」。list「～を一覧表に載せる，リストアップする」，arrange for＋人＋to do「人が～できるよう手配する」も押さえておこう。(A) arrange「～を手配する」，(B) line「並ぶ，～を並べる」，(D) pretend「～のふりをする」。

語句 □vacant 空いている　□as of ～ ～以後は，～の時点で

36. Would you check with Mr. Yoshida or one of his ------- to see if they have any extra paper for printing flyers?

(A) submissions　(B) subordinates
(C) subjects　(D) subscriptions

Yoshidaさんか彼の部下の1人に，チラシを印刷するための余分な紙があるかどうかを確認していただけますか。

正解 **(B)**

解説 「Yoshidaさんか彼の------- の中の1人に確認する」とあり，選択肢の中で人を表すものは(B)のsubordinate「部下」だけである。sub–で始まる語でsubsidiary「子会社」やsubsidy「補助金」などはTOEIC頻出だ。(A) submission「服従，提出」，(C) subject「主題，題材，被験者」，(D) subscription「予約購読」。

語句 □check with ～ ～に確認する，相談する　□extra 余分な　□flyer チラシ

37. The supplier packages every item very carefully to ------- nothing is damaged in transit.

(A) assure　(B) ensure
(C) censure　(D) unsure

供給業者は，配送中に破損するようなことがないことを保証するために，どの商品も非常に注意深く包装している。

正解 **(B)**

解説 商品を注意深く包装するとあり，その理由は配送中に破損しないことを「保証する」ためだと判断する。選択肢には「～を保証する」という意味を持つ(A) assureと(B) ensureがあるが，空所以下が節なので，直後に節をとるensureが正解だ。assureが節をとる場合は，〈assure＋人＋that ...〉「人に…ということを自信を持って言う」の形で用いることも押さえておこう。(C) censure「～を厳しく批判する」，(D) unsure「不確かな」。

語句 □in transit 輸送中で，乗り継ぎの，通過中で

38. The factory director ------- his assistants to inspect the factory thoroughly because some inspectors were coming the next day.

(A) commenced　(B) commented
(C) commanded　(D) commended

その翌日に検査官が来ることになっていたため，工場長はアシスタントたちに工場を徹底的にチェックしておくよう指示を出した。

正解 **(C)**

解説 空所後がhis assistants to inspectで〈人＋to do〉の形になっているため，この形をとる動詞を選ぶ。(C)は〈command＋人＋to do〉で「人に～するように命じる」という意味になるので，これが正解だ。(D)は〈commend＋人＋for [on, upon] ～〉「人の～を褒める」の形をとる。(A) commence「～を開始する」，(B) comment「コメントする」。

語句 □thoroughly 完全に，すっかり

39.

It is important to give the person in charge a clear ------- for choosing equipment when you make a presentation at an unfamiliar place.

(A) rationale　(B) fraction
(C) outfit　(D) inception

なじみのない場所でプレゼンテーションをする際は，備品選びについて明確な理由付けを担当者に伝えることが大切だ。

正解 **(A)**

解説 (A)のrationaleは「理由付け，論理的根拠」という意味で，「担当者に明確な理由付けを与える」とすれば文意が通じる。(C)のoutfit「衣服，用具（装備）一式」は，動詞だとoutfit A with B「AにBを取り付ける」のように使う。(D)のinception「始まり，発端」はsince its inception in 2013「2013年の設立以来」という形で押さえておこう。(B) fraction「破片，ごく少量」。

40.

Everyone in our company knows that Ms. Shirakawa is the ------- behind the company's marketing strategy.

(A) masterstroke　(B) mastery
(C) masterpiece　(D) mastermind

会社の販売戦略の真の立案者はShirakawaさんだということを，社内の誰もが知っている。

正解 **(D)**

解説 選択肢には全てmasterが付く名詞が並んでいる。文脈から，空所には「人」を表す語が入るが，この中で人を表すものは(D)のmastermind「立案者，指導者」だけだ。(A) masterstroke「見事な腕前」はHer idea was a masterstroke.「彼女のアイデアは大変素晴らしかった」，(B) mastery「熟達，精通」はmastery of a skill「技能の熟達」という表現を覚えておくとよいだろう。(C) masterpiece「名作，傑作」。

Part

6

長文穴埋め問題

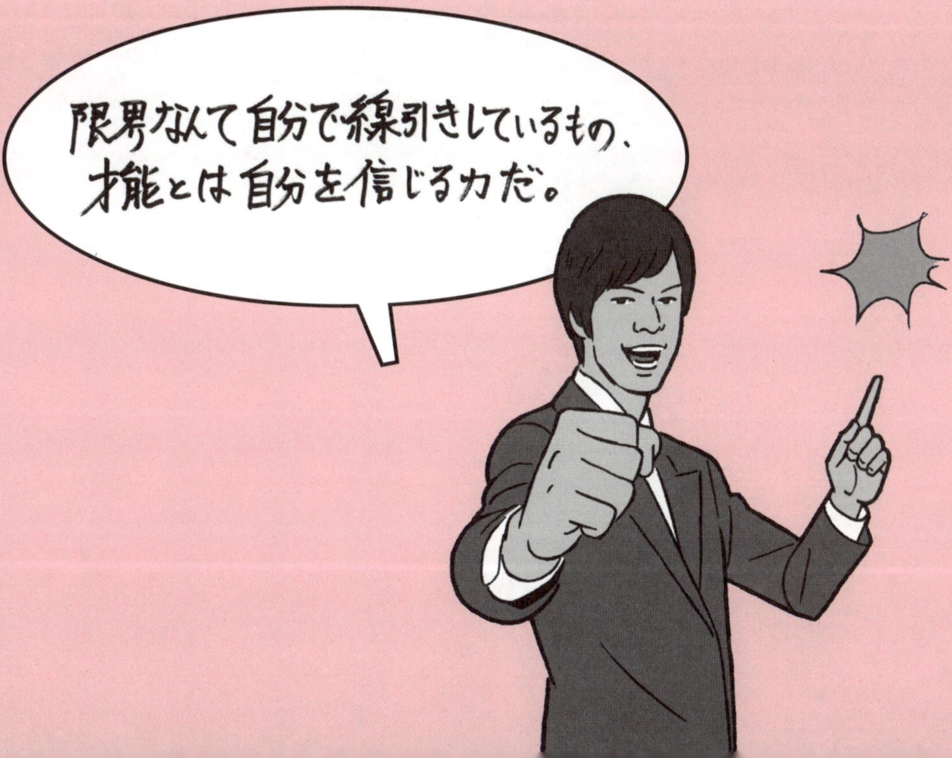
限界なんて自分で線引きしているもの、
才能とは自分を信じる力だ。

Part
6
長文穴埋め問題
990点獲得のポイントと攻略法

Part 6では特別な技術や解法は不要だ。空所前後だけでなく，英文を最初から最後まで全て読み，内容を完璧に理解しよう。空所の部分に来たら**文脈・文法・語法**の3つの切り口で正解を選べばよい。ただし，正解の根拠が空所のすぐ近くにあるとは限らないことに注意したい。**Delayed Clue（遅れて登場する手掛かり）問題**が登場するということを常に意識しておこう。

990点獲得のポイント

1. **空所前後だけでなく，英文を最初から最後まで全て読む**
2. **Delayed Clue 問題の存在を意識する**

まずは例題を解いてみよう。

例 **Questions 141-143** refer to the following letter.

July 14

Mr. Rafael Clark
Deliah, Inc.
7 Rainbow Street
Nashville, TN 37245

Dear Mr. Clark,

I have been informed that the first shipment from Deliah, Inc. ------- as scheduled.

141. (A) arrives
(B) would have arrived
(C) will be arriving
(D) has arrived

Let me remind you that these items will be used in our guest rooms and must be of excellent quality to meet the high standards our guests have come to expect from the Appleberry Hotel.

At Appleberry Hotel, we value a strong working relationship with our suppliers. This is why we have worked with the same supplier, Trenton, Ltd., for twenty years until the unfortunate closure of ------- factory last month. We hope we will have a similar

142. (A) our
(B) his
(C) your
(D) its

long-lasting relationship with the supplier that will replace Trenton, Ltd.

I am pleased to say that our executives were delighted with your products, and we have decided to expand our initial purchase, provided you can deliver them by the end of this month. Details of additional goods we require can be found in the enclosed order form. Please let us know if you are able to meet the abovementioned -------.

143. (A) approval
(B) deadline
(C) persons
(D) expenses

Sincerely,

Miranda Leslie, Manager
Appleberry Hotel

141. Ⓐ Ⓑ Ⓒ Ⓓ
142. Ⓐ Ⓑ Ⓒ Ⓓ
143. Ⓐ Ⓑ Ⓒ Ⓓ

Part 6

これがHUMMER式アプローチ！

Part 6は**空所を含む段落全て**を一通り読んだ上で空所に適切な選択肢はどれなのかを考えるとよい。ただし，**正解の根拠が空所からかなり離れたところに登場する場合がある**ことを意識しておこう。

以下に，問題を読む流れを番号で示し，右ページで各ステップについて解説した。❶から→❷へと読み進め，続いて❷から→❸へ，❸から→❹へと読んでいってほしい。

例

❶ July 14

Mr. Rafael Clark
Deliah, Inc.
7 Rainbow Street
Nashville, TN 37245

Dear Mr. Clark,

❹ I have been informed that the first shipment from Deliah, Inc. -------

141. (A) arrives (B) would have arrived (C) will be arriving (D) has arrived

as scheduled. →❺ Let me remind you that these items will be used in our guest rooms and must be of excellent quality to meet the high standards our guests have come to expect from the Appleberry Hotel. →❷

❷ At Appleberry Hotel, we value a strong working relationship with our suppliers. This is why we have worked with the same supplier, Trenton, Ltd., for twenty years until the unfortunate closure of -------

142. (A) our (B) his (C) your (D) its

factory last month. We hope we will have a similar long-lasting relationship with the supplier that will replace Trenton, Ltd. →❸

❸ I am pleased to say that our executives were delighted with your products, →❹ ❺ and we have decided to expand our initial purchase, provided you can deliver them by the end of this month. Details of additional goods we require can be found in the enclosed order form. Please let us know if you are able to meet the abovementioned -------.

143. (A) approval (B) deadline (C) persons (D) expenses

Sincerely,

Miranda Leslie, Manager
Appleberry Hotel

7月14日

Rafael Clark様
Deliah社
Rainbow Street 7番地
Nashville,TN 37245

Clark様
Deliah社からの初めての出荷品が予定通り到着したと連絡を受けました。確認させていただきたいのですが，これらの商品は客室で使う予定ですから，お客さまが当Appleberryホテルに期待するようになった高水準に見合う卓越した品質のものでなければなりません。
Appleberryホテルでは，納入業者と仕事上の安定した関係を築くことを重んじています。そのため同じ納入業者であるTrenton社と20年間，残念ながら先月その工場が閉鎖となるまで一緒に仕事をさせていただきました。私どもは，Trenton社に代わる納入業者とも，同様の息の長いお付き合いができればと思っています。
弊社の役員は，貴社の製品に満足しておりますので，もし今月末までに納品していただけるなら，初期購入分を増やすことに決めました。追加で必要な商品の詳細については，同封の注文用紙をご覧ください。上記の期日に間に合うかどうかをお知らせください。

敬具

支配人 Miranda Leslie
Appleberryホテル

正解 **141. (D) 142. (D) 143. (B)**

語句 □as scheduled 予定通り □remind ～に思い出させる □item 商品 □value ～を尊重する □supplier 供給業者 □long-lasting 長続きする □replace ～に取って代わる □executive 幹部，重役 □initial 最初の □provided もし～ならば □abovementioned 上記の

❶ July 14からDear Mr. Clarkまでの日付や受取人の名前などは「読まずに見るだけ」という感覚でよい。続いて，本文冒頭のI have been informedから読み進めていく。すると「初めての出荷品が予定通り -------」という部分に空所が登場する。選択肢から時制が問われていると分かるが，この段落には荷物が届いたのか，これから届くのかを判断できる情報がない。解答を一度保留にして次の段落を読み進めていく。

❷ Appleberry ホテルの納入業者に対するスタンスが書かれた第1文に続き，空所を含む文が登場する。大意は「先月 ------- の工場が閉鎖されるまで，私たちはTrenton社と20年間お付き合いをしてきた」である。閉鎖されたのはTrenton 社の工場なので(D)のitsが正解だ。

❸ 第3段落に入ってすぐに**141.**の正解の根拠が登場する。第3段落第1文のour executives were delighted with your productsのyour productsは第1段落のthe first shipment from Deliah, Inc.のことなので→❹から❹へと戻る。その品物を受け取った人たちが喜んでいることから，荷物はすでに到着していると分かるので，**141.**の正解は(D)のhas arrivedだ。

❺ 第3段落の続きに戻ると，第1文後半にwe have decided to expand our initial purchase「初期購入分を増やすことに決めた」とあり，その条件としてprovided you can deliver them by the end of this month.「今月末までに納品が可能なら」とある。同じ内容が，空所を含む文のif you are able to meet the abovementioned -------.で繰り返されているので，(B)のdeadlineが正解だ。

990点獲得への道

Part 6には，Part 5とPart 7を解くために必要なことが凝縮されている。問題は**空所を含む英文だけで解答可能な独立型**と，**空所前後の話の流れをきちんと理解しているかを問う文脈依存型**の2パターンだ。**独立型**はPart 5と同様に解答すればよい。**文脈依存型**は語彙や時制の問題が多いが，**Delayed Clue問題**はPart 7における両文書参照型問題の基本になると言ってもよいだろう。

Part 6ではトレーニングを設けず，Delayed Clue問題を含む実戦問題を用意した。拾い読みではなく，頭から英文を全て読む「ベタ読み」をし，全問正解を目指そう。

まとめ

Part 6はDelayed Clue問題を意識して読み進めよう。英文は基本的に全文「ベタ読み」し，「文脈・文法・語法」の3つの切り口で攻めるという意識を忘れずに。

Practice Test

空所に入る最も適切なものを (A) (B) (C) (D) の中から 1 つ選びなさい（マークシートは別冊 p.158 にあります）。

Questions 1-3 refer to the following article.

MONTREAL, 4 April — Air Karin, which ------- to regain its spot as the number one

1. (A) had struggled
(B) struggles
(C) will struggle
(D) is struggling

airline in Canada, announced a major expansion in its flights to Asia in order to boost revenue. New routes include flights to Seoul, Beijing and Tokyo.

"Asia Pacific routes are important if Air Karin hopes to become profitable," says Ronald Chang, manager of an airline consultation company based in Montreal.

"In the past, Air Karin had implemented cost-cutting measures in order to turn a profit. -------, there is a limit to this approach."

2. (A) Conversely
(B) Likewise
(C) However
(D) Incidentally

Last year, Air Karin came third among Canadian airlines in terms of profit and load factor, after five years of being at the top. With many low-cost airlines competing for customers especially on domestic flights, Air Karin seems to have placed its future on ------- flights. The new schedule will take effect in October.

3. (A) existing
(B) internal
(C) inexpensive
(D) long-haul

Practice Test　正解と解説

設問 1-3 は次の記事に関するものである。

モントリオール，4月4日――Air Karinは，カナダでナンバーワンの航空会社としての地位を回復しようと必死に努めているが，収益を押し上げるため，アジアへの路線を大々的に拡大することを発表した。新たな飛行ルートとしては，ソウル，北京，東京行きを含む。
モントリオールに本拠地を置く航空会社関連のコンサルティング会社部長のRonald Chang氏は，「Air Karinが利益を出したいと願うなら，アジア太平洋路線が重要である」と述べている。
「Air Karinはこれまで，利益を出すためにコスト削減策をとってきた。しかしながら，このやり方には限界がある」とも続けた。
Air Karinは，収益と座席利用率に関して，カナダの航空会社の中で5年間トップの座を守り続けたが，昨年は3位に転落した。特に国内線の乗客に関しては競合する低価格の航空会社が多いので，Air Karinはその将来を長距離路線に据えたようだ。新しいスケジュールは10月より実施される。

語句　□struggle もがく，奮闘する　□boost ～を押し上げる　□revenue 収益
□consultation company　コンサルティング会社　□based in ～ ～を拠点としている
□cost-cutting measures 経費削減措置　□turn a profit 利益を出す
□in terms of ～ ～に関して　□load factor 座席利用率　□low-cost 低価格の
□take effect 実施される

1.

正解　**(D)**

解説　空所の少し後に，announced a major expansion in its flights to Asia in order to boost revenue. とある。「収益を押し上げるための路線拡大」は決定事項であり，その方針で会社が現在動いていることが文脈から判断できる。よって正解は現在進行形の(D)だ。

2.

正解　**(C)**

解説　空所の直前では「Air Karinは利益を出すためにコスト削減を行ってきた」と述べられているが，空所の後では「この手法には限界がある」と直前の内容を否定している。選択肢の中で，それまでの内容を否定する意味を持っているのは，(C)のhoweverである。(A)のconverselyは「逆に」という意味だが，前に書かれている内容を否定する意味を持っているわけではないのでここでは使えない。(B) likewise「同様に」，(D) incidentally「ちなみに，偶然に」。

3.

正解　**(D)**

解説　第1段落で「アジアへの大規模な路線の拡大を発表した」とあり，空所を含む文にも「国内線(domestic flights)は低価格航空会社が多い」とあるので，Air Karinは「国際線」に活路を見出そうとしたと考えられる。選択肢に「国際線の」にあたる語はないが，(D)のlong-haul「長距離の」を入れれば同様の内容を表せるので，これが正解。(A) existing「現存の」，(B) internal「国内の」，(C) inexpensive「安価な」ではいずれも文脈に合わない。

Questions 4-6 refer to the following letter.

June 30

Mr. Abraham Berkowitz
Bowman Industries
Blueridge Drive
Fairview 2190

Dear Mr. Berkowitz,

I am writing to inform you of a unique opportunity to contribute to the community by donating prizes for the Fairview Elementary School photographic competition focused on local -------.

4. (A) children
(B) welfare
(C) nature
(D) wildlife

This is the fifth time our school is hosting this event as a way to encourage children to express their creativity ------- to collect funds necessary for the school. This

5. (A) since
(B) also
(C) moreover
(D) as well as

year, the money raised through the entrance cost, which is 3 dollars each, will be put towards purchasing new library equipment.

The competition will take place on September 12, and the artwork will be displayed in the City Hall Atrium from September 15 to 30. We hope that the photographs of the forests and landscapes of Fairview taken ------- Fairview Elementary students

6. (A) from
(B) of
(C) by
(D) to

will also help increase environmental awareness.

We look forward to hearing from you soon.

Sincerely,
Sky Holland
Fairview Elementary School

設問 4-6 は次の手紙に関するものである。

6月30日

Abraham Berkowitz 様
Bowman Industries 社
Blueridge Drive
Fairview 2190

Berkowitz 様

地元の自然をテーマにしたFairview小学校写真コンテストのために，賞品を寄付していただくことによって地域に貢献できるという，またとない機会をご案内申し上げます。
学校に必要な資金を集めるためだけでなく，子どもたちにその創造性を発揮させるための手段として，当校がこのイベントを主催するのは今回で5回目です。今年は，1人3ドルの入場料によって集まった資金は，図書館の新しい備品の購入に充てられる予定です。
コンテストは9月12日に開催され，作品は市役所のアトリウムに9月15日から30日まで展示されます。Fairview小学校の児童が撮ったFairviewの森や風景の写真が，環境意識の向上にも一役買ってくれればと思っています。
お返事をお待ちしております。

敬具
Sky Holland
Fairview 小学校

語句 □photographic competition　写真コンテスト
□atrium アトリウム（ビルの吹き抜けの空間）　□awareness 意識，認知度

Part 6

4.

正解 **(C)**

解説 地元の何に焦点を合わせた写真コンテストなのかが空所の前後では述べられていないので，これを意識しつつ続きを読み進めていく。最後の段落のthe photographs of the forests and landscapes of Fairviewから，写真の被写体は「Fairviewの森と風景」だと分かる。抽象的に言い換えた(C)のnatureが正解だ。

5.

正解 **(D)**

解説 空所を含む文の中盤にas a way「方法として」とあり，to以下からイベントが「子どもたちにその創造性を発揮させること」と「学校に必要な資金を集めること」のための手段であることが分かる。(D)のas well as「（A as well as Bで）BだけでなくAも」でつなげば，文法的に適切であり文意も通る。

6.

正解 **(C)**

解説 これは小学校が主催する写真コンテストであり，第2段落にencourage children to express their creativity「子どもたちにその創造性を発揮させる」とあるため，写真の撮影者は小学生だと考えられる。the photographs of the forests and landscapes of Fairviewは「小学生によって撮影される」ため，空所には(C)のbyを入れ，taken by Fairview Elementary studentsとすれば文意が通る。

Questions 7-9 refer to the following e-mail.

To: Charles Le Point <clepoint@pammail.com>
From: David Newman <dnewman@TYGlobal.com>
Date: December 12
Subject: Employee Training

Dear Dr. Le Point,

I am truly glad that you have accepted to lead our employee training session. We have been looking for someone who is truly passionate about ------- their

7. (A) furthering
(B) recording
(C) transferring
(D) concealing

knowledge, and your reputation for holding engaging classes as an Economics professor at JM University is well-known.

It is perhaps ------- to hire someone outside the industry to teach employees. In

8. (A) scarce
(B) customary
(C) unconventional
(D) external

fact, this is the first time our company has attempted this, but I have a feeling it will be a great success.

As a first time trainer, you will be presented with appropriate information pertaining to our company well ahead of the session. You will also have a chance to meet with Jonathan Wales, who ------- all our training sessions before he took on another

9. (A) will arrange
(B) has been arranging
(C) had arranged
(D) would have arranged

role, on January 20.

Let me know if you have any questions.

David Newman
Human Resources
Ext. 287

設問 7-9 は次のEメールに関するものである。

宛先：Charles Le Point 〈clepoint@pammail.com〉
送信者：David Newman 〈dnewman@TYGlobal.com〉
日付：12月12日
件名：社員研修

Le Point 先生

弊社の社員研修会の指導をお引き受けくださり，心よりうれしく思っております。私どもは，知識を伝えることに真の情熱を傾けてくださる方をずっと探しておりまして，JM大学の経済学教授として魅力あふれる授業をなさっているという先生の評判は知れ渡っています。
従業員を教育するために業界外の方を雇うのは，おそらく異例のことです。事実，これは弊社にとって初めての試みですが，大成功するような気がしています。
初回の指導者である先生には，研修会よりかなり前に，弊社に関する適切な情報をお伝えします。また，今は別の職務に就いていますが，弊社の全ての研修会を手配していたJonathan Walesにも，1月20日にお会いいただく機会を設けるつもりです。
何かご質問がございましたら，お知らせください。

David Newman
人事部
内線 287

語句 □passionate 情熱的な □engaging 魅力のある □be presented with ～ ～を提示される □pertaining to ～ ～に関する □well ahead of ～ ～よりかなり前に，早く □Ext. 内線番号

Part 6

7.

正解 **(C)**

解説 第1段落第1文に「弊社の社員研修会の指導を引き受けた」とあり，空所を含む次の文ではその企業が探し続けていた人材について書かれている。このことから，空所を含む部分 ------- their knowledge は「研修会を指導する」と同様の内容になると考えられる。「指導する」＝「知識を伝える」ということなので，正解は(C)の transfer だ。(A) further「～を推進する」，(B) record「～を記録する」，(D) conceal「～を隠す」。

8.

正解 **(C)**

解説 空所を含む文では「従業員を教育するために，業界外の方を雇うのはおそらく -------なこと」だと述べられている。その次の文で「事実，これは弊社にとって初めての試みだ」とあるため，空所には「初めて」か「普通ではない」という意味を持つ単語を選べばよい。(C)の unconventional「異例の」を入れると文意が通る。(A) scarce「乏しい」，(B) customary「普通の」，(D) external「外部の」。

9.

正解 **(C)**

解説 Jonathan Wales, who ------- all our training sessions before he took on another role から，空所には took on another role「他の職務を引き受けた」よりも前に「Jonathan Walesはこの会社の全ての研修会を手配していた」ということが分かる。tookという過去よりも前に行われた動作なので，(C)の過去完了形 had arranged を空所に入れれば文法的にも文脈的にも適切だ。

Questions 10-12 refer to the following article.

Many passers-by stopped ------- the beautiful miniature copies of famous

10. (A) admiring
(B) are admiring
(C) to admire
(D) admired

architecture on display at the Terry Smith Department Store windows this month.

The installation was created by John Brown, who started making miniature -------

11. (A) supplements
(B) reproductions
(C) paintings
(D) reprints

of buildings and bridges twenty years ago after graduating with a degree in Architectural Design from Taito College. Now he runs a successful company with twenty designers on his team.

John Brown is planning to retire in May at which time he will ------- the responsibility

12. (A) oblige
(B) return
(C) delegate
(D) represent

of head designer to his son, Percy Brown. The Rainville Show in June will be the first time Percy will work on his own, but he says he already has some new ideas he is eager to try out.

設問 10-12 は次の記事に関するものである。

たくさんの通行人が，今月 Terry Smith デパートのショーウィンドウに展示されている有名な建築物の美しいミニチュアの複製の前に立ち止まり，感嘆の声をあげた。
この展示は，Taito 大学の建築デザイン学科を卒業後，20 年前に建物や橋のミニチュアの複製品を作り始めたという John Brown 氏によるものだ。今や彼は会社を経営して成功を収めており，20 人のデザイナーチームを擁している。
John Brown 氏は 5 月に引退し，その時点で，チーフデザイナーの職務を息子の Percy Brown 氏に委譲する予定だ。Percy 氏が独力で手がける初めての仕事は 6 月の Rainville Show だが，彼は，ぜひとも試してみたいアイデアがすでにいくつかあると語っている。

語句 □ miniature copy ミニチュアの複製 □ admire ～を称賛する，感心する
□ architecture 建築物 □ be eager to do しきりに～したがっている

10.

正解 **(C)**

解説 stop の後には，doing も to 不定詞もどちらも置くことができるが，〈stop ＋ doing〉は「(継続的にしてきたこと) をやめる」であり，〈stop ＋ to 不定詞〉は「～するために立ち止まる」という意味である。文脈から「多くの通行人はデパートに展示されているミニチュアを見るために立ち止まった」となる (C) が正解だ。この文の主語である passers-by は passer-by「通行人」の複数形である。

11.

正解 **(B)**

解説 miniature reproduction は「ミニチュアでの複製品」という意味だ。John Brown は建築物のミニチュアを制作している人物であるため，(A) supplement「補足，補完」，(C) painting「絵画」，そして (D) reprint「再版」だといずれも文意が通らない。

12.

正解 **(C)**

解説 第 3 段落の最初の文に「John Brown は 5 月に引退し，その時点でチーフデザイナーの職務を息子である Percy Brown に ------- するだろう」とある。(C) の delegate は delegate A to B「A (権限・職務など) を B (人) に委譲する，委託する」のように使い，空所に入れると文意が通る。(A) oblige「(受身形で) 感謝を示す」，(B) return「～を戻す」，(D) represent「～を表す」。

Column 4

本気で挑戦を続ければ，必ず結果は手に入る。

A Road to TOEIC 990

2010年9月，僕は初めてTOEICテストで990点を獲得した。ここでは僕が990点を取るまでのスコアの変遷と，飛躍に直結したテキストを精選して紹介しよう。

TOEICテスト スコア変遷

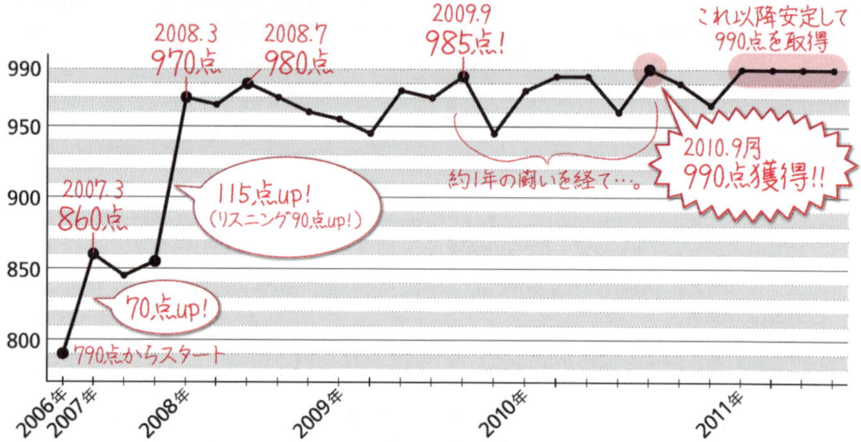

飛躍に直結した精選テキスト ベスト5

『TOEICテスト新公式問題集』(Vol.1, 2, 3)（国際ビジネスコミュニケーション協会刊）

『Tactics for TOEIC Listening and Reading Test』（Oxford University Press刊）

こう使った▶ 上記4冊分のPart 2計240問を，毎日連続1時間シャドーイング。

『新TOEIC TEST 英文法 出るとこだけ! —直前5日間で100点差がつく鉄則27』（小石 裕子著　アルク刊）

＊他に『新TOEIC TEST英単語出るとこだけ!』『新TOEIC TESTリスニング出るとこだけ!』

こう使った▶ もはや自分は著者よりもその本について詳しいというぐらい，何周も復習。

『新TOEIC TEST出まくり英文法』（早川 幸治，高橋 基治，武藤 克彦著　コスモピア刊）

こう使った▶ どんなに仕事で遅くなっても1冊まるごと音読。音読効果で，Part 5満点獲得。

『新TOEICテスト 速読速解7つのルール』（Daniel Warriner，神崎 正哉著　朝日出版社刊）

こう使った▶ Part 7へのアプローチ法を網羅的に体得。解答スタイルを身に付けるのに役立つ。

どのテキストに取り組む場合でも，僕は**信頼できる本を徹底的に何周も学習すること**を鉄則としている。働きながら独学で990点を取得できたのも，日々真摯に挑戦を続けてきた結果だと思う。985点から伸び悩んだときも，**「限界なんて自分で線引きしているだけ」「自分だけが唯一，自分自身を変えられる人間だ」**と自分に言い聞かせて，いつも本気で勉強を続けてきた。今，990点を目指している方々も，徹底的にやれば必ず報われる。ぜひ自分を信じて本気で挑戦してほしい。

Part

7
読解問題

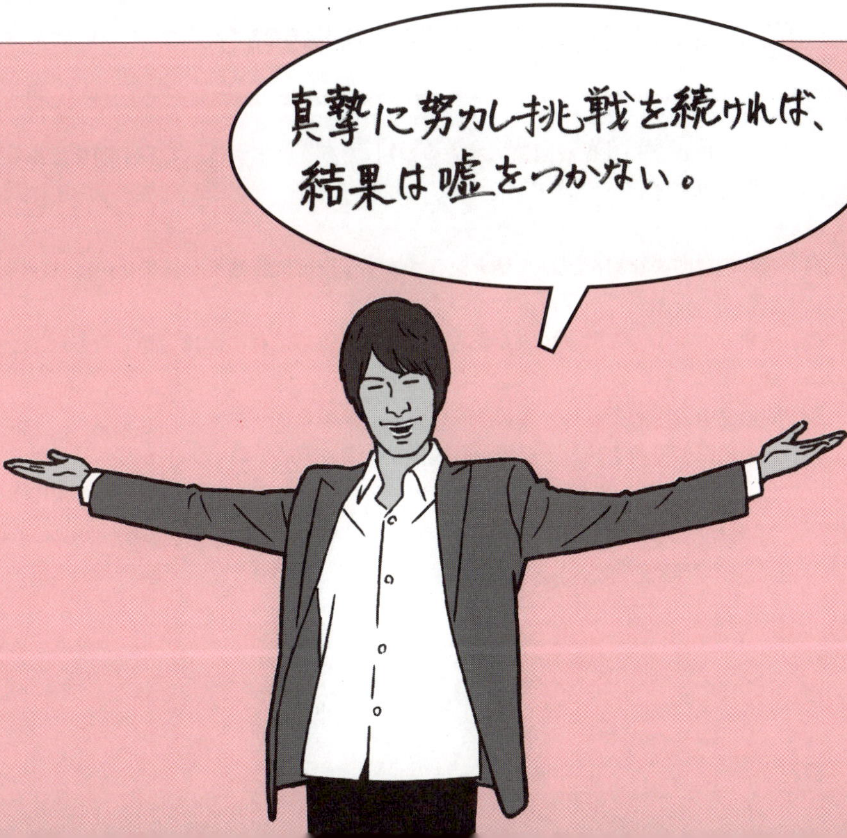
真摯に努力し挑戦を続ければ、結果は嘘をつかない。

Part 7

読解問題

990点獲得のポイントと攻略法

Part 7は**速く正確に読んで解答する**ことが求められる。**「正解回路（解答の型）」**を作ることで解答のプロセスを自動化し，効率良く読み進めて解答の精度とスピードを上げよう。全文を飛ばし読みせず丁寧に読み，正解の根拠を明確に提示する訓練を積めば，速く正確なリーディングが可能になってくる。この章で，それをしっかりと体得してほしい。

990点獲得のポイント

1. **「正解回路（解答の型）」を確立する**
2. **正解の根拠を明確に提示する訓練を積む**

以下は，Part 7の**「正解回路（解答の型）」**である。まずは，この手順を意識して例題を解いてみてほしい。

(1) **最初の設問の質問**を読み，**リテンション**する（選択肢はまだ読まない）。
(2) 問題文を冒頭から**ベタ読み**していく。
(3) **区切りの良いところ**まで読んだら（または，**正解の根拠**が見つかったら）**選択肢に移動**する。
(4) 問題文中の**正解の根拠と選択肢を照合し，正解をマーク**する。
(5) **次の設問の質問**を読み，**続きから**問題文を読み進めていく。
（上記を設問ごとに繰り返し，そのセットの問題を全問解答し終えたら次のセットに進む）

例 **Questions 153-155** refer to the following article.

Bexi.com to Open New Warehouse

Bexi.com, the world's third largest online retailer, has announced the opening of a new warehouse in Berlin, Germany, in May. Bexi.com currently has forty warehouses strategically placed around the world to fulfill orders from its customers. Last year, Bexi.com sold around 15 million items a day over the holiday season and this winter they expect the figure to rise to 20 million per day.

The new warehouse will be built on the site of an old brewery and will be Bexi.com's biggest shipping center in Europe. Nelly Wilde, who works at Bexi.com's headquarters in Phoenix, says that many people are astonished when they hear that there are no robots within Bexi.com's immense warehouses. Instead, hundreds of workers use bar codes to find and ship the ordered items. According to Wilde, this is more economical than implementing and using automated systems. Reportedly, Bexi.com will need an additional 200 workers to staff its latest warehouse.

153. What is indicated about Bexi.com?
(A) It made 15 million dollars last year.
(B) It runs an Internet shopping business.
(C) It has forty storage buildings in the U.S.
(D) Its head office is located in Berlin.
Ⓐ Ⓑ Ⓒ Ⓓ

154. According to Nelly Wilde, what are people surprised by?
(A) The low prices they can find on Bexi.com
(B) The complex machines used at Bexi.com's shipping centers
(C) The lack of robots in Bexi.com's warehouses
(D) The number of items sold by Bexi.com per day
Ⓐ Ⓑ Ⓒ Ⓓ

155. What is suggested about the Berlin warehouse?
(A) It will be built next to a brewery.
(B) It will be the largest in the world.
(C) It will create a lot of jobs.
(D) It is the only shipping center in Europe.
Ⓐ Ⓑ Ⓒ Ⓓ

これがHUMMER式アプローチ！

例

❷ *Bexi.com to Open New Warehouse*

Bexi.comの新しい倉庫がオープン

Q153 Bexi.com, the world's third largest online retailer, has announced the opening of a new warehouse in Berlin, Germany, in May. Bexi.com currently has forty warehouses strategically placed around the world to fulfill orders from its customers. Last year, Bexi.com sold around 15 million items a day over the holiday season and this winter they expect the figure to rise to 20 million per day. →❸

世界で3番目に大きなオンライン小売業者のBexi.comは，5月にドイツのベルリンに新しい倉庫をオープンすることを発表した。Bexi.comは現在，顧客からの注文に応えるため，戦略的に40の倉庫を世界中に保持している。昨年，Bexi.comは休暇シーズン中に1日約1,500万個もの商品を売り，今年の冬，その数字は1日2,000万個に上る見込みだ。

❺ The new warehouse will be built on the site of an old brewery and will be Bexi.com's biggest shipping center in Europe. Nelly Wilde, who works at Bexi.com's headquarters in Phoenix, says that Q154 many people are astonished when they hear that there are no robots within Bexi.com's immense warehouses. →❻ ❽ Instead, hundreds of workers use bar codes to find and ship the ordered items. According to Wilde, this is more economical than implementing and using automated systems. Reportedly, Q155 Bexi.com will need an additional 200 workers to staff its latest warehouse. →❾

新しい倉庫は旧醸造所跡地に建設され，Bexi.comのヨーロッパ最大の配送センターになる予定。フェニックスにあるBexi.com本社で働くNelly Wilde氏は，Bexi.comの巨大倉庫内部にロボットが1台もないことを聞くと，多くの人は驚くと言う。その代わり，数百人もの従業員がバーコードを使って，注文品を見つけたり配送したりしている。Wilde氏によると，これは自動システムを実施したり使用したりするよりも経済的だという。伝えられるところによると，Bexi.comは最新の倉庫に配置する200人の従業員を，追加で雇用する必要があるという。

153. ❶ What is indicated about Bexi.com? →❷
(A) ❸ It made 15 million dollars last year.
(B) It runs an Internet shopping business. →❹
(C) It has forty storage buildings in the U.S.
(D) Its head office is located in Berlin.

Bexi.comについてどんなことが示されているか。
(A) 昨年1,500万ドルの売り上げを達成した。
(B) ネットショッピングのビジネスをしている。
(C) アメリカ国内に40の貯蔵庫を所有している。
(D) 本社はベルリンにある。

154. ❹ According to Nelly Wilde, what are people surprised by? →❺
(A) ❻ The low prices they can find on Bexi.com
(B) The complex machines used at Bexi.com's shipping centers
(C) The lack of robots in Bexi.com's warehouses →❼
(D) The number of items sold by Bexi.com per day

Nelly Wildeによると，人々は何に驚くか。
(A) Bexi.comで見つけられる低価格
(B) Bexi.comの配送センターで使用されている複雑な機械
(C) Bexi.comの倉庫にロボットがないこと
(D) Bexi.comが1日に売る商品の数

155. ❼ What is suggested about the Berlin warehouse? →❽
(A) ❾ It will be built next to a brewery.
(B) It will be the largest in the world.
(C) It will create a lot of jobs. →正解，このセットの解答終了
(D) It is the only shipping center in Europe.

ベルリンの倉庫についてどんなことが分かるか。
(A) 醸造所の隣に建設予定である。
(B) 世界最大となる。
(C) たくさんの仕事を生み出す。
(D) ヨーロッパで唯一の配送センターである。

正解 **153. (B)　154. (C)　155. (C)**

語句 □brewery 醸造所，ビール会社　□immense 非常に大きな，巨大な　□storage building 貯蔵庫

Part 6と同様に，問題を読む流れを番号で示した。❶から→❷へ，❷から→❸へと読み進めていってほしい。

❶最初の設問の質問を読み，リテンションする。選択肢は読まずに問題文へ進む。
★質問は簡単な言葉に置き換えて記憶するとよい。例えばこの問題の場合 indicate「示唆する」が使われているが，「Bexi.comについて何が書いてある？」となる。

❷冒頭から問題文をベタ読みしていく。**153.** のような indicate，suggest，infer などの問題は，キーワードが出てきたらすぐに選択肢を見るのではなく，区切りの良いところまで問題文を読み進めてから選択肢と照合するとよい。段落がある問題文の場合は設問1つにつき段落1つ，段落がない問題文の場合は，例えば設問が3つであれば問題文の3分の1程度まで，といった具合である。
★ベタ読みすることで，「読んでいないところに正解の根拠があるのでは」という疑念を持たずに読み進めることができる。
★問題文を最後まで読んでから解答する方法だと，問題文の最初の方の内容を忘れてしまったり，正解の根拠が書かれている箇所に戻るのに手間取ったりしてしまう。しかし，この方法だとそのロスを防ぐことができる。

❸**153.** の選択肢を(A)から順番に確認していく。(B)の It runs an Internet shopping business. が，冒頭の Bexi.com, the world's third largest online retailer と一致しているので正解だ。この時点でマークシートの(B)を塗りつぶし，この問題に関するタスクは終了。選択肢の(C)と(D)は確認程度に目をやるだけにして❹に進む。
★不正解の選択肢が不正解である根拠を探す必要はない。それによって貴重な時間をロスしないようにしたい。

❹**154.** の質問を読み，「人々はなぜ驚いている？」とリテンションして問題文に戻る。

❺第2段落の中盤に正解の根拠となりそうな部分が登場。**154.** の選択肢へ。

❻**154.** の選択肢を(A)から読み進めていくと，(C)の The lack of robots in Bexi.com's warehouses が第2段落中盤にある there are no robots within Bexi.com's immense warehouses. と一致する。

❼**155.** の質問を読み，「Berlin warehouseについて何が書いてある？」とリテンションして先ほど中断したところから問題文を読み進めていく。
★**153.** 同様，suggest「示唆する」は簡単な言葉に置き換えて差し支えない。

❽第2段落を読み終えたら **155.** の選択肢へ。

❾(C) It will create a lot of jobs. が，問題文の最後にある Bexi.com will need an additional 200 workers to staff its latest warehouse. と一致するので正解だ。latest warehouse が Berlin warehouse であることは，第1段落から分かる。

990点獲得への道

あらためて，Part 7の正解回路のポイントをまとめておこう。

(1) **最初の設問の質問**を読み，**リテンション**する（選択肢はまだ読まない）。
- 質問はリテンションしやすいよう簡潔な日本語に置き換えるとよい。

(2) 問題文を冒頭から**ベタ読み**していく。
- 全文をきっちり読むことで，自信を持って解答できる。

(3) **区切りの良いところ**まで読んだら（または，**正解の根拠**が見つかったら）**選択肢に移動**する。
- 段落分けされていない文章は，設問の数で問題文を割って読むとよい。
- 設問ごとに解答することで，全文を覚えておく負担や，正解の箇所を探すロスを回避できる。

(4) 問題文中の**正解の根拠と選択肢を照合し，正解をマーク**する。
- 不正解の選択肢が不正解である根拠は探しても見つからない場合が多いので，最初から探さない。

(5) **次の設問の質問**を読み，**続きから**問題文を読み進めていく。
- 1つの段落に複数の問題の正解の根拠がくる場合もあるので，必ず続きから読む。

Part 7は上記（1）～（5）の繰り返しだ。ベタ読みしても**時間内に全問解答できる速さ**を身に付けよう。そのためには，日々の学習で英文を読む時間・回数を増やすことが必須である。英文を読む速度は，反復練習によって徐々に身に付いてくる。

この後に行うTrainingでは，正解の根拠を正確に把握することを意識して解答にあたってもらう。900点台の学習者でも，全ての問題の正解の根拠を，ピンポイントでしっかりと押さえられている人は多くはない。TOEICの問題では，正解の選択肢と不正解の選択肢の違いがハッキリしているので，文脈を大体追うことができれば正解できてしまうことも多々あるからだ。

だが，その程度の精度のリーディング力では990点は取れない。正解の根拠をピンポイントで押さえ，**不正解の選択肢を自信を持ってスルーする力**を身に付けられるよう，本書できっちり練習しよう。NOT問題などの「手間がかかる問題」に関しても，この後のTrainingやPractice Testで豊富に扱うので期待してほしい。

まとめ

Part 7は正解回路（解答の型）をしっかりと確立することが肝要である。また，正解の根拠を明確に示せるよう意識すること。

Training

次の問題に解答し，正解の根拠を示しなさい（マークシートは別冊 p.157 にあります）。

Questions 1-4 refer to the following article.

Baruti Wildlife Park

By Dingane Mbeki

For 36 years, Baruti Wildlife Park in South Africa has been providing sanctuary to orphaned and injured animals from South Africa and beyond, including cheetahs, lions, marmosets, and many species of birds. The 1,000-acre park is privately owned and relies heavily on donations from individuals, companies and organizations.

David Seaberg, best known as a director of the popular science fiction series *Solar Adventures*, donated €2 million to the Baruti Wildlife Park after spending a two-week family holiday at the luxurious lodge located within the park's grounds. "I was moved by the passion of the volunteers and employees at the park and wanted to show my support," Seaberg commented.

In an effort to finance the growing maintenance costs, Baruti Wildlife Park also partnered with Sunrise Travels, which now organizes various tours to the park. Besides enjoying the spectacular nature and wildlife, visitors can participate in a wildlife photography course or explore the grounds with a certified field guide to learn about local ecology and culture.

1. The word "sanctuary" in paragraph 1, line 1, is closest in meaning to
(A) medicine
(B) goods
(C) shelter
(D) prayer

2. What is indicated about David Seaberg?
(A) He participated in a volunteer program.
(B) He is famous for his love of animals.
(C) He shot a film about Baruti Wildlife Park.
(D) He took a vacation to South Africa.

3. What is NOT true about Baruti Wildlife Park?
(A) It takes care of animals that got hurt.
(B) It has been operating for more than a decade.
(C) It works together with a travel agency.
(D) It breeds endangered species.

4. According to the article, what can visitors do at Baruti Wildlife Park?
(A) Adopt an orphaned animal
(B) Be certified as a park ranger
(C) Take a guided tour
(D) Study how to paint

Questions 5-8 refer to the following letter.

Lo-Mart

May 15

Mr. Larry Arroyo
78 Candy Lane
Dallas, TX 75982

Dear Mr. Arroyo,

Congratulations!
Your essay has been awarded third prize in the parent category of the Lo-mart and I contest sponsored by Lo-Mart. We wish to celebrate your accomplishment at an award ceremony on Sunday, June 1, at Kosting Elementary School. Upon entering the school's North gate, turn left and walk past the vegetable garden to get to the school's auditorium, where the ceremony will be held.
The winning essays, including yours, will be published in the Lo-Mart Newsletter, which is delivered to members every month, and put on our Web site. Additionally, they will be printed and displayed in every Lo-Mart store. As a third place winner, you will receive a 50-dollar gift voucher redeemable at any Lo-Mart store before December 31. You can pick it up at the award ceremony, or provide us with an address where you want it to be sent.
Again, congratulations on your achievement!

Sincerely,
Arthur Lucero
Arthur Lucero, Manager,
Lo-Mart, Inc.

5. Who most likely is Mr. Arroyo?
(A) A winner of a lucky draw
(B) A teacher at an elementary school
(C) A participant in a competition
(D) An employee of Lo-Mart

6. What is NOT provided in the letter?
(A) The date of an award event
(B) The content of a prize
(C) Directions to the event venue
(D) The names of award winners

7. According to the letter, how can people read the essays?
(A) By obtaining a local newspaper
(B) By visiting a Lo-Mart store
(C) By sending an e-mail request
(D) By going to the school library

8. What can be inferred about the voucher?
(A) It only applies to an order of over 50 dollars.
(B) It should be used at a particular outlet.
(C) It will be given out at a Lo-Mart store.
(D) It must be used by a certain date.

Questions 9-12 refer to the following e-mail.

From: Matt Juliano [Mjuliano@kg.com]
To: Customer Service [customerservice@elecABC.com]
Subject: Alarmio 2109
Date: October 6

I purchased the Alarmio 2109 from your online store after browsing the Internet to find a replacement for my old alarm clock which I accidentally broke a few months ago.

I have no complaints about the alarm clock itself. I always wanted an alarm clock that could project the time on the wall, which is why I bought the Alarmio 2109. I also found the functions which allow me to set two separate wake times and change the intensity of the night light very useful. However, on your Web site, some of the customer reviews for Alarmio 2109 mention how it automatically adjusts to daylight-saving time. It is the Alarmio 2110 that has this function and not the Alarmio 2109. I thought this was rather confusing and hope you will take down these reviews from the site, or move them to the reviews for Alarmio 2110.

Matt Juliano

9. The word "browsing" in paragraph 1, line 1, is closest in meaning to
(A) wondering
(B) searching
(C) comparing
(D) connecting

10. According to the e-mail, what happened a few months ago?
(A) An order was delivered.
(B) A device was upgraded.
(C) An item stopped working.
(D) A watch went missing.

11. Which function is indicated as the reason for the purchase?
(A) Time projection
(B) Dual wake time
(C) Night light adjustment
(D) Automatic daylight-saving time adjustment

12. What is suggested about the reviews?
(A) Some of them are offensive.
(B) Some of them are misleading.
(C) Some of them are outdated.
(D) Some of them are too long.

Questions 13-17 refer to the following e-mail.

From: Peter Gomez [Pgomez@tg.com]
To: Kelly Brown [Kbrown@tg.com]
Subject: Dr. Annie Boonsung
Date: August 10

Kelly,

Dr. Annie Boonsung has informed me that due to a previous commitment, she won't be able to travel to Bangkok to give a presentation at our Annual Pharmaceutical Conference starting on September 1.

At the request of Dr. Boonsung, I have rescheduled her presentation a week later on September 7, and notified all persons involved in the organization of the original conference. Attached is the revised itinerary for Dr. Boonsung. The Belladonna Inn has also been informed of the change, and the hotel will confirm the new reservation by e-mail before August 31.

Incidentally, I have booked the Lindman Hall for her talk. However, I'm concerned that the seating capacity of the hall will not be sufficient. As she is one of the forerunners in the field of genetics, I expect many people to turn up. If you can think of a better venue for her presentation, please let me know. I will get back to you with the administrative details by August 30.

Thanks,

Peter Gomez
Assistant Manager,
TG Pharmaceuticals

13. Why is the e-mail being sent?
(A) To schedule a multi-day workshop
(B) To inform a colleague of a changed schedule
(C) To organize a telephone conference
(D) To decline a conference invitation

14. The word "request" in paragraph 2, line 1, is closest in meaning to
(A) inquiry
(B) wish
(C) offer
(D) demand

15. When will the presentation take place?
(A) On August 30
(B) On August 31
(C) On September 1
(D) On September 7

16. What can be inferred about Dr. Boonsung?
(A) She lives in Bangkok.
(B) She founded TG Pharmaceuticals.
(C) She is a leading philosopher.
(D) She will stay at Belladonna Inn.

17. What is suggested about Lindman Hall?
(A) Its location is inconvenient.
(B) It is expensive to rent.
(C) It is not very big.
(D) It doesn't have good equipment.

Questions 18-22 refer to the following advertisement and e-mail.

Travel with UTC Insurance!

A traveller's nightmare is a perfect vacation or an important business trip ruined because of an unforeseen accident or emergency health issue. Minimize your risk! Call us now at 555-2789.

Our policy covers:
✓ Loss of luggage
✓ Pre-trip cancellations
✓ Overseas medical expenses
✓ High value personal items

Please note that our policy does not cover pre-existing medical conditions or flight delays due to bad weather.

Returning customer? Call 555-3990 and receive a pre-filled application form. Just check it, make necessary changes and send it back to us! You will also receive a coupon book which can be used to get a discount in 100 hotels around the world!

To: Emma Sanders [esanders@utcinsurance.com]
From: Nirada Reed [NReed@lefman.org]
Date: June 12
Subject: Your service

Dear Ms. Sanders,

I went on a trip to Phuket last month with a colleague of mine, and while we were riding rented motorcycles, a bird suddenly flew right in front of us. My colleague hit the brakes, and he was thrown off the motorcycle. Fortunately, he was not badly injured, but he still needed to get medical attention right away. We had no contact in Thailand and we didn't know what to do. We called the ambulance, and then we called your 24-hour emergency support number. While we were waiting for the ambulance to arrive, your customer representative told us which hospital is highly regarded in the area. More than anything, I was glad I bought your policy as it was vital to know where we could find a good doctor.

When we returned to the U.S., my colleague filled the claim form, which he said was a little complicated. Regardless, I plan to take out a policy with you for my trip to Panama in autumn. I feel confident that should anything go wrong, I would be in good hands.

Thanks,
Nirada Reed

18. What is NOT covered by UTC Insurance's policy?
(A) A baggage not arriving at the airport
(B) A flight being postponed due to a storm
(C) A sudden fever that requires hospitalization
(D) A trip called off due to a family emergency

19. In the advertisement, the word "unforeseen" in paragraph 1, line 2, is closest in meaning to
(A) unfounded
(B) unconscious
(C) surprising
(D) expectant

20. What is indicated about Ms. Reed?
(A) She was visiting Phuket for the first time.
(B) She was in a jet-skiing accident.
(C) She did not know anyone in Thailand.
(D) She injured her leg while travelling.

21. What did Ms. Reed appreciate?
(A) The quick arrival of the emergency vehicle
(B) The information about medical institutions
(C) The friendliness of the customer representative
(D) The simplicity of the claim procedure

22. What can be inferred about Ms. Reed's next trip?
(A) She will get a free novelty stationery set.
(B) She will not need to submit an application form.
(C) She will acquire a booklet with discount coupons.
(D) She will be able to buy insurance for a cheaper price.

Questions 23-27 refer to the following article and e-mail.

NEW YORK — Hudson Air's popular calendar came about due to a digital photography competition for crew members ten years ago. As part of a learning incentive program, Hudson Air let their crews showcase their best photographs taken at its destination cities, with a €50 gift voucher for the best one. The idea of turning the top 13 pictures into a charity calendar followed.

The calendars were printed and sold onboard Hudson Air flights. To the surprise and delight of airline staff, the first 570 copies sold out in just 2 days. Judith Oak, the Managing Director of Hudson Air donated the €6,840 proceeds to Determined Kids, a global charity focusing on children's education, a few months later at a ceremony in New York.

Since then, the airline has been producing the charity calendar every year. This year's calendar features an extra 3 pages containing a map of New York, London and Beijing, the three most frequent destinations of Hudson Air. Copies are available onboard Hudson Air flights, at hudsonair.com and in Determined Kids' charity shops in the U.S., Canada and Europe.

To: Penelope Ward [pward@hudsonair.com]
From: Deborah Hugh [Hugh@dk.org]
Date: August 3, 11:25 A.M.
Subject: Thank you for your support

Dear Ms. Ward,

Thank you for your continued support of Determined Kids. Because of your company's generous donation, this year our organization was able to offer scholarships to 5 students who face financial difficulties, and help establish two new children's learning centers in India. Please know that your company's efforts made a big difference in the lives of these children.

On a more personal note, I purchased several copies of your calendar for myself as well as for my friends, and was very impressed. The maps are beautiful, and I have hung them in my living room. I have never travelled much myself, but the pictures truly inspire imagination. Moreover, my friends who travel have found the added bonus to be extremely useful and I hope it will be a recurring feature.

Sincerely,
Deborah Hugh
Determined Kids

23. What does the article imply about the calendar?
(A) It costs €50 for each copy.
(B) It originated from a photo contest.
(C) It contains pictures of flight attendants.
(D) It had been planned for many years.

24. Where are people NOT able to purchase the calendar?
(A) Inside Hudson Air airplanes
(B) At major international airports
(C) From a company's Web site
(D) At an organization's store

25. What is indicated about Determined Kids?
(A) It focuses on adult learning.
(B) It operates domestically.
(C) It runs a business in Beijing.
(D) It provides aid to students.

26. What feature of the calendar did Ms. Hugh's friends find helpful?
(A) City maps
(B) Fridge magnets
(C) Logo stickers
(D) World atlas

27. What can be inferred about Ms. Hugh?
(A) She works at Hudson Air.
(B) She does not fly frequently.
(C) She received a financial reward.
(D) She is interested in local arts.

Training 正解と解説

Questions 1-4 refer to the following article.
設問 1-4 は次の記事に関するものである。

❷Baruti Wildlife Park
By Dingane Mbeki

Q3(B) For 36 years, Baruti Wildlife Park in South Africa Q3(A) has been providing sanctuary to orphaned and injured animals from South Africa and beyond, including cheetahs, lions, marmosets, and many species of birds. The 1,000-acre park is privately owned and relies heavily on donations from individuals, companies and organizations. →❸

❺David Seaberg, best known as a director of the popular science fiction series *Solar Adventures*, donated €2 million to the Baruti Wildlife Park Q2 after spending a two-week family holiday at the luxurious lodge located within the park's grounds. "I was moved by the passion of the volunteers and employees at the park and wanted to show my support," Seaberg commented. →❻

❾In an effort to finance the growing maintenance costs, Q3(C) Baruti Wildlife Park also partnered with Sunrise Travels, which now organizes various tours to the park. Besides enjoying the spectacular nature and wildlife, visitors can participate in a wildlife photography course or Q4 explore the grounds with a certified field guide to learn about local ecology and culture. →❿

Baruti野生動物公園
Dingane Mbeki記

36年間，南アフリカのBaruti野生動物公園は，南アフリカやその他の地域から来た，親がいなかったり傷ついたりしている動物たちの保護区となっている。動物にはチーター，ライオン，マーモセットや多くの種類の鳥を含む。広さ1,000エーカーの公園は民間の所有で，個人や会社，団体からの寄付に大いに頼っている。

人気SFシリーズ*Solar Adventures*の監督としてもっとも知られているDavid Seaberg氏は，Baruti野生動物公園内の高級ロッジで家族と2週間休暇を過ごした後，公園に200万ユーロを寄付した。「私は公園のボランティアや従業員の情熱に感動して，支援の気持ちを示したくなったのです」とSeaberg氏はコメントしている。

Baruti野生動物公園は増大し続ける維持費を調達するために，同公園を巡るさまざまなツアーを現在企画しているSunrise旅行社とも提携した。来園者は素晴らしい自然と野生動物を楽しむだけでなく，野生動物撮影講座に参加したり，現地の生態系や文化を学ぶために，資格を持ったフィールドガイドと敷地内を探検することができる。

語句 □orphaned 親を失った □marmoset マーモセット（動物） □acre エーカー（面積の単位）

1. ❶The word "sanctuary" in paragraph 1, line 1, is closest in meaning to →❷
(A) ❸medicine
(B) goods
(C) shelter 正解，次の設問へと進む →❹
(D) prayer

第1段落・1行目のsanctuaryに最も近い意味の語は
(A) 薬
(B) 商品
(C) 避難所
(D) 祈り

正解 **(C)**

解説 parkがorphaned and injured animalsに提供しているものがsanctuaryだ。sanctuaryには「自然保護区，避難所」という意味があり，最も意味が近いのは(C)のshelterになる。sanctuaryについて「聖域」という意味しか知らなくても，文脈から推測することができる。

2. ❹What is indicated about David Seaberg?
「David Seabergに関する記述？」とリテンションして問題文へ →❺
(A) ❻He participated in a volunteer program.
(B) He is famous for his love of animals.
(C) He shot a film about Baruti Wildlife Park.
(D) He took a vacation to South Africa.
正解，次の設問へと進む →❼

David Seabergについてどんなことが述べられているか。
(A) ボランティアプログラムに参加した。
(B) 動物が大好きなことで有名である。
(C) Baruti野生動物公園についての映画を撮った。
(D) 休暇を取って南アフリカに行った。

正解 (D)

解説 第2段落のspending a two-week family holidayをtook a vacationと言い換えた(D)が正解だ。(A)～(C)の選択肢の内容は，いずれもどこか一部が問題文の内容とズレている。

3. ❼What is NOT true about Baruti Wildlife Park?
NOT問題の場合はそのまま選択肢に進む →❽
(A) ❽It takes care of animals that got hurt.
(B) It has been operating for more than a decade.
(C) It works together with a travel agency.
(D) ❿It breeds endangered species.
4つの選択肢の内容をリテンションして問題文へ →❾
正解，次の設問へと進む →⓫

Baruti野生動物公園について，正しくないのはどれか。
(A) けがをした動物の世話をしている。
(B) 10年以上操業している。
(C) 旅行代理店と協力関係にある。
(D) 絶滅危惧種を繁殖させている。

正解 (D)

解説 NOT問題は先に選択肢を読んで内容を頭に入れてから問題文を読み，3つの選択肢の情報が登場した時点で残った1つが正解，と考えるとよい。2.で中断したところから問題文を読み進めると，最後の段落に(C)の内容が登場する。また，(A)，(B)の内容が第1段落に書かれていたことを思い出し，確認程度にさっと読む。全文をきちんと読んで覚えておくと効率的である。

4. ⓫According to the article, what can visitors do at Baruti Wildlife Park?
すでに正解の根拠が登場しているので選択肢へ →⓬
(A) ⓬Adopt an orphaned animal
(B) Be certified as a park ranger
(C) Take a guided tour →正解，このセットの解答終了
(D) Study how to paint

記事によると，訪問者はBaruti野生動物公園で何をすることができるか。
(A) 親のいない動物を引き取る
(B) 公園の監視員としての資格を取る
(C) ガイドツアーに参加する
(D) 絵の描き方を学ぶ

正解 (C)

解説 最終段落にvisitorsはexplore the grounds with a certified field guideができるとある。これをTake a guided tourと言い換えた(C)が正解だ。(B)にあるpark rangerは「公園監視員，公園保護官」のことだが，時々TOEICに登場する表現なので知っておきたい。

Questions 5-8 refer to the following letter.

設問 5-8 は次の手紙に関するものである。

❷ Lo-Mart May 15 Mr. Larry Arroyo 78 Candy Lane Dallas, TX 75982	Lo-Mart 5月15日 Larry Arroyo 様 Candy Lane 78 番地 Dallas, TX 75982
Dear Mr. Arroyo, Congratulations! Q5 Your essay has been awarded third prize in the parent category of the Lo-Mart and I Contest sponsored by Lo-Mart. →❸ ❻We wish to celebrate your accomplishment at an award ceremony on Sunday, Q6(A) June 1, Q6(C) at Kosting Elementary School. Upon entering the school's North gate, turn left and walk past the vegetable garden to get to the school's auditorium, where the ceremony will be held. The winning essays, including yours, will be published in the Lo-Mart Newsletter, which is delivered to members every month, and put on our Web site. Additionally, Q7 they will be printed and displayed in every Lo-Mart store. As a third place winner, you will receive Q6(B) a 50-dollar gift voucher Q8 redeemable at any Lo-Mart store before December 31. →❼ You can pick it up at the award ceremony, or provide us with an address where you want it to be sent. Again, congratulations on your achievement! Sincerely, Arthur Lucero Arthur Lucero, Manager, Lo-Mart, Inc.	Arroyo 様 おめでとうございます！ あなたのエッセーが, Lo-Mart提供のLo-Mart and Iコンテストの保護者部門で3位に入賞いたしました。私たちは, 6月1日の日曜日にKosting小学校で行われる授賞式で, あなたの偉業をたたえたいと思います。小学校の北門を入りましたら左に曲がり, 菜園を通り抜けて講堂にお越しください。そこで授賞式が行われます。 あなたのエッセーを含む受賞作品は, 毎月会員に配布されるLo-Mart会報と, 私たちのウェブサイトに掲載されます。また, 印刷されてLo-Mart各店に展示される予定です。3位入賞者として, 12月31日までLo-Mart全店でご利用いただける50ドル分の商品券が贈られます。授賞式でお受け取りになるか, ご送付を希望される住所をお知らせください。 あらためまして, 受賞おめでとうございます！ 敬具 Arthur Lucero（署名） Arthur Lucero, 部長 Lo-Mart社

語句 □auditorium 講堂, 公会堂 □redeemable 換金できる, 商品に換えられる

5. ❶Who most likely is Mr. Arroyo?

Arroyoさんとは誰だと考えられるか。

「Arroyoは誰？」とリテンションし, 問題文を冒頭から読み始める →❷

(A) ❸A winner of a lucky draw

(B) A teacher at an elementary school

(C) A participant in a competition

正解, 次の設問へと進む →❹

(D) An employee of Lo-Mart

(A) 抽選会の当選者

(B) 小学校の先生

(C) コンテストの参加者

(D) Lo-Martの従業員

正解 (C)

解説 Your essay has been awarded third prize から，Arroyo さんはコンテストの受賞者だと判断できるので，(C) が正解。(A) は a lucky draw「抽選会」が誤り。

6. ❹What is NOT provided in the letter? 手紙に書かれていないものはどれか。

NOT 問題の場合はそのまま選択肢に進む →❺

(A) ❺The date of an award event (A) 授賞イベントの日付

(B) The content of a prize (B) 賞品の中身

(C) Directions to the event venue (C) イベント会場への行き方

(D) ❼The names of award winners (D) 受賞者の名前

4 つの選択肢の内容をリテンションして問題文へ →❻

正解，次の設問へ進む →❽

正解 (D)

解説 (A)，(C)，(B) の順に情報が現れ，この時点でタスク終了。残った (D) の情報が本文中に登場していないことは確認せず，すぐに次の設問へと進むこと。

7. ❽According to the letter, how can people read the essays? 手紙によると，人々はどのようにしてエッセーを読むことができるか。

すでに正解の根拠が登場しているので選択肢へ →❾

(A) ❾ By obtaining a local newspaper (A) 地元新聞を手に入れることで

(B) By visiting a Lo-Mart store (B) Lo-Mart の店舗を訪れることで

正解，次の設問へ進む →❿

(C) By sending an e-mail request (C) E メールのリクエストを送ることで

(D) By going to the school library (D) 学校の図書館に行くことで

正解 (B)

解説 第 2 段落中ほどに they will be printed and displayed in every Lo-Mart store. とあるので，正解は (B)。they は第 2 段落冒頭の the winning essays のこと。エッセーが掲載される Lo-Mart Newsletter は Lo-Mart の会員に配布されるもので，local newspaper ではないので (A) を選ばないようにしたい。Web site で見ることもできるが，e-mail でリクエストする必要はないので (C) は不正解。

8. ❿What can be inferred about the voucher? 商品券についてどんなことが推測されるか。

すでに正解の根拠が登場しているので選択肢へ→⓫

(A) ⓫It only applies to an order of over 50 dollars. (A) 50 ドル以上の注文にのみ適用される。

(B) It should be used at a particular outlet. (B) 特定の店舗で使用しなければならない。

(C) It will be given out at a Lo-Mart store. (C) Lo-Mart の店舗で配布される予定だ。

(D) It must be used by a certain date. (D) 特定の日までに使用しなければならない。

→正解，このセットの解答終了（残りの問題文は読まなくてよい）

正解 (D)

解説 問題文中の before December 31 を by a certain date と抽象的に言い換えた (D) が正解だ。(B) は particular が誤り。

Questions 9-12 refer to the following e-mail.
設問9-12は次のEメールに関するものである。

❷From: Matt Juliano [Mjuliano@kg.com]
To: Customer Service [customerservice@elecABC.com]
Subject: Alarmio 2109
Date: October 6

I purchased the Alarmio 2109 from your online store after browsing the Internet to find a replacement for my old alarm clock which Q10 I accidentally broke a few months ago. →❸

❼I have no complaints about the alarm clock itself. Q11 I always wanted an alarm clock that could project the time on the wall, which is why I bought the Alarmio 2109. →❽ ❿I also found the functions which allow me to set two separate wake times and change the intensity of the night light very useful. However, on your Web site, some of the customer reviews for Alarmio 2109 mention how it automatically adjusts to daylight-saving time. It is the Alarmio 2110 that has this function and not the Alarmio 2109. Q12 I thought this was rather confusing and hope you will take down these reviews from the site, or move them to the reviews for Alarmio 2110. →⓫

Matt Juliano

送信者：Matt Juliano [Mjuliano@kg.com]
宛先：顧客サービス係[customerservice@elecABC.com]
件名：Alarmio 2109
日付：10月6日

私は数カ月前にうっかり壊してしまった古い目覚まし時計の代わりを探してインターネットを閲覧し，御社のオンラインストアでAlarmio 2109を購入しました。

目覚まし時計自体には不満はありません。私は壁に時刻を投影できる目覚まし時計が欲しいと常に思っており，それがAlarmio 2109を購入した理由です。また，2つの異なった起床時刻を設定したり，常夜灯の明るさを変えたりすることができる機能は，大変便利だと思いました。しかしながら，御社のウェブサイトにあるAlarmio 2109のカスタマーレビューの中には，自動的に夏時間に調節されるという言及があります。この機能があるのはAlarmio 2110で，Alarmio 2109ではありません。これは多少分かりにくいため，これらのレビューをサイトから削除するか，Alarmio 2110のレビューに移動していただけると幸いです。

Matt Juliano

語句　□project ～を投影する　□intensity 明度，強烈さ　□night light 常夜灯
□daylight-saving time 夏時間

9. ❶The word "browsing" in paragraph 1, line 1, is closest in meaning to →❷
(A) ❸wondering
(B) searching 正解，次の設問へと進む→❹
(C) comparing
(D) connecting

第1段落・1行目のbrowsingに最も近い意味の語は
(A) ～だろうかと考える
(B) ～を検索する
(C) ～を比較する
(D) ～をつなぐ

正解　**(B)**

解説　after browsing the Internetとあり，ここでのbrowseは「～を閲覧する」だ。これに近い意味を持つ(B)のsearchが正解となる。browseは「(店で商品を) 見て回る」という意味でPart 1にも登場する表現なので覚えておこう。

10. ❹According to the e-mail, what happened a few months ago?

Eメールによると，数カ月前に何が起こったか。

すでに正解の根拠が登場しているので選択肢へ →❺

(A) ❺An order was delivered.
(B) A device was upgraded.
(C) An item stopped working.
正解，次の設問へと進む →❻
(D) A watch went missing.

(A) 注文品が配達された。
(B) 装置がアップグレードされた。
(C) 商品が作動しなくなった。
(D) 腕時計が行方不明になった。

正解 **(C)**

解説 10.の質問を読んだ瞬間に「この内容については9.の問題を解く際に問題文で読んだので覚えている」と思いたい。そうすれば問題文に戻らずそのまま選択肢に進むことができる。I accidentally broke a few months ago.から，(C)のAn item stopped working.が正解だ。

11. ❻Which function is indicated as the reason for the purchase?

どの機能が購入の理由になったと述べられているか。

「購入の理由，何？」とリテンションして問題文へ →❼

(A) ❽Time projection 正解，次の設問へと進む →❾
(B) Dual wake time
(C) Night light adjustment
(D) Automatic daylight-saving time adjustment

(A) 時刻の投影
(B) 2つの起床時刻
(C) 常夜灯の調節
(D) 夏時間への自動調節

正解 **(A)**

解説 I always wanted an alarm clock that could project the time on the wall, which is why I bought the Alarmio 2109.と，購入した理由を明確に述べているため，迷うことなく(A)のTime projectionを選べるだろう。(B)，(C)も便利だと述べられているが，購入の理由ではない。(D)は別の時計が持つ機能である。

語句 □dual 2つの

12. ❾What is suggested about the reviews?

レビューについてどんなことが分かるか。

「reviewsに関する記述？」とリテンションして問題文へ →❿

(A) ⓫Some of them are offensive.
(B) Some of them are misleading.
→正解，このセットの解答終了
(C) Some of them are outdated.
(D) Some of them are too long.

(A) いくつかは無礼である。
(B) いくつかは誤解を招く恐れがある。
(C) いくつかは時代遅れである。
(D) いくつかは長すぎる。

正解 **(B)**

解説 Alarmio 2110に書くべきであるreviewが，Alarmio 2109に書いてあると述べられており，I thought this was rather confusingとも言及されている。それを言い換えた(B)のSome of them are misleading.が正解だ。問題文にあるconfusingがmisleadingにつながる決定的な表現だ。

語句 □offensive 無礼な，不愉快な

Questions 13-17 refer to the following e-mail.
設問 13-17 は次のEメールに関するものである。

❷From: Peter Gomez [Pgomez@tg.com]
To: Kelly Brown [Kbrown@tg.com]
Subject: Dr. Annie Boonsung
Date: August 10

Kelly,

Dr. Annie Boonsung has informed me that due to a previous commitment, she won't be able to travel to Bangkok to give a presentation at our Annual Pharmaceutical Conference starting on September 1.

At the request of Dr. Boonsung, Q13 Q15 I have rescheduled her presentation a week later on September 7, and notified all persons involved in the organization of the original conference. Q16 Attached is the revised itinerary for Dr. Boonsung. The Belladonna Inn has also been informed of the change, and the hotel will confirm the new reservation by e-mail before August 31. →❸

⓫Incidentally, I have booked the Lindman Hall for her talk. However, Q17 I'm concerned that the seating capacity of the hall will not be sufficient. As she is one of the forerunners in the field of genetics, I expect many people to turn up. If you can think of a better venue for her presentation, please let me know. I will get back to you with the administrative details by August 30. →⓬

Thanks,

Peter Gomez
Assistant Manager,
TG Pharmaceuticals

送信者：Peter Gomez [Pgomez@tg.com]
宛先：Kelly Brown [Kbrown@tg.com]
件名：Annie Boonsung 医師
日付：8月10日

Kellyさん

Annie Boonsung医師が知らせてきたところによると，先約があるため，9月1日から始まる年次医薬会議で発表をするためにバンコクへ行くことはできないということです。

Boonsung医師の要請を受けて，私は彼女の発表を1週間後の9月7日に変更し，当初の会議の準備関係者全員に知らせました。添付はBoonsung医師の変更後の日程表です。Belladonnaホテルにも変更を知らせており，ホテルは8月31日より前に新しい予約の確認をEメールで送ってくると思います。

ちなみに，彼女の発表のためにLindmanホールを予約しました。しかしながら，ホールの収容人数が十分ではないことを心配しています。彼女は遺伝学の分野では先駆者の1人ですので，たくさんの人が出席すると思います。発表にもっと適切な会場を思いついたら，どうか私に知らせてください。8月30日までに運営の詳細について折り返し連絡します。

よろしくお願いします。

Peter Gomez
係長
TG製薬会社

語句 □incidentally ちなみに □forerunner 先駆者 □genetic 遺伝子の

13. ❶Why is the e-mail being sent?
「Eメールの目的は？」とリテンションして問題文へ→❷
(A) ❸To schedule a multi-day workshop
(B) To inform a colleague of a changed schedule
正解，次の設問へと進む→❹
(C) To organize a telephone conference
(D) To decline a conference invitation

なぜEメールが送られているか。
(A) 数日間にわたる研修の日程を決めるため
(B) 同僚に変更後の日程を知らせるため
(C) 電話会議の準備をするため
(D) 会議への招待を断るため

正解 **(B)**

解説 第2段落の内容から，EメールEの目的はDr. Boonsungのプレゼンの日程変更を伝えるものだと分かる。

語句 □a multi-day workshop 数日間にわたる研修

14. ❹The word "request" in paragraph 2, line 1, is closest in meaning to →❺

第2段落・1行目のrequestに最も近い意味の語は

(A) ❺inquiry (A) 質問
(B) wish 正解，次の設問へと進む →❻ (B) 要請
(C) offer (C) 申し出
(D) demand (D) 要求

正解 **(B)**

解説 at somebody's requestはbecause someone asks for it to be doneという意味である。正解は(B)のwishだ。(D)のdemandはa very firm request for something that you believe you have the right to getという意味で，ここでは強すぎる。

15. ❻When will the presentation take place?

発表はいつ行われる予定か。

すでに正解の根拠が登場しているので選択肢へ →❼

(A) ❼On August 30 (A) 8月30日
(B) On August 31 (B) 8月31日
(C) On September 1 (C) 9月1日
(D) On September 7 正解，次の設問へと進む →❽ (D) 9月7日

正解 **(D)**

解説 第2段落前半にI have rescheduled her presentation a week later on September 7とあり，(D)が正解。複数の設問に対する正解の根拠が部分的に集中することもある。

16. ❽What can be inferred about Dr. Boonsung?

Boonsung医師について何が推測できるか。

すでに正解の根拠が登場しているので選択肢へ →❾

(A) ❾She lives in Bangkok. (A) バンコクに住んでいる。
(B) She founded TG Pharmaceuticals. (B) TG製薬会社を設立した。
(C) She is a leading philosopher. (C) 優れた哲学者である。
(D) She will stay at Belladonna Inn. 正解，次の設問へと進む →❿ (D) Belladonnaホテルに宿泊する予定である。

正解 **(D)**

解説 第2段落でthe hotel will confirm the new reservationと述べていることから，Dr. Boonsungは日程変更前と同じホテル（Belladonna Inn）に宿泊するだろうと判断できる。

17. ❿What is suggested about Lindman Hall?

Lindmanホールについてどんなことが分かるか。

「Lindman Hallに関する記述？」とリテンションして問題文へ →⓫

(A) ⓬Its location is inconvenient. (A) 場所が不便である。
(B) It is expensive to rent. (B) 借料が高い。
(C) It is not very big. →正解，このセットの解答終了 (C) あまり広くない。
(D) It doesn't have good equipment. (D) 良い装置がそろっていない。

正解 **(C)**

解説 第3段落のthe seating capacity of the hall will not be sufficient.を，It is not very big.と簡潔に言い換えた(C)が正解だ

Part 7

Questions 18-22 refer to the following advertisement and e-mail.

設問 18-22 は次の広告と E メールに関するものである。

❸ *Travel with UTC Insurance!*

A traveller's nightmare is a perfect vacation or an important business trip ruined because of an unforeseen accident or emergency health issue. Minimize your risk! Call us now at 555-2789.

Our policy covers:

✓ Q18 (A) Loss of luggage
✓ Q18 (D) Pre-trip cancellations
✓ Q18 (C) Overseas medical expenses →❹
✓ ❽ High value personal items

Please note that our policy does not cover pre-existing medical conditions or flight delays due to bad weather.

Q22 Returning customer? Call 555-3990 and receive a pre-filled application form. Just check it, make necessary changes and send it back to us! Q22 You will also receive a coupon book which can be used to get a discount in 100 hotels around the world!

ご旅行には UTC 保険を！

旅行者にとって最悪の事態は，完璧な休暇や重要な出張が，思いがけない事故や突発的な健康問題によって台無しになることです。リスクを最小限にしましょう！　すぐに 555-2789 にお電話ください。

われわれの保険は次のものをカバーしています：

✓ 荷物の紛失
✓ 旅行前のキャンセル
✓ 海外医療費
✓ 高額個人携行品

われわれの保険は，持病や悪天候による飛行機の遅延はカバーいたしませんので，ご注意ください。

リピートのお客さまでしょうか？　555-3990 に電話して，以前お書きいただいた申込書をお受け取りください。ご確認の上，必要な変更をした後，ご返送いただくだけで結構です！　世界中のホテル 100 カ所で割引が受けられるクーポンブックももらえます！

To: Emma Sanders [esanders@utcinsurance.com]
From: Nirada Reed [NReed@lefman.org]
Date: June 12
Subject: Your service

Dear Ms. Sanders,

I went on a trip to Phuket last month with a colleague of mine, and while we were riding rented motorcycles, a bird suddenly flew right in front of us. My colleague hit the brakes, and he was thrown off the motorcycle. Fortunately, he was not badly injured, but he still needed to get medical attention right away. Q20 We had no contact in Thailand and we didn't know what to do. We called the ambulance, and then we called your 24-hour emergency support number. While we were waiting for the ambulance to arrive, your customer representative told us

宛先：Emma Sanders [esanders@utcinsurance.com]
送信者：Nirada Reed [NReed@lefman.org]
日付：6 月 12 日
件名：御社のサービス

Sanders 様

私は先月，同僚とプーケットに旅行に行きました。レンタルバイクに乗っているとき，1 羽の鳥が突然私たちの目の前に飛んできました。同僚は急ブレーキをかけ，彼はバイクから投げ出されてしまいました。幸いひどいけがではありませんでしたが，彼はすぐに治療が必要でした。私たちはタイではつてがなく，どうすればよいか分かりませんでした。救急車を呼び，それから御社の 24 時間緊急サポート番号に電話をしました。救急車の到着を待つ間，御社の顧客係はどの病院がその地域で評判が良いかを教えてくれました。何よりも，

which hospital is highly regarded in the area. More than anything, Q21 I was glad I bought your policy as it was vital to know where we could find a good doctor. →❾	私は御社の保険に加入したことをうれしく思いました。というのも，私たちがどこで良い医者を見つけることができるかを知ることは，不可欠だったからです。
⓭When we returned to the U.S., my colleague filled the claim form, which he said was a little complicated. Regardless, Q22 I plan to take out a policy with you for my trip to Panama in autumn. I feel confident that should anything go wrong, I would be in good hands. →⓮	アメリカに戻ってから，同僚が請求書に記入しましたが，彼は少し分かりにくいと言っていました。それでも，秋のパナマ旅行には御社の保険に加入する予定です。万一何かがあっても，心配することはないと心強く思っています。
Thanks,	ありがとうございます。
Nirada Reed	Nirada Reed

語句 □nightmare 悪夢　□ruined 台無しになった，損なわれた　□unforeseen 予期せぬ　□pre-existing 前から存在する　□pre-filled 記入済みの　□hit the brakes 急ブレーキを踏む　□ambulance 救急車　□vital 必須の，不可欠な　□in good hands 何も心配することがなくて，安泰で

18. ❶What is NOT covered by UTC Insurance's policy? NOT問題の場合はそのまま選択肢に進む →❷

UTC保険がカバーしていないのはどれか。

(A) ❷A baggage not arriving at the airport
(B) ❹A flight being postponed due to a storm
正解，次の設問へと進む →❺
(C) A sudden fever that requires hospitalization
(D) A trip called off due to a family emergency
4つの選択肢の内容をリテンションして問題文へ →❸

(A) 空港に到着しない荷物
(B) 嵐のために遅延した飛行機
(C) 入院が必要な突然の発熱
(D) 家族の緊急事態による旅行の中止

正解 **(B)**

解説 (A)，(D)，(C)の順に情報が現れている。言い換えに戸惑うかもしれないが，Please note that ... 以下に(B)が補償対象でないことがはっきりと書かれているので解きやすい。

語句 □hospitalization 入院　□call off ～ ～を中止する

19. ❺In the advertisement, the word "unforeseen" in paragraph 1, line 2, is closest in meaning to →❻

広告の第1段落・2行目のunforeseenに最も近い意味の語は

(A) ❻unfounded
(B) unconscious
(C) surprising 正解，次の設問へと進む →❼
(D) expectant

(A) 根拠のない
(B) 意識を失った
(C) 意外な
(D) 期待する

正解 **(C)**

解説 unforeseenを空所と考え，その空所に最もふさわしい単語を選ぶとよい。perfect vacationがnightmareとなる原因はどのようなaccidentなのかを考えると，(C)が適切。

20. ❼What is indicated about Ms. Reed?
「Reedに関する記述？」とリテンションして問題文へ→❽
(A) ❾She was visiting Phuket for the first time.
(B) She was in a jet-skiing accident.
(C) She did not know anyone in Thailand.
正解，次の設問へと進む→❿
(D) She injured her leg while travelling.

Reedさんについてどんなことが述べられているか。
(A) 初めてプーケットを訪れた。
(B) ジェットスキーの事故にあった。
(C) タイで誰も知らなかった。
(D) 旅行中，足にけがをした。

正解 **(C)**
解説 EメールのWe had no contactを，She did not know anyoneと言い換えた(C)が正解だ。(A)は初めてとは書かれておらず，(B)は乗り物が，(D)はけがをした人が異なる。

21. ❿What did Ms. Reed appreciate?
すでに正解の根拠が登場しているので選択肢へ→⓫
(A) ⓫The quick arrival of the emergency vehicle
(B) The information about medical institutions
正解，次の設問へと進む→⓬
(C) The friendliness of the customer representative
(D) The simplicity of the claim procedure

Reedさんは何に感謝したか。
(A) 緊急車両の素早い到着
(B) 医療機関についての情報
(C) 顧客係の親しみやすさ
(D) 請求手順の簡潔さ

正解 **(B)**
解説 where we could find a good doctorをThe information about medical institutionsと言い換えた(B)が正解。(C)は，customer representativeのfriendlinessについての言及はないため不正解。(D)は次の段落に反対の記述がある。

22. ⓬What can be inferred about Ms. Reed's next trip? Ms. Reed's next tripをリテンションして問題文へ→⓭
(A) ⓮She will get a free novelty stationery set.
(B) She will not need to submit an application form.
(C) She will acquire a booklet with discount coupons. →正解，このセットの解答終了
(D) She will be able to buy insurance for a cheaper price.

Reedさんの次の旅行について何が推測できるか。
(A) 彼女は無料の新型文具セットをもらえる。
(B) 彼女は申込書を提出する必要がなくなる。
(C) 彼女は割引クーポン付きの小冊子を手に入れる。
(D) 彼女は割安の値段で保険に加入することができる。

正解 **(C)**
解説 2つ目の文書後半の下線部からMs. Reedがこの保険会社のリピーターになることが分かるので，1つ目の文書に戻ってReturning customer?を参照する。正解は(C)。(B)のShe will not need to submit an application form.を選んでしまいそうになるかもしれないが，a pre-filled application formは返送する必要があるので不正解だ。
語句 □novelty 目新しい，変わった

Questions 23-27 refer to the following article and e-mail.
設問 23-27 は次の記事とEメールに関するものである。

❷NEW YORK— Q23 Hudson Air's popular calendar came about due to a digital photography competition for crew members ten years ago. As part of a learning incentive program, Hudson Air let their crews showcase their best photographs taken at its destination cities, with a €50 gift voucher for the best one. The idea of turning the top 13 pictures into a charity calendar followed. →❸

ニューヨーク―10年前，Hudson航空の人気カレンダーが作られたきっかけは，乗務員のデジタル写真コンテストだった。学習奨励プログラムの一環として，Hudson航空は乗務員に就航先で撮った最高の写真を展示させ，一番良い写真には50ユーロの商品券が贈られるというものだ。その後，上位13枚の写真をチャリティーカレンダーにするというアイデアが出た。

❻The calendars were printed and sold onboard Hudson Air flights. To the surprise and delight of airline staff, the first 570 copies sold out in just 2 days. Judith Oak, the Managing Director of Hudson Air donated the €6,840 proceeds to Q25 Determined Kids, a global charity focusing on children's education, a few months later at a ceremony in New York.

カレンダーは印刷されて，Hudson航空の機内で販売された。乗務員が驚き喜んだことに，最初の570部はたった2日で売り切れた。Hudson航空取締役のJudith Oak氏は，ニューヨークで開かれた数カ月後の式典で，子どもたちの教育に尽力する国際慈善団体Determined Kidsに6,840ユーロの収益金を寄付した。

Since then, the airline has been producing the charity calendar every year. Q26 This year's calendar features an extra 3 pages containing a map of New York, London and Beijing, the three most frequent destinations of Hudson Air. Copies are available Q24(A) onboard Hudson Air flights, Q24(C) at hudsonair.com and Q24(D) in Determined Kids' charity shops in the U.S., Canada and Europe. →❼

それ以降，その航空会社は毎年チャリティーカレンダーを作成している。今年のカレンダーの特徴は追加された3ページ分で，Hudson航空が最も頻繁に就航する3都市，ニューヨーク，ロンドン，北京の地図を含む。カレンダーはHudson航空の機内か，hudsonair.com，またアメリカ・カナダ・ヨーロッパのDetermined Kidsのチャリティーショップで入手可能だ。

⓫To: Penelope Ward [pward@hudsonair.com]
From: Deborah Hugh [Hugh@dk.org]
Date: August 3, 11:25 A.M.
Subject: Thank you for your support

宛先：Penelope Ward [pward@hudsonair.com]
送信者：Deborah Hugh [Hugh@dk.org]
日付：8月3日，午前11時25分
件名：ご支援ありがとうございます

Dear Ms. Ward,

Ward様

Thank you for your continued support of Determined Kids. Because of your company's generous donation, this year our organization was able to offer scholarships to 5 students who face financial difficulties, and help establish two new children's learning centers in India. Please know that your company's efforts made a big

Determined Kidsへの引き続きのご支援をありがとうございます。御社の寛大な寄付により，今年私たちの団体は，経済的に困難な5人の生徒に奨学金を提供することができました。また，インドに新しい子ども用学習センターを2カ所創設するのに役立ちました。御社の努力がこうした子どもたちの生活に大きな違いをもたらし

Part 7

difference in the lives of these children.

On a more personal note, I purchased several copies of your calendar for myself as well as for my friends, and was very impressed. The maps are beautiful, and I have hung them in my living room. Q27 I have never travelled much myself, but the pictures truly inspire imagination. Moreover, Q26 my friends who travel have found the added bonus to be extremely useful and I hope it will be a recurring feature. →⓬

Sincerely,
Deborah Hugh
Determined Kids

たことを知っていただければと思います。

個人的なお知らせですが，私は友人や自分自身のために御社のカレンダーを数部購入し，大変感動いたしました。地図は美しく，私はそれを居間に掛けています。私はあまり旅行をしたことがないのですが，その写真は本当に想像力をかきたてます。さらに，旅行をする私の友人は今年の追加されたおまけのページは大変便利だと言っていましたので，この特徴がまた採用されることを希望します。

敬具
Deborah Hugh
Determined Kids

語句 □showcase ～を見せる，展示する □make a difference 相違を生じる，良くする □recur 繰り返す

23. ❶What does the article imply about the calendar? 「calendarに関する記述？」とリテンションして問題文へ →❷

(A) ❸It costs €50 for each copy.
(B) It originated from a photo contest.
正解，次の設問へと進む →❹
(C) It contains pictures of flight attendants.
(D) It had been planned for many years.

カレンダーについて記事から何が推測されるか。

(A) 1部50ユーロである。
(B) 写真コンテストから始まった。
(C) 客室乗務員の写真が含まれている。
(D) 数年にわたり準備されていた。

正解 (B)

解説 1つ目の文書の第1段落の冒頭に，calendar came about due to a digital photography competitionとある。came about due toをoriginated fromと言い換えている(B)が正解だ。(A)の€50は贈られる商品券の値段。客室乗務員が写った写真ではないので(C)は不正解。

語句 □originate from ～ ～が起源である

24. ❹Where are people NOT able to purchase the calendar? NOT問題の場合はそのまま選択肢に進む →❺

(A) ❺Inside Hudson Air airplanes
(B) ❼At major international airports
正解，次の設問へと進む →❽
(C) From a company's Web site
(D) At an organization's store
4つの選択肢の内容をリテンションして問題文へ →❻

人々がカレンダーを買うことができないのはどこか。

(A) Hudson航空の機内
(B) 主要国際空港
(C) 会社のウェブサイト
(D) 団体の店舗

正解 (B)

解説 1つ目の文書の最後の段落に，カレンダーを購入できる場所についての情報がまとめて述べられている。(B)のAt major international airportsは，いかにもこの商品が売られていそうな場所に思えるかもしれないが，問題文中では一切述べられていない。

25. ❽What is indicated about Determined Kids?
すでに正解の根拠が登場しているので選択肢へ→❾
(A) ❾It focuses on adult learning.
(B) It operates domestically.
(C) It runs a business in Beijing.
(D) It provides aid to students.
正解，次の設問へと進む→❿

Determined Kidsについてどんなことが述べられているか。
(A) 大人の学習に尽力している。
(B) 自国で活動している。
(C) 北京でビジネスをしている。
(D) 生徒に援助をしている。

正解 **(D)**
解説 Determined Kidsがどのような団体であるのかについては，1つ目の文書に書かれている。a global charity focusing on children's educationを言い換えた(D)が正解。(A)のadult learning，(B)のdomesticallyは問題文と反する内容であり，(C)のBeijingはカレンダーに追加された地図の場所である。

26. ❿What feature of the calendar did Ms. Hugh's friends find helpful?「Ms. Hugh's friends, calendar, 特徴は？」とリテンションして問題文へ→⓫
(A) ⓬City maps 正解，次の設問へと進む→⓭
(B) Fridge magnets
(C) Logo stickers
(D) World atlas

Hughさんの友人たちは，カレンダーのどんな特徴が役立つと気づいたか。
(A) 都市の地図
(B) 冷蔵庫のマグネット
(C) ロゴステッカー
(D) 世界地図

正解 **(A)**
解説 2つ目の文書の終わりの方にmy friends who travel have found the added bonus to be extremely usefulとあり，bonusの内容は1つ目の文書にあったのでそれを確認しにいく。This year's calendar features an extra 3 pages containing a map of New York, London and Beijingがbonusなので(A)が正解だ。このように，1セットの問題を全て解き終えるまでは，全ての内容を頭に残すつもりで問題文を読み進めよう。

27. ⓭What can be inferred about Ms. Hugh?
すでに正解の根拠が登場しているので選択肢へ →⓮
(A) ⓮She works at Hudson Air.
(B) She does not fly frequently.
→正解，このセットの解答終了
(C) She received a financial reward.
(D) She is interested in local arts.

Hughさんについて何が推測できるか。
(A) Hudson航空で働いている。
(B) 頻繁には飛行機に乗らない。
(C) 金銭的報酬を受けた。
(D) 地域の芸術に興味がある。

正解 **(B)**
解説 2つ目の文書の最後の段落にI have never travelled much myselfとあり，それを言い換えた(B)のShe does not fly frequently.が正解だ。

Practice Test

英文を読み，質問に対して最も適切な答えを (A) (B) (C) (D) の中から 1 つ選びなさい（マークシートは別冊 p.158 にあります）。

Questions 1-3 refer to the following article.

Book of the Month

by Jason Kang

One of the industries most radically transformed by the development of the Internet was investment. Today, many private individuals buy and sell stocks and bonds online with little help from professional brokers. However, with an overwhelming amount of information available at a click of a finger, the average first-time investor is at a loss as to where to start. Such investors will find *The Happy Person's Guide to Investing Online* by Tito Bergman most helpful. The guide provides basic instructions, such as how to choose online banking services and where to get the facts. It is very well-written overall. The chapter on preparation is a must-read for all first-time investors. In this chapter, Bergman warns people to be mindful of investment risks and to safeguard themselves from Internet scams. He also encourages novice investors to practice first, for example, by playing online investment games.

1. What is the purpose of the article?
(A) To advertise a book sale
(B) To review a publication
(C) To rate a travel guide
(D) To criticize a new novel

2. What is suggested about investing online?
(A) It is quickly losing popularity.
(B) It should be done by specialists.
(C) It is hard to obtain related information.
(D) It can be confusing for beginners.

3. What is NOT indicated as advice from Tito Bergman?
(A) Save up enough money
(B) Play online games
(C) Protect against fraud
(D) Be aware of possible risks

設問 1-3 は次の記事に関するものである。

Q1 今月の一冊

Jason Kang 記

インターネットの発達により最も根本的な変貌を遂げた業界の1つは，投資でした。今日では，多くの個人がプロのブローカーからほとんど助けを得ることなくオンラインで株や債券を売買しています。しかしながら，指先でワンクリックするだけで膨大な量の情報が得られるため，Q2 一般的な投資初心者はどこから始めたらよいのか分からなくて困ってしまうものです。Q1 そのような投資家には，Tito Bergman 著 *The Happy Person's Guide to Investing Online* が大変役に立つでしょう。本書は，オンライン銀行サービスをどのように選ぶかや，事実をどこで把握することができるかといった基礎知識を提供してくれるのです。全体的にとてもよく書かれています。準備編は全ての投資初心者にとって必読の章です。この章で，Bergman 氏は Q3(D) 投資リスクに注意し，Q3(C) インターネット詐欺から自分を守るよう人々に警告しています。また，例えば Q3(B) オンライン投資ゲームをするなど，投資初心者はまず練習してみるようにとも勧めています。

語句　□radically 徹底的に，根本的に　□overwhelming 圧倒的な
□as to ～に関しては，～については　□scam 詐欺　□novice 初心者

1. 記事の目的は何か。

(A) 書籍のセールを宣伝すること　(B) 出版物の論評をすること

(C) 旅行ガイドを評価すること　(D) 新しい小説を批評すること

正解　**(B)**

解説　タイトルがBook of the Monthであり，問題文の5行目にもSuch investors will find *The Happy Person's Guide to Investing Online* by Tito Bergman most helpful. とあるため，正解は(B)のTo review a publicationだ。この問題文には段落が1つしかないので，まずは1.の設問に対する正解の根拠が登場するまで読み進めてみる，というアプローチがよいだろう。

2. オンライン投資についてどんなことが分かるか。

(A) 急速に人気が落ちている。　(B) 専門家が行うべきである。

(C) 関連情報を得るのが難しい。　(D) 初心者にとっては分かりにくいことがある。

正解　**(D)**

解説　問題文の4行目にthe average first-time investor is at a loss as to where to start.とあるので，それを言い換えた(D)のIt can be confusing for beginners.が正解だ。at a loss「途方に暮れて」がconfusing「混乱させるような」に言い換えられている。

3. Tito Bergman からのアドバイスとして述べられていないものはどれか。

(A) 十分な貯金をする　(B) オンラインゲームをする

(C) 詐欺から身を守る　(D) 起こり得るリスクに注意する

正解　**(A)**

解説　問題文の下から4行目では，Bergman warns people to be mindful of investment risks and to safeguard themselves from Internet scams. He also encourages novice investors to practice first, for example, by playing online investment games.と締めくくっている。(B)～(D)の内容は，全てアドバイスとしてこの中に登場しているが，(A)のSave up enough moneyについては言及がない。

語句　□fraud 詐欺

Part 7

Questions 4-7 refer to the following letter.

March 21

Mr. Jordan White
LTK Corporation
6 York Street, Richmond
Victoria 3887

Dear Sir,

I wish to register my opposition to the proposed Potham Beach Revitalization Project. As a property owner and long-time resident of Potham Beach, I am concerned about the numerous adverse impacts the proposed project may have on our community. Although the construction of a large-scale shopping mall may seem attractive as it brings in more visitors and energizes the community, it may also cause road congestion, and impose a serious burden on the town's existing Fire, Police and Medical services that are already operating at maximum capacity as it is.

Further, the nearby Potham Beach Forest which presently supports a variety of birds, snakes and lizards may be adversely affected by the development. I feel we should be working to preserve nature instead of jeopardizing it.

I plan to formally voice my concerns at the resident meeting held by LTK Corporation on April 3, and hope that LTK Corporation will provide further details on how it plans to address these issues at that time.

Sincerely,
Maggy Grant
Maggy Grant

4. What is the purpose of the letter?
(A) To announce a meeting for the residents
(B) To inform a company of a change in property price
(C) To express discontent about a plan
(D) To make a complaint regarding an employee

5. What can be inferred about Ms. Grant?
(A) She runs a souvenir store in Potham Beach.
(B) She visits Potham Beach every year.
(C) She recently moved to Potham Beach.
(D) She has lived in Potham Beach for years.

6. What does LTK Corporation plan to do?
(A) Open a resort hotel
(B) Build a shopping center
(C) Develop a golf course
(D) Set up a power plant

7. What is NOT mentioned as a concern of Ms. Grant?
(A) The project may lessen the number of tourists.
(B) The project may increase vehicular traffic.
(C) The project may overload local resources.
(D) The project may negatively affect wildlife.

設問 4-7 は次の手紙に関するものである。

3月21日

Jordan White 様
LTK Corporation
York Street 6番地, Richmond
Victoria 3887

拝啓

Q4 私は，提案されているPotham海岸再生計画に反対の申し立てをしたいと思います。Q5 Potham海岸に土地を所有し，長年住んでいる者として，提案されている計画がわれわれの地域社会に及ぼす可能性のある多くの悪影響について心配しています。Q6 大規模ショッピングモールの建設は，より多くの訪問客を呼び込み，地域社会を活性化するため魅力的に思えるかもしれませんが，Q7(B) それはまた道路渋滞を生み，すでに最大限で稼働しているQ7(C) 町の消防，警察や医療サービスに深刻な負担をかける可能性があります。

さらに，Q7(D) 近隣のPotham海岸森林地区では現在，さまざまな鳥，ヘビ，トカゲなどが生息していますが，それらは開発により悪影響を受けるかもしれません。私たちは自然を脅かすのではなく，保護するべきであると私は思います。

4月3日にLTK Corporationが開催する住民会議で，私の懸念を正式に述べる予定です。そのときにLTK Corporationが，これらの問題にどのように対処する予定なのかについて，さらに詳しい説明をくださることを希望します。

敬具
Maggy Grant（署名）
Maggy Grant

語句 □energize ～に活力を吹き込む □lizard トカゲ □adversely 逆に，不利に
□jeopardize ～を危険にさらす

4. 手紙の目的は何か。
(A) 住民のための会議の告知をすること
(B) 企業に不動産価格の変更を知らせること
(C) 計画についての不満を述べること
(D) 従業員に関する苦情を言うこと

正解 **(C)**

解説 問題文1行目I wish to register my opposition to the proposed Potham Beach Revitalization Project.から，手紙を書いた人はPotham海岸再生計画に反対していると伝えようとしていることが分かる。

語句 □discontent 不満

5. Grantさんについて，何が推測できるか。

(A) Potham海岸で土産物店を経営している。
(B) 毎年Potham海岸を訪れている。
(C) 最近Potham海岸に引っ越してきた。
(D) Potham海岸に長年住んでいる。

正解 **(D)**

解説 4.の正解の根拠の直後に根拠が登場する。問題文2行目でlong-time resident of Potham Beachと述べているため，これを言い換えた(D)のShe has lived in Potham Beach for years.が正解だ。(C)にあるmove to～「～に引っ越す」は同義語のrelocate to ～も一緒に押さえておこう。

6. LTK Corporationは何をしようと計画しているか。

(A) リゾートホテルをオープンする
(B) ショッピングセンターを建設する
(C) ゴルフコースを開発する
(D) 発電所を建設する

正解 **(B)**

解説 GrantさんはLTK Corporationによる海岸再生計画に反対する手紙を書いており，4行目のthe construction of a large-scale shopping mallから，再生計画にはショッピングセンターの建設が含まれていることがわかる。よって正解は(B)。

7. Grantさんの懸念として述べられていないものはどれか。

(A) 計画により旅行者数が減少するかもしれない。
(B) 計画により車の往来が増えるかもしれない。
(C) 計画により地域資源に負担がかかるかもしれない。
(D) 計画により野生動物に悪い影響を与えるかもしれない。

正解 **(A)**

解説 問題文6行目以降に正解の根拠がまとまって述べられている。cause road congestionが(B)，impose a serious burden on the town's existing Fire, Police and Medicinal servicesが(C)，a variety of birds ... may be adversely affected by the developmentが(D)にあたる。

Questions 8-11 refer to the following letter.

September 21

Mr. Alexis Mattice
3 Park Street, New Jersey
Jackson 2776

Dear Mr. Mattice,

Regarding your recent interview, I am pleased to offer you the position of network specialist at Kris International. I am sure the 13 years you spent maintaining network integrity at our competitor, B&E Corporation, will be an asset to our IT team.

As an employee, you are eligible for medical and dental insurance, sick leave and vacation time. In your first year, you are entitled to two weeks of vacation. For more information on this subject, please consult the enclosed booklet.

At Kris International, we encourage our personnel to take advantage of various business skills courses offered in the vicinity. Available courses and registration dates are listed on the employee bulletin board for your review. Should you decide to attend one of the courses, please inform Anita Berg in Human Resources, who will make the necessary arrangements. Please let me know if you have any further questions.

Kind regards,

Gus Linscott

Gus Linscott
Human Resources Department
Kris International

8. Why most likely did Mr. Linscott send the letter to Mr. Mattice?
(A) To invite a candidate for an interview
(B) To introduce a new employee
(C) To inform him of a successful registration
(D) To welcome a new team member

9. What is suggested about Mr. Mattice?
(A) He has a background in event planning.
(B) He is known for his honest character.
(C) He is a veteran in his field.
(D) He will join a rival company of Kris International.

10. What is probably provided in the booklet?
(A) A list of recreational facilities
(B) Details of employee benefits
(C) An outline of company goals
(D) Specifics of staff training

11. What is indicated about the courses?
(A) They are mandatory for employees.
(B) They are taught by Anita Berg.
(C) They are held at nearby locations.
(D) They are reviewed annually by management.

設問 8-11 は次の手紙に関するものである。

9月21日

Alexis Mattice 様
Park Street 3 番地, New Jersey
Jackson 2776

Mattice 様

Q8 先日の面接を受けて，Kris International でのネットワークスペシャリストとして貴殿の採用が決定しましたのでお知らせいたします。Q9 我が社のライバル会社である B&E Corporation で貴殿がネットワークの保全に費やした 13 年間は，我が社の情報技術チームにとって貴重なものとなるでしょう。

Q10 従業員として，貴殿は医療保険，歯科保険，病気休暇，休暇の適用を受けられます。初年度は，2 週間の休暇が付与されます。この件についての詳しい説明は，同封の小冊子をご覧ください。

Q11 Kris International では，近隣で提供されているさまざまなビジネススキル講座を活用するよう従業員に勧めています。受講可能な講座と登録日時は，閲覧ができるように従業員用掲示板に掲載されています。講座のどれかに出席することを決めた場合には，人事部の Anita Berg まで連絡してください。彼女が必要な手続きをしてくれます。
さらに質問がある場合はご連絡ください。

敬具
Gus Linscott（署名）
Gus Linscott
人事部
Kris International

語句　□ vicinity 周辺，近所，付近

8. Linscott さんはなぜ Mattice さんに手紙を送ったと思われるか。
(A) 候補者を面接に呼ぶため
(B) 新入社員を紹介するため
(C) 無事に登録できたことを彼に知らせるため
(D) 新入社員を歓迎するため

正解　**(D)**

解説　手紙を送った目的は，面接を受けた人に採用を通知することである。(D) を積極的に正解とするのは難しいが，(A)～(C) の内容は問題文中で言及されていない。TOEIC では 100% 正解だとは思えないものが正解になることがある。その場合，他の選択肢は問題文に全く言及がないか，部分的に矛盾しているかのどちらかなので，消去法での解答が有効である。

9. Matticeさんについてどんなことが分かるか。

(A) イベント企画の職歴がある。

(B) 誠実な人柄で知られている。

(C) 彼の分野ではベテランである。

(D) Kris Internationalのライバル会社に入社する予定である。

正解 **(C)**

解説 第1段落2行目にあるI am sure the 13 years you spent maintaining network integrity at our competitor, B&E Corporation, will be an asset to our IT team.から，Matticeさんはライバル会社で13年間，ネットワーク保全のキャリアがあることが分かるので，(C)が正解である。

10. 小冊子の中に書かれていると思われることは何か。

(A) 娯楽施設のリスト

(B) 従業員の福利厚生についての詳細

(C) 会社の目標の概要

(D) 社員研修の詳細

正解 **(B)**

解説 第2段落2行目にFor more information on this subject, please consult the enclosed booklet.とあり，これ以前では従業員の保険や休暇が話題だったので，(B)のDetails of employee benefitsが正解だ。(A)も福利厚生の一部と考えられるが，問題文中に明記されていないので不適切。推測で解答せず，問題文中に書かれていることを必ず根拠にして解答しよう。

語句 □specifics 詳細

11. 講座について，どんなことが述べられているか。

(A) 従業員は受講義務がある。

(B) Anita Bergが指導する。

(C) 近隣の場所で行われる。

(D) 経営陣が毎年見直している。

正解 **(C)**

解説 最後の段落冒頭でAt Kris International, we encourage our personnel to take advantage of various business skills courses offered in the vicinity.と述べられていることから，講座はin the vicinity，つまり近くで開催されると分かる。したがって，正解は(C)だ。

語句 □mandatory 義務的な，命令の

Questions 12-16 refer to the following e-mail.

From: Edward Gregory [egreg@greenvilleu.edu]
To: Ian North [Inorth@legacytor.com]
Subject: Structural Bracing II
Date: March 5

Dear Mr. Ian North,

I received your e-mail inquiry dated March 1, and contacted Mr. Weisman, who will be teaching *Structural Bracing II*. He says that although you have not taken *Structural Bracing I*, which is indicated as a prerequisite for the course in the catalogue, because of your extensive experience as a municipal engineer, he is happy to accept you as a student in his class.

The course takes place on April 11-12 at Hara Center. It focuses on creating efficient bracing systems and is intended mainly for structural designers, consultants, practicing architects, and other professionals who design or evaluate structures.

The course fee is $750, but will be reduced to $600 each when two or more people from the same organization enroll together. The fee includes a notebook and pen, break refreshments, lunches and a certificate. Normally we ask our students to contact Mr. Chang at Beckson Bookstore to order the required texts. However, since Mr. Chang is away, please contact your course teacher directly to purchase *Structural Bracing and Stability* written by Dr. Ben Martin, which is required for this course.

If you cannot attend the course, please notify us by April 1 to get a full refund. You may also enroll a substitute at any time before the course begins at no extra charge.

We have also reserved a block of guest rooms at Cairo Center. The room rates start from $75, and you can reserve a room by calling 555-2789.
If you have any questions, please do not hesitate to contact me.

Sincerely,
Edward Gregory
Administration Office
Greenville University

12. What is the purpose of the e-mail?
(A) To promote an upcoming training course
(B) To answer a question from a prospective student
(C) To arrange a tour of the university campus
(D) To request submission of an application form

13. What is indicated about Mr. Ian North?
(A) He graduated from Greenville University.
(B) He has not attended a required course.
(C) He is an international exchange student.
(D) He has passed a difficult entrance exam.

14. Who most likely is the course NOT intended for?
(A) Professional architects
(B) Civil engineers
(C) Graphic designers
(D) Structural inspectors

15. What can be inferred about the course fee?
(A) It will not be refunded under any circumstances.
(B) It includes transportation, food and accommodation.
(C) It will be reduced if the same person enrolls in another course.
(D) It will be cheaper for multiple enrollments from the same company.

16. Who should Mr. North contact to obtain the course material?
(A) Mr. Weisman
(B) Mr. Chang
(C) Dr. Martin
(D) Mr. Gregory

設問 12-16 は次のEメールに関するものである。

送信者：Edward Gregory [egreg@greenvilleu.edu]
宛先：Ian North [Inorth@legacytor.com]
件名：構造物の筋かい2
日付：3月5日

Ian North 様

Q12 3月1日付のお問い合わせメールを拝受し，Q16「構造物の筋かい2」を教える予定のWeisman氏に連絡を取りました。氏によれば，Q13 あなたは講座要覧で必修となっている「構造物の筋かい1」を受講されていませんが，市の技術者として豊富な経験をお持ちなので，Q12 喜んで受講者として受け入れるとのことです。

講座は4月11日から12日にHaraセンターで行われます。効率的な筋かいシステムを作ることを中心に扱う講座で，主に構造デザイナー，コンサルタント，Q14(A) 現役の建築家や，Q14(B)(D) その他，構造をデザインしたり評価したりする専門家向けとなっています。

Q15 講座料金は750ドルですが，同じ団体から2人以上で同時に申し込まれた場合は，1名さま600ドルになります。料金にはノートとペン，休憩時間中の軽食，昼食，および修了証が含まれています。通常，受講者には，Beckson書店のChang氏に連絡して，必要な教科書を注文するようにお願いをしています。しかしながらChang氏が不在なので，Q16 受講講座の教授に直接連絡して，この講座に必要なBen Martin博士著 *Structural Bracing and Stability* を購入してください。

講座に出席できなくなった場合は，4月1日までにお知らせいただけば，全額が払い戻されます。講座開始前であれば，いつでも追加料金なしで代理人に受講いただくこともできます。

また，Cairoセンターに客室をまとめて予約してあります。部屋の料金は75ドルからです。555-2789に電話すれば部屋を予約することができます。
ご質問があれば，遠慮なく私までご連絡ください。

敬具
Edward Gregory
管理事務所
Greenville大学

語句 □bracing 筋かい　□prerequisite 必修科目，必須条件　□municipal 市の，都市の

12. Eメールの目的は何か。
(A) 次回のトレーニング講座を宣伝する
(B) 受講者になりそうな人からの質問に答える
(C) 大学のキャンパスツアーを準備する
(D) 申込書の提出を要求する

正解 **(B)**

解説 最初の段落の冒頭でI received your e-mail inquiry dated March 1と述べており，同じ段落の

最後にhe is happy to accept you as a student in his classと言っていることから，(B) のTo answer a question from a prospective studentが正解となる。

13. Ian Northさんについてどんなことが述べられているか。
(A) Greenville大学を卒業した。
(B) 必須講座に出席していない。
(C) 海外からの交換留学生である。
(D) 難しい入学試験に合格した。

正解 **(B)**

解説 第1段落2行目にyou have not taken *Structural Bracing I*, which is indicated as a prerequisite for the course in the catalogueとあり，このEメールはIan Northさん宛てのものであることから，彼は必須の講座を取っていなかったことが分かる。正解は(B)だ。

14. 講座は誰に対しては向いていないと考えられるか。
(A) プロの建築家
(B) 土木技師
(C) グラフィックデザイナー
(D) 構造検査官

正解 **(C)**

解説 第2段落に，この講座が誰に向けたものなのかが書かれている。2行目にintended mainly for structural designers, consultants, practicing architects, and other professionals who design or evaluate structures.とあり，これらに該当しないのは(C)のgraphic designerだけだ。

15. 講座料金について何が推測できるか。
(A) どんな場合でも返金はされない。
(B) 交通費，食費，宿泊費が含まれる。
(C) 同じ人が他の講座に申し込んだ場合に減額される。
(D) 同じ会社から複数の申し込みがあれば安くなる。

正解 **(D)**

解説 第3段落1行目にThe course fee is $750, but will be reduced to $600 each when two or more people from the same organization enroll together.とある。本来，講座料金は750ドルだが，同じ団体から2人以上一緒に申し込みをした場合には1人当たり600ドルで受講できることが分かる。正解は(D)だ。

16. 講座の教材を手に入れるために，Northさんは誰に連絡を取らなければならないか。
(A) Weisman氏
(B) Chang氏
(C) Martin博士
(D) Gregory氏

正解 **(A)**

解説 第3段落5行目にplease contact your course teacher directly to purchase *Structural Bracing and Stability* written by Dr. Ben Martin, which is required for this courseとあり，講座の担当教授に直接連絡を取らなければならないとある。第1段落1行目にMr. Weisman, who will be teaching *Structural Bracing II.* とあるので，正解は(A)のWeisman氏だと分かる。

Part 7

Questions 17-21 refer to the following letters.

March 21

Kix Outing Center

Ms. Aditi Baboor
MT Exchange Bank
8 Bridge Street, Cavendish
Newfoundland

Dear Madam,

Thank you for considering Kix Outing Center for your event this year. We are confident that your guests and employees will enjoy a memorable day at the Center.

Below are the plans we offer:

Included in your private site:	Plan #1	Plan #2	Plan #3	Plan #4
Pavilion	✓	✓	✓	✓
Swimming pool			✓	✓
Sand volleyball court		✓		✓
Miniature golf course	✓		✓	✓
Tennis court	✓	✓	✓	✓
Max. number of guests	120	120	240	240
Max. Price	$1,500	$2,000	$3,200	$3,800

All private sites are available for rent from 9 A.M. to 5 P.M. Please ask about our free usage of game equipment. We are also happy to arrange a disk jockey service, pony rides and air bounces to meet your outing themes for a minimal fee. For your safety, we also provide lifeguards at the pools at no extra cost. All plans are available Tuesday through Sunday. Every Monday the Center is closed for maintenance.

Kind regards,
Jing Malm
Jing Malm, Director of Operations

March 29

Kix Outing Center

Ms. Aditi Baboor
MT Exchange Bank
8 Bridge Street, Cavendish
Newfoundland

Dear Ms. Baboor,

Thank you for choosing Kix Outing Center! We have received your signed contract with a deposit of $2,000. The remaining balance can be paid on the day of the outing. Please note that the plan you have chosen does not include a sand volleyball court. As you have requested that we include pony rides, an extra $300 will be added to the total.

We understand that your corporate outing theme for this year is "Family Fun". Although Kix Outing Center is suitable for people of all ages, we excel at providing an enjoyable occasion to families. This is why, with your permission, we will set up a crafts corner for free for your event. Crafts corner is an attraction for children where they can create paper hats, friendship bracelets and egg carton animals.

Sincerely,
Jing Malm
Jing Malm, Director of Operations

17. Who most likely are the letters addressed to?
(A) An organizer of a company banquet
(B) A captain of a local sports team
(C) An employee at a financial institution
(D) A member of a luxury fitness club

18. What is NOT true about Kix Outing Center?
(A) Some music can be arranged.
(B) An employee will watch over swimmers.
(C) Maintenance is performed on weekends.
(D) Visitors can borrow game equipment.

19. What is the purpose of the second letter?
(A) To confirm a receipt of first payment
(B) To ask a customer to sign a contract
(C) To provide a client with a price quote
(D) To give an overview of Kix Outing Center

20. Which plan did Ms. Baboor choose?
(A) Plan 1 (B) Plan 2 (C) Plan 3 (D) Plan 4

21. What can be inferred about the event?
(A) The entrance fee will be charged at the gate.
(B) The pony rides will be provided for free.
(C) The children of staff members are invited.
(D) The drinks will be catered by a different company.

設問 17-21 は次の2つの手紙に関するものである。

3月21日

Kix Outing Center

Q17 Aditi Baboor 様
MT 為替銀行
Bridge Street 8番地, Cavendish
Newfoundland

拝啓

今年の貴行のイベントにKix Outing Centerをご検討いただき，ありがとうございます。Q21 貴行のお客様と従業員の皆様はきっと当センターで 思い出に残る1日をお楽しみいただけると思います。
以下は私どもがご提案するプランです。

貸し切り会場に含まれるもの：	Q20 プラン #1	プラン #2	Q20 プラン #3	プラン #4
大型テント	✓	✓	✓	✓
スイミングプール			✓	✓
ビーチバレーコート		✓		✓
ミニチュアゴルフコース	✓		✓	✓
テニスコート	✓	✓	✓	✓
最大収容人数	120	120	240	240
最高料金	Q20 1,500 ドル	2,000 ドル	Q20 3,200 ドル	3,800 ドル

貸し切り会場は全て，午前9時から午後5時までご利用になれます。Q18(D) ゲーム設備の無料でのご利用についてはお問い合わせください。Q18(A) また，レクリエーションのテーマに合うようなDJサービス，ポニー乗馬，エア遊具も最小限の費用でご用意できます。Q18(B) お客様の安全のために，追加料金なしでプールに監視員を配置いたします。全てのプランは火曜日から日曜日まで利用可能です。毎週月曜日は，センターは整備のため休館となります。

敬具
Jing Malm（署名）
Jing Malm，事業部長

3月29日

Kix Outing Center

Q17 Aditi Baboor 様
MT 為替銀行
Bridge Street 8番地, Cavendish
Newfoundland

Baboor 様

Kix Outing Centerをお選びいただき，ありがとうございます！ Q19 2,000 ドルの手付金と署名入りの契約書を受け取りました。残額はレクリエーションの当日にお支払いください。Q20 お客様がお選びになったプランにはビーチバレーコートが含まれておりませんのでご注意ください。ポニー乗馬の追加をリクエストいただきましたので，合計金額に300ドルが加算されます。

Q21 今年の貴行のレクリエーションのテーマは「家族で楽しむ」だと心得ています。Kix Outing Centerはあらゆる年代の人が楽しめますが，家族連れに楽しく過ごす時間を提供することを得意としています。ですので，よろしければ，今回のイベント用に無料の工作コーナーを設けるつもりです。Q21 工作コーナーは，子どもたちが，紙の帽子や友情のブレスレット，卵ケースからできた動物を作ることができるアトラクションとなります。

敬具
Jing Malm（署名）
Jing Malm，事業部長

17. 2つの手紙は誰に向けて書かれたものだと思われるか。
(A) 会社の宴会の主催者
(B) 地元のスポーツチームのキャプテン
(C) 金融機関の従業員
(D) 高級フィットネスクラブの会員

正解 **(C)**

解説 手紙の宛て先はどちらもMs. Aditi Baboor, MT Exchange Bankとなっているので，これを言い換えた(C)のAn employee at a financial institutionが正解だ。このようにヘッダーにヒントがある場合もあるので，必ず目を通すようにしよう。

18. Kix Outing Centerについて，正しくないのはどれか。
(A) 音楽を用意できる。
(B) 従業員が水泳をしている人を監視する予定だ。
(C) 整備は週末に行われる。
(D) 利用者はゲーム設備を借りることができる。

正解 **(C)**

解説 1つ目の手紙の最後の段落に，正解の根拠がまとめて述べられている。free usage of game equipment.が(D)，arrange a disk jockey serviceが(A)，we also provide lifeguards at the pools at no extra cost.が(B)にあたる。

19. 2つ目の手紙の目的は何か。
(A) 初回支払いの受領を確認する
(B) 契約書に署名することを顧客に頼む
(C) 取引先に見積もり額を知らせる
(D) Kix Outing Centerの概要を知らせる

正解 **(A)**

解説 2つ目の手紙の冒頭にThank you for choosing Kix Outing Center! We have received your signed contract with a deposit of $2,000.とある。2,000ドルの手付金と署名入りの契約書を受け取ったことを述べており，これを簡潔に言い換えた(A)が正解だ。

20. Baboorさんはどのプランを選んだか。
(A) プラン1
(B) プラン2
(C) プラン3
(D) プラン4

正解 **(C)**

解説 2つ目の手紙の最初の段落3行目にPlease note that the plan you have chosen does not include a sand volleyball court.とある。sand volleyball courtが含まれないプランは1と3だ。Baboorさんは手付金をすでに2,000ドル支払っているので，最高料金が1,500ドルであるプラン1は消える。よって，正解は(C)のプラン3だ。

21. イベントについて何が推測できるか。
(A) 入場料はゲートで徴収される。
(B) ポニー乗馬は無料で提供される。
(C) 従業員の子どもたちが招待される。
(D) 飲み物は別会社によって提供される。

正解 **(C)**

解説 1つ目の手紙の前半から，イベントは銀行の客と従業員向けだということ，2つ目の手紙の後半からイベントのテーマが"Family Fun"であり，大人も子どもも楽しめるものだということが分かる。下から2行目に子ども用のアトラクションとして工作コーナーの提案もあることから，(C)が正解だ。

Questions 22-26 refer to the following e-mails.

To: Isabel Hernandez [Iherz@dtfoods.com]
From: Lionel Price [Lprc@dtfoods.com]
Date: October 1
Subject: Dorinkos

This year we will celebrate the 30th anniversary of our flagship beverage product, Dorinkos. We believe Dorinkos has attained its full market potential and profitability, so our task now is to sustain the product at this stage. In order to do so, our team has come up with an idea of developing line extensions. This means implementing new tastes for Dorinkos; more specifically, adding blueberry and strawberry flavored Dorinkos to the orange and apple flavored ones we already produce. The plan is still at an early stage of development, and creating new flavors takes considerable time. However, we would like to present some ideas for maintaining Dorinkos' popularity at the annual stockholders' meeting next month. Therefore, we would like some feedback from all of you regarding this idea before October 6. Thank you for your cooperation.

Lionel Price
Product Development Dept.
D&T Foods

To: Lionel Price [Lprc@dtfoods.com]
From: Isabel Hernandez [Iherz@dtfoods.com]
Date: October 3
Subject: Re:Dorinkos

Mr. Price,
I am writing this message in response to your e-mail on October 1. In my humble opinion, implementing new flavors to Dorinkos is not the best way to retain its popularity in the market. Instead, I'd like to suggest a renewal of its packaging.

While I am not a marketing expert, I worked for a few years as a cashier at a supermarket where they sold Dorinkos. In the past, special editions of Dorinkos have been sold, including banana and lemon flavors, but most consumers preferred the traditional flavors. I have attached the sales report of these past special editions, which supports my point, to this e-mail.

On the other hand, changing the packaging is less costly and an attractive design will not only increase customers, but improve the brand image of D&T Foods. Moreover, since no new content needs to be developed, we will be able to present the new packaging design at the upcoming meeting which you mentioned.

Isabel Hernandez
Accounting Dept.
D&T Foods

22. In the first e-mail, the word "flagship" in paragraph 1, line 1, is closest in meaning to
(A) advanced (B) primary (C) endless (D) latest

23. What is suggested about Dorinkos?
(A) Its sales are declining.
(B) It has reached a mature stage.
(C) It currently comes in four flavors.
(D) It has been developed by Mr. Price.

24. What can be inferred about Ms. Hernandez?
(A) She consulted marketing specialists about the issue.
(B) She wants to put forward an alternative strategy.
(C) She works at a store that stocks D&T Foods' products.
(D) She wishes to join the product development team.

25. What is attached to Ms. Hernandez's e-mail?
(A) An in-depth report on the benefits of drinking Dorinkos
(B) A study which shows how consumers view D&T Foods
(C) A schedule that indicates when different tasks should be completed
(D) A record which states how many products were sold

26. According to Ms. Hernandez, at which event can the new design be presented?
(A) At an event to celebrate the founding of D&T Foods
(B) At a meeting for people who have shares in D&T Foods
(C) At a gathering for store owners that sell Dorinkos
(D) At a media event attended by press members

設問22-26 は次の2つのEメールに関するものである。

宛先：Isabel Hernandez [Iherz@dtfoods.com]
送信者：Lionel Price [Lprc@dtfoods.com]
日付：10月1日
件名：Dorinkos

今年はわれわれの主力飲料製品であるDorinkosの30周年にあたります。Q23 Dorinkosはその市場潜在力と採算性が上限に達しているので，今われわれがすべきことは，当該商品をこの段階で維持し続けることです。そのために，われわれのチームはラインナップを拡充するというアイデアを考え付きました。これはDorinkosに新しい味を加えるということです。具体的に言えば，すでに生産しているオレンジ味とリンゴ味のDorinkosに，ブルーベリー味とイチゴ味のDorinkosを加えるのです。この計画はまだ開発の初期段階にあり，新しい味を作り出すには相当な時間がかかります。Q26 しかしながら，われわれはDorinkosの人気を維持するためのアイデアを，来月の年次株主総会でいくつか発表したいと思っています。ですので，10月6日までにこのアイデアに関して皆さんの意見をいただければと思います。ご協力ありがとうございます。

Lionel Price
製品開発部
D&T Foods

宛先：Lionel Price [Lprc@dtfoods.com]
送信者：Isabel Hernandez [Iherz@dtfoods.com]
日付：10月3日
件名：Re:Dorinkos

Price様

10月1日付けのあなたのEメールに応えるべくこのメッセージを書いています。私見ですが，Dorinkosに新しい味を加えることは，市場での人気を維持するための最良の方法ではないと思います。Q24 代わりに，私はパッケージの刷新を提案したいと思います。

私はマーケティングの専門家ではありませんが，Dorinkosを販売するスーパーのレジで数年間働きました。過去に，バナナ味とレモン味などのDorinkosの特別版が販売されましたが，ほとんどの消費者は昔ながらの味を好みました。Q25 過去に出された限定味の売上報告書をこのEメールにを添付しましたが，それは私の意見を裏付けています。

一方，パッケージの変更はコストも少なくすみ，魅力的なデザインは顧客を増やすだけでなく，D&T Foodsのブランドイメージも向上させるでしょう。さらに，新たな内容物を開発する必要がないので，Q26 あなたのおっしゃった次回の総会で新しいパッケージデザインを発表することができるでしょう。

Isabel Hernandez
経理部
D&T Foods

語句 □in my humble opinion 私のつたない意見によれば，私見ですが

22. 最初のEメールの第1段落・1行目のflagshipに最も近い意味の語は

(A) 進歩した　(B) 主要な　(C) 終わりのない　(D) 最新の

正解 **(B)**

解説　1つ目のEメールの冒頭This year we will celebrate the 30th anniversary of our flagship beverage product, Dorinkos.から，Dorinkosは30周年を迎える商品だということが分かる。flagshipは「主要商品（の）」という意味。正解は(B)のprimary「主要な」だ。

23. Dorinkosについてどんなことが分かるか。

(A) 売上が落ちている。　(B) 成熟期に達した。
(C) 現在4つの味で売られている。　(D) Priceさんによって開発された。

正解　**(B)**

解説　1つ目のEメールの2行目に，Dorinkos has attained its full market potential and profitabilityとあるため，Dorinkos は市場潜在力と採算性の上限に達しているということが分かる。これを言い換えた，(B)のIt has reached a mature stage.「成熟期に達した」が正解となる。

語句　□mature 成熟した

24. Hernandezさんについて何が推測できるか。

(A) その問題についてマーケティングの専門家に意見を求めた。
(B) 代替戦略を提案したいと思っている。
(C) D&T Foodsの商品を置く店で働いている。
(D) 製品開発チームに加わりたいと願っている。

正解　**(B)**

解説　Hernandezさんは2つ目のEメールの3行目でInstead, I'd like to suggest a renewal of its packaging.と述べている。新しい味のDorinkosを販売する代わりに，パッケージの刷新を提案しているため，(B)のShe wants to put forward an alternative strategy.が正解となる。

語句　□put forward～ ～を提案する，提出する

25. HernandezさんのEメールには何が添付されているか。

(A) Dorinkosを飲むことによって得られる利点についての詳細な報告書
(B) 消費者のD&T Foodsに対する見方を示す調査報告書
(C) さまざまな仕事を完了すべき時期を示す計画表
(D) 商品がどれだけ売れたかを記載した記録

正解　**(D)**

解説　2つ目のEメールの7行目で，HernandezさんはI have attached the sales report of these past special editions, which supports my point, to this e-mail.と述べている。過去に出された限定味の販売報告書を言い換えた(D)が正解だ。

語句　□in-depth 掘り下げた，徹底的な，綿密な

26. Hernandezさんによると，新しいデザインはどのイベントで発表できるか。

(A) D&T Foodsの創立記念イベント　(B) D&T Foodsの株式を所有する人々の会議
(C) Dorinkosを販売する店主の集まり　(D) 報道関係者が出席するマスコミ向けイベント

正解　**(B)**

解説　Hernandezさんは2つ目のEメールの下から3行目でwe will be able to present the new packaging design at the upcoming meeting which you mentioned.と述べている。次回のmeetingは，1つ目のEメールの下から3行目にあるthe annual stockholders' meeting next month.のことを指す。これを言い換えた(B)のAt a meeting for people who have shares in D&T Foodsが正解だ。

おわりに

僕がこれまでやってきたこと。

990点をコンスタントに取れるようになるためにやってきたこと。

それは決して誰にも真似することができないような，一握りの限られた人間だけにしかできないような，「あり得ないレベルの努力」ではないということを，ここで再度述べておきたいと思う。

かなりの時間と労力を費やしてきたが，一切の妥協をせずに，最後まで原稿を書き上げることができた。

それを支え続けてくださった，旺文社の岩村明子さん，山田弘美さん。

正直，途中で何度もプレッシャーに負けそうになった。

だが，その都度誰かが協力してくれた。

何かが僕を支えてくれた。

コラムを書いてくださったメディアビーコンの高木恭子さん，アスク出版の竹田直次郎さん，推薦コメントを書いてくださった清水直彦さん，渋谷奈津子さん，そして江川真由さんをはじめとする明海大学HT学部の教え子たち。

Part 1に使用する写真を提供してくださった中経出版の細田朋幸さん，この企画を僕に繋いでくださったメディアビーコンの藤桂輔さんにも，心よりお礼を申し上げたい。

990点を取るために何が必要か。

それは「己を律する力」である。

リスニングセクションで確実に97問以上正解し，リーディングセクションでは全問正解できる実力をつけるために，日々「普通の人ができる範囲内ギリギリの努力」を続けていくことである。

素材はTOEIC対策専用の教材だけで必要十分であり，「TOEICに出題される問題レベルであれば，まず間違えない」実力をつければよいのだ。

心の底から「高嶺の花」を手に入れたいのかどうか。

それを再度自分に問い掛けてみてほしい。

そしてそれが本心であるならば，人生を懸ける意気込みで挑戦してみてもいいんじゃないかと僕は思う。

本書があなたを変えるきっかけになること，そしてあなたの願いが叶うことを心から願っている。

挑戦し続けようとするあなたの人生を，これからも僕は全力で応援し続けていきたい。

濵﨑潤之輔

新TOEIC®テストスコア別攻略シリーズ 5

新TOEIC®テスト 990点攻略

別冊

旺文社

Final Test

Listening Test
Reading Test

LISTENING TEST

CD 2 [2]~[12]

In the Listening test, you will be asked to demonstrate how well you understand spoken English. The entire Listening test will last approximately 45 minutes. There are four parts, and directions are given for each part. You must mark your answers on the separate answer sheet. Do not write your answers in your test book.

PART 1

Directions: For each question in this part, you will hear four statements about a picture in your test book. When you hear the statements, you must select the one statement that best describes what you see in the picture. Then find the number of the question on your answer sheet and mark your answer. The statements will not be printed in your test book and will be spoken only one time.

Example

Sample Answer

Ⓐ Ⓑ ● Ⓓ

Statement (C), "They're standing near the table," is the best description of the picture, so you should select answer (C) and mark it on your answer sheet.

1.

2.

GO ON TO THE NEXT PAGE

3.

4.

5.

6.

GO ON TO THE NEXT PAGE

7.

8.

9.

10.

GO ON TO THE NEXT PAGE

PART 2

CD 2 13 ~ 43

Directions: You will hear a question or statement and three responses spoken in English. They will not be printed in your test book and will be spoken only one time. Select the best response to the question or statement and mark the letter (A), (B), or (C) on your answer sheet.

Sample Answer

Example Ⓐ ● Ⓒ

You will hear: Where is the meeting room?

You will also hear: (A) To meet the new director.

(B) It's the first room on the right.

(C) Yes, at two o'clock.

The best response to the question "Where is the meeting room?" is choice (B), "It's the first room on the right," so (B) is the correct answer. You should mark answer (B) on your answer sheet.

11. Mark your answer on your answer sheet.

12. Mark your answer on your answer sheet.

13. Mark your answer on your answer sheet.

14. Mark your answer on your answer sheet.

15. Mark your answer on your answer sheet.

16. Mark your answer on your answer sheet.

17. Mark your answer on your answer sheet.

18. Mark your answer on your answer sheet.

19. Mark your answer on your answer sheet.

20. Mark your answer on your answer sheet.

21. Mark your answer on your answer sheet.

22. Mark your answer on your answer sheet.

23. Mark your answer on your answer sheet.

24. Mark your answer on your answer sheet.

25. Mark your answer on your answer sheet.

26. Mark your answer on your answer sheet.

27. Mark your answer on your answer sheet.

28. Mark your answer on your answer sheet.

29. Mark your answer on your answer sheet.

30. Mark your answer on your answer sheet.

31. Mark your answer on your answer sheet.

32. Mark your answer on your answer sheet.

33. Mark your answer on your answer sheet.

34. Mark your answer on your answer sheet.

35. Mark your answer on your answer sheet.

36. Mark your answer on your answer sheet.

37. Mark your answer on your answer sheet.

38. Mark your answer on your answer sheet.

39. Mark your answer on your answer sheet.

40. Mark your answer on your answer sheet.

GO ON TO THE NEXT PAGE →

PART 3

CD 2 44 ~ 54

Directions: You will hear some conversations between two people. You will be asked to answer three questions about what the speakers say in each conversation. Select the best response to each question and mark the letter (A), (B), (C), or (D) on your answer sheet. The conversations will not be printed in your test book and will be spoken only one time.

41. What is the problem?
(A) A flight has been canceled.
(B) A hat is missing.
(C) A ticket has been misplaced.
(D) A passenger is late for a party.

42. What information does the woman request?
(A) The airline name
(B) The passenger name
(C) The seat number
(D) The flight number

43. According to the woman, how long will the man need to wait?
(A) Around 5 minutes
(B) Around 10 minutes
(C) Around 30 minutes
(D) Around 60 minutes

44. What is the advantage of the recently available apartment?
(A) It is in a quiet neighborhood.
(B) It has many lighting fixtures.
(C) It is within Ms. Short's budget.
(D) It has lots of space.

45. What does Lisa offer?
(A) To fax an application form
(B) To take Ms. Short for a viewing
(C) To stop by Ms. Short's home
(D) To reserve the property on Augustus Lane

46. What does Ms. Short want to confirm?
(A) If she can play the piano
(B) If she can have two vehicles
(C) If she can have pets
(D) If she can renovate

47. Where most likely are the speakers?
(A) At a street corner
(B) In a shopping mall
(C) In a museum
(D) In a parking lot

48. What is happening on George Avenue?
(A) A store opening
(B) A road resurfacing
(C) A street performance
(D) A building construction

49. What will the man probably do next?
(A) Give a speech
(B) Return a car key
(C) Collect his belongings
(D) Pick out a gift

---

50. Where most likely does the man work?
(A) At an elementary school
(B) At a kitchen appliance store
(C) At a hotel
(D) At a muffin shop

51. What problem does the woman mention?
(A) An item is currently out of stock.
(B) A product is no longer available.
(C) A worker is temporarily occupied.
(D) A client is making unreasonable demands.

52. Why does the woman discourage self-installation?
(A) To protect the equipment
(B) To avoid injuries
(C) To secure employment
(D) To speed up the process

---

53. What type of business do the speakers probably work for?
(A) A cleaning service
(B) A paper mill
(C) A convenience store
(D) A technology company

54. What does the man suggest?
(A) Replacing the device
(B) Using larger items
(C) Consulting the label
(D) Dispatching staff more often

55. What does the woman say she will do?
(A) Order new supplies
(B) Get in touch with the staff
(C) Train the workers
(D) Check the shipment

GO ON TO THE NEXT PAGE

56. Why did the woman make the call?
(A) To arrange a day trip
(B) To inquire about transportation costs
(C) To discuss a business partnership
(D) To ask about a group tour

57. What can customers receive at an additional cost?
(A) An extended stay
(B) Late check-out option
(C) Nightly meals
(D) Tour guide service

58. What does the woman ask for?
(A) An e-mail address
(B) A company brochure
(C) A cost estimate
(D) A travel itinerary

---

59. Why is the man pessimistic?
(A) He doesn't have enough qualifications.
(B) He thinks he won't get the job.
(C) He failed an important exam.
(D) He received a bad evaluation.

60. What does the woman say about a follow-up call?
(A) It gives a good impression.
(B) It is better than sending an e-mail.
(C) It should be made as soon as possible.
(D) It demonstrates his responsibility.

61. What does the man say he has done?
(A) Phoned the employer
(B) Sent a recommendation letter
(C) Applied to other places
(D) Consulted a professional

---

62. What is the problem?
(A) A coffee machine is out of order.
(B) A wrong type of material has been used.
(C) A device is not working properly.
(D) A piece of equipment does not turn off.

63. Where most likely does Mark work?
(A) At an electronics store
(B) At a school office
(C) At a school cafeteria
(D) At a stationery company

64. What will the technician most likely do?
(A) Visit the office tomorrow
(B) Bring another kind of paper
(C) Replace old components
(D) Order a new unit

---

65. What will probably happen next month?
(A) An employee will be transferred.
(B) A staff member will go on holiday.
(C) Some duties will be outsourced.
(D) Some departments will be merged.

66. What does the woman say about her department?
(A) It is heavily cluttered.
(B) It lacks sufficient manpower.
(C) It will get some new recruits.
(D) It will move to another location.

67. How did the man know payroll associated tasks would be outsourced?
(A) He heard rumors about it.
(B) He saw a notice on the bulletin board.
(C) He read about it in a publication.
(D) He received a memo from his boss.

68. What is the man concerned about?
(A) A misprint on an invoice
(B) An error on an inventory record
(C) A mistake in the amount of labels
(D) An inaccuracy on an order form

69. What does the woman suggest the man do?
(A) Consult another source
(B) Question his colleagues
(C) Double-check the stockroom
(D) Correct the inventory

70. What will the woman do next?
(A) Enter a password
(B) Give authorization
(C) Return some items
(D) Update the records

GO ON TO THE NEXT PAGE →

PART 4

CD 2 55～65

Directions: You will hear some talks given by a single speaker. You will be asked to answer three questions about what the speaker says in each talk. Select the best response to each question and mark the letter (A), (B), (C), or (D) on your answer sheet. The talks will not be printed in your test book and will be spoken only one time.

71. What is being advertised?
(A) Custom-made bracelets
(B) Professional photo frames
(C) Customized stamps
(D) Birthday cards

72. What is the minimum order?
(A) 2 sheets
(B) 10 sheets
(C) 20 sheets
(D) 40 sheets

73. What is available on the Web site?
(A) Sample designs
(B) Discount vouchers
(C) How-to guidelines
(D) Store directions

74. Why is the speaker calling the man?
(A) He failed to meet a deadline.
(B) He missed a meeting.
(C) He performed poorly on a test.
(D) He has not returned a message.

75. What will the man most likely do next week?
(A) Take a business trip
(B) Present a report
(C) Have an interview
(D) Go on vacation

76. According to the woman, what will happen to the forms?
(A) They will be reviewed by the board of directors.
(B) They will be sent to headquarters.
(C) They will be used at a performance.
(D) They will be handed to Erik Cole.

77. What type of business is being advertised?
(A) A hotel chain
(B) A textile corporation
(C) A food delivery service
(D) A laundry company

78. According to the speaker, what is flexible?
(A) Payment method
(B) Delivery time
(C) Service costs
(D) Pick-up location

79. What does the speaker suggest about the cleaning process?
(A) It only takes a short time.
(B) It is fully automated.
(C) It involves using cutting-edge computers.
(D) It is environmentally friendly.

---

80. How long does the tour last?
(A) Quarter of an hour
(B) One hour
(C) Two hours
(D) Three hours

81. What is manufactured at the Redville Plant?
(A) Car parts
(B) Airplane engines
(C) Motorcycles
(D) Stereo components

82. What will the listeners probably do next?
(A) Proceed to the factory floor
(B) Visit the gift shop
(C) Watch an introductory video
(D) See a current production

---

83. What is the purpose of the telephone message?
(A) To make a reservation
(B) To give details about a booking
(C) To change an order
(D) To provide a cost estimate

84. How much is the penalty charge?
(A) 10 dollars
(B) 15 dollars
(C) 24 dollars
(D) 40 dollars

85. What can the listener obtain from the Web site?
(A) A form for making an inventory
(B) A worksheet to calculate the total cost
(C) A timetable to facilitate moving
(D) A copy of the rental agreement

GO ON TO THE NEXT PAGE

86. What is the news broadcast about?
(A) Increased international shipping costs
(B) Global environmental protection programs
(C) New promotional strategies for companies
(D) Relocation of employees to foreign countries

87. What does Mr. Chang say about last year?
(A) Demand for Glomore's products increased.
(B) Business was slow for Glomore.
(C) Glomore had to lay off some employees.
(D) Glomore had to close down its overseas office.

88. Which area is Glomore increasingly involved with?
(A) Asia
(B) The United States
(C) Western Europe
(D) Africa

---

89. What is the purpose of the call?
(A) To arrange an appointment
(B) To inform a client of an upcoming project
(C) To notify a client of a change of personnel
(D) To announce a promotional event

90. What does the caller think will happen to the two companies?
(A) They will start official support shortly.
(B) They will keep growing together.
(C) They will become leaders in many countries.
(D) They will merge into one company.

91. Who most likely is Jon Brooks?
(A) A customer of Magda International
(B) A colleague of Mr. Blake
(C) An employee of LEEMA Electronics
(D) A staff member at Magda International

---

92. Why has the speaker been busy?
(A) A new publication has been released.
(B) An establishment is being renovated.
(C) New stock has been delivered.
(D) Several courses have been canceled.

93. Who most likely is the listener?
(A) A worker at a book store
(B) An instructor of a new course
(C) A staff member at a school library
(D) An owner of used textbooks

94. What does the speaker advise the listener to do?
(A) Visit the office to apply for an identification card
(B) Obtain the list of books being used for next term
(C) Sell the books while he can get better prices for them
(D) Purchase all the items he needs for his courses at once

95. What is the main purpose of the talk?
(A) To tell employees about the speaker herself
(B) To announce that the speaker is leaving a job
(C) To motivate team members to work harder
(D) To brainstorm ideas for an advertisement

96. What type of industry does the speaker probably work for?
(A) Finance
(B) Construction
(C) Mass media
(D) Electronics

97. What does the speaker request team members to do?
(A) Inform her of their availability
(B) Come up with topics for discussion
(C) Write down their e-mail addresses
(D) Work on their communication skills

98. What is the talk about?
(A) Customer relations
(B) Security measures
(C) Emergency procedures
(D) Wellness guidelines

99. What happened last week?
(A) An updated version of a product was released.
(B) Construction of some buildings began.
(C) Electronic devices were installed.
(D) A professional assessment was conducted.

100. What are employees asked to do?
(A) Attend a photo session
(B) Back up important files
(C) Lock the break room doors
(D) Keep the office tidy

This is the end of the Listening test. Turn to Part 5 in your test book.

READING TEST

In the Reading test, you will read a variety of texts and answer several different types of reading comprehension questions. The entire Reading test will last 75 minutes. There are three parts, and directions are given for each part. You are encouraged to answer as many questions as possible within the time allowed.

You must mark your answers on the separate answer sheet. Do not write your answers in your test book.

PART 5

Directions: A word or phrase is missing in each of the sentences below. Four answer choices are given below each sentence. Select the best answer to complete the sentence. Then mark the letter (A), (B), (C), or (D) on your answer sheet.

101. A restructuring of the major divisions will end up taking place after SO & T ------- Supersoft next month.

(A) foresees
(B) acquires
(C) rests
(D) merges

102. The annual shareholders' meeting will be held in the Hamptons in ------- with company tradition.

(A) connecting
(B) keeping
(C) realizing
(D) concluding

103. For being a senior partner at Berizon and Rukoil Law Firm, frequent travel to other countries is one of the -------.

(A) recoupment
(B) requirements
(C) reflections
(D) refurbishment

104. Mr. Moskovitz reviewed the latest proposal and ------- it to the manager for approval.

(A) continued
(B) extinguished
(C) forwarded
(D) converted

105. Von Vai Industry's new fall line of siding for houses is guaranteed to ------- the look of your house.
(A) quicken
(B) depict
(C) exemplify
(D) enhance

106. Please print your address on the label in the space provided and ------- it to the top of the bottle.
(A) abide
(B) affix
(C) detach
(D) confine

107. Donations to the Takashi Tanaka & Family Home will be greatly appreciated, yet are only -------.
(A) optional
(B) usable
(C) individual
(D) candid

108. The new attorneys and counselors must be under the supervision of a senior manager for several months before they are ------- any clients.
(A) garnered
(B) assumed
(C) incurred
(D) assigned

109. This will be the ------- biggest merger in the history of our company.
(A) one
(B) any
(C) single
(D) most

110. Due to the ------- of a self-development training program at Ballmer Company, staff absenteeism has been reduced to 10 percent.
(A) implementation
(B) temptation
(C) independency
(D) indemnity

111. Follow the ------- of steps to unlock the emergency exit door, or you will not be able to open it again.
(A) orbit
(B) sequence
(C) instruction
(D) expertness

112. The mayor said that ------- should be placed on public health and security, rather than on the preservation of local traditions.
(A) tenseness
(B) priority
(C) routine
(D) measurement

GO ON TO THE NEXT PAGE →

113. Bale Energy is seeking an alternative lubricant that is ------- in quality to the brand that they have been using over the past decade.
(A) quantity
(B) comparable
(C) pilot
(D) substantial

114. Tokyo has an ------- public transit system with many subway, train and bus lines.
(A) attachable
(B) ensuing
(C) assertive
(D) extensive

115. The next business trip to the city of New York conveniently ------- with the Fourth of July weekend celebration.
(A) subscribes
(B) consists
(C) partners
(D) coincides

116. Fortunately, the readings for the chemical analysis were well ------- the acceptable range for safety.
(A) within
(B) slight
(C) amid
(D) mutually

117. Melbourne ------- the most livable city in Australia for the fifth successive year according to a readers' poll in today's newspaper.
(A) remains
(B) materializes
(C) requires
(D) votes

118. Jeff Thompson took two weeks off work for the birth of his third child but will return next Monday to ------- his former duties here.
(A) resume
(B) assemble
(C) extract
(D) operate

119. The manager spoke most ------- about focusing on customer satisfaction, although he failed to address several topics during the last meeting.
(A) independently
(B) previously
(C) eloquently
(D) evasively

120. The area has the largest ------- of coffee plants in the country due to the favorable climate in the southern hills.
(A) concentration
(B) conversion
(C) compost
(D) correspondence

121. Please consider the mountains along Austria's western ------- before making vacation plans for summer.
(A) deadline
(B) border
(C) exposition
(D) domicile

122. ------- of consumers who bought Berizon's new laptop were not entirely satisfied with the quality.
(A) Some
(B) Any
(C) A large number
(D) Many

123. On November 20, the sales department is going to ------- a new policy that will take effect as soon as the current one expires.
(A) chaperon
(B) introduce
(C) derive
(D) command

124. Unless oak doors are treated with a chemical stabilizer, they have a tendency to ------- in a humid climate.
(A) append
(B) intensify
(C) expand
(D) inflate

125. BNP Foods states that for a healthier meal, you can ------- grape seed oil for common cooking oil.
(A) sustain
(B) substitute
(C) amend
(D) grade

126. All the recipes in this book are ------- enough to be adjusted to individual preferences.
(A) miscellaneous
(B) versatile
(C) prototypical
(D) unabridged

127. To help ------- our educational program for children of low-income families, Mr. Walton has made a sizable donation to our foundation.
(A) gratify
(B) support
(C) rely
(D) confide

128. The amber grapes are used to make ice wine, the most ------- and expensive wine in the world.
(A) renowned
(B) utter
(C) seasoned
(D) devoted

GO ON TO THE NEXT PAGE →

129. The manager said that the company outing next month, including a visit to a famous museum, is ------- to all staff and their families.

(A) deliberate
(B) open
(C) virtuous
(D) summoned

130. Actually, ------- all the applications reviewed, Mr. Persson's is by far the most impressive one.

(A) out
(B) toward
(C) of
(D) onto

131. In preparation for the arrival of the DM25, the older version, the DM20 will be ------- phased out over the next three months.

(A) sufficiently
(B) excessively
(C) gradually
(D) inadvertently

132. Most of the workers may find the daily tasks ------- due to the intrinsic nature of work.

(A) disposed
(B) repetitive
(C) unfortunate
(D) preceding

133. Students who have yet to submit their plans for their next research project must submit those documents ------- after the completion of them this evening.

(A) exceptionally
(B) particularly
(C) promptly
(D) inwardly

134. The Italian food festival downtown has become so popular that almost all local residents avoid going into the city -------.

(A) never
(B) slightly
(C) scarcely
(D) altogether

135. Before we make a decision on purchasing the property, we are currently having an ------- undertaken to determine the true value of it.

(A) advantage
(B) appraisal
(C) aggregate
(D) absorption

136. The manager of the restaurant has requested a complete ------- of the restaurant's daily routines and costs.

(A) role
(B) fluctuation
(C) evaluation
(D) alternative

137. The extra 30-minute break time added to the workday may explain the facility's high ------- over the last year.

(A) entry
(B) induction
(C) mandate
(D) output

138. City officials ------- to widen the road in order to ease traffic congestion in this area.

(A) proposed
(B) braced
(C) advocated
(D) asserted

139. Several industry analysts predict the market is heading into the worst recession ------- the last decade.

(A) for
(B) in
(C) during
(D) to

140. Berkshire Group will try to offer consumers more accurate information on a wide range of goods so that they can make an ------- decision.

(A) informal
(B) informed
(C) informative
(D) informing

GO ON TO THE NEXT PAGE

PART 6

Directions: Read the texts that follow. A word or phrase is missing in some of the sentences. Four answer choices are given below each of the sentences. Select the best answer to complete the text. Then mark the letter (A), (B), (C), or (D) on your answer sheet.

Questions 141-143 refer to the following memo.

MEMO

From: Roberto Segura
To: All MTK employees
Date: July 20
Re: Employee Safety

At MTK Industries, safety is not a goal but a requirement. -------, employees must

141. (A) Thereafter
(B) Instead
(C) Therefore
(D) Nevertheless

strictly adhere to safety regulations and procedures as stated in the attached guideline. Please be warned that failure to do so may result in disciplinary action.

Further, to ensure a safe working environment, employees should report hazardous activities of other employees to appropriate personnel, should such actions -------.

142. (A) observing
(B) to observe
(C) have been observed
(D) be observed

All non-MTK personnel, including suppliers, subcontractors and regulatory authorities are also required to follow the safety rules during their -------.

143. (A) inspections
(B) visits
(C) deliveries
(D) recesses

Questions 144-146 refer to the following e-mail.

To: Sean Cox <scox@kyleman.com>
From: Paul Gray <pgray@kyleman.com>
Date: December 7
Subject: Social Committee

Dear Mr. Cox,

I'd like to inform you that three new members ------- the Social Committee. This is

144. (A) have joined
(B) to join
(C) would have joined
(D) will be joining

due to the fact that the number of employees has doubled since last year.

The committee has been organizing golf outings, barbecue lunches and bowling nights. All of these ------- activities aim to strengthen the bond among

145. (A) competitive
(B) cultural
(C) recreational
(D) inter-office

employees and boost work output.

The list of new committee members will be sent to you in January after interviewing prospective members. -------, I'd like to discuss the budget for the upcoming

146. (A) Conversely
(B) Meanwhile
(C) Besides
(D) Likewise

year's activities, so please let me know your availability.

Thank you,

Paul Gray
Human Resources
Ext. 989

GO ON TO THE NEXT PAGE →

Questions 147-149 refer to the following letter.

February 2

Dr. Mitchell Young
Taikon Alloys
201 Alfred Street
Sydney, NSW 2890

Dear Dr. Young,

We would like to invite you to attend the Environment and Industrial Infrastructure Workshop organized by the Graham Earth Institute. The objective of the workshop is to bring together the knowledge and experience of professionals from around the country. -------, the workshop will pay special attention to critical issues that

147. (A) Rather
(B) Additionally
(C) Embarrassingly
(D) Comparatively

has developed in the last 6 months. The list of selected ------- will be sent by the

148. (A) products
(B) locations
(C) topics
(D) editions

organizing committee shortly.

For the purpose of communication, a dedicated e-mail address has been set up at workshop@grahamearth.com. Please use this e-mail address for all future communications ------- to the workshop.

149. (A) relate
(B) to relate
(C) will relate
(D) related

Sincerely,
Harry Yates
Harry Yates
Graham Earth Institute

Questions 150-152 refer to the following article.

The Ortiz Library Project announced last month has been receiving a lot of -------.

150. (A) praise
(B) criticism
(C) instructions
(D) donations

The £10 million project centers around the renovation of its main building on Snowpike Avenue.

According to the plan, the building, which is currently used for reference operation only, will be ------- into a hybrid that also contains a circulating library and an

151. (A) inspired
(B) converted
(C) reverted
(D) grown

exhibition space.

Many users are concerned about the decrease in the library's holdings. 3 million books and manuscripts will be moved to another library as a consequence of the renovation. Although the library assures users that these items can be obtained within 2 days of request, many are ------- as to the necessity of the renovation,

152. (A) unhappy
(B) doubtful
(C) assured
(D) convinced

and wonder whether the money would have been better spent elsewhere.

GO ON TO THE NEXT PAGE

PART 7

Directions: In this part you will read a selection of texts, such as magazine and newspaper articles, letters, and advertisements. Each text is followed by several questions. Select the best answer for each question and mark the letter (A), (B), (C), or (D) on your answer sheet.

Questions 153-154 refer to the following article.

Density-2000 Wins Again

Globe-biz.net has released its list of top-selling mobile phones for this month. According to the list, Density-2000 by Bensen is in first place for the third consecutive month. In second place is Hyuwa-90 by Hyuwa Electronics.

It has been quite a year for Bensen, with its Density-2000 selling 35 million units worldwide. Bensen also overtook Hyuwa, becoming the biggest mobile phone manufacturer in January this year.

More details on Density-2000 are available on page 27—find out if the features that attract thousands are suitable for you.

153. Where would the article most likely appear?
(A) In a technology magazine
(B) In a historical novel
(C) In a scholarly journal
(D) In a business report

154. What is indicated in the article?
(A) Hyuwa-90 has sold more than Density-2000.
(B) Hyuwa is the largest mobile phone manufacturer.
(C) Density-2000 has been a best-selling product for 3 months.
(D) Bensen sold less than 35 million mobile phones last year.

Questions 155-156 refer to the following advertisement.

Get the Professional Look with MP Solutions!

How can MP Solutions improve your business?
The way in which you present your material says a lot about your company. Create sophisticated, professional-looking documents by using our thermal binding system. We offer only the highest performance machines in the market.

We provide:

Fast delivery
The machines are normally delivered and are ready for use within 2-3 days from the time of your call.

User support
Customers will be provided with an exclusive phone number where an expert will answer any questions you may have.

Flexible lease terms
Our machines are available for short or long-term lease. At this time, items are not available for retail purchases.

155. What type of service does MP Solutions offer?
(A) Document shipping service
(B) Equipment rental service
(C) Printer maintenance service
(D) Fashion consultation service

156. What is suggested in the advertisement?
(A) Orders are delivered to destinations overnight.
(B) A support service is available to customers.
(C) Payment can be made in installments.
(D) Support is offered to users 24 hours a day.

GO ON TO THE NEXT PAGE

Questions 157-159 refer to the following Web page.

Pinecone Entertainment

Home
About us
Rates
DJs

Our entertainment division offers tailor-made packages to suit functions of up to 300 people. Our four DJs devote an enormous amount of time to music research and meet with clients beforehand to discuss requests. Our goal is your satisfaction! With our lighting and audio-visual effects, we can create just the mood you are looking for!

Mr. Enzo Rankin, Dacota Financial Institute, says,

"Thank you for your performance at our gala dinner. Judging from the fact that you were able to extend your services for a few hours and from the compliments we received from guests, I must say hiring you was a great idea. Our guests came from all walks of life and all of them were happy."

157. What is NOT provided by Pinecone Entertainment?
(A) Lighting adjustment
(B) Market research
(C) Audio-visual effects
(D) Pre-event meeting

158. What is indicated about Pinecone Entertainment's service?
(A) It is customized for each client.
(B) It guarantees 100 percent satisfaction.
(C) It is suitable for events of all sizes.
(D) It must be reserved one week in advance.

159. What is mentioned in Mr. Rankin's comment?
(A) The event ended earlier than expected.
(B) The attendants were happy with the food quality.
(C) The guests came from a variety of backgrounds.
(D) The company had been recommended by a guest.

GO ON TO THE NEXT PAGE →

Questions 160-163 refer to the following e-mail.

From: Margaret Klimov [Mklimov@lonetech.com]
To: Jim Barros [Jbarros@lonetech.com]
Subject: Ice Hockey Event
Date: Wednesday, March 7

Hi Jim,

I wonder if you got the message I left on your desk on Monday. Have you already reserved the bus to Yolanda Ice Hockey Stadium? If so, please notify me of the pick-up time and meeting point as I am making the final copy of the itinerary of the event to distribute to staff members at tomorrow's meeting.

Incidentally, there are a few dozen sheets of name tag stickers in the storage room if you need them for the event. I thought there were some paper cups and napkins left over from last year's picnic but didn't find any. The storage room is usually open on weekdays, but if it's locked, you can get the key from Elena in the accounting department.

I read in the newspaper that it will be nice weather on Friday. I hope you will all enjoy yourselves, and I look forward to hearing all about it when you return!

Margaret

160. What is the purpose of the e-mail?
(A) To inform a colleague of an office clean-up
(B) To reserve a bus for a sports team
(C) To obtain missing information
(D) To ask about existing stocks

161. When will the outing take place?
(A) Monday
(B) Wednesday
(C) Friday
(D) Sunday

162. What can be found in the storage room?
(A) Adhesive labels
(B) Disposable cups
(C) Picnic baskets
(D) Paper towels

163. What is probably NOT true about the event?
(A) Transportation will be arranged.
(B) Schedules will be handed out beforehand.
(C) All employees will participate.
(D) The weather is expected to be sunny.

GO ON TO THE NEXT PAGE →

Questions 164-166 refer to the following e-mail.

From: Jimmy Chang [Jchang@ssf.com]
To: Colin Peters [Cpeters@osc.org]
Subject: GMT Technologies
Date: April 29

Dear Mr. Peters,

Following the near miss incident at the Abo factory last week, I was assigned to conduct an assessment of worker safety in twelve GMT factories. Upon careful inspection, I found all safety equipment at the factories in good working condition. However, twenty-five accidents and ten near misses were reported within GMT facilities last year. This year, there have so far been a total of five accident reports. The analysis of incidents shows that 40 percent of the injuries were caused by falling. This included falling from steps, chairs, stools and slipping on wet or uneven surfaces on the floor. Regrettably, many of the reported incidents could have been avoided if workers followed basic safety rules, such as using ladders to reach higher shelves, wiping any spills on the floor and not leaving unnecessary tools lying around. My conclusion is that the number of accidents can be significantly lowered by reinforcing workplace safety through rewarding workers who demonstrate safe behaviors, encouraging workers to participate in developing safety programs, and placing signs and guidelines in appropriate locations. My full report is attached to this e-mail for the review of the Oakland Safety Commission.

Jimmy Chang
SSF, Inc.

164. What was the content of Mr. Chang's assignment?
(A) To negotiate better working conditions
(B) To investigate the cause of a lone accident
(C) To evaluate the safety of working environments
(D) To implement a new security policy

165. What is indicated as the main reason for the incidents?
(A) A malfunction in the machinery
(B) Failure to follow regulations
(C) Lack of human resources
(D) Too much overtime work

166. What is NOT a suggestion made by Mr. Chang?
(A) Putting up signs on site
(B) Getting workers involved in some programs
(C) Making stricter rules to protect confidentiality
(D) Rewarding employees who act safely

GO ON TO THE NEXT PAGE →

Questions 167-168 refer to the following book review.

Book of the Month

Reviewed by Michael Gottenberg

Meals and Magic

By Lorenzo Carreras

Illustrated. 258 pages

Don Juan Publishing. £19.99

Bookstores today are filled with stacks of books dedicated to helping you with creating great healthy dishes in no time. But have you ever wondered how those images of steaming home-cooked pasta or lamb curry that make your mouth water are taken?

Wonder no more —Lorenzo Carreras takes you behind the scenes in his new book *Meals and Magic*. A self-confessed food enthusiast, Carreras interviews chefs, photographers and editors to discover the secret behind creating magnificent food photographs.

The book is filled with tricks experienced photographers use to make the dishes look fresh, such as brushing oil over finished food to add shine, and hiding hot towels behind the plate to create steam. Even if you are not a professional cook, it will be simple to apply the tips in the book to take amazing snapshots of your own culinary handiwork.

167. What is indicated about Mr. Carreras?
(A) He is a skilled photographer.
(B) He works with Michael Gottenberg.
(C) He is passionate about food.
(D) He cooks delicious meals.

168. What is suggested about the photographic techniques described in the book?
(A) They were developed over many years.
(B) They determine the sales of a product.
(C) They require professional equipment.
(D) They can easily be adopted by amateurs.

Questions 169-171 refer to the following article.

Drought Affects Milk Production

The drought over much of the south-eastern region is putting pressure on dairy farmers. Over the last seven months, the region has experienced a 35 percent decrease in the production of crops such as corn and soybeans. This has resulted in the doubling of crop prices, which in turn has affected the price of animal feed.

Compared to last year, the cost of animal feed has increased by 20 percent and many farmers are being forced to use cheaper, less nutritious cattle feed. Not only has this lead to a drop in the total production of milk, but it is affecting the density and creaminess of the product.

Those who refuse to compromise on quality are driven to take on more debt, or to simply leave the field. Analysts say many of the small dairy farmers will be forced out of business while larger farms and corporate milking operations may manage to get through, but then, only just.

169. How much did crop prices increase?
(A) 20 percent
(B) 35 percent
(C) 50 percent
(D) 100 percent

170. What is indicated about animal feed?
(A) It is mainly manufactured in the south-eastern region.
(B) It is in low supply across the world.
(C) It generally does not contain a lot of vitamins.
(D) It has gotten more expensive than before.

171. What is suggested by analysts?
(A) Larger corporations should help small farmers.
(B) Both small and large farmers will have a hard time.
(C) Small farmers will need to make more products.
(D) Large farms will be hit the hardest by the drought.

GO ON TO THE NEXT PAGE

Questions 172-175 refer to the following letter.

March 28

Mr. Jonathan Lee
767 Kensington Drive
Springfield, VT 05465

Dear Mr. Lee,

After house hunting for several months, I was delighted to discover your beautiful home located at 767 Kensington Drive. Since I enjoy hiking as a hobby, the wooded surroundings near the house is perfect for me. It is rare to find such nature and calm so close from downtown Springfield, where incidentally my office is located. Moreover, I was impressed by the consideration given to the floor layout. The location of the two bedrooms on the upper floor gives a lot of privacy and shuts out noise from the living room on the first floor.

I have carefully considered my offering price and have decided to offer $139,000. My reason for not offering the asking price of $143,000 is because I noticed that the floorboards in several rooms need to be fixed, and the living room wall needs a new paint job. I think it is a fair offer compared to local housing prices. For example, a similar two-bedroom house just one block away on Dexter Avenue sold for $128,000.

Thank you for considering my offer. I look forward to hearing from you.

Sincerely,

Russ Taylor

Russ Taylor

172. Who most likely wrote the letter?
(A) A property owner
(B) A real estate agent
(C) A home buyer
(D) A next-door neighbor

173. What is NOT indicated about the house?
(A) It has a well thought-out layout.
(B) It is surrounded by woods.
(C) It has more than one floor.
(D) It has been soundproofed.

174. What is suggested about the asking price of the house?
(A) It has been reduced.
(B) It is comparatively high.
(C) It is similar to others on the market.
(D) It is not negotiable.

175. What can be inferred about Mr. Taylor?
(A) He is retiring from his job.
(B) He plans to repair the house.
(C) He is a native of Springfield.
(D) He expects housing values to fall.

GO ON TO THE NEXT PAGE

Questions 176-180 refer to the following letter.

August 1

Mr. Albert Shea
178 Orange Street
Orlando, FL 36729

Dear Mr. Shea,

Please be advised that the monthly magazine, *Boating Today*, will cease publication after the September issue. However, we are happy to announce that the magazine *Seamaster* has agreed to fulfill your subscription for the remaining term of six months.

Where *Boating Today* brought you insights into the world of cruisers and yachts, *Seamaster* brings you the same deep insights into the world of fishing. We are sure *Seamaster* will light the same passion in you for fishing that you have for boating.

You will receive an issue of *Seamaster* for every remaining issue of *Boating Today* that you were entitled to receive. If you are already subscribed to *Seamaster*, your subscription will be extended for the term left on your original *Boating Today* subscription.

If you are not satisfied with this arrangement and wish to receive a refund, please contact the Subscription Department at 555-2790 before September 15.

Sincerely,

Willie Boggs

Willie Boggs
Subscription Department

176. What is the purpose of the letter?
(A) To advertise a newly inaugurated publication
(B) To inform a reader of a magazine discontinuance
(C) To subscribe to a daily newspaper
(D) To recommend an interesting article

177. The word "fulfill" in paragraph 1, line 3, is closest in meaning to
(A) charge
(B) reward
(C) deliver
(D) compromise

178. What is indicated about *Seamaster*?
(A) Its first edition is coming out in September.
(B) It contains articles on ships and boats.
(C) It will be sent in the place of *Boating Today*.
(D) It has the same theme as *Boating Today*.

179. What is suggested in the letter?
(A) Boating and fishing are similar activities.
(B) Readers of *Boating Today* will also enjoy *Seamaster*.
(C) Both of the magazines are aimed at novice fishermen.
(D) Fishing is more enjoyable than boating.

180. According to the letter, who should contact the Subscription Department?
(A) People wishing to subscribe to *Boating Today*
(B) Clients who already have a subscription with *Seamaster*
(C) Customers wanting reimbursement of the subscription fee
(D) Subscribers who need to change the delivery address

GO ON TO THE NEXT PAGE →

Questions 181-185 refer to the following notice and e-mail.

Posted Date: May 7
KGK, Inc.
Now Hiring

Job Description: KGK, Inc. is a prominent independent oil and gas company based in Texas. We are seeking a manufacturing engineer whose primary responsibility will be to assist in the development and implementation of production techniques. The individual will need to coordinate with other engineers to achieve clearly defined goals.

Qualifications:
Bachelor's degree in engineering
3-5 years relative experience

Documents required:
Application letter
Comprehensive résumé with picture

Deadline of submission of required documents is May 15. A 3-hour written examination will be administered on the following day. Qualified persons can take the exam anytime between 10 A.M. and 5 P.M.

Clark Gold
CGold@kgk.com
Human Resources
KGK, Inc.

To: Clark Gold [CGold@kgk.com]
From: Edward Wise [ewise@zennifer.com]
Date: May 10
Subject: Manufacturing Engineer Position

Dear Mr. Gold,

I am writing in response to a notice posted on Jobwide.com.
My name is Edward Wise and as you can see from my CV, I have graduated from Hopeton University with a degree in engineering. I received top marks in my classes as is shown on the attached transcript.

While I was a student, I interned at the oil plant of Thames Global in Singapore every summer. After graduation, I joined Blare Corporation, where I have been working as a manufacturing engineer for three years. I have a reputation of being reliable, hard-working and passionate about my work. Reference letters are available upon request. Also, please find my application letter attached to this e-mail.
Thank you for your consideration, and I look forward to hearing from you.

Sincerely,
Edward Wise

181. In the notice, the word "primary" in paragraph 1, line 2, is closest in meaning to
(A) basic
(B) leading
(C) peripheral
(D) social

182. What is suggested about the job?
(A) It is temporary.
(B) It involves team work.
(C) It offers a high salary.
(D) It requires traveling.

183. When will candidates take a written exam?
(A) May 7
(B) May 10
(C) May 15
(D) May 16

184. What unrequired document is sent with the e-mail?
(A) An application letter
(B) A medical form
(C) Academic records
(D) A letter of reference

185. What can be inferred about Mr. Wise?
(A) He recently graduated from university.
(B) He does not have the appropriate experience.
(C) He is familiar with KGK, Inc.'s line of work.
(D) He read the notice in the newspaper.

GO ON TO THE NEXT PAGE →

Questions 186-190 refer to the following article and e-mail.

New Grafton Community Center Opens

Over a year after Miles Hall was damaged by a passing tornado, the town of Grafton opened the doors to its new community center on Thursday, October 6.

The cost of building the center was initially estimated to reach $1,200,000, which was over the town's already stretched budget of $920,000. The town then decided to use municipal employees to complete the project. Through using town labor, the total cost was held at $920,000.

The new community center, housing a multi-purpose room, several program spaces, a fully-equipped kitchen and a children's learning center, was built on the south corner of Grafton Park.

Recently, there has been much debate about the fate of the original hall. The initial plan was to demolish it completely, but this has been met with strong opposition from the local community. Grafton Residents' Association member Carrie Houston says, "Miles Hall has been a part of the Grafton community for over 50 years. We hope to keep it that way for future generations."

To: Tim Watkins [twatkins@gpnews.com]
From: Carrie Houston [Houston@teb.com]
Date: December 20, 9:00 A.M.
Subject: Follow-up

Dear Mr. Watkins,

Hello. You may remember me from the ribbon-cutting ceremony of the Grafton Community Center. I am writing with an update on Miles Hall, in case you would be interested in writing an article about it.

Over the past few months, the Grafton Residents' Association has hosted several fundraising events to help preserve Miles Hall. We also repeatedly held discussions with town officials, and last week, they finally agreed to move the structure to its new home on 567 Haybale Avenue by the end of February next year. If you have any questions, please contact me at 555-2768.

Carrie Houston

186. How was the town able to complete the building of the center without a proper budget?
(A) By changing contractors
(B) By using existing workers
(C) By applying for a grant
(D) By gathering volunteers

187. In the article, the word "held" in paragraph 2, line 4, is closest in meaning to
(A) maintained
(B) approximated
(C) released
(D) compensated

188. What is indicated about Ms. Houston?
(A) She has been living in Grafton for 50 years.
(B) She attended an event on October 6.
(C) She is a member of the town council.
(D) She runs a children's learning center.

189. Why did Ms. Houston send the e-mail to Mr. Watkins?
(A) To ask for some assistance
(B) To follow up on a job interview
(C) To inform him of a new development
(D) To inquire about an ongoing issue

190. According to the e-mail, what will happen next year?
(A) Miles Hall will be renovated.
(B) A meeting will take place.
(C) A fundraiser will be organized.
(D) A building will be relocated.

GO ON TO THE NEXT PAGE →

Questions 191-195 refer to the following e-mails.

To: Joanna Flore [jflore@lgar.com]
From: Erika Smith [SmithE@joosta.com]
Date: November 1, 10:25 A.M.
Subject: Introducing Joosta, Inc.

Dear Ms. Flore,

Hello! I am writing to introduce you to our company, Joosta, Inc. We are a German company which designs and produces top quality wooden toys. Our products have been widely enjoyed in Germany for over fifteen years. All our toys are made from safe, premium quality material and each one is crafted by hand by an expert toymaker in Germany. Within the country, our products are sold in such reputable department stores as Axi and Rian Guus.

Currently, we are working to develop our clientele in the North American region. This is why we have prepared a sample package which you, as a retailer in North America, can receive for free by filling out the attached form and sending it back to us. It is important that you fill out all the entries on the form to ensure a swift delivery. Included in the package are a few of our most popular toys and some items from our brand-new children's apparel line. After you experience our products first-hand, you can then decide whether to place further orders with us.

We look forward to working with you.

Sincerely,
Erika Smith, Manager
Joosta, Inc.

To: Joanna Flore [jflore@lgar.com]
From: Adrian Appel [AppelA@joosta.com]
Date: November 7, 9:00 A.M.
Subject: Sample Pack

Dear Ms. Flore,

We are delighted to hear of your interest in our products. A sample package is on its way! Should you decide to place an order, simply fill out and return the order sheet enclosed in the package.

In an effort to reduce our carbon footprint, we no longer provide printed literature with our sample packs. However, detailed product information and technical documentation can be downloaded from our Web site.

Regarding your question concerning high-volume order discount, the manager will get back to you with details in a separate e-mail which will be sent shortly.

Thank you.

Adrian Appel, Customer Representative
Joosta, Inc.

191. Who most likely is Ms. Flore?
(A) A representative of a manufacturing company
(B) A customer of a department store
(C) A store owner in North America
(D) A wood supplier based in Germany

192. What can be inferred about Joosta, Inc.?
(A) It is a family-owned company.
(B) It is expanding its business.
(C) Its products are manufactured abroad.
(D) Its main customer base is in North America.

193. What is Ms. Flore encouraged to do?
(A) Let customers try out Joosta, Inc. products
(B) Return a document to receive complimentary samples
(C) Complete and send a form to enter a contest
(D) Read customer reviews on Joosta, Inc.'s Web site

194. What is NOT included in the package?
(A) Some garments
(B) Handmade toys
(C) A product catalogue
(D) An order form

195. What is indicated about high-volume orders?
(A) A separate price list will be sent.
(B) The toy designs do not allow for mass production.
(C) Joanna Flore will need to meet with the manager.
(D) Erika Smith will provide more information.

GO ON TO THE NEXT PAGE

Questions 196-200 refer to the following article and letter.

NEWPORT—Potential visitors to the Newport Flower Show are not the only ones hoping for better summer weather. As the unusually rainy summer forces many flower shows to be canceled, organizers hope the same won't happen to their show which brings in approximately 40,000 visitors to the town each year. The show, which is hosted by the Newport Horticultural Society and costs £300,000 to stage, is a big boost to Newport's economy.

"I don't think the event will be canceled totally, but I'm afraid it will be severely curtailed like the flower shows at Stony Shade or Templeton." said Rolf Kelly, a Newport business owner.

This year at the Newport Flower Show, on top of the usual display of various flowers and over 100 fantastic English-style gardens, a demonstration by the rescue dog team will take place. Also, a glass pavilion has once again been set up to house the many species of roses.

Bob Martin, President of the Newport Horticultural Society says, "We have prepared a stunning range of events with the help of the local community. For example, this is our first attempt to incorporate animals into our show, which we hope will be appreciated by people of all ages but especially by our younger guests."

August 31

Mr. Bob Martin
Newport Horticultural Society
287 Bane Street
Newport, South Wales
NP18 6G5

Dear Mr. Martin,

I would like to congratulate you on the success of last week's flower show. I'm happy to hear that you had a turnout of around 40,000 visitors despite adverse weather conditions. I visited the show twice during its opening days myself. I loved the glass pavilion section last year and the roses were magnificent this year as well.

I deeply appreciate the kind suggestion by the Newport Horticultural Society of donating flowers and plants for the Newport Hospital playground. Unfortunately, however, at this time we do not have enough funds or manpower to plant and maintain them. Nevertheless, we thank you for thinking of us.

Sincerely,

Jing Wong

Jing Wong, Director

196. Why is Mr. Kelly concerned?
(A) A major town event has been canceled.
(B) The water shortage has damaged plants.
(C) Business has been slow in Newport.
(D) Some other flower shows were cut short.

197. What feature is new to this year's show?
(A) Glass pavilion
(B) English gardens
(C) Rescue dog demonstration
(D) Children's playground

198. What can be inferred about the turnout?
(A) It was poorer than expected.
(B) It was more than usual.
(C) It was less than last year.
(D) It was about the same as usual.

199. What is the purpose of the letter?
(A) To congratulate an award winner
(B) To report on the outcome of an event
(C) To thank for a monetary donation
(D) To decline a proposed offer

200. What type of organization does Mr. Wong most likely work for?
(A) A regional committee
(B) A local school
(C) A health service
(D) A charity organization

Stop! This is the end of the test. If you finish before time is called, you may go back to Part 5, 6, and 7 and check your work.

Final Test 解答・解説 解答一覧

設問	正解	設問	正解	設問	正解	設問	正解	設問	正解
1	D	41	B	81	C	121	B	161	C
2	B	42	D	82	C	122	C	162	A
3	D	43	C	83	B	123	B	163	C
4	B	44	C	84	D	124	C	164	C
5	A	45	C	85	A	125	B	165	B
6	C	46	C	86	D	126	B	166	C
7	C	47	C	87	B	127	B	167	C
8	B	48	B	88	D	128	A	168	D
9	C	49	C	89	C	129	B	169	D
10	A	50	C	90	B	130	C	170	D
11	A	51	C	91	D	131	C	171	B
12	A	52	A	92	B	132	B	172	C
13	C	53	A	93	D	133	C	173	D
14	A	54	B	94	C	134	D	174	B
15	B	55	B	95	A	135	B	175	B
16	C	56	D	96	B	136	C	176	B
17	B	57	C	97	A	137	D	177	C
18	C	58	C	98	B	138	A	178	C
19	B	59	B	99	C	139	B	179	B
20	C	60	A	100	D	140	B	180	C
21	A	61	C	101	B	141	C	181	B
22	C	62	C	102	B	142	D	182	B
23	B	63	B	103	B	143	B	183	D
24	B	64	C	104	C	144	D	184	C
25	C	65	B	105	D	145	C	185	C
26	A	66	B	106	B	146	B	186	B
27	A	67	C	107	A	147	B	187	A
28	C	68	B	108	D	148	C	188	B
29	A	69	A	109	C	149	D	189	C
30	A	70	D	110	A	150	B	190	D
31	B	71	C	111	B	151	B	191	C
32	C	72	A	112	B	152	B	192	B
33	B	73	C	113	B	153	A	193	B
34	B	74	A	114	D	154	C	194	C
35	C	75	A	115	D	155	B	195	D
36	A	76	B	116	A	156	B	196	D
37	B	77	D	117	A	157	B	197	C
38	B	78	B	118	A	158	A	198	D
39	A	79	D	119	C	159	C	199	D
40	C	80	C	120	A	160	C	200	C

予想スコア換算表

Final Testの答え合わせを終えたら，下の表を参考に正解数をスコアに換算して，予想スコアを出してみましょう。

この表は，旺文社が独自に作成したものであり，実際のTOEICテストのスコア算出方法とは異なりますので，あくまで現在の実力を推し量る目安としてください。

リスニング・セクション

正解数	予想スコア	正解数	予想スコア
100	495	74	395
99	495	73	390
98	495	72	385
97	495	71	380
96	495	70	375
95	495	69	370
94	495	68	365
93	490	67	360
92	485	66	355
91	480	65	350
90	475	64	345
89	470	63	340
88	465	62	335
87	460	61	330
86	455	60	325
85	450	59	320
84	445	58	315
83	440	57	310
82	435	56	305
81	430	55	300
80	425	54	295
79	420	53	290
78	415	52	285
77	410	51	280
76	405	50	275
75	400		

リーディング・セクション

正解数	予想スコア	正解数	予想スコア
100	495	74	380
99	495	73	375
98	495	72	370
97	495	71	365
96	490	70	360
95	485	69	355
94	480	68	350
93	475	67	345
92	470	66	340
91	465	65	335
90	460	64	330
89	455	63	325
88	450	62	320
87	445	61	315
86	440	60	310
85	435	59	305
84	430	58	300
83	425	57	295
82	420	56	290
81	415	55	285
80	410	54	280
79	405	53	275
78	400	52	270
77	395	51	265
76	390	50	260
75	385		

リスニング		リーディング		予想スコア
正解数（　　）／点	+	正解数（　　）／点	=	正解数（　　）／点

Final Test 正解と解説

PART 1

CD 2 [2]～[12]

1.

[3]

(A) They're climbing up the staircase.
(B) They're repairing a heavy device outdoors.
(C) They have finished working at the construction site on the hill.
(D) They're climbing up the mountain in a group.
(A) 彼らは階段を上っている。
(B) 彼らは屋外で重機を修理している。
(C) 彼らは丘にある建設現場での作業を終えたところだ。
(D) 彼らは集団で山の斜面を登っている。

正解 **(D)**

解説 何人かの人たちが石の転がった山の斜面を歩いている。これを適切に描写している(D)が正解だ。(A)はstaircase，(B)はrepairing a heavy device，(C)はconstruction siteが聞こえた時点で不正解と判断できる。

語句 □staircase（壁や手すりを含む）階段

2.

[4]

(A) Some plants are being watered in a flower bed.
(B) Some shrubs are being trimmed in a yard.
(C) Some water hoses are being sold at an open-air market.
(D) Some flowers are being planted in a garden by the man.
(A) 植物が花壇の中で水を与えられているところだ。
(B) 庭で低木が刈られているところだ。
(C) 戸外の市場で水道用のホースが売られているところだ。
(D) 花が男性によって庭に植えられているところだ。

正解 **(B)**

解説 男性が庭で枝にはさみを入れている写真だ。受け身の進行形「～されているところだ」を使ってこの状況を描写している(B)が正解である。他の選択肢にも受け身の進行形が使われており，写真に登場しているものの関連語を含んでいるが，写真の状況を描写するには不適切なものとなっている。

語句 □flower bed 花壇　□shrub 低木　□trim ～を刈る　□open-air market 屋外の市場

3.

[5]

(A) The woman is talking with her co-workers at a service station.
(B) The woman is rearranging some equipment in the vehicle.
(C) The woman is removing her necklace from her neck.
(D) The woman is putting gas into the vehicle at the gas station.

(A) 女性がガソリンスタンドで同僚たちと話をしている。
(B) 女性が車の中で備品を並べ直している。
(C) 女性がネックレスを首から外している。
(D) 女性がガソリンスタンドで乗り物にガソリンを入れている。

正解 **(D)**

解説 ガソリンスタンドで女性が車に給油をしている。put A into B「AをBに入れる」を使ってこの状況を描写している(D)が正解となる。ガソリンスタンドはservice stationともgas stationとも表現できることを覚えておこう。Part 1では主語はもちろんのこと，動詞や目的語，そして場所まできちんと聞き取って確実に理解すること。

4.

6

(A) The man is gathering up some electrical wires on the ground.
(B) Some boxes are being loaded in the back of the truck.
(C) The man is labeling the packages.
(D) Some storage warehouses have been constructed in the field.

(A) 男性が地面にある電線をまとめている。
(B) 箱がトラックの後部に積み込まれているところだ。
(C) 男性がパッケージにラベルを付けている。
(D) 倉庫が野原に建てられている。

正解 **(B)**

解説 後部が開いているトラックに箱が積み込まれている。この状況を受け身の進行形で表している(B)が正解だ。人が登場して何らかの動作を行っている写真の場合，このように物を主語にして受け身の形で出題されることが多々ある。音声が流れる前からそのことを意識しておこう。

語句 □electrical wire 電線

5.

7

(A) Rows of lights are over both edges of the platform.
(B) A train station is closed for renovations.
(C) Some people are purchasing tickets from vending machines.
(D) Some passengers are exiting the train.

(A) ライトの列がホーム両端の上方に設置されている。
(B) 駅が改修のために閉鎖されている。
(C) 人々が自動券売機で券を購入している。
(D) 乗客が電車から降りている。

正解 **(A)**

解説 人がメインで写っていない問題は，難易度が高めとなる傾向がある。場面は駅であり，ホーム両端の上方にライトが並んでいる。これを描写している(A)が正解だ。(B)はrenovationsを行っているかどうかは写真から判断できない。(C)と(D)も写真とは状況が異なる。

語句 □rows of ～ ～の列

6.

8

(A) Some pottery is being cleared from the rack.
(B) Some pots have fallen on the ground.
(C) Various kinds of pots are being displayed on the shelves.
(D) Some mirrors are being hung on the wall.

(A) 陶器が棚から撤去されているところだ。
(B) 鉢が地面に落ちている。
(C) さまざまな種類の鉢が棚に並んでいる。
(D) 鏡が壁に掛けられているところだ。

正解 **(C)**

解説 (A)～(C)の選択肢には，写真に写っている「鉢」を表すpotteryやpotが登場している。(A)のbe being clearedは「撤去中」という意味なので，作業中の人が写っている必要があり不正解だ。(B)は現在完了形で，鉢が地面にすでに落ちてしまっている状態を表している。(C)は受け身の進行形だが，be being displayedは展示された「状態」が続いていることを表し，これが正解となる。

語句 □pottery 陶器

7.

9

(A) A woman is looking at some trees outdoors.
(B) Some chairs remain empty on the terrace.
(C) There are some potted plants sitting on the ledge side by side.
(D) A woman is turning off a bedside lamp.

(A) 女性が戸外の木を見ている。
(B) テラスの椅子は空いたままである。
(C) 壁面の出っ張りに鉢植えが並んでいる。
(D) 女性がベッドの脇にあるライトを消そうとしている。

正解 **(C)**

解説 ledgeは壁面の棚状の出っ張りを表す。ledgeに鉢植え（potted plants）が並んでいる様子を描写している(C)が正解だ。(A)と(D)はa womanが，(B)はchairsが出てくるので写真の状況とは合わない。

語句 □ledge 壁面の棚状の出っ張り，突き出た棚

8.

10

(A) The women are relaxing under some umbrellas near the water.
(B) Some bicycles are under the lamppost.
(C) Some bicycles are parked next to each other at the beach.
(D) The lampposts are casting shadows on the road.

(A) 女性たちが水辺の傘の下でリラックスしている。
(B) 自転車が街灯の下にある。
(C) 自転車が浜辺に隣り合わせで駐輪されている。
(D) 街灯が道路に影を投げかけている。

正解 **(B)**

解説 自転車が街灯の下にあるので，(B)が正解となる。(A)はThe womenが出てくる時点で不正解だ。(C)は浜辺での様子，(D)は複数の街灯が影を投げかけている状況を表しているので不正解である。この問題のように遠くまで写っている写真は，背景も意識して音声を聞こう。

9.

11

(A) Some waiters are carrying some menus to the customers.

(B) The woman is taking something from the backpack.

(C) A pair of customers is examining the menus at the restaurant.

(D) The couple is reading a sign near the water.

(A) ウエーターが客にメニューを運んでいる。

(B) 女性がバックパックから何かを取り出している。

(C) 1組の客がレストランでメニューを見ている。

(D) カップルが水辺で標識を読んでいる。

正解 **(C)**

解説 レストランで男女のペアがメニューを眺めている。Part 1に時々登場する動詞examineを使って写真の状況を的確に表している(C)が正解だ。examineには「調査する，診察する，試験を行う」などの意味があるが，Part 1では本やメニューなどを見ている写真にも使われるので覚えておこう。

10.

12

(A) A line of customers is waiting at the counter.

(B) An assortment of reading materials is sitting in the rack.

(C) A woman is putting something into the paper bag.

(D) A variety of items is being removed from the rack.

(A) 客の列がカウンターで並んで待っている。

(B) さまざまな読み物がラックに並んでいる。

(C) 女性が紙袋に何かを入れている。

(D) さまざまな商品がラックから撤去されているところだ。

正解 **(A)**

解説 カウンターに何人かの客が並んでいる写真だ。これを正しく描写しているのは(A)だ。(B)のreading materialsは本や新聞などの読み物全般を指す表現だが写真には写っておらず，(C)の動作を行っている女性も写っていないため不正解。ラックから商品が撤去されている最中でもないので(D)も正解にはならない。

語句 □an assortment of ～ 各種の～

11.

14

New notices will soon be posted on the message board, won't they?	新しいお知らせはすぐにメッセージボードに掲示されますよね。
(A) Yes, I think so.	(A) はい，そうだと思います。
(B) Thank you so much for calling me on such short notice.	(B) こんなにすぐにお電話いただきありがとうございます。
(C) Due to the bad weather.	(C) 悪天候のせいです。

正解 **(A)**

解説 新しいお知らせが掲示されることを確認する問いかけであり，これに素直に応答している(A)が正解だ。(B)は問いかけの中にあるnoticeを使った応答だが，内容が全くかみ合っていないため不正解。(C)は原因や理由を答えているのでこちらも不適切である。

12.

15

All your new laptops come with some free software, right?	そちらの新しいノートパソコンには皆，フリーソフトが付いてくるのですね。
(A) Several of the new models we carry do.	(A) こちらで扱っているいくつかの新製品には付きます。
(B) It'll be set up on February 16.	(B) 2月16日にセットアップされる予定です。
(C) Mr. Smith will fix the broken one as soon as possible.	(C) Smithさんが壊れたものをできるだけ早く直す予定です。

正解 **(A)**

解説 「全てのノートパソコンにフリーソフトが付属するのですよね」という問いかけに対して，「いくつかには付属しています」と返している(A)が会話として自然なので正解だ。doはcome (with some free software) を表している。(B)と(C)はパソコンに関連する表現が含まれているが問いかけに対する応答になっておらず，不正解。

13.

16

The concert was really awful, wasn't it?	コンサートは本当にひどかったですね。
(A) Yes, it's a very successful film.	(A) はい，それは大成功した映画です。
(B) No, I'm very struck by your work.	(B) いいえ，私はあなたの作品に非常に感銘を受けています。
(C) It wasn't good at all, I think.	(C) 全く良くなかったと私は思います。

正解 **(C)**

解説 コンサートの感想を，同意を求めるニュアンスで問いかけている。これに対してnot～at all「全く～ではない」を使って「コンサートは良くなかった」と応答している(C)が正解となる。(A)はfilm「映画」，(B)はwork「作品」に対しての感想なのでいずれも不正解だ。

語句 □awful ひどい　□be struck by ～ ～に感銘を受ける

14.

17

That company's earnings should be recalculated by next week.	会社の収益は来週までに再計算されなければなりません。
(A) I have no idea if that can be done by next week.	(A) 来週までにできるかどうかは分かりません。
(B) Heavier paper will work better, I think.	(B) より重い紙の方がよりよく機能すると思います。
(C) They work at a large legal office, I heard.	(C) 彼らは大きな法律事務所で働いていると聞いています。

正解 **(A)**

解説 平叙文に対する応答は予想しにくいので注意が必要だ。「来週までに収益を再計算しなければいけない」という内容に対し「できるかどうか分からない」と答えている(A)が正解だ。(B)は全く内容のかみ合わない応答であり，(C)もcompanyの関連表現であるofficeという語は登場するものの，内容のつながりがなく適切ではない。

語句 □recalculate ～を再計算する

15.

18

Every sales representative seemed to make it to the conference on time.	営業担当者は全員時間通り会議に到着したようです。
(A) No, it's in the filing cabinet in the corner, isn't it?	(A) いいえ，それは隅のファイリングキャビネットにありますよね。
(B) I just heard that Ms. Johnson was slow in arriving.	(B) Johnsonさんが遅れたと聞いたばかりです。
(C) Was it true that you missed the conference yesterday?	(C) あなたが昨日会議に行かなかったというのは本当ですか。

正解 **(B)**

解説 発言にあるmake it to～は「～に到着する」という意味を表す。「営業担当者は全員時間通り会議に到着したようだ」という発言に対し，「Johnsonさんが遅れたと聞いたばかりだ」と答えている(B)の応答が自然だ。(A)は何かが置かれている場所を示す内容であり，(C)は相手が会議に行かなかったことを確認する内容であるため，いずれも不正解だ。

16.

19

His team's new product is being unveiled next month.	彼のチームの新製品は来月公開される予定です。
(A) He'll renew his membership next month.	(A) 彼は来月会員権を更新する予定です。
(B) It's the second largest assembly facility around there.	(B) それはあの辺りで2番目に大きい組立工場です。
(C) They're excited to show it.	(C) 彼らはそれを紹介することに興奮しています。

正解 **(C)**

解説 「彼のチームの新製品が来月公開される」という発言に対して，They're excitedと応答している(C)が正解だ。(A)と(B)は，最初の発言にあるproductやnext monthなどから関連しそうな内容に思えるが，いずれも会話として成立しないので不正解。(B)のthe second largest「2番目に大きい」という表現は覚えておくとよいだろう。

17. 20

Mr. Johnson will be returning to work from vacation next Tuesday.	Johnsonさんは来週の火曜日に休暇から仕事へ戻ってくる予定です。
(A) We are planning to open new stores next Tuesday.	(A) 来週の火曜日に新しい店舗をオープンする予定です。
(B) Yes, I'll see him back at our office.	(B) はい，戻ってきた彼とオフィスで会うことになるでしょう。
(C) No, I forgot to bring his camera.	(C) いいえ，私は彼のカメラを持ってくるのを忘れました。

正解 **(B)**

解説 「Johnsonさんが戻ってくる」という事実に対して，自然な応答になっているものを選択する。「戻ってきた彼とオフィスで会うことになる」と答えている(B)が正解だ。(A)はnext Tuesdayが登場するもののそれ以外の接点がなく，(C)は内容に関連がないため不正解だ。

18. 21

You called Mr. Williams back this afternoon, right?	今日の午後，Williamsさんに折り返し電話をかけましたよね。
(A) No, in the back seat, I think.	(A) いいえ，後部座席だと思います。
(B) I have to put off the teleconference until Wednesday.	(B) 水曜日までテレビ会議を延期しなければなりません。
(C) Not yet, I'll call him tomorrow morning.	(C) まだです。明日の朝，彼に電話をするつもりです。

正解 **(C)**

解説 Williamsさんに折り返し電話をかけたかどうかの確認をしている最初の発言に対し，「まだなので，明日の朝かける予定だ」と応答している(C)が正解になる。(A)のback, (B)のteleconferenceは関連語を使ったひっかけである。put off～「～を延期する（＝postpone）」は基本表現として押さえておこう。

19. 22

The novel by Ignazio Fellini got terrific reviews.	Ignazio Fellini氏の小説は素晴らしい書評をもらいました。
(A) You can get a great view of the ocean from the terrace.	(A) テラスから素晴らしい海の景色を見ることができます。
(B) Oh, have you already read his book?	(B) ああ，もう彼の本を読みましたか。
(C) Actually, I've been working at the publishing company.	(C) 実は出版社にずっと勤めています。

正解 **(B)**

解説 ある作家の本に対する書評がとても良いということを伝える発言だ。これに対して「もう読みましたか」と質問している(B)が正解だ。(A)はviewやterraceなど，最初の発言に登場している単語の音に似た語を使ったひっかけの選択肢であり，(C)はnovelに関連するpublishing companyを使って解答者を惑わせている。

語句 □terrific 素晴らしい

20. 23

I was very pleased with your presentation at the conference.	会議でのあなたのプレゼンを大変気に入りました。
(A) Sorry, we can no longer use the conference room.	(A) すみません，もう会議室は使うことができません。
(B) Sorry, I already have other plans next month.	(B) すみません，来月はすでに他の予定が入っています。
(C) I worked very hard. Thank you so much for your compliment.	(C) 一生懸命やりました。お褒めいただき本当にありがとうございます。

正解 **(C)**

解説 最初の発言は相手に「プレゼンが素晴らしかった」ということを伝える内容だ。これに対して素直にお礼を伝えている(C)が正解だ。(A)はpresentationに関連するconference roomが登場しているが，適切な応答になっていない。(B)は来月の予定を聞かれたときなどに，誘いを断る場合の応答である。

21. 24

The insurance on your car expired last month, didn't it?	あなたの車の保険契約は先月切れたんですよね。
(A) That reminds me, I need to renew it as soon as possible.	(A) それで思い出した。すぐに更新しなければ。
(B) No, our company guarantees you are getting the lowest price.	(B) いいえ，当社はあなたに最低価格を保証いたします。
(C) The expiration date can be found at the bottom of the bottle.	(C) 賞味期限は瓶の底に書いてあります。

正解 **(A)**

解説 相手の車の保険が切れてしまっていることを確認する問いかけだ。問いかけをきっかけに，自分の保険の更新を思い出したという(A)が正解となる。(B)は客に最低価格の保証を伝える内容であり，(C)は賞味期限の確かめ方を伝えている。

22. 25

We'll be able to inspect the facility tomorrow.	明日は施設の検査を行うことができるでしょう。
(A) I'll buy you a novel tomorrow.	(A) 明日小説を買ってあげます。
(B) No, they'll shut down the facility next year.	(B) いいえ，彼らは来年その施設を閉鎖する予定です。
(C) OK, what time should I go there?	(C) 分かりました，何時にそこに行けばよいですか。

正解 **(C)**

解説 自分たちが行うであろう明日の施設の検査に関する確認に対し，OKと答え，集合時間に関する問いかけをしている(C)が正解だ。この問題のように，平叙文に対して問いかけで応答する場合もある。常に，文意を瞬時に把握することを念頭に置いて，音声を聞くようにしよう。

23.

26

Please be on time for your appointment.	約束の時間通りに来てくださいね。
(A) Actually, you missed your appointment last time.	(A) 実際，前回あなたは約束通りに来ませんでした。
(B) OK, I'll be there at ten sharp.	(B) はい，10時ちょうどにそこに行きます。
(C) For at least four months, it won't be available.	(C) 少なくとも4カ月間，それは使えません。

正解 **(B)**

解説 約束の時間通りに来るよう相手に念を押す内容の発言だ。「10時ちょうどに行く」と述べている(B)が正解だ。時刻の後にくるsharpは副詞で「～ちょうどに」という意味。

24.

27

They're flying to Sydney via Singapore today.	彼らは今日，シンガポール経由でシドニーに飛行機で行く予定です。
(A) They had a nice time in Sydney.	(A) 彼らはシドニーで楽しい時間を過ごしました。
(B) I heard they're looking forward to it so much.	(B) 彼らはとても楽しみにしていると聞いています。
(C) I tried to buy some travel guidebooks.	(C) 私は旅行ガイドブックを何冊か買おうとしました。

正解 **(B)**

解説 第三者の予定を簡潔に伝える発言に対して，その人たちに関する情報をシンプルに伝えている(B)が正解だ。(A)も(C)も旅行に関するものであるため，最初の発言をきちんと理解してリテンションする必要がある。

25.

28

What should we name our new mountaineering boots?	新作の登山用ブーツの名前は何にしましょうか。
(A) You'd better put yourself in his shoes.	(A) 彼の立場になって考えた方がいいですよ。
(B) We never knew you had mountaineering boots.	(B) あなたが登山用ブーツを持っていることを知りませんでした。
(C) Something fashionable.	(C) ファッショナブルなものにしましょう。

正解 **(C)**

解説 新製品の名前をどうするかという相談の問いかけだ。これに対してシンプルに意見を述べている(C)が正解だ。短い選択肢なのでこれだけでは選びにくいかもしれないが，(A)，(B)と合わせて考えれば問題ないだろう。(A)のin someone's shoesは「～の立場になって」という意味。

語句 □mountaineering boots 登山用ブーツ

26.

29

The presentation will be about forty minutes long.
(A) Maybe, it'll be longer than that.
(B) Yes, for about four hours.
(C) My colleague did it yesterday at the conference.

プレゼンは約40分間の予定です。
(A) それよりももっと時間がかかるかもしれません。
(B) はい，約4時間です。
(C) 私の同僚が昨日会議でそれを行いました。

正解 **(A)**

解説 プレゼンの所要時間に関する発言に対し，「もっと時間がかかるかもしれません」と答えている(A)を選択すれば会話が成立する。(B)はYesで受けているにも関わらず所要時間が違っており，(C)は時制が違っているため正解にはなり得ない。

27.

30

I'll give you some time to go over the terms and conditions of the contract.
(A) OK, I'll call you again in a few minutes.
(B) Sorry, I don't have contact with the attorney.
(C) Yes, it was discussed at the last meeting.

契約の条件を詳しく調べる時間を差し上げます。
(A) 分かりました。すぐにかけ直します。
(B) すみません，弁護士とは連絡を取っていません。
(C) はい，それは前回の会議で話し合われました。

正解 **(A)**

解説 聞き手は契約に関して調べる時間を与えられ，それに対して「すぐに（電話を）かけ直す」と応答している(A)が正解だ。(B)はcontractに似た音を持つcontactや，contractから連想されるattorneyを含んでいるが，会話がつながらない。(C)は時制が一致しておらず，会話も続かないので不正解である。

語句 □attorney 弁護士

28.

31

Tom, some fluorescent lights are dead and need to be replaced now.
(A) Dinner will need to be served promptly at 9 P.M.
(B) I think you are missing Jack.
(C) OK, I'll get them fixed right away.

Tom，蛍光灯が何本か切れているので，すぐ交換しないといけません。
(A) ディナーは午後9時ちょうどに提供する必要があるでしょう。
(B) あなたはJackがいなくて寂しいのだと思います。
(C) はい，今すぐ修理してもらいます。

正解 **(C)**

解説 最初の発言にあるfluorescent lightは蛍光灯であり，それがdead，つまり切れているので暗に交換をお願いしている発言だ。〈get＋目的語＋過去分詞〉で「～を…の状態にする」だが，これを使って応答している(C)が正解だ。(A)の〈promptly at＋時刻〉は「～時きっかりに」という意味であり，23.の(B)のように〈時刻＋sharp〉と言い換えることができる。

語句 □fluorescent light 蛍光灯

29.

32

I should have caught some sleep because it was a long flight.
(A) You can get some sleep now.
(B) I'd like you to show me your passport.
(C) For about eight hours.

長いフライトだったので少し眠ればよかったです。
(A) 今，少し眠ってもいいですよ。
(B) パスポートを見せていただきたいのですが。
(C) 約8時間です。

正解 **(A)**

解説 眠ればよかったという最初の発言に対し，今睡眠を取るよう勧めている(A)が適切な応答だ。(B)と(C)もフライトに関係する表現ではあるが，いずれも会話がかみ合わないため不適切である。

30.

33

I've lost the combination for my locker.
(A) Why don't you tell Ms. Brown at the front desk about that?
(B) Please pass this document to Ms. Jones.
(C) I'm so sorry, she's on another line now.

ロッカーのパスワードをなくしてしまいました。
(A) 受付のBrownさんにそのことを話してみてはいかがですか。
(B) Jonesさんにこの書類をお渡しください。
(C) すみません，彼女は今，他の電話に出ています。

正解 **(A)**

解説 パスワードをなくして困っているという発言に対して，「Brownさんに相談してみては」と解決策を提案している(A)が正解だ。(B)，(C)は全く関係のない応答であるため，いずれも不正解である。

語句 □combination（錠前など鍵を開けるための）文字や数字の組み合わせ

31.

34

Mr. Rodriguez's speech is supposed to start at ten o'clock, right?
(A) During the teleconference last weekend.
(B) I have no idea, so I'll find out and let you know soon.
(C) We'll hire ten new employees as soon as we can.

Rodriguezさんのスピーチは10時から始まる予定ですよね。
(A) 先週末のテレビ会議の間でした。
(B) 分からないので，調べてすぐにお知らせいたします。
(C) できるだけ早く10人の従業員を新たに採用する予定です。

正解 **(B)**

解説 スピーチの開始時刻を確認する問いかけに対して「分かりません」と答えている(B)が適切な応答だ。be supposed to do「～することになっている」は，今後の予定を伝えるときに頻繁に使う表現である。(A)はwhenに対する応答の一例，(C)は人手不足が話題のときの応答であり，いずれも応答としては不適切である。

32. 35

We have to talk about making some changes to the new personnel system.
(A) It's in this year's general budget report.
(B) I have to convert the local currency into Australian dollars.
(C) Is there something wrong with it?

新しい人事制度にいくつか変更を加えることについて話し合う必要があります。
(A) それは今年の一般予算報告書の中にあります。
(B) 自国の通貨をオーストラリアドルに両替しなければいけません。
(C) 制度には何か問題があるのですか。

正解 **(C)**

解説 人事制度を変更する必要があると提案している発言に対して,「何か問題があるのですか」と答えている(C)が応答として適切だ。(B)の選択肢にあるconvert A into B「AをBに変える」は「(通貨など)を両替する」の意味を押さえておこう。

語句 □convert ～を両替する

33. 36

Our team's weekly profits have decreased by three percent.
(A) I heard the outlet sold it at a discount.
(B) Oh, that's unfortunate.
(C) In three weeks.

わがチームの週間の利益は3%減りました。
(A) 直売店ではそれを割引価格で売っていると聞きました。
(B) ああ,それは残念です。
(C) 3週間後にです。

正解 **(B)**

解説 チームの利益が落ちたことを伝える発言だ。これに対してシンプルに感想を伝えている(B)が適切な応答になる。簡単な返答はうっかり聞き逃しがちなので,各選択肢の音声が流れてくるたびに呼吸を整えて,内容を100%キャッチするように努めよう。

語句 □outlet 直売店,アウトレット

34. 37

You're going to the company picnic, aren't you?
(A) I took her to the picnic last week.
(B) Yes, I'd like to go.
(C) She went on an outing last Saturday.

会社のピクニックに行きますよね。
(A) 先週彼女をピクニックに連れて行きました。
(B) はい,行きたいです。
(C) 彼女は先週の土曜日に行楽に行きました。

正解 **(B)**

解説 これから開催されるピクニックに行くかどうかの確認をしている問いかけで,素直に「行きたい」という意思を伝えている(B)が正解だ。(A)と(C)はいずれもピクニックに関連する内容ではあるが,時制や内容が合わないため不適切な応答である。

語句 □outing 遠足,行楽

35.

38

I've been to Rio de Janeiro three times.
(A) Oh, where was that?
(B) That'll be during your next vacation.
(C) So have I, twice.

私はリオデジャネイロに3回行ったことがあります。
(A) ああ，それはどこでしたか。
(B) それはあなたの次の休暇中です。
(C) 私もです。2回行きました。

正解 **(C)**

解説 経験を報告している発言に対し，So have I（＝I have been to Rio de Janeiro, too）と，自分も同じ経験があると伝えている(C)が応答として適切である。(A)は場所を尋ねる内容，(B)は何かの時期を伝える内容なので，いずれも会話が成立しない。

36.

39

The thesis is about five hundred pages long.
(A) Ms. Hernandez's is much longer, I heard.
(B) Did you report it to the front desk?
(C) She said that the year-end sale will begin next week.

その論文は約500ページあります。
(A) Hernandezさんのはもっとずっと長いと聞いています。
(B) フロントに報告しましたか。
(C) 年末セールが来週から始まると彼女が言っていました。

正解 **(A)**

解説 thesis「論文」のページ数を伝える発言に対して，「Hernandezさんの（論文）はもっとずっと長いと聞いている」と応答している(A)が適切だ。(B)は報告する対象がprofessorなど論文に関係する人であれば正解となり得るが，フロントという対象が不自然である。(C)は発言に全く関係のない内容である。

語句 □thesis 論文

37.

40

The department manager notified you of the sales goals, didn't she?
(A) I read the parking notice last Friday.
(B) We were told about them at the meeting yesterday.
(C) They are all working toward the same goal.

部長が売上目標をあなたにお伝えしましたよね。
(A) 先週の金曜日に駐車に関する通知を読みました。
(B) 昨日の会議でそれについて聞きました。
(C) 彼らは皆，同じ目標に向かって仕事をしています。

正解 **(B)**

解説 相手に情報が伝わっているかどうかを確認する問いかけだ。(B)が素直に「昨日の会議で聞いた」と答えているので，これが正解となる。(A)はnotifiedに似ている音のnoticeを使ったひっかけの選択肢であり，(C)もsales goalsとsame goalを使って解答者を惑わそうとしている選択肢である。

38.

41

The entrance ticket is ten dollars, isn't it?	入場券は10ドルですよね。
(A) We'll offer you better quality products at reasonable prices.	(A) 私たちはお手頃な値段でより良い品質の製品を提供します。
(B) The sign at the box office says it costs twelve.	(B) 入場券売り場の看板に，それは12（ドル）だと書いてあります。
(C) You had to pay it before entering the movie theater.	(C) 映画館に入る前にそれを支払わなくてはなりませんでした。

正解 **(B)**

解説 入場券の値段を確認する，付加疑問文を使った問いかけだ。「box officeにあるsignには12(ドル)と書いてある」と，正しい情報を伝えている(B)が適切な応答になる。(A)はreasonable pricesという値段に関する表現を使っているが，問いかけには関係のない内容なので不正解。(C)は入場時に関する内容ではあるが，値段ではなく手続きについて述べているので不適切な応答である。

語句 □box office 入場券売り場

39.

42

Ms. Ortiz will order office supplies this afternoon.	Ortizさんは今日の午後に事務用品を注文します。
(A) She already did yesterday, I heard.	(A) 彼女はすでに昨日そうしたと聞いています。
(B) She's older than she looks.	(B) 彼女は見かけよりも年を取っています。
(C) That's not so expensive, right?	(C) それほど高くありませんよね。

正解 **(A)**

解説 Ortizさんが事務用品を注文するという情報を伝えている発言だ。「もう昨日（注文）した」と述べている(A)が自然な応答である。(B)はorderに音が似ているolderを使った選択肢，(C)はorderと関連したexpensiveを使った選択肢で，いずれもひっかけの典型である。

40.

43

The organization was established about thirty years ago.	その組織は約30年前に設立されました。
(A) Over the next thirteen months.	(A) 次の13カ月にわたってです。
(B) I'm in very good condition.	(B) 私はとても調子が良いです。
(C) I think so.	(C) そうだと思います。

正解 **(C)**

解説 組織が約30年前に設立されたという事実を伝える発言で，この発言をシンプルに肯定している(C)が正解だ。(A)のoverは「～を越えて」ではなく「～にわたって」という意味であることに注意。また，thirtyとthirteenを混同させようとしている。(B)の内容は発言とは全くかみ合わない。

PART 3

CD 2 44～54

Questions 41 through 43 refer to the following conversation.

設問41-43 は次の会話に関するものである。

45

M: Hello. I just got off a flight from Lisbon but Q41 I realized I left my cap in the cabin. I got it 10 years ago as a birthday present and it's my favorite. Could you please help me get it back?

W: Of course. Q42 May I have your flight number? If you take a seat, I'll call the staff and one of them can bring it to you.

M: Here's my ticket. Well, I still need to get my luggage. Can I come back after I pick it up?

W: Sure. Q43 It'll probably take half an hour or so.

M: こんにちは。たった今, Lisbon発の便から降りたところなのですが，機内に帽子を忘れてきたことに気が付きました。10年前に誕生日プレゼントとしてもらったもので，お気に入りなのです。取り戻せるよう手助けしていただけないでしょうか。

W: もちろんできます。便名を教えていただけますか。お掛けいただければ，スタッフに連絡をして, お客さまのところまで届けさせます。

M: こちらが私の航空券です。ああ，まだ手荷物を引き取らなくてはなりません。引き取ってから戻って来てもいいですか。

W: 承知いたしました。恐らく30分ほどかかるでしょう。

41. What is the problem?

(A) A flight has been canceled.
(B) A hat is missing.
(C) A ticket has been misplaced.
(D) A passenger is late for a party.

何が問題か。

(A) 航空便が欠航となった。
(B) 帽子が見つからない。
(C) 券が置き忘れられた。
(D) 乗客がパーティーに遅れている。

正解 **(B)**

解説 男性の最初の発言のI realized I left my cap in the cabin.を言い換えた(B)が正解だ。capをhatと言い換えているため, 一瞬判断に迷うかもしれない。(A), (C), (D)はflight, ticket, passengerと，いずれも飛行機に関連する表現が含まれてはいるが，会話の内容とは一致しないので不正解である。

語句 □misplace ～を置き忘れる

42. What information does the woman request?
(A) The airline name
(B) The passenger name
(C) The seat number
(D) The flight number

女性が要求している情報は何か。
(A) 航空会社名
(B) 乗客名
(C) 座席番号
(D) 便名

正解 **(D)**

解説 女性が最初の発言で男性に対して May I have your flight number? と質問しているため，(D) が正解となる。下線部の直後にある If you take a seat から (C) を選ばないように気を付けよう。

43. According to the woman, how long will the man need to wait?
(A) Around 5 minutes
(B) Around 10 minutes
(C) Around 30 minutes
(D) Around 60 minutes

女性によると，男性はどのくらいの時間待たなければならないか。
(A) 約5分
(B) 約10分
(C) 約30分
(D) 約60分

正解 **(C)**

解説 女性の2回目の発言に It'll probably take half an hour or so. とあるため，男性が帽子を受け取るまでにかかる時間は約30分であることが分かる。half an hour を 30 minutes と言い換えた (C) が正解だ。時間関連の表現は言い換えが多いので，頻出表現を一つ一つしっかりと押さえていく必要がある。half past ten「10時30分」，quarter to five「4時45分」なども覚えておこう。

Questions 44 through 46 refer to the following conversation.
設問 44-46 は次の会話に関するものである。

46

W1: Hello, Ms. Short. This is Lisa Green calling from Tyler Real Estate Agent. An apartment on Augustus Lane just became available for rent. It's in the same building as the one we went to look at on Saturday. Although it's a little smaller than the one we saw, it's cheaper and it has more windows so you get plenty of sunlight. I hope you received the details I faxed you earlier.

W2: Yes, I'm very interested. Q44 I liked the apartment we saw last week but unlike this one it was too expensive for me. Shall I come to your office to sign the application?

W1: Well, I'm showing a property in your neighborhood to some clients this morning, Q45 so I can stop by afterward with the papers.

W2: That's great. Q46 By the way, I just want to make sure that the apartment allows cats, as I have two tabbies.

W1: もしもし，Shortさん。Tyler不動産のLisa Greenです。たった今，Augustus Lane沿いのアパートの部屋が借りられる状態になりました。私たちが土曜日に見に行った部屋と同じ建物内です。見た部屋より少し狭いですが，家賃はもっと安く，窓が多いので日当たりがいいです。先ほどファクスでお送りした詳細が届いているといいのですが。

W2: はい，とても興味があります。先週見た部屋は気に入っていたのですが，今回の部屋と違って，私には家賃が高過ぎました。申込書にサインするために，そちらのオフィスに伺いましょうか。

W1: そうですね，午前中はShortさんの近所の物件を何人かのお客さまに案内する予定ですので，後で書類を持ってそちらに立ち寄ることができます。

W2: それはよかったわ。ところで，そのアパートでは猫を飼うことが認められていることをちょっと確認したいのですが。虎猫を2匹飼っていますので。

語句 □afterward 後で，後ほど　□tabby 虎猫，ぶち猫

44. What is the advantage of the recently available apartment?
(A) It is in a quiet neighborhood.
(B) It has many lighting fixtures.
(C) It is within Ms. Short's budget.
(D) It has lots of space.

最近空いた部屋の利点は何か。
(A) 閑静な地域にある。
(B) 照明器具がたくさんある。
(C) Shortさんの予算の範囲内である。
(D) スペースが広い。

正解 **(C)**

解説 アパートの部屋の利点に関する情報を待ち構えながら会話を聞く。1人目の女性が最初の発言で家賃が安いことや日当たりに触れているが，それに該当する選択肢はないのでそのまま聞き続ける。2人目の女性がI liked the apartment we saw last week but unlike this one it was too expensive for me.と言っており，先週見た部屋を気に入っていたが，今回話題にしている部屋と違って家賃が高かったことが分かる。ここから，今回話題になっているアパートは予算内だと推測できるので，(C)が正解だ。

語句 □lighting fixture 照明器具

45. What does Lisa offer?
(A) To fax an application form
(B) To take Ms. Short for a viewing
(C) To stop by Ms. Short's home
(D) To reserve the property on Augustus Lane

Lisaは何を申し出ているか。
(A) 申込書をファクスで送信する
(B) Shortさんを下見に連れて行く
(C) Shortさんの自宅に立ち寄る
(D) Augustus Lane沿いの物件を予約する

正解 **(C)**

解説 最初に登場した女性がLisaである。2回目の発言でso I can stop by afterward with the papers.と述べている。stop byは「立ち寄る」という意味なので，申込書を持って後ほど立ち寄るということ。正解は(C)だ。他の選択肢の内容はいずれもこの状況で話題になりそうなものばかりだが，会話の内容を理解していれば惑わされないはずだ。

語句 □viewing 調査，検分，見ること

46. What does Ms. Short want to confirm?
(A) If she can play the piano
(B) If she can have two vehicles
(C) If she can have pets
(D) If she can renovate

Shortさんは何を確かめたがっているか。
(A) ピアノを弾けるか
(B) 乗り物を2台持てるか
(C) ペットを飼えるか
(D) 改修できるか

正解 **(C)**

解説 最初に登場する女性がHello, Ms. Short.と呼びかけているため，Ms. Shortは2人目の女性のことだと分かる。同性同士による会話では，どちらが誰なのかをきちんと把握するように努める必要がある。Shortさんは2回目の発言でBy the way, I just want to make sure that the apartment allows cats, as I have two tabbies.と述べているため，(C)が正解だ。

Questions 47 through 49 refer to the following conversation.

設問 47-49 は次の会話に関するものである。 47

M: Excuse me, do you happen to know where the parking lot is? It's my first time here. I wanted to take a good look around but I just remembered I'm supposed to be at the Togo Mall opening ceremony at five.	M: すみませんが，駐車場がどこにあるかご存じないですか。ここは初めてなんです。じっくりと見て回りたかったのですが，5時にTogoモールのオープニングセレモニーに行かなければならないことをたった今思い出したのです。
W: That's too bad. Q47 To get to the parking lot, take a left there by the museum gift shop, and then go through the African mammals' section until you get to the elevator. It's two floors down. By the way, if you're heading to the new mall in a hurry, Q48 I would avoid George Avenue. They are repaving the street today.	W: それは残念ですね。駐車場に行くには，博物館のギフトショップのそばを左に曲がり，次にアフリカの哺乳類のセクションを通り抜けると，エレベーターに着きます。駐車場はエレベーターで2つ下の階です。ところで，新しいモールに急いで向かうのであれば，私ならGeorge Avenueを避けますよ。今日は通りの再舗装が行われていますので。
M: I'll remember that, thanks. Well, Q49 I better go and get my things from the coat check now.	M: 覚えておきます，ありがとうございます。さて，そろそろ手荷物預かり所に行って，預けていたものを返してもらうようにします。

語句　□mammal 哺乳類　□repave ～を再舗装する　□coat check 手荷物預かり所

47. Where most likely are the speakers?
(A) At a street corner
(B) In a shopping mall
(C) In a museum
(D) In a parking lot

2人はどこにいると考えられるか。
(A) 街角
(B) ショッピングモール
(C) 博物館
(D) 駐車場

正解　**(C)**

解説　女性が最初の発言でTo get to the parking lot, take a left there by the museum gift shop, and then go through the African mammals' section と言っているため，博物館での会話だということが推測できる。正解は(C)だ。駐車場への行き方についての会話であることをきちんと理解していれば，(D)を選んでしまうことはないだろう。

48. What is happening on George Avenue?
(A) A store opening
(B) A road resurfacing
(C) A street performance
(D) A building construction

George Avenueでは何が行われているか。
(A) 店のオープン
(B) 道路の再舗装
(C) 路上パフォーマンス
(D) 建物の建設

正解 **(B)**

解説 固有名詞であるGeorge Avenueの登場を待ち構えながら会話を聞こう。女性が発言の後半でI would avoid George Avenue. They are repaving the street today.と述べているため，(B)が正解だ。repave「～を再舗装する」がresurfaceに置き換えられているので一瞬迷うかもしれないが，resurfaceという単語を知らなくてもre-「再び」+surface「表面」から容易に想像することができるだろう。

語句 □resurface ～を再舗装する，再浮上する，再び現れる

49. What will the man probably do next?
(A) Give a speech
(B) Return a car key
(C) Collect his belongings
(D) Pick out a gift

男性は次に何をすると思われるか。
(A) 演説を行う
(B) 車の鍵を返す
(C) 所持品を取りに行く
(D) ギフトを選ぶ

正解 **(C)**

解説 do nextの問題はPart 3 & 4では頻出である。このタイプの問題の正解の根拠はほとんどの場合，会話の後半に登場する。この会話のすぐ後に何が行われるのかをしっかりとイメージしよう。この問題では男性が2回目の発言でI better go and get my things from the coat check now.と述べているため，get my thingsをcollect his belongingsと言い換えた(C)が正解だ。

語句 □belongings 所持品

Questions 50 through 52 refer to the following conversation.

設問 50-52 は次の会話に関するものである。

48

M: This is Lionel Donovan Q50 from Paradise Grand Resort. I'd like to order a new convection oven for our kitchen, please. The product number is WA789S.	M: Paradise Grand ResortのLionel Donovanと申します。キッチン用に新しい対流式オーブンを注文したいのですが。製品番号はWA789Sです。
W: Certainly, Mr. Donovan. Oh, but Tom, Q51 our installation specialist, is working for another client until Thursday. Is it alright if he comes to install the product on Friday?	W: かしこまりました, Donovanさん。ああ, でも専門の取り付けスタッフであるTomが木曜日まで他のお客さまのための作業をしているのです。金曜日にTomが製品の取り付けに伺うということでもよろしいでしょうか。
M: Can't one of our staff install it? It seems pretty straightforward.	M: うちのスタッフでは取り付けできないのでしょうか。かなり簡単に見えるのですが。
W: We strongly recommend that our customers do not attempt to install the equipment themselves. Q52 It can seriously damage the product.	W: 当社では, お客さまご自身での製品の取り付けはされませんよう強くお勧めしております。製品がひどく損傷を受けてしまう恐れがありますので。

語句 □convection oven 対流式オーブン　□straightforward 簡単な, 分かりやすい

50. Where most likely does the man work?
(A) At an elementary school
(B) At a kitchen appliance store
(C) At a hotel
(D) At a muffin shop

男性はどこで働いていると考えられるか。
(A) 小学校
(B) 台所用品店
(C) ホテル
(D) マフィン屋

正解 **(C)**

解説 男性が最初の発言でfrom Paradise Grand Resort.と言っている。ここから男性の職場はホテルだと考えられるので, 正解は(C)だ。場所を問う問題はPart 3 & 4で頻出である。この問題では1回しか登場しないが, 正解の根拠は会話の中で何回か登場する場合もあるので,「聞き逃した」と思ったときも諦めずに音声に集中しよう。

語句 □kitchen appliance 台所用品

51. What problem does the woman mention?
(A) An item is currently out of stock.
(B) A product is no longer available.
(C) A worker is temporarily occupied.
(D) A client is making unreasonable demands.

女性はどのような問題を述べているか。
(A) 商品が現在，在庫切れである。
(B) 製品がもう入手できない。
(C) 作業員が当面は手いっぱいである。
(D) 顧客が不当な要求をしている。

正解 **(C)**

解説 女性が述べている問題を問われているので，女性の発言に正解の根拠が登場するはずだ。女性は最初の発言で our installation specialist, is working for another client until Thursday. と言っている。これを簡単に言い換えた (C) が正解となる。

語句 □make unreasonable demand 不当な要求をする

52. Why does the woman discourage self-installation?
(A) To protect the equipment
(B) To avoid injuries
(C) To secure employment
(D) To speed up the process

女性はなぜ顧客自身での取り付けをやめさせようとしているか。
(A) 装置を保護するため
(B) けがを防ぐため
(C) 雇用を確保するため
(D) 工程を迅速化するため

正解 **(A)**

解説 質問の主語が女性なので，女性の発言に正解の根拠が登場するはずだ。女性の2回目の発言の最後で It can seriously damage the product. と述べており，この It は自分で装置を取り付けることを意味している。購入者が自分で取り付けると装置が損傷する恐れがあるので，それを防ぐために専門の作業員による取り付けを勧めているのである。正解は (A) だ。

語句 □self-installation 自分で取り付けること

Questions 53 through 55 refer to the following conversation.

設問 53-55 は次の会話に関するものである。 49

W: Jack, Q53 we've been getting complaints from DTC Technologies about their roll towel dispensers. They say they're always empty. Q53 I've considered sending our cleaning crew on a more frequent basis, but I don't think we can afford that.

M: Hmm ... Q54 how about replacing the rolls with larger ones? Most dispensers can handle more than what's indicated on the label.

W: Great idea. Q55 I'll ask our staff which models they use at their office.

M: Good. It's important we respond to complaints quickly to keep our customers happy.

W: Jack，ロールタオル・ディスペンサーのことでDTC Technologiesから苦情を受けているわ。ディスペンサーがいつも空だって言うのよ。清掃員を派遣する頻度をもっと増やすことも考えたんだけど，コスト的にその余裕がないわね。

M: うーん…，もっと大きいロールに取り換えるのはどうだろう。ほとんどのディスペンサーはラベルに表示されているよりも大きいものでも利用できるよ。

W: いい考えね。スタッフにどのモデルをオフィスで使っているか尋ねてみるわ。

M: いいね。お客さまを満足させ続けるには，苦情に素早く対応することが重要だからね。

語句 □roll towel dispenser ロールタオル・ディスペンサー □cleaning crew 清掃員
□on a more frequent basis もっと高い頻度で

53. What type of business do the speakers probably work for?

(A) A cleaning service
(B) A paper mill
(C) A convenience store
(D) A technology company

2人はどのような種類の会社で働いていると思われるか。

(A) 清掃サービス
(B) 製紙工場
(C) コンビニエンスストア
(D) 技術系企業

正解 **(A)**

解説 職業・職種を問う問題は，場所を問う問題と同様，ヒントが会話中に複数回登場することが多い。女性の最初の発言のwe've been getting complaints ... about their roll towel dispensers. とI've considered sending our cleaning crewから，話者たちの会社は清掃サービスを行っているということが分かる。よって正解は(A)だ。roll towel dispenserに関する苦情が話題になっているからといって，(B)を選ばないように。paper mill「製紙工場」という表現は覚えておこう。

54. What does the man suggest?
(A) Replacing the device
(B) Using larger items
(C) Consulting the label
(D) Dispatching staff more often

男性は何を提案しているか。
(A) 装置を取り換える
(B) より大きい製品を使用する
(C) ラベルを参照する
(D) スタッフをより頻繁に派遣する

正解 **(B)**

解説 男性の提案は，彼の最初の発言中に登場する。how about replacing the rolls with larger ones? とあり，ロールを今までの物よりも大きいサイズに交換することを提案している。正解は(B)だ。larger itemsのitemsはrollsのことを指す。device（＝roll towel dispenser）を交換するわけではないため(A)は不正解。

語句 □dispatch ～を派遣する

55. What does the woman say she will do?
(A) Order new supplies
(B) Get in touch with the staff
(C) Train the workers
(D) Check the shipment

女性は何をすると言っているか。
(A) 新しい備品を注文する
(B) スタッフに連絡する
(C) 作業員を教育する
(D) 積み荷を確認する

正解 **(B)**

解説 do nextの問題と同様，will doの問題も，会話の後半に正解の根拠が登場することが多い。女性の2回目の発言にI'll ask our staff which models they use at their office.とある。ask our staffをGet in touch with the staffと言い換えた(B)が正解だ。get in touch with～「～と連絡を取る」という表現を押さえておこう。

Questions 56 through 58 refer to the following conversation.

設問 56-58 は次の会話に関するものである。 50

M: Ambient Travels. How may I help you?
W: Hi. Q56 We're planning a trip for our sales team of around seven people to reward them for reaching a sales goal. What kind of travel packages do you offer?
M: We have several choices depending on your preferences, but one of our most popular packages is the five nights six days at Laguna Beachside Spa. It includes transfers, accommodation, guides, and two evening programs. Q57 For a small additional fee, we can also provide gourmet dinners during your stay.
W: It sounds like just the thing we are looking for. Q58 Could you send a quote by e-mail?

M: Ambient Travelsでございます。どのようなご用件でしょうか。
W: もしもし。営業目標を達成したことをねぎらって，営業チーム7人程度での旅行を計画しています。そちらではどのようなパック旅行がありますか。
M: こちらではお客さまのお好みに応じていくつかのパックをご用意しておりますが，最も人気があるのは，Laguna Beachside Spaの5泊6日のパックです。このパックには，移動，宿泊，ガイドと，イブニング・プログラム2回分が含まれています。わずかな追加費用で，滞在期間を通してグルメディナーを提供させていただくこともできます。
W: まさに私たちが求めているもののようです。見積もりをEメールで送っていただけますか。

56. Why did the woman make the call?
(A) To arrange a day trip
(B) To inquire about transportation costs
(C) To discuss a business partnership
(D) To ask about a group tour

女性はなぜ電話をしたか。
(A) 日帰り旅行を手配するため
(B) 交通費について尋ねるため
(C) 事業提携について話し合うため
(D) 団体旅行について尋ねるため

正解 **(D)**

解説 女性の最初の発言の中にWe're planning a trip for our sales team of around seven people to reward them for reaching a sales goal.とある。営業チーム7人程度で行く旅行をa group tour「団体旅行」と言い換えた(D)が正解だ。(A)が不正解かどうかはその後の会話を聞かなくては判断できないが，男性が勧める5泊6日の旅行に対して女性がIt sounds like just the thing we are looking for.と答えていることから，日帰り旅行を希望しているのではないと分かる。

語句 □business partnership 事業提携

57. What can customers receive at an additional cost?
(A) An extended stay
(B) Late check-out option
(C) Nightly meals
(D) Tour guide service

顧客は追加費用で何を受けることができるか。
(A) 滞在の延長
(B) レイトチェックアウトのオプション
(C) 毎晩の食事
(D) 観光ガイドのサービス

正解 **(C)**

解説 additional costに関する発言を待ち構えて会話を聞く。男性の2回目の発言にFor a small additional fee, we can also provide gourmet dinners during your stay.とある。追加費用で滞在中にgourmet dinnersが提供されるが，dinnersと複数形になっていることがポイント。dinnerが複数回あることを言い換えた(C)のNightly mealsが正解だ。nightlyはここでは「毎晩の」という形容詞で，副詞だと「毎晩」という意味になる。

語句 □extended stay 滞在の延長

58. What does the woman ask for?
(A) An e-mail address
(B) A company brochure
(C) A cost estimate
(D) A travel itinerary

女性は何を求めているか。
(A) Eメールアドレス
(B) 会社のパンフレット
(C) 費用の見積もり
(D) 旅行日程

正解 **(C)**

解説 女性の発言中に，相手に求めるものが出てくるのを待ち構えて会話を聞く。女性の2回目の発言にCould you send a quote by e-mail?とあるため，女性は見積もりをEメールで送ってほしいと考えているということが分かる。正解は(C)だ。quoteを選択肢ではestimateと言い換えており，どちらもTOEICでは頻出の表現である。

Questions 59 through 61 refer to the following conversation.

設問 59-61 は次の会話に関するものである。 51

W: Say, Miles, I heard you went for an interview last week. How did it go?

M: Not so well, I guess. Q59 There were dozens of other candidates, and I haven't heard anything from them since.

W: Well, you are qualified enough, so I wouldn't be so pessimistic if I were you. Why don't you give them a follow-up call? Q60 It will show them how much you would like to get the job and that's always a good thing.

M: I really don't think there's much point. However, Q61 I sent my résumé to several other companies, so let's hope for the best.

W: ねえ，Miles，先週面接を受けに行ったって聞いたけど，どうだったの？

M: あまり良くないんじゃないかな。他にも面接を受けに来ている人がたくさんいたし，全く音沙汰がないんだ。

W: うーん，あなたは十分に能力があるから，もし私があなただったら，そんなに悲観的にならないわ。経過確認の電話をしてみたらどうかしら。そうすればどれほどその仕事に就きたいかが伝わるし，絶対にいいと思うわ。

M: 意味があるとは全く思えないな。でも，他の数社にも履歴書を送ったから，最善の結果を期待することにしよう。

語句 □dozens of ～ 数十の～，多数の～ □qualified 能力のある，資格要件を満たした
□pessimistic 悲観的な □follow-up call 経過確認の電話
□there's much point 意味がある

59. Why is the man pessimistic?

(A) He doesn't have enough qualifications.
(B) He thinks he won't get the job.
(C) He failed an important exam.
(D) He received a bad evaluation.

男性はなぜ悲観的なのか。

(A) 十分な能力がないから。
(B) 仕事に就くことができないと思っているから。
(C) 重要な試験に落ちたから。
(D) 悪い評価を受けたから。

正解 **(B)**

解説 男性の心情に関する問題だ。心情を問う問題は，頻度は高くはないが時々出題される。男性の最初の発言にThere were dozens of other candidates, and I haven't heard anything from them since.とあり，男性は面接に行った会社から全然連絡が来ないことを悲観している。これを言い換えた(B)が正解だ。dozenは「12個，12の」という意味だが，dozens of ～で「数十の～，多数の～」という意味になる。

60. What does the woman say about a follow-up call?
(A) It gives a good impression.
(B) It is better than sending an e-mail.
(C) It should be made as soon as possible.
(D) It demonstrates his responsibility.

女性は経過確認の電話をかけることについて何と言っているか。
(A) 好印象を与える。
(B) Eメールを送るよりもよい。
(C) できるだけ早くした方がよい。
(D) 彼の責任を示すことになる。

正解 **(A)**

解説 2回目の発言で, 女性は経過確認の電話をかけるよう提案した後, It will show them how much you would like to get the job and that's always a good thing. と言っていて,「絶対にいいと思う」と肯定的に考えている。これを言い換えた(A)のIt gives a good impression. が正解だ。

61. What does the man say he has done?
(A) Phoned the employer
(B) Sent a recommendation letter
(C) Applied to other places
(D) Consulted a professional

男性は何をしたと言っているか。
(A) 雇用者に電話をした
(B) 推薦状を送った
(C) 他の複数の場所に応募した
(D) 専門家に相談した

正解 **(C)**

解説 男性は2回目の発言でI sent my résumé to several other companiesと述べている。履歴書をいくつかの会社に送ったとのことなので, (C)が正解となる。(B), (D)に関しては, もっともらしい内容ではあるが, 会話中では全く言及されていない。

Questions 62 through 64 refer to the following conversation.

設問 62-64 は次の会話に関するものである。

52

M1: Hi. This is Mark Cooper. Q63 We have a BEX-2000 copy machine at our office. Q62 It had been working fine for years until yesterday when it stopped working properly. When we put paper into the feed, it comes out crumpled and then the whole machine shuts off.	M1: もしもし。Mark Cooperと申します。事務室でBEX-2000コピー機を使っております。何年も順調に作動していたのですが，昨日正常に作動しなくなってしまいました。紙を用紙送りに入れると，紙がクシャクシャになって出てきて，コピー機全体が停止してしまいます。
M2: I see. Did you use any kind of special paper other than standard copier paper when this happened?	M2: そうでしたか。そのようなことが起きたときは，標準のコピー用紙ではない何らかの特殊な紙を使いましたか。
M1: We only buy our copier paper from BEX stores. Q63 We need to print out hundreds of course guidelines to hand out to our students tomorrow. Can you fix it as soon as possible?	M1: うちではコピー用紙はBEXの店舗からしか買っていません。明日，生徒たちに配布するために，講義要領を数百部印刷する必要があります。できるだけ早く修理していただけないでしょうか。
M2: It sounds like a case of a worn-out paper feed or exit rollers. Q64 We'll send one of our technicians this afternoon and he can change them for you.	M2: 用紙送りか排紙ローラーがすり減っている事例のようですね。今日の午後に技術者を1人派遣して，それらを交換できるようにしましょう。

語句　□feed 供給装置　□crumpled しわくちゃの　□hand out ～ ～を配る
□worn-out すり減った　□exit roller 排紙ローラー

62. What is the problem?
(A) A coffee machine is out of order.
(B) A wrong type of material has been used.
(C) A device is not working properly.
(D) A piece of equipment does not turn off.

問題は何か。
(A) コーヒーメーカーが故障している。
(B) 間違った種類の材料が使用されている。
(C) 装置が適切に作動していない。
(D) 機器の電源が切れない。

正解　**(C)**

解説　話者の1人が直面している問題が何かを問うのは，定番の出題パターンだ。最初に登場した男性がIt had been working fine for years until yesterday when it stopped working properly.と言っている。ずっと順調に動いていたコピー機が，昨日正常に作動しなくなったというのが今回起きた問題だ。よって正解は(C)である。

63. Where most likely does Mark work?
(A) At an electronics store
(B) At a school office
(C) At a school cafeteria
(D) At a stationery company

Markはどこで働いていると考えられるか。
(A) 電器店
(B) 学校の事務室
(C) 学生食堂
(D) 文房具メーカー

正解 **(B)**

解説 最初に出てくる男性がMarkである。We have a BEX-2000 copy machine at our office. と述べており, また2回目の発言でWe need to print out hundreds of course guidelines to hand out to our students tomorrow. と言っているため, 正解は(B)だ。

語句 □stationery company 文房具メーカー

64. What will the technician most likely do?
(A) Visit the office tomorrow
(B) Bring another kind of paper
(C) Replace old components
(D) Order a new unit

技術者は何をすると考えられるか。
(A) 明日, 事務室を訪れる
(B) 別の種類の紙を持って来る
(C) 古い部品を交換する
(D) 新しい装置を注文する

正解 **(C)**

解説 technicianがすることに関する情報を待ち構えて会話を聞く。2人目の男性の2回目の発言にWe'll send one of our technicians this afternoon and he can change them for you. とあるため, technicianはthem (= paper feed or exit rollers) を交換しに行くということが分かる。よって正解は(C)だ。(A)はtomorrowではなくtodayであれば正解となる。

語句 □component 部品

Questions 65 through 67 refer to the following conversation.

設問 65-67 は次の会話に関するものである。

53

W: Sam, Q65 here's the form you need to fill out before you take your vacation leave next month.

M: Thanks, Lena. Hey, what's wrong? You look tired. Is the department still understaffed?

W: Yes. Q66 We have too much work and not enough workers. But I heard that next year we will hire an outside company to take care of all payroll associated tasks, so it should get better.

M: Oh yes, Q67 I remember there was an announcement about that in the company newsletter. People say that it's common for companies to do that these days.

W: Sam，これが来月休暇を取る前に記入しなければならない用紙よ。

M: ありがとう，Lena。おい，どうしたんだい。疲れているようだね。部署はまだ人員不足なのかな？

W: そうなのよ。仕事が多過ぎるのに，スタッフが足りないの。でも，来年は外部の会社を雇って給与関連の業務を全て担当してもらうと聞いているので，改善されるはずよ。

M: うん，そうだね。それについては社内報に告知が載っていたのを覚えている。最近は企業がそうするのは一般的なんだってね。

語句 □payroll associated task 給与関連の業務

65. What will probably happen next month?

(A) An employee will be transferred.

(B) A staff member will go on holiday.

(C) Some duties will be outsourced.

(D) Some departments will be merged.

来月には何が起こると思われるか。

(A) 従業員が異動する。

(B) スタッフが休暇で出掛ける。

(C) いくつかの業務が外部に委託される。

(D) いくつかの部署が合併される。

正解 **(B)**

解説 next monthに関する情報を待ち構えて音声を聞く。冒頭で女性がhere's the form you need to fill out before you take your vacation leave next month.と言っている。休暇を取るのは次に登場する，同じ会社に勤めている男性だ。take your vacation leaveをgo on holidayと言い換えている(B)が正解。会話の後半で(C)に当たる内容が出てくるが，これは来月ではなく来年のことである。

語句 □outsource ～を外注する

66. What does the woman say about her department?
(A) It is heavily cluttered.
(B) It lacks sufficient manpower.
(C) It will get some new recruits.
(D) It will move to another location.

女性は自分の部署について何と言っているか。
(A) ひどく散らかっている。
(B) 人手が十分に足りていない。
(C) 新人が入る予定である。
(D) 他の場所に移転する予定である。

正解 **(B)**

解説 女性の発言に正解の根拠が登場するはずだと予測し，待ち構える。女性は2回目の発言で部署についてWe have too much work and not enough workers.と言っている。仕事が多過ぎるのに，働き手が足りていないのだ。これを簡潔に言い換えた(B)が正解である。(A)の選択肢にあるcluttered「散らかった」は，時々登場する重要な表現なので押さえておこう。

語句 □cluttered 散らかった　□manpower 人手　□recruit 新メンバー，新入社員

67. How did the man know payroll associated tasks would be outsourced?
(A) He heard rumors about it.
(B) He saw a notice on the bulletin board.
(C) He read about it in a publication.
(D) He received a memo from his boss.

男性は給与関連の業務が外注されることをどのようにして知ったか。
(A) うわさを聞いた。
(B) 掲示板で告知を見た。
(C) 刊行物で読んだ。
(D) 上司から社内文書をもらった。

正解 **(C)**

解説 男性は2回目の発言でI remember there was an announcement about that in the company newsletter.と述べている。このthatは直前の女性の発言中にあるnext year we will hire an outside company to take care of all payroll associated tasksのことを指している。company newsletterをpublicationと言い換えている(C)が正解だ。

Questions 68 through 70 refer to the following conversation.

設問68-70は次の会話に関するものである。 54

M: Ms. Young, I need to talk to you about the stock. When I went to get the building parts from the stockroom, Q68 I noticed that there's a discrepancy between the quantity on the bin card and the actual number of stored parts. What would you like me to do?

W: Q69 Why don't you check the inventory record in the computer? That might sort it out.

M: But I don't have access to the file. Can you type in the code? Thanks. Well ... according to this record, we should have 2,000 parts. But we only have 150 in the stockroom.

W: Oh, sorry, I completely forgot. Q70 Those parts were pulled out of stock three weeks ago. I'll correct it right away.

M: Youngさん，在庫についてお話ししなければならないことがあります。倉庫に建築用の部品を取りに行ったときに，在庫表上の数量と実際に保管されている部品の数が一致していないことに気付いたのです。どうすればいいですか。

W: コンピューターで在庫記録を確認してみたらどうかしら。それで解決するかもしれないわ。

M: でも私にはファイルへのアクセス権がないのです。コードを入力していただけないでしょうか。ありがとうございます。ええと…，記録によると，部品は2,000個あるはずです。でも倉庫には150個しかありません。

W: あら，ごめんなさい。完全に忘れていたわ。その部品は3週間前に在庫から取り出したのよ。すぐに修正するわ。

語句 □stockroom 倉庫 □discrepancy 食い違い □bin card 在庫表 □inventory record 在庫記録 □sort ～ out ～を解決する □pull out ～ ～を取り出す

68. What is the man concerned about?

(A) A misprint on an invoice
(B) An error on an inventory record
(C) A mistake in the amount of labels
(D) An inaccuracy on an order form

男性は何を心配しているか。

(A) 送り状の間違い
(B) 在庫記録の間違い
(C) ラベルの量の間違い
(D) 注文書の間違い

正解 **(B)**

解説 男性は最初の発言でI noticed that there's a discrepancy between the quantity on the bin card and the actual number of stored parts. と述べている。これは，実際の部品の数と在庫表の数字に食い違いがあるということを表しているので，それを端的に言い換えた(B)が正解だ。discrepancy「食い違い」は確実に覚えておきたい単語だ。

語句 □inaccuracy 誤り

69. What does the woman suggest the man do? 女性は男性に何をするように提案しているか。

(A) Consult another source　(A) 他の情報源を参照する
(B) Question his colleagues　(B) 同僚に質問する
(C) Double-check the stockroom　(C) 倉庫を再確認する
(D) Correct the inventory　(D) 在庫一覧表を修正する

正解 **(A)**

解説 女性が何を提案しているのかに意識を向けつつ会話を聞く。女性は最初の発言でWhy don't you check the inventory record in the computer? と言っているため，コンピューターで在庫記録を確認するようアドバイスをしていることが分かる。これを抽象的に言い換えている(A)が正解だ。

70. What will the woman do next? 女性は次に何をすると思われるか。

(A) Enter a password　(A) パスワードを入力する
(B) Give authorization　(B) 権限を与える
(C) Return some items　(C) いくつかの物品を戻す
(D) Update the records　(D) 記録を更新する

正解 **(D)**

解説 do nextの問題なので，会話の後半，女性の発言を待ち構えよう。女性の2回目の発言にThose parts were pulled out of stock three weeks ago. I'll correct it right away. とある。itは前に登場しているrecordのことを指す。在庫数をきちんと入力していなかったため，その数字を訂正すると言っているのだ。これを言い換えた(D)が正解となる。

語句 □authorization 権限

Questions 71 through 73 refer to the following advertisement.
設問 71-73 は次の宣伝に関するものである。 56

Q71 PhotoStamps.com brings to you this season the chance to create your own original stamps! Create stamps with family photos to send to loved ones, or use your company logo to enhance correspondence with your customers. What's more, we provide a 10 percent discount for first time purchases. Each sheet contains 20 stamps of the same design, and Q72 the minimum order for each design is 2 sheets. Q73 Visit our Web site at www.photostamps.com and follow the easy instructions to create your own unique stamps.

PhotoStamps.comでは，この季節，あなた自身のオリジナル切手を作ることができます！ ご家族の写真入りの切手を作って最愛の人たちに送ってみてください。あるいは，会社のロゴを使って顧客との手紙のやりとりをより良いものにしてください。さらに，初回の購入時は1割引きとなります。各シートには同じデザインの切手が20枚入っていて，各デザインは最低2シートから注文できます。弊社ウェブサイト www.photostamps.com をご覧いただき，簡単な説明に従ってあなたらしい独自の切手を作ってみてください。

語句 □loved one 最愛の人 □enhance ～を高める，さらに良くする
□correspondence with ～ ～とのやりとり

71. What is being advertised?
(A) Custom-made bracelets
(B) Professional photo frames
(C) Customized stamps
(D) Birthday cards

何が宣伝されているか。
(A) 特別注文のブレスレット
(B) 本格的なフォトフレーム
(C) 注文に応じて作られた切手
(D) 誕生日カード

正解 **(C)**

解説 設問からトークの内容は何かの宣伝だということが分かる。冒頭でPhotoStamps.com brings to you this season the chance to create your own original stamps!とあるため，この会社はオリジナルの切手を制作しているということが分かる。これをcustomizedで言い換えた(C)が正解だ。

語句 □custom-made 特別注文の □bracelet ブレスレット

72. What is the minimum order?
(A) 2 sheets
(B) 10 sheets
(C) 20 sheets
(D) 40 sheets

最低発注量はどれくらいか。
(A) 2シート
(B) 10シート
(C) 20シート
(D) 40シート

正解 **(A)**

解説 minimum orderを意識に留めておきつつ音声を待ち構える。トークの後半でthe minimum order for each design is 2 sheets.と述べられているため，正解は(A)だ。この直前でEach sheet contains 20 stamps of the same designと言っているが，これは1シート当たりの切手の枚数である。惑わされて(C)を選ばないように。

73. What is available on the Web site?
(A) Sample designs
(B) Discount vouchers
(C) How-to guidelines
(D) Store directions

ウェブサイトでは何が入手できるか。
(A) 見本デザイン
(B) 割引券
(C) やり方の指針
(D) 店までの道順

正解 **(C)**

解説 Web siteに関する情報を待ち構えながらトークを聞く。トーク終盤のVisit our Web site at www.photostamps.com and follow the easy instructions to create your own unique stamps. から，ウェブサイトでは自分独自の切手の「作り方」を知ることができると分かる。これを簡潔に言い換えた(C)が正解である。

語句 □how-to 手引きの，手引書

Questions 74 through 76 refer to the following telephone message.

設問74-76 は次の電話のメッセージに関するものである。 57

Hi. This is Denise Erasmo from Human Resources with a message for Erik Cole. Erik, Q74 we haven't received your self-evaluation form yet, and it was due on Wednesday. I know Q75 you have your hands full preparing for the conference in Singapore, but can you send it to us before you leave for the conference next week? The formal performance review is coming up next month and Q76 headquarters has requested that all forms be sent to them before then. Thanks.	もしもし。こちらは人事部のDenise Erasmoです。Erik Coleに伝言があります。Erik，あなたの自己評価シートをまだ受け取っていません。その締め切りは水曜日でした。シンガポールでの会議の準備で手いっぱいなのは分かりますが，来週会議に出発する前に送ってくれませんか。正式な勤務評価が来月に迫っていて，それまでにシートを全て送るようにと本社から要求されているのです。よろしくお願いします。

語句 □self-evaluation form 自己評価シート □formal 正式な
□performance review 勤務評価

74. Why is the speaker calling the man?
(A) He failed to meet a deadline.
(B) He missed a meeting.
(C) He performed poorly on a test.
(D) He has not returned a message.

話し手はなぜ男性に電話をしているか。
(A) 締め切りを守れなかったから。
(B) 会議に欠席したから。
(C) 試験の成績が悪かったから。
(D) メッセージを返さなかったから。

正解 **(A)**

解説 設問のthe manは，この留守番電話を聞く男性のことである。あいさつの直後に，we haven't received your self-evaluation form yet, and it was due on Wednesday.と言っている。受け手の男性は，自己評価シートをどうやらまだ提出していないらしいということが分かるため，これを遠回しに言い換えた(A)が正解となる。留守番電話のメッセージは，冒頭部を特に注意して聞き逃さないようにすること。

75. What will the man most likely do next week?
(A) Take a business trip
(B) Present a report
(C) Have an interview
(D) Go on vacation

男性は来週何をすると考えられるか。
(A) 出張する
(B) 報告書を提出する
(C) 面接を受ける
(D) 休暇を取る

正解 **(A)**

解説 next weekが重要なキーワードだと意識してトークを聞こう。トークの中盤でyou have your hands full preparing for the conference in Singapore, but can you send it to us before you leave for the conference next week?と言っているため，受け手の男性はSingaporeでの会議に出席することと，その会議が来週開催されることが分かる。正解は(A)だ。

76. According to the woman, what will happen to the forms?

(A) They will be reviewed by the board of directors.
(B) They will be sent to headquarters.
(C) They will be used at a performance.
(D) They will be handed to Erik Cole.

女性によると，シートはどうなるか。

(A) 役員会で検討される。
(B) 本社に送られる。
(C) 公演の際に使用される。
(D) Erik Coleに手渡される。

正解 **(B)**

解説 formsに関する情報を待ち構えながらトークを聞く。トークの最後にheadquarters has requested that all forms be sent to themとあるため，本社が全ての用紙を送ってほしいと要求していることが分かる。headquartersがそのまま登場している(B)が正解だ。

Questions 77 through 79 refer to the following advertisement.
設問 77-79 は次の宣伝に関するものである。 58

For more than 25 years, Q77 Whitecare Laundry Service has provided Ottawa's hospitality industries with top quality services. To make life easier for our clients, Q78 we provide flexible collection and delivery hours. After the linens are collected they go through Q77 a variety of cleaning processes which ensure the highest level of disinfection without damaging the textiles. Q79 We use energy efficient machinery with low water usage and near zero emissions to protect the environment around us. You can depend on Q77 Whitecare Laundry Service for all your linen needs. Call 555-1892 to request our professional services or to learn more about us.

Whitecare Laundry Serviceは25年以上にわたって，オタワの接客業界に最高品質のサービスを提供してまいりました。お客さまの利便性を考慮し，融通の利いた集配時間を設定しております。リネンが回収された後は，布地を痛めない最高レベルの消毒を保証する，クリーニングのさまざまな工程を通過することになります。また，水の使用量を抑えて排ガスがゼロに近い，エネルギー効率の良い機械を使うことで，周囲の環境を保護しています。リネンのどのようなご要望に関しても，Whitecare Laundry Serviceにお任せください。専門的なサービスのご依頼やお問い合わせについては，555-1892までお電話ください。

語句 □hospitality industry 接客業界 □collection and delivery hours 集配時間
□linen リネン，敷布 □disinfection 消毒 □textile 布地
□energy efficient エネルギー効率の良い □emissions 排ガス

77. What type of business is being advertised?
(A) A hotel chain
(B) A textile corporation
(C) A food delivery service
(D) A laundry company

どのような種類の会社が宣伝されているか。
(A) ホテルチェーン
(B) 繊維会社
(C) 食事の配達サービス
(D) クリーニング業者

正解 **(D)**

解説 トークの冒頭でWhitecare Laundry Serviceと言っている。これだけでも正解を選ぶことはできるが，万が一これを聞き逃したとしても，トークの中盤でa variety of cleaning processes，終盤でも，再度Whitecare Laundry Serviceと言っているため，リカバリーの利く問題だ。正解は(D)。

語句 □textile corporation 繊維会社

78. According to the speaker, what is flexible?
(A) Payment method
(B) Delivery time
(C) Service costs
(D) Pick-up location

話し手によると，何について融通が利くか。
(A) 支払い方法
(B) 配達時間
(C) サービス費用
(D) 受け取り場所

正解 **(B)**

解説 意識すべきキーワードは flexible だ。トークの前半で we provide flexible collection and delivery hours. と言っている。融通の利く集配時間を設定しているということから，正解は (B) の Delivery time だ。collection and delivery hours で「集配時間」という意味になる。

79. What does the speaker suggest about the cleaning process?
(A) It only takes a short time.
(B) It is fully automated.
(C) It involves using cutting-edge computers.
(D) It is environmentally friendly.

話し手はクリーニングの工程についてどんなことを示唆しているか。
(A) 短い時間しかかからない。
(B) 完全に自動化されている。
(C) 最先端のコンピューターの使用を伴う。
(D) 環境に配慮している。

正解 **(D)**

解説 トークの終盤で We use energy efficient machinery with low water usage and near zero emissions to protect the environment around us. と述べている。作業工程において，周囲の環境の保護を優先しているということが分かるため，これを簡潔に言い換えた (D) が正解となる。energy efficient machinery「エネルギー効率の良い機械」を使ってはいるが，(C) の cutting-edge computers の使用に関しては言及がない。

語句 □cutting-edge 最先端の　□environmentally friendly 環境に優しい

Questions 80 through 82 refer to the following talk.
設問80-82は次の話に関するものである。 59

Good morning everyone, and welcome to the Yamabuki Corporation factory tour. Here at the Redville Plant, a variety of manufacturing processes are performed. Q80 During the 2-hour tour, Q81 you will see frames, fenders and fuel tanks assembled to create brand-new Yamabuki motorcycles. Get excited, because in the showroom you will have a chance to sit on our current production motorcycles. At the end of the tour, you can visit the factory gift shop to purchase souvenirs. Q82 We will start by showing a 15-minute introductory video, and then continue on to the factory floor.

皆さん，おはようございます。Yamabuki社の工場見学ツアーへようこそ。このRedville工場では，さまざまな製造工程が行われています。2時間のツアーの間に，フレーム，フェンダー，燃料タンクが組み立てられ，新品のYamabuki製オートバイが製造される様子がご覧いただけます。ショールームでは現行製品のオートバイにお乗りになるチャンスもありますので，ご期待ください。ツアーの終わりには，お土産のご購入に工場のギフトショップへお立ち寄りになれます。まずは15分間の紹介ビデオの上映から開始し，その後，引き続き作業場へと向かいます。

語句 □current 現行の，現在の □introductory 紹介の，導入の

80. How long does the tour last?
(A) Quarter of an hour
(B) One hour
(C) Two hours
(D) Three hours

ツアーはどのくらいの時間続くか。
(A) 15分間
(B) 1時間
(C) 2時間
(D) 3時間

正解 **(C)**

解説 トークの前半で，この工場見学のツアーに関してDuring the 2-hour tourと言及している。よって正解は(C)だ。(A)のQuarter of an hour「15分間」は，紹介ビデオの上映時間のことである。

81. What is manufactured at the Redville Plant?
(A) Car parts
(B) Airplane engines
(C) Motorcycles
(D) Stereo components

Redville工場では何が製造されているか。
(A) 自動車の部品
(B) 飛行機のエンジン
(C) オートバイ
(D) ステレオの部品

正解 **(C)**

解説 何が製造されているのかを考えながらトークを聞く。前半でyou will see frames, fenders and fuel tanks assembled to create brand-new Yamabuki motorcycles.と述べているので，Redville工場ではオートバイを製造しているということが分かる。正解は(C)だ。

語句 □manufacture ～を製造する

82. What will the listeners probably do next?
(A) Proceed to the factory floor
(B) Visit the gift shop
(C) Watch an introductory video
(D) See a current production

聞き手は次に何をすると思われるか。
(A) 作業場へと進む
(B) ギフトショップを訪れる
(C) 紹介ビデオを鑑賞する
(D) 現行製品を見る

正解 **(C)**

解説 do next の問題なので，トークの終盤に正解の根拠が登場すると予想しつつ音声を聞こう。We will start by showing a 15-minute introductory video と言っているため，最初にビデオの上映が行われるということが分かる。よって正解は (C) だ。その後 continue on to the factory floor となるため，(A) はビデオ上映後に行われる予定を表す。

語句 □proceed 進む

Questions 83 through 85 refer to the following telephone message.

設問83-85は次の電話のメッセージに関するものである。

60

Good afternoon, Mr. Long. This is Peter Hummel from Nick's Truck Rentals. Q83 We received your online reservation, and we're happy to confirm that a cargo van has been reserved for you for September 15 from 10 A.M. The vehicle can be picked up at your nearest Nick's Truck Rental Center, which is on Jardine Avenue. Since you have chosen the same drop-off location option, please return the vehicle to the same Rental Center. Please be warned that if you cancel within 24 hours of pick-up time, Q84 a 40-dollar penalty fee will be assessed. We'd also like to tell you that Q85 we provide printable worksheets which you can use to list articles belonging to your household to make your moving easier, at www.nickstruckrentals.com.

こんにちは，Longさん。こちらはNick's Truck RentalsのPeter Hummelと申します。オンラインでご予約をいただきましたが，9月15日午前10時からカーゴバンの予約が確認できましたのでお知らせいたします。車両はJardine Avenue沿いの最寄りのNick's Truck Rental Centerでお受け取りいただけます。返却場所は同じ所をご希望とのことですので，同Rental Centerにご返却ください。受取時刻の24時間以内にキャンセルされた場合は，40ドルの違約金が課せられますのでご注意ください。また，移転をより快適にするために，ご家庭にある品目をリスト化するのに使用できる印刷可能なワークシートのこともお知らせしたいと思います。こちらはwww.nickstruckrentals.comでご利用になれます。

語句 □cargo van カーゴバン（車の種類） □drop-off location 返却場所，引き渡し場所 □pick-up time 受取時刻 □assess ～を課する □printable 印刷可能な □list ～をリスト化する □article 品目，品物 □household 家庭，世帯

83. What is the purpose of the telephone message?

(A) To make a reservation

(B) To give details about a booking

(C) To change an order

(D) To provide a cost estimate

電話のメッセージの目的は何か。

(A) 予約をする

(B) 予約の詳細を知らせる

(C) 注文を変更する

(D) 費用の見積もりを提示する

正解 **(B)**

解説 電話の用件，つまりトークの目的を問う問題は，Part 4では頻出の問題の1つだ。トークの最初の方にWe received your online reservation, and we're happy to confirm that a cargo van has been reserved for you for September 15 from 10 A.M.とあるため，予約が取れたことを知らせるために電話をかけたことが分かる。その後，レンタル方法やキャンセルなど詳細を説明しているため，正解は(B)だ。(A)は予約すること自体を表しているので混同しないように。

84. How much is the penalty charge?
(A) 10 dollars
(B) 15 dollars
(C) 24 dollars
(D) 40 dollars

違約金はいくらか。
(A) 10ドル
(B) 15ドル
(C) 24ドル
(D) 40ドル

正解 **(D)**

解説 penalty chargeに関する話題を待ち構えながら聞く。メッセージの終盤でa 40-dollar penalty fee will be assessed.と言っているので，正解は(D)だ。assessには「～を評価する，見積もる」という意味の他に「(税金・費用など) を課する」という意味があるということを押さえておきたい。

語句 □penalty charge 違約金

85. What can the listener obtain from the Web site?
(A) A form for making an inventory
(B) A worksheet to calculate the total cost
(C) A timetable to facilitate moving
(D) A copy of the rental agreement

聞き手はウェブサイトから何を入手できるか。
(A) 品目の一覧表を作るための用紙
(B) 総費用を計算するためのワークシート
(C) 移転を楽にする予定表
(D) レンタル契約書のコピー

正解 **(A)**

解説 Web siteに関する部分を待ち構えて確実に聞き取る。話し手は，トークの最後をwe provide printable worksheets which you can use to list articles belonging to your household to make your moving easier, at www.nickstruckrentals.com.と締めくくっている。印刷できるワークシートを提供し，品目のリストを作成することができると述べているため，これを，inventoryを使って言い換えた(A)が正解だ。

語句 □inventory 一覧表，在庫　□facilitate ～を楽にする，促進する

Questions 86 through 88 refer to the following news broadcast.

設問86-88は次のニュース放送に関するものである。 61

And now for business news. More and more Q86 companies are using global mobility programs to effectively utilize their workforce on an international scale. Glomore is a company which helps employers run these programs by offering relocation solutions that fit the companies' policies and budgets. Glomore spokesperson Andrew Chang says Q87 they did see a slowdown in business last year due to the economic crisis, but demands for their services are rising rapidly and it is expected to continue. And he points out that although the primary business centers like Hong Kong, Singapore, New York and London are still popular destinations, Q88 they have been dealing increasingly with relocations to African and Eastern European countries.	ではここで，ビジネスニュースの時間です。ますます多くの企業が，地球規模での移動性プログラムを使って，国際的な規模で労働力を効果的に活用しています。Glomore社は，企業の方針や予算に合った配置転換のソリューションを提供することで，雇用主がこうしたプログラムを実施する手助けをする会社です。Glomore社の広報担当，Andrew Chang氏は，昨年は経済恐慌により社の業績は低迷したが，このサービスに対する需要は急増していて，これからもまだ増え続ける見込みだと述べています。Chang氏はまた，香港，シンガポール，ニューヨーク，ロンドンなどビジネスの主要な中心地は今でも人気のある目的地だが，Glomore社ではアフリカ諸国や東ヨーロッパ諸国への配置転換を扱うことが次第に増えてきていると指摘しています。

語句 □global mobility 地球規模での移動性 □utilize ～を利用する，活用する
□workforce 労働力，全従業員 □slowdown 低迷 □primary 第一の，主要な

86. What is the news broadcast about?
(A) Increased international shipping costs
(B) Global environmental protection programs
(C) New promotional strategies for companies
(D) Relocation of employees to foreign countries

何に関するニュース放送か。
(A) 国際輸送費の価格上昇
(B) 地球規模の環境保護プログラム
(C) 企業向けの新たな販売促進戦略
(D) 従業員の外国への配置転換

正解 **(D)**

解説 Part 4で頻出の，トークの目的・内容に関する問題だ。冒頭でcompanies are using global mobility programs to effectively utilize their workforce on an international scale.と言っているため，正解は(D)だ。global mobility programs「地球規模での移動性プログラム」と聞いても具体的にどのようなことなのかイメージしにくいが，その直後でto effectively utilize their workforce on an international scaleと説明しているので，プログラムの内容のおおよその想像がつくだろう。

87. What does Mr. Chang say about last year?
(A) Demand for Glomore's products increased.
(B) Business was slow for Glomore.
(C) Glomore had to lay off some employees.
(D) Glomore had to close down its overseas office.

Changさんは昨年について何と言っているか。
(A) Glomore社製品への需要が増加した。
(B) Glomore社の業績は低迷していた。
(C) Glomore社は一部の従業員を一時解雇しなければならなかった。
(D) Glomore社は海外支店を閉鎖しなければならなかった。

正解 **(B)**

解説 last yearをキーワードにして，正解の根拠が登場するのを待ち構えよう。中盤でthey did see a slowdown in business last yearとあるため，昨年は会社の業績が低迷したということが理解できる。これを端的に言い換えた(B)が正解となる。

語句 □lay off ～ ～を一時解雇する

88. Which area is Glomore increasingly involved with?
(A) Asia
(B) The United States
(C) Western Europe
(D) Africa

Glomoreが次第に関与してきている地域はどこか。
(A) アジア
(B) アメリカ
(C) 西ヨーロッパ
(D) アフリカ

正解 **(D)**

解説 地域に関連する内容が登場するのを待ち構えよう。ニュースの終盤でthey have been dealing increasingly with relocations to African and Eastern European countries.と言っている。アフリカと東ヨーロッパへの配置転換を扱うようになってきていると述べているので，正解は(D)だ。(C)はWestern Europeなので不正解である。細かい部分も確実に聞き取って100%理解した上で解答しよう。

語句 □be involved with ～ ～に関与している

Questions 89 through 91 refer to the following telephone message.
設問89-91 は次の電話のメッセージに関するものである。

62

Hello, Mr. Blake. Q91 This is Ron Tyrell from Magda International. Q89 I would like to inform you that I will be transferring to another department within the company next month. I just wanted to say a personal thank you for your support to date. Your help has been invaluable to me and Q90 I believe Magda International and LEEMA Electronics will continue to prosper together. Q91 My colleague, Jon Brooks will be taking over my responsibilities as a contact person with LEEMA Electronics. I assure you that he is a very capable person, and the transition will be very smooth. However, if there is anything you'd like to talk to me about, please feel free to call me at any time.

もしもし，Blakeさん。こちらはMagda InternationalのRon Tyrellです。来月，社内の別の部署に異動することになりましたので，お知らせいたします。これまでお世話になったことに対して，ただ個人的にお礼を言いたかったのです。いただいたご支援は私にとって非常に貴重なものでした。Magda InternationalとLEEMA Electronicsは今後も共に繁栄していくことと思います。LEEMA Electronicsとの連絡窓口としての職務は，私の同僚であるJon Brooksが引き継ぎます。彼が非常に有能であることは保証できますので，引き継ぎはとても円滑に行われるでしょう。ですが，もし何か私にお話がございましたら，いつでもお気軽にお電話ください。

語句 □to date これまで，今まで □invaluable 非常に貴重な □capable 有能な □transition 引き継ぎ，移行

89. What is the purpose of the call?
(A) To arrange an appointment
(B) To inform a client of an upcoming project
(C) To notify a client of a change of personnel
(D) To announce a promotional event

電話の目的は何か。
(A) 約束を取り決める
(B) 顧客に次回のプロジェクトを知らせる
(C) 顧客に人事異動を知らせる
(D) 販売促進イベントを告知する

正解 **(C)**

解説 留守番電話のメッセージの目的を問う問題だ。名乗った直後にI would like to inform you that I will be transferring to another department within the company next month. と言っている。電話をかけた人は，来月他の部署への異動が決まったのだ。これを言い換えた(C)が正解である。a change of personnelで「人事異動」という意味だ。

90. What does the caller think will happen to the two companies?

(A) They will start official support shortly.
(B) They will keep growing together.
(C) They will become leaders in many countries.
(D) They will merge into one company.

電話をかけている人は2つの会社がどのようになると考えているか。

(A) 間もなく公的なサポートを開始する。
(B) 一緒に成長し続ける。
(C) 多くの国で指導的立場に就く。
(D) 1つの会社に合併する。

正解 **(B)**

解説 話し手はトークの中盤で，I believe Magda International and LEEMA Electronics will continue to prosper together. と言って，自分の所属しているMagda Internationalと聞き手が所属すると思われるLEEMA Electronicsの両方が共に繁栄していくだろうと述べている。よって正解は(B)だ。他の選択肢の内容は，全てメッセージ内での言及がないので不正解である。

91. Who most likely is Jon Brooks?

(A) A customer of Magda International
(B) A colleague of Mr. Blake
(C) An employee of LEEMA Electronics
(D) A staff member at Magda International

Jon Brooksは誰だと考えられるか。

(A) Magda Internationalの顧客
(B) Blakeさんの同僚
(C) LEEMA Electronicsの従業員
(D) Magda Internationalのスタッフ

正解 **(D)**

解説 Jon Brooksという名前を待ち構えながら音声を聞く。冒頭のThis is Ron Tyrell from Magda International. から，電話をかけている人がMagda Internationalの社員だと把握していれば，トークの中盤でMy colleague, Jon Brooksと言った時点で，Jon BrooksもMagda Internationalの社員だと分かり，すぐに(D)が正解と判断できる。また，Jon Brooksがas a contact person with LEEMA Electronics. と紹介されていることから，彼がLEEMA Electronicsの社員ではないことが分かり，(C)は不正解であると判断できる。

Questions 92 through 94 refer to the following voice-mail message.
設問 92-94 は次の音声メッセージに関するものである。

63

Hello. This is Lindsey from Lamdsey University Book Store with a message for Jonathan Leeds. Jonathan, sorry for not getting back to you sooner, but Q92 we have been very busy since the book store is undergoing renovations and we need to move our stock. Q93 To answer your question about selling back the textbooks you will no longer use, you can do that by bringing them in person to the book store. Remember, you'll need to present your student ID at that time. Q94 I recommend you sell your books now, since the departments have turned in the list of books being used for next term, and you may get higher buyback values for the books.

もしもし。こちらはLamdsey大学書店のLindseyと申します。Jonathan Leedsに伝言があります。Jonathan, もっと早くに折り返しのお電話ができず，すみません。当書店は現在改装中で，在庫を移動させる必要があるため非常に忙しいのです。使わなくなった教科書の売り戻しについてのご質問にお答えいたします。当書店にご自分で直接本をご持参いただければ可能です。その際に学生証の提示が必要となることをお忘れなく。教科書は今すぐお売りになることをお勧めいたします。というのも，各学部が来学期に使用する教科書のリストを提出したところなので，買い戻しの価格が高くなる可能性があるからです。

語句 □at that time そのとき，その際　□turn in ～ ～を提出する　□buyback 買い戻し

92. Why has the speaker been busy?
(A) A new publication has been released.
(B) An establishment is being renovated.
(C) New stock has been delivered.
(D) Several courses have been canceled.

話し手はなぜ忙しいのか。
(A) 新刊書が出版されたから。
(B) 施設が改装中だから。
(C) 新たな在庫が配送されたから。
(D) いくつかの課程が取り消されたから。

正解 **(B)**

解説 busyをキーワードとして意識しておく。トークの前半でwe have been very busy since the book store is undergoing renovationsと述べているので，忙しい理由は改装中のためだと分かる。正解は(B)だ。book storeが(B)ではestablishmentと言い換えられていることに注意。また，トークの続きにwe need to move our stockとあるが，new stockが配送されたとは言っていないので，(C)は不正解である。

93. Who most likely is the listener?
(A) A worker at a book store
(B) An instructor of a new course
(C) A staff member at a school library
(D) An owner of used textbooks

聞き手は誰だと考えられるか。
(A) 書店の従業員
(B) 新しい課程の講師
(C) 学校図書館の職員
(D) 使用済み教科書の所有者

正解 (D)

解説 トークの中盤でTo answer your question about selling back the textbooks you will no longer useと述べている。ここから分かることは，聞き手がtextbooksを使っていたという事実だ。それを簡単に言い換えた(D)のAn owner of used textbooksが正解となる。(A)と(C)が紛らわしいかもしれないが，その後もRemember, you'll need to present your student ID at that time.と学生証の提示を求めているので，問題なく除外できるはずだ。

94. What does the speaker advise the listener to do?
(A) Visit the office to apply for an identification card
(B) Obtain the list of books being used for next term
(C) Sell the books while he can get better prices for them
(D) Purchase all the items he needs for his courses at once

話し手は聞き手に何をするように勧めているか。
(A) 身分証明書の申し込みのために事務所を訪れる
(B) 来学期に使用される教科書のリストを入手する
(C) よりよい価格で売れるうちに教科書を売却する
(D) 自分の課程に必要なもの全てをすぐに購入する

正解 (C)

解説 トークの最後に，話し手はI recommend you sell your books now, since the departments have turned in the list of books being used for next term, and you may get higher buyback values for the books.と述べている。これは，買い戻しの価格が高くなる可能性があるため，本を売るなら今だというアドバイスをしているのだ。よって正解は(C)。

語句 □at once すぐに

Questions 95 through 97 refer to the following announcement.
設問 95-97 は次のお知らせに関するものである。 64

Hello, team. Q95 I'd like to take a few minutes to introduce myself. My name is Sydney Chang and I have been appointed as the new PR and Communications manager. For the last 5 years Q96 I worked as a public relations officer at Hendel Global, so I have a deep understanding of the construction industry as well as good communication skills. Q96 My goal here at RT Constructions is to create a stronger brand image and maintain a positive relationship with customers, stockholders, the media and the public. I will spend the coming week meeting with each of you separately to get to know you better and to discuss topics of concern. Q97 Please e-mail me your availability after this meeting is over.

こんにちは，チームの皆さん。少しお時間をいただき，自己紹介したいと思います。私の名前はSydney Changです。新たに広報部長に任命されました。この5年間はHendel Global社で広報担当をしていたので，建設業界について深く理解しており，またコミュニケーション能力に長けています。ここRT建設での私の目標は，より強力なブランドイメージを構築し，顧客，株主，メディア，そして一般の方々との良好な関係を維持することです。皆さんのことをよりよく知り，関心のある話題について話し合うために，来週は1週間かけて一人一人と個別に面談します。この会議の終了後，Eメールでご都合をお知らせください。

語句 □topic of concern 関心のある話題

95. What is the main purpose of the talk?
(A) To tell employees about the speaker herself
(B) To announce that the speaker is leaving a job
(C) To motivate team members to work harder
(D) To brainstorm ideas for an advertisement

話の主な目的は何か。
(A) 話し手自身について従業員に話す
(B) 話し手が辞職することを告知する
(C) より一生懸命働くようにチームメンバーにやる気を出させる
(D) 宣伝のためのアイデアを出し合う

正解 **(A)**

解説 トークの目的は，冒頭に登場することが多い。I'd like to take a few minutes to introduce myself. と話し手は言っているので，自己紹介のトークだと分かる。正解は(A)だ。

語句 □motivate ～にやる気を出させる　□brainstorm idea アイデアを出し合う

96. What type of industry does the speaker probably work for?
(A) Finance
(B) Construction
(C) Mass media
(D) Electronics

話し手はどのような業界で働いていると思われるか。
(A) 金融
(B) 建設
(C) マスコミ
(D) 電子

正解 **(B)**

解説 職業・職種に関する内容を待ち構えて聞き取る。前半でI worked as a public relations officer at Hendel Global, so I have a deep understanding of the construction industryと述べていること，またMy goal here at RT Constructionsとあることから，話し手は建設業界で働いていると判断することが可能だ。正解は(B)。話し手はPR and Communications managerだと自己紹介をしているが，これは社内での立場であって，その業界の人間であるわけではないため(C)は誤り。

97. What does the speaker request team members to do?
(A) Inform her of their availability
(B) Come up with topics for discussion
(C) Write down their e-mail addresses
(D) Work on their communication skills

話し手はチームメンバーに何をするように求めているか。
(A) 彼女に都合を知らせる
(B) 話し合いの議題を考え出す
(C) Eメールアドレスを書き留める
(D) コミュニケーション能力の改善に取り組む

正解 **(A)**

解説 トークの最後を，話し手はPlease e-mail me your availability after this meeting is over.と言って締めくくっている。聞き手の都合をEメールで知らせてほしいと頼んでいるため，これを言い換えた(A)が正解となる。

語句 □come up with ～ ～を考え出す　□write down ～ ～を書き留める
□work on ～ ～の改善に取り組む

Questions 98 through 100 refer to the following talk.

設問98-100は次の話に関するものである。

65

Good morning, all. Following last month's security assessment, Q98 OMAR Technologies has decided to upgrade its perimeter control systems. Some of you may have noticed Q98 Q99 intercoms and surveillance cameras being set up in buildings A and B last week. In addition, we will be enforcing stricter rules. Currently, the access control badges issued to employees and authorized contractors are updated annually. But under the new policy, they will be updated every 6 months. On top of that, we'd like to ask all our employees to keep important papers locked up in secure cabinets and Q100 keep their work stations neat and orderly to make identifying strange objects or unauthorized persons easier. Thank you.

皆さん，おはようございます。OMAR Technologiesは，先月の安全評価を受けて，周辺制御システムをアップグレードすることに決めました。一部の方はお気付きかもしれませんが，先週，A棟とB棟にインターホンと監視カメラを設置しました。加えて，より厳しい規則を施行します。現在，従業員と認可された請負業者に発行されるアクセス制御用のカードの更新は1年ごとですが，新しい方針では半年ごととします。さらに，全ての従業員にお願いしたいのですが，重要書類は安全なキャビネットの中に鍵を掛けて保管してください。また，不審物や許可されていない人物をより簡単に識別できるように，作業場を整然とした状態に保ってください。よろしくお願いします。

語句 □perimeter control system 周辺制御システム　□intercom インターホン
□surveillance camera 監視カメラ　□enforce ～を施行する　□on top of ～ ～に加えて
□lock up ～ ～を鍵を掛けて保管する　□neat and orderly 整然として

98. What is the talk about?
(A) Customer relations
(B) Security measures
(C) Emergency procedures
(D) Wellness guidelines

話は何についてか。
(A) 顧客との関係
(B) 安全対策
(C) 応急処置
(D) 健康に関する指針

正解 **(B)**

解説 冒頭で話し手はOMAR Technologies has decided to upgrade its perimeter control systems.と言っている。perimeter control systemsが何なのか理解できない場合でも，直後にintercoms and surveillance cameras being set up in buildings A and B last week.とあるので，安全面に関する設備のアップグレードの話だということが理解できるはずだ。これを簡単に言い換えた(B)が正解である。

語句 □security measures 安全対策　□wellness 健康であること

99. What happened last week?

(A) An updated version of a product was released.
(B) Construction of some buildings began.
(C) Electronic devices were installed.
(D) A professional assessment was conducted.

先週何があったか。

(A) 更新版の製品が発売された。
(B) 建物の建築が始まった。
(C) 電子装置が設置された。
(D) 専門的な評価が行われた。

正解 **(C)**

解説 last week に関する内容は，トークの前半，98. の正解の根拠ともなり得る部分に登場している。intercoms and surveillance cameras being set up in buildings A and B last week. とあるため，インターホンや監視カメラが取り付けられたことが分かる。これらの装置を electronic devices と言い換えている (C) が正解だ。

100. What are employees asked to do?

(A) Attend a photo session
(B) Back up important files
(C) Lock the break room doors
(D) Keep the office tidy

従業員は何をするように求められているか。

(A) 撮影会に参加する
(B) 重要なファイルをバックアップする
(C) 休憩室のドアに鍵を掛ける
(D) オフィスを整然とした状態に保つ

正解 **(D)**

解説 トークの最後の方で，聞き手に対して keep their work stations neat and orderly と話し手は述べている。作業場を整然とした状態に保っておいてほしいと伝えていることから，neat and orderly を tidy と言い換えている (D) が正解となる。

語句 □ tidy きちんとした，整然とした

PART 5

101. A restructuring of the major divisions will end up taking place after SO & T ------- Supersoft next month.

(A) foresees (B) acquires
(C) rests (D) merges

主要部門の再編成は，結局はSO & T社がSupersoft社を来月買収した後に行われることになるだろう。

正解 (B)

解説 文脈から(B) acquire「～を買収する」と(D) merge「合併する」のいずれかが正解になると考えられる。空所直後にSupersoftという目的語があるので他動詞を正解に選ぶ必要がある。よって，正解は(B)。(D)はmerge with ～ で「～と合併する」という意味になる。(A) foresee「～を予想する」，(C) rest「～を置く，休む」。

語句 □restructuring 再編成，リストラ □end up doing 結局～することになる
□take place 行われる

102. The annual shareholders' meeting will be held in the Hamptons in ------- with company tradition.

(A) connecting (B) keeping
(C) realizing (D) concluding

会社の慣例に従って，年次株主総会はHamptonsで開かれる予定である。

正解 (B)

解説 選択肢に動詞の-ing形が並んでいる語彙問題だ。空所の前後がin ------- withになっていることに注目して(B) keepingを入れると「～に従って」という意味になる。(A) connect「接続する」，(C) realize「～を悟る，気付く」，(D) conclude「結論に達する」。

103. For being a senior partner at Berizon and Rukoil Law Firm, frequent travel to other countries is one of the -------.

(A) recoupment (B) requirements
(C) reflections (D) refurbishment

Berizon and Rukoil法律事務所のシニアパートナーになるためには，必要条件の1つに頻繁な海外への出張がある。

正解 (B)

解説 選択肢にはre-から始まる名詞が並んでいる。空所の前がone of theなので，正解の候補は名詞の複数形である(B)と(C)に絞られる。文脈から「頻繁な海外出張」は「条件」の1つだと判断することができるので，正解は(B)のrequirements「必要条件，要件」だ。(A) recoupment「埋め合わせ」，(C) reflection「反射」，(D) refurbishment「改装」。

104. Mr. Moskovitz reviewed the latest proposal and ------- it to the manager for approval.

(A) continued (B) extinguished
(C) forwarded (D) converted

Moskovitzさんは最新の提案書を検討し，承認を得るためにそれを部長に転送した。

正解 (C)

解説 選択肢に動詞の過去形が並んでいる語彙問題だ。空所の後がA to Bの形になっているので，目的

語以降がこの形になり，かつ文意が通る(C)のforwardが正解。forward A to Bで「AをBに転送する」という意味だ。(D)のconvertもA to Bを続けられるが，convert A to Bで「AをBに転換させる，変える」という意味なので文脈に合わない。(A) continue「～を続ける」，(B) extinguish「～を消滅させる」。

105.

Von Vai Industry's new fall line of siding for houses is guaranteed to ------- the look of your house.

(A) quicken (B) depict
(C) exemplify (D) enhance

Von Vai産業の秋の新製品である住宅用羽目板は，家の見栄えを良くすることを保証する。

正解 (D)

解説 new fall line「秋の新製品」はthe look of your house「家の見栄え」をどうすることを保証するのかを考える。文意が通るのは(D) enhance「～を高める」だ。(A) quicken「～を速める」，(B) depict「～を描く」，(C) exemplify「～を例証する，例示する」。

語句 □siding 羽目板 □guarantee ～を保証する

106.

Please print your address on the label in the space provided and ------- it to the top of the bottle.

(A) abide (B) affix
(C) detach (D) confine

ラベル上の空欄に住所を活字体で書き，瓶のふたにそれを貼り付けてください。

正解 (B)

解説 「ラベルに住所を活字体で書き，それを瓶のふたに ------- してください」という内容だ。文脈から(B)が正解で，affix A to Bで「AをBに貼り付ける」という意味だ。(A)のabideは「～を我慢する」という意味であり，(C) detachはaffixの反意語で「～を外す」，(D) confineは「～を限定する」という意味なので，文脈から考えると正解にはなり得ない。

107.

Donations to the Takashi Tanaka & Family Home will be greatly appreciated, yet are only -------.

(A) optional (B) usable
(C) individual (D) candid

Takashi Tanaka & Family Homeへの寄付は大いに感謝されるが，それは任意にすぎない。

正解 (A)

解説 空所には補語になる形容詞が並んでいる。逆接のyetがあるため「寄付は感謝されるが -------」という内容だ。(A)のoptional「任意の，選択できる」を入れれば文意が通る。(B) usable「使用できる」，(C) individual「個人の」，(D) candid「率直な」。

語句 □donation 寄付 □appreciate ～を感謝する

108.

The new attorneys and counselors must be under the supervision of a senior manager for several months before they are ------- any clients.

(A) garnered (B) assumed
(C) incurred (D) assigned

新人の弁護士とカウンセラーは，依頼人を割り当てられる前に数カ月間シニアマネージャーの管理下に置かなければならない。

正解 **(D)**

解説 選択肢には-ed形が並んでおり，空所の前にbe動詞があるので受動態である。受動態の後にany clientsという目的語がきているため，目的語を2つ取る動詞が正解となる。正解は(D)のassignで，assign A Bで「AにBを割り当てる」という意味だ。(A) garner「～を獲得する」，(B) assume「～を引き受ける，仮定する」，(C) incur「～を負う，被る，招く」。

語句 □attorney 弁護士 □supervision 監督，監視

109.

This will be the ------- biggest merger in the history of our company.

(A) one (B) any
(C) single (D) most

我が社の歴史において，これは単独で最も大きな合併になるだろう。

正解 **(C)**

解説 最上級biggestの直前に置いて修飾できるものを選ぶ問題で，正解は(C)のsingleだ。the single biggestで「単独で最も大きい」という意味になるので押さえておこう。(A)と(B)では文意が通らず，bigの最上級に(D)のmostは不要だ。

語句 □merger 合併

110.

Due to the ------- of a self-development training program at Ballmer Company, staff absenteeism has been reduced to 10 percent.

(A) implementation (B) temptation
(C) independency (D) indemnity

Ballmer社での自己啓発トレーニングプログラムの実行によって，スタッフの欠勤率は10%に下がった。

正解 **(A)**

解説 「プログラムの-------で，スタッフの欠勤が減った」というのが問題文の内容だ。プログラムの「実行」と考えれば文意が通るため，正解は(A) implementation「実行」。あわせて，動詞implement「（計画や政策など）を実行する」も覚えておきたい。(B) temptation「誘惑」，(C) independency「独立」，(D) indemnity「損害補償，賠償金」。

語句 □self-development 自己啓発 □absenteeism 常習的欠勤 □reduce ～を減らす

111.

Follow the ------- of steps to unlock the emergency exit door, or you will not be able to open it again.

(A) orbit (B) sequence
(C) instruction (D) expertness

非常口のドアを開錠するためには，一連の手順に従ってください。さもないと二度と開けることができなくなってしまいます。

正解 **(B)**

解説 非常口のドアを開錠するためには，何に従う必要があるのか。正解は(B)で，the sequence of

stepsで「一連の手順」という意味である。形容詞形のsequent「続いて起こる」や関連語のconsequent「結果として起こる」, consequently「その結果，従って」もTOEICによく登場する表現なので一緒に覚えておこう。(A) orbit「軌道」, (C) instruction「指示」, (D) expertness「熟練，熟達」。

語句 □unlock ～の鍵を開ける □emergency exit 非常口

112. The mayor said that ------- should be placed on public health and security, rather than on the preservation of local traditions.

(A) tenseness (B) priority
(C) routine (D) measurement

地域の伝統を守ることよりも，市民の健康と安全に優先順位を置くべきだと市長は述べた。

正解 **(B)**

解説 選択肢には名詞が並んでおり，それがshould be placedの主語となっている。「地域の伝統よりも，市民の健康や安全に ------- を置くべきだ」という文脈から，(B) priority「優先順位」が正解だ。(A) tenseness「緊張」, (C) routine「決まり切った仕事」, (D) measurement「測定，寸法」。

113. Bale Energy is seeking an alternative lubricant that is ------- in quality to the brand that they have been using over the past decade.

(A) quantity (B) comparable
(C) pilot (D) substantial

Bale Energyは，過去10年間使用してきた銘柄に質が匹敵するような，代替の潤滑油を探している。

正解 **(B)**

解説 ヒントは空所の後に登場するtoだ。(B)を選択し，be comparable to ～「～に匹敵する」とすれば文意が通るので正解だ。空所直後にin qualityがありtoを意識しづらいかもしれないが，このような副詞句の挿入が時々登場することを頭に入れておこう。(A) quantity「量」, (C) pilot「案内人，試験的な」, (D) substantial「かなりの」。

語句 □alternative 代替となる □lubricant 潤滑油

114. Tokyo has an ------- public transit system with many subway, train and bus lines.

(A) attachable (B) ensuing
(C) assertive (D) extensive

東京にはたくさんの地下鉄と電車，バス路線といった広範囲にわたる公共交通機関がある。

正解 **(D)**

解説 public transit system「公共交通機関」を修飾する適切な形容詞を選ぶ。選択肢の中で文脈に合うのは，(D)のextensive「広範囲にわたる」だ。(B)のensuingは「結果として起こる，次の」という意味の形容詞である。ensure「～を保証する」と混同しないように注意して覚えておくこと。(A) attachable「取り付けることができる」, (C) assertive「断定的な」。

115.

The next business trip to the city of New York conveniently ------- with the Fourth of July weekend celebration.

(A) subscribes (B) consists
(C) partners (D) coincides

ニューヨーク市への次の出張は，7月4日(アメリカ独立記念)の週末の祝典にうまく時期が一致している。

正解 (D)

解説 coincide with ～で「～と同時に起こる」という意味になる。「出張が祝典と同時期に起こる」とすれば文意が通るため，正解は(D)だ。(A)はsubscribe to ～「～を定期購読する」，(B)はconsist of ～「～から成る」，(C)はpartner with ～「～と組む」のように使うので，押さえておこう。

116.

Fortunately, the readings for the chemical analysis were well ------- the acceptable range for safety.

(A) within (B) slight
(C) amid (D) mutually

幸運にも，化学分析の測定値は十分に安全基準の範囲内であった。

正解 (A)

解説 問題文の内容は「幸運にも測定値は安全基準の範囲の -------であった」だ。(A)のwithin「～の範囲内で」を空所に入れると文意が通るので，これが正解となる。(C)のamidは「～の中に，まっただ中に」という意味の前置詞であり，wellで修飾することができないため不正解だ。(B) slight「わずかな」，(D) mutually「相互に」。

語句 □reading（計器などの）示度，表示数値

117.

Melbourne ------- the most livable city in Australia for the fifth successive year according to a readers' poll in today's newspaper.

(A) remains (B) materializes
(C) requires (D) votes

今日の新聞の読者投票によると，メルボルンは5年連続で，オーストラリアで最も住みやすい都市のままだ。

正解 (A)

解説 空所に動詞が並んでおり，空所の前後が主語と補語の関係になっているので，自動詞で文意の通る(A) remain「～のままである」が正解。(B) materialize「現実に起こる」，(C) require「～を必要とする」，(D) vote「投票する」。

語句 □livable 住みやすい　□poll 投票

118.

Jeff Thompson took two weeks off work for the birth of his third child but will return next Monday to ------- his former duties here.

(A) resume (B) assemble
(C) extract (D) operate

Jeff Thompsonは，3人目の子どもが生まれたため2週間の休暇を取っていたが，来週の月曜日にここで以前の仕事を再開するために戻ってくる予定だ。

正解 (A)

解説 「Thompsonさんは休暇を取っていたが，来週戻ってきて以前の仕事を-------する」という内容だ。文脈から(A)のresume「～を再開する」が正解。(C)のextractは「～を抽出する」という

意味を持つが，関連語としてexcerpt「抜粋，～を抜粋する」も押さえておくとよいだろう。(B) assemble「～を組み立てる」，(D) operate「～を操作する」。

119. The manager spoke most ------- about focusing on customer satisfaction, although he failed to address several topics during the last meeting.

(A) independently (B) previously
(C) eloquently (D) evasively

部長は前回のミーティングでいくつかの話題を取り上げ損ねたが，顧客満足に焦点を当てることに関しては最も雄弁に語った。

正解 **(C)**

解説 接続詞のalthoughに正解の鍵がある。「彼はいくつかの話題を取り上げ損ねたが，顧客満足については最も -------に話した」という内容だ。(C)のeloquently「雄弁に」を選択すると，2つの節の内容が対比されて文脈が適切につながるため正解となる。(A) independently「独立して」，(B) previously「前もって」，(D) evasively「回避的に」。

120. The area has the largest ------- of coffee plants in the country due to the favorable climate in the southern hills.

(A) concentration (B) conversion
(C) compost (D) correspondence

南部の丘陵地帯は気候が良いため，その地域は国内で最もコーヒー畑が集中した地域になっている。

正解 **(A)**

解説 「気候が良いのでコーヒー畑が-------である」というのが問題文の内容だ。the largestによって修飾でき，かつ文意が通る名詞は，(A)のconcentrationだ。the largest concentration of ～で「～の最大の集中（地）」という意味。(C)のcompost「堆肥」は見慣れない単語かもしれないが，押さえておこう。(B) conversion「転換」，(D) correspondence「通信」。

121. Please consider the mountains along Austria's western ------- before making vacation plans for summer.

(A) deadline (B) border
(C) exposition (D) domicile

夏期休暇の計画を立てる前に，オーストリアの西部国境に沿った山をご検討ください。

正解 **(B)**

解説 空所はthe mountainsを修飾する前置詞句の一部である。along Austria's western -------「オーストリア西部の-------に沿った」から，(B)のborder「国境」を空所に入れると文意が通る。(A) deadline「締め切り」，(C) exposition「展示会」，(D) domicile「居住地」。

122.

------- of consumers who bought Berizon's new laptop were not entirely satisfied with the quality.

(A) Some　(B) Any
(C) A large number　(D) Many

Berizonの新しいノートパソコンを買った多くの消費者は，その質に完全に満足しているわけではなかった。

正解　(C)

解説　some of ～，any of ～，そして many of ～ の後には，いずれも限定を示す冠詞の the や its, their などが必要だ。a large number of ～ は冠詞がいらないので，正解は (C) だ。

語句　□entirely 全く，完全に

123.

On November 20, the sales department is going to ------- a new policy that will take effect as soon as the current one expires.

(A) chaperon　(B) introduce
(C) derive　(D) command

11月20日に，営業部は，現行の方針が終了するとすぐに発効する新しい方針を取り入れることになっている。

正解　(B)

解説　new policy「新しい方針」を目的語にとり，なおかつ文意が通るのは (B) の introduce「～を取り入れる」だ。(A) chaperon「～に付き添う」, (C) derive「～を引き出す」, (D) command「～を命令する」。

語句　□take effect 効力を発する

124.

Unless oak doors are treated with a chemical stabilizer, they have a tendency to ------- in a humid climate.

(A) append　(B) intensify
(C) expand　(D) inflate

オーク材のドアは化学安定剤で処理されないと，湿気の多い気候では大きくなる傾向がある。

正解　(C)

解説　「オーク材のドアは湿気の多い気候では ------- する傾向がある」という内容から，空所には「(湿気を吸って) 大きくなる」という意味を持つ単語が入るのではないかと予想できる。(C) と (D) が候補になりそうだが，(D) の inflate は「(空気・ガスなどで) 膨らむ」という意味なので，正解は (C) の expand「広がる，大きくなる」だ。(A) append「～を付け加える，付加する」, (B) intensify「いっそう強くなる，激しくなる」。

語句　□oak オーク材　□chemical stabilizer 化学安定剤　□tendency 傾向

125.

BNP Foods states that for a healthier meal, you can ------- grape seed oil for common cooking oil.

(A) sustain　(B) substitute
(C) amend　(D) grade

より健康的な食事のために，普通の調理用油をグレープシードオイルで代用することができるとBNP Foodsは言っている。

正解　(B)

解説　空所の後に for があることに注目し，substitute A for B「A を B の代わりに用いる」ではないかと予想する。「普通の調理用油の代わりにグレープシードオイルを使えば健康的な食事になる」となり文意も通るので，正解は(B)だ。(A) sustain「～を維持する」，(C) amend「～を修正する」，(D) grade「～を格付けする」。

126.

All the recipes in this book are ------- enough to be adjusted to individual preferences.

(A) miscellaneous　(B) versatile
(C) prototypical　(D) unabridged

この本にある全てのレシピは，個人の好みに合わせることができるくらい万能だ。

正解 **(B)**

解説 「個人の好みに合わせることができる」という内容から，これを表す形容詞として(B)のversatile「万能の」を入れると文意が通る。(A) miscellaneous「種々雑多な」，(C) prototypical「典型の」，(D) unabridged「省略されていない，完全な」。

127.

To help ------- our educational program for children of low-income families, Mr. Walton has made a sizable donation to our foundation.

(A) gratify　(B) support
(C) rely　(D) confide

所得が少ない家庭の子どもへの教育プログラムを支援することを手伝うために，Waltonさんはわれわれの基金に多額の寄付をした。

正解 **(B)**

解説 〈help＋動詞の原形〉で「～することを助ける，手伝う」のパターンだ。our educational programを目的語にとり，なおかつ文脈にふさわしいのは，(B)のsupport「～を支援する」だけだ。(A)のgratifyは「(人）を喜ばせる」という意味であり，目的語は基本的に人になる。(C)のrely「頼る」は自動詞なので，目的語を直接はとれない。(D) confide「～を打ち明ける」。

語句 □sizable かなり大きな

128.

The amber grapes are used to make ice wine, the most ------- and expensive wine in the world.

(A) renowned　(B) utter
(C) seasoned　(D) devoted

その琥珀色に熟したブドウは，世界で最も有名で高価なワインであるアイスワインを作るために使われている。

正解 **(A)**

解説 wineをexpensiveと共に修飾する形容詞を選ぶ問題だ。(A)のrenowned「名高い」以外はこの文脈でwineを修飾するには不適当であるため，正解は(A)だ。(B)のutterは「全くの」という形容詞だが，「～を口に出す」という動詞でもあることを押さえておこう。(C)のseasoned「経験豊富な」，(D)のdevoted「専念した，献身的な」はTOEIC頻出の単語だ。

語句 □amber grapes 琥珀色に熟したブドウ

129.

The manager said that the company outing next month, including a visit to a famous museum, is ------- to all staff and their families.

(A) deliberate (B) open
(C) virtuous (D) summoned

来月の社員旅行では有名な博物館への訪問もあり，全スタッフとその家族が参加可能だと部長が言った。

正解 **(B)**

解説 選択肢には形容詞が並んでいる。that節内の主語the company outing next monthに対して補語になるものは，文脈から(B)のopen。be open to ～で「～に対して開かれている」という意味になる。(A)のdeliberateは「熟考された，慎重な」という形容詞だが，「～を熟考する」という動詞でもある。(C)のvirtuousは「立派な」という意味であり，名詞形のvirtue「美徳」と一緒に覚えておこう。(D)のsummonは「～を招集する」という意味だ。

語句 □company outing 社員旅行

130.

Actually, ------- all the applications reviewed, Mr. Persson's is by far the most impressive one.

(A) out (B) toward
(C) of (D) onto

実は，検討済みの全ての応募書類の中でPerssonさんのものが群を抜いて印象的なものだった。

正解 **(C)**

解説 最上級を表す文だが，「どの範囲の中で1番なのか」を表すof ～の部分が先に登場する形になっている。よって正解は(C)だ。問題文中に登場するby farは最上級を強調し，「群を抜いて」という意味になる。

131.

In preparation for the arrival of the DM25, the older version, the DM20 will be ------- phased out over the next three months.

(A) sufficiently (B) excessively
(C) gradually (D) inadvertently

DM25の到着に備えて，旧バージョンのDM20は，今後3カ月間で徐々に姿を消していくことになる。

正解 **(C)**

解説 「今後3カ月をかけて-------にDM20は姿を消す」という内容だ。選択肢の中である程度の期間にわたる状況を修飾する副詞は，(C)のgradually「徐々に」である。(A) sufficiently「十分に」，(B) excessively「過度に，甚だしく」，(D) inadvertently「うっかり」。

語句 □in preparation for ～ ～に備えて □phase out ～ ～を段階的に減らす

132.

Most of the workers may find the daily tasks ------- due to the intrinsic nature of work.

(A) disposed (B) repetitive
(C) unfortunate (D) preceding

ほとんどの従業員は，仕事に元々備わっている性質から，日常業務は同じことの繰り返しであると分かるかもしれない。

正解 **(B)**

解説 空所後にあるintrinsic nature「元々備わっている性質」が理解できなかったとしても，the daily tasksの補語としてふさわしいものが何かと考えれば正解を選べる問題だ。日々行っていることを表すのは，(B)のrepetitive「繰り返しの」だ。(D)のpreceding「先立つ」はthe preceding year「前年」という形で出題されやすいので注意しよう。(A) disposed「～する傾向がある」, (C) unfortunate「不運な, 残念な」。

語句 □intrinsic 本来備わっている, 固有の

133.

Students who have yet to submit their plans for their next research project must submit those documents ------- after the completion of them this evening.

(A) exceptionally (B) particularly
(C) promptly (D) inwardly

次の調査プロジェクトの計画をまだ提出していない学生は, 今晩の完成後すぐに書類を提出しなければならない。

正解 (C)

解説 空所直後のafter以下を修飾し, 文意が通じる副詞を選択する。promptly after ～ で「～の後すぐに」となるので, 正解は(C)だ。immediately after ～ としてもほぼ同様の意味になるので, 一緒に押さえておこう。(A) exceptionally「例外的に」, (B) particularly「特に」, (D) inwardly「内部で, ひそかに」。

134.

The Italian food festival downtown has become so popular that almost all local residents avoid going into the city -------.

(A) never (B) slightly
(C) scarcely (D) altogether

中心街でのイタリアンフードフェスティバルは非常に人気が出てきたので, 地元のほとんどの住民はすっかり市内に行くことを避けている。

正解 (D)

解説「フードフェスティバルが非常に人気となったため, 地元の住民は ------- 市内に行くのを避けている」が大意だ。avoid「～を避ける」を修飾し, なおかつ文脈に合った意味になるのは, (D)のaltogether「すっかり」だ。(B)のslightly「わずかに」はavoidを修飾するには不適切。(A) never「少しも～ない」, (C) scarcely「ほとんど～ない」。

語句 □resident 住民

135.

Before we make a decision on purchasing the property, we are currently having an ------- undertaken to determine the true value of it.

(A) advantage (B) appraisal
(C) aggregate (D) absorption

物件を購入する判断をする前に, その本当の価値を見極めるため, 私たちは現在査定をしてもらっている。

正解 (B)

解説 空所を含む節は「物件の本当の価値を見極めるために, 私たちは現在 ------- をしてもらっている」という内容だ。物件の価値を「査定」してもらっているとすれば文意が通るため, 正解は(B)のappraisalとなる。(D) absorption「吸収」は, 動詞形のabsorb「～を吸収する」も一緒に覚えておこう。(A) advantage「有利な点」, (C) aggregate「集合」。

語句 □property 物件 □determine ～を正確に知る

136. The manager of the restaurant has requested a complete ------- of the restaurant's daily routines and costs.

(A) role　(B) fluctuation
(C) evaluation　(D) alternative

レストランの支配人は，レストランの日々の業務とコストの評価がまとめてあるものを要求した。

正解 (C)

解説 complete「完全な」が修飾し，なおかつ「日々の業務とコストの -------」に当てはまるのは，(C)のevaluation「評価」だ。(D)のalternativeは名詞では「代替物」，形容詞だと「代替の」という意味であり，両方とも公開テストに登場する表現なので押さえておこう。(A) role「役割」，(B) fluctuation「変動」。

137. The extra 30-minute break time added to the workday may explain the facility's high ------- over the last year.

(A) entry　(B) induction
(C) mandate　(D) output

1日の労働時間に追加の休憩時間が30分加わったことは，昨年1年間におけるその施設の高い生産高の理由となっているかもしれない。

正解 (D)

解説 労働時間に対し休憩が30分長くなったことから，仕事の生産性が上がったと推測できる。正解は(D)のoutput「生産高」だ。(C)のmandate「委任，命令」は「～の統治を委任する，～を命令する」という動詞の意味も覚えておきたい。(A) entry「入場，登録」，(B) induction「誘導」。

138. City officials ------- to widen the road in order to ease traffic congestion in this area.

(A) proposed　(B) braced
(C) advocated　(D) asserted

市当局はその地域の交通渋滞を緩和するために，その道路を拡張することを提案した。

正解 (A)

解説 空所の後がto widenであるため，後にto不定詞をとることができ，なおかつ文脈に適切な動詞を選択する。選択肢の中ではpropose「～を選択する」だけがそれに該当するため，正解は(A)だ。(B)のbraceはto不定詞を後にとるが「～に備える」という意味なので空所に入れても文意が通らない。(C) advocate「～を主張する，指示する」，(D) assert「～を断言する，強く主張する」。

語句 □city officials 市当局　□widen ～を広げる

139. Several industry analysts predict the market is heading into the worst recession ------- the last decade.

(A) for　(B) in
(C) during　(D) to

何人かの業界アナリストは，市場は過去10年間の中で最悪の不況に向かいつつあると予測している。

正解 (B)

解説 「アナリストは市場が最悪の不況に向かっていると予測している」という内容だ。the last

decadeの前に置いて文脈が通じるのは(B)のinであり,「過去10年の間に」という意味になる。

語句 □industry analyst 業界アナリスト □predict ～を予想する
□head into ～ ～に向かって進む □recession 景気後退，不景気

140. Berkshire Group will try to offer consumers more accurate information on a wide range of goods so that they can make an ------- decision.

(A) informal (B) informed
(C) informative (D) informing

Berkshire Groupは,消費者が詳細な情報を得た上で決断できるように,幅広い種類の商品に関するより正確な情報を提供しようと努めていくだろう。

正解 (B)

解説 問題文は「-------の決断ができる状況になるように，Berkshire Groupは商品に関するより正確な情報を提供しようと努めていくだろう」という内容だ。informed decisionで「詳細な情報を得た上での決断」という意味になり，so that以下の内容としてこれが適切である。よって正解は(B)だ。(A) informal「形式ばらない,非公式の」,(C) informative「(情報などが) 役に立つ」,(D) inform「～を通知する」。

語句 □accurate 正確な □a wide range of ～ さまざまな～，幅広い～

Questions 141-143 refer to the following memo.
設問 141-143 は次のメモに関するものである。

MEMO

From: Roberto Segura
To: All MTK employees
Date: July 20
Re: Employee Safety

At MTK Industries, safety is not a goal but a requirement. -------, employees must strictly adhere to

141. (A) Thereafter
(B) Instead
(C) Therefore
(D) Nevertheless

safety regulations and procedures as stated in the attached guideline. Please be warned that failure to do so may result in disciplinary action.

Further, to ensure a safe working environment, employees should report hazardous activities of other employees to appropriate personnel, should such actions -------.

142. (A) observing
(B) to observe
(C) have been observed
(D) be observed

All non-MTK personnel, including suppliers, subcontractors and regulatory authorities are also required to follow the safety rules during their -------.

143. (A) inspections
(B) visits
(C) deliveries
(D) recesses

メモ

発信者：Roberto Segura
宛先：MTKの全従業員
日付：7月20日
件名：従業員の安全

MTK Industriesでは，安全は目標ではなく，必要不可欠なことです。そのため，従業員は添付のガイドラインで述べられているように，安全基準と安全手順を厳格に順守してください。守らなかった場合は懲戒処分になりますのでご注意ください。

さらに，安全な職場環境を確保するため，他の従業員の危険な行為については，そのような行動が見られた場合，適切な職員に報告してください。

納入業者，下請け業者，規制当局などMTKの社員でない方々にも全員，来社中は当安全規則に従っていただきますようお願いいたします。

語句 □strictly 厳重に，厳しく　□adhere to ～ ～を忠実に守る　□disciplinary action 懲戒処分
□observe ～を見る，に気付く　□subcontractor 下請け業者
□regulatory 規制する，取り締まる

141.

正解 **(C)**

解説 空所の前では「安全は目標ではなく，必要不可欠なことです」と述べており，空所後では「従業員は安全基準と安全手順を厳格に順守してください」とある。空所の前後が順接の関係なので，(C)のtherefore「そのため」を入れれば文脈が正しくつながる。(A) thereafter「その後は」, (B) instead「その代わりに」, (D) nevertheless「それにもかかわらず」。

142.

正解 **(D)**

解説 空所の主語は直前にあるsuch actionsである。such actions「そのような行動」はobserveされることなので受動態が正解の候補となる。(C)と(D)が受動態だが，安全な職場環境を確保するための一般的な話を伝えているだけなので，現在完了形を使う必要性はない。正解は(D)だ。空所前後はif such actions should be observedのifが省略され，shouldが倒置で前に出た仮定法である。

143.

正解 **(B)**

解説 職場環境の安全基準に関してのメモなので，All non-MTK personnel, including suppliers, subcontractors and regulatory authoritiesがその規則を守らなければならない場所は，当然MTK社内においてであると判断できる。納入業者，下請け業者，規制当局などMTKの社員でない人たちがMTK社を(B) visit「訪問」しているときに規則を守る，と考えるのが自然だ。(A) inspection「点検，検査」, (C) delivery「配達」, (D) recess「休憩」。

Questions 144-146 refer to the following e-mail.

設問 144-146 は次のEメールに関するものである。

To: Sean Cox <scox@kyleman.com>
From: Paul Gray <pgray@kyleman.com>
Date: December 7
Subject: Social Committee

Dear Mr. Cox,

I'd like to inform you that three new members -------

144. (A) have joined
(B) to join
(C) would have joined
(D) will be joining

the Social Committee. This is due to the fact that the number of employees has doubled since last year.

The committee has been organizing golf outings, barbecue lunches and bowling nights. All of these ------- activities aim to strengthen the bond

145. (A) competitive
(B) cultural
(C) recreational
(D) inter-office

among employees and boost work output.

The list of new committee members will be sent to you in January after interviewing prospective members. -------, I'd like to discuss the budget for the upcoming

146. (A) Conversely
(B) Meanwhile
(C) Besides
(D) Likewise

year's activities, so please let me know your availability.

Thank you,

Paul Gray
Human Resources
Ext. 989

宛先：Sean Cox <scox@kyleman.com>
送信者：Paul Gray <pgray@kyleman.com>
日付：12月7日
件名：親睦委員会

Cox様

親睦委員会に新たに3人のメンバーが加わる予定であることをお知らせいたします。これは昨年来，従業員数が倍増したことによるものです。

当委員会では，ゴルフイベント，バーベキューランチ，夜のボウリング大会を企画してきました。これらのレクリエーション活動は全て，従業員間の絆を強くし，労働生産高を増やす狙いがあります。

新しい委員会メンバーのリストは，メンバー候補と面談してから，1月に送付するつもりです。その間に，来年の活動に対する予算について話し合いたいと思いますので，ご都合をお知らせください。

よろしくお願いします。

Paul Gray
人事部
内線 989

語句 □double 倍になる □aim to do ～することを目標としている □strengthen ～を強化する
□bond 結束，絆 □boost ～を引き上げる
□work output 労働生産高 □prospective 見込みのある，見込まれる

144.

正解 **(D)**

解説 時制の問題だが，正解の根拠が第3段落に登場するDelayed Clueの問題だ。The list of new committee members will be sent to you in January after interviewing prospective members.から，まだメンバー候補者への面談は行われておらず，委員会のメンバーには加わっていないことが分かる。正解は未来時制の(D) will be joiningだ。

145.

正解 **(C)**

解説 空所直前のtheseは，golf outings, barbecue lunches and bowling nights.のことを指している。(C)のrecreationalを空所に入れれば，recreational activities「レクリエーション活動」となり，上記の活動の言い換えになる。(A) competitive「競争の」，(B) cultural「文化の」，(D) inter-office「社内の」。

146.

正解 **(B)**

解説 空所の前では新メンバーのリスト送付が1月になること，空所後では委員会の予算の相談をしたいことが書かれており，全く別の話が登場している。「その間に」という意味を持つ(B)のmeanwhileを入れれば文脈が正しくつながる。(A) conversely「反対に，逆に」，(C) besides「加えて」，(D) likewise「同じく，同様に」。

Questions 147-149 refer to the following letter.
設問 147-149 は次の手紙に関するものである。

February 2

Dr. Mitchell Young
Taikon Alloys
201 Alfred Street
Sydney, NSW 2890

Dear Dr. Young,

We would like to invite you to attend the Environment and Industrial Infrastructure Workshop organized by the Graham Earth Institute. The objective of the workshop is to bring together the knowledge and experience of professionals from around the country. -------, the workshop will pay special attention to

147. (A) Rather
(B) Additionally
(C) Embarrassingly
(D) Comparatively

critical issues that has developed in the last 6 months. The list of selected ------- will be sent by the organizing

148. (A) products
(B) locations
(C) topics
(D) editions

committee shortly.

For the purpose of communication, a dedicated e-mail address has been set up at workshop@grahamearth.com. Please use this e-mail address for all future communications ------- to the workshop.

149. (A) relate
(B) to relate
(C) will relate
(D) related

Sincerely,
Harry Yates
Harry Yates
Graham Earth Institute

2月2日

Mitchell Young 博士
Taikon Alloys
Alfred Street 201 番地
シドニー，NSW 2890

Young 博士

Graham Earth Institute主催の環境と産業基盤のワークショップにご出席いただきたくご案内申し上げます。このワークショップの目的は，全国から集まったプロフェッショナルの知識と経験を結集することにあります。加えて，ワークショップでは，この6カ月の間に生じた重要問題にも特別に注目するつもりです。選び出されたテーマのリストは，組織委員会が近いうちにお送りする予定です。

連絡用に，専用Eメールアドレス workshop@grahamearth.com を設けました。ワークショップに関連する今後のご連絡は全て，このEメールアドレスをお使いください。

敬具

Harry Yates（署名）
Harry Yates
Graham Earth Institute

語句 □industrial infrastructure 産業基盤 □objective 目的，目標 □critical 重要な，重大な

147.

正解 **(B)**

解説 空所の前では「ワークショップの目的は，全国から集まったプロフェッショナルの知識と経験を結集することにある」と述べ，空所後では「ワークショップでは，この6カ月の間に生じた重要問題に特別に注目する」と述べている。ワークショップで扱う2つの別の事項に続けて触れているため，(B) のadditionally「加えて」を入れれば文意が通る。(A) rather「それどころか」，(C) embarrassingly「とまどうほど」，(D) comparatively「比較的には」。

148.

正解 **(C)**

解説 空所の前のThe listは，直前で言及されているcritical issues that has developed in the last 6 monthsのリストだと文脈から読み取ることができる。issuesをtopicsと言い換えた(C)が正解だ。(A) product「製品」，(B) location「位置」，(D) edition「版，部数」。

149.

正解 **(D)**

解説 空所を含む文Please use this e-mail address for all future communications ------- to the workshop.には，すでにuseという動詞が存在するため，(B)のto relateと(D)のrelatedが正解の候補となる。related to ～で「～に関係のある」という意味になり名詞を後ろから修飾するので(D)が正解。

Questions 150-152 refer to the following article.
設問 150-152 は次の記事に関するものである。

The Ortiz Library Project announced last month has been receiving a lot of -------. The £10 million project

150. (A) praise
(B) criticism
(C) instructions
(D) donations

centers around the renovation of its main building on Snowpike Avenue.

先月発表されたOrtiz図書館プロジェクトには，たくさんの批判が寄せられている。この1,000万ポンドのプロジェクトは，Snowpike Avenueにある本館の改築を軸として展開している。

According to the plan, the building, which is currently used for reference operation only, will be ------- into a

151. (A) inspired
(B) converted
(C) reverted
(D) grown

hybrid that also contains a circulating library and an exhibition space.

計画によれば，本館は，現状はレファレンス業務だけに使われているが，これを貸出し図書館と展示スペースも含む多目的なものに変える。

Many users are concerned about the decrease in the library's holdings. 3 million books and manuscripts will be moved to another library as a consequence of the renovation. Although the library assures users that these items can be obtained within 2 days of request, many are ------- as to the necessity of the renovation,

152. (A) unhappy
(B) doubtful
(C) assured
(D) convinced

and wonder whether the money would have been better spent elsewhere.

多くの利用者は，図書館の蔵書が減るのではないかと心配している。改築によって，300万冊の本や原稿は，別の図書館へ移されることになる。これらの本は，リクエストすれば2日以内に入手できると図書館側は利用者に言っているが，多くの人は改築の必要性に関して疑問に思っており，そのお金は他に良い使い道があったのではないかと思っている。

語句 □reference operation レファレンス業務　□hybrid 混成物
□circulating library（有料の）貸出し図書館　□holdings 所有物
□manuscript 原稿，写本　□as a consequence of ～ ～の結果として
□as to ～ ～に関して　□necessity 必要性　□wonder ～かどうかと思う
□elsewhere 他のどこかで，他の場所に

150.

正解 (B)

解説 正解の根拠がかなり後に登場するDelayed Clueの問題だ。第3段落から人々がこのプロジェクトに否定的な意見を持っていることが分かるため，正解は(B)のcriticism「批判」だ。(A) praise「賞賛」，(C) instruction「指図」，(D) donation「寄付」。

151.

正解 (B)

解説 the buildingが空所を含む一文の主語だ。will be ------- into a hybrid that also contains a circulating library and an exhibition space.のintoに注目し，convert A into B「AをBに変える」の受動態だと考えると文脈が正しくつながる。よって，正解は(B)だ。(A) inspire「～に活気を与える」，(C) revert「戻る」，(D) grow「～を育てる」。

152.

正解 (B)

解説 many are ------- as to the necessity of the renovation, and wonder whether the money would have been better spent elsewhere.のカンマの後ろから，多くの人たちはお金を何か他のことに使った方が良かったと考えていること，つまり改築の必要性について疑問に思っていることが分かるので，正解は(B)のdoubtful「疑わしい」だ。(A) unhappy「不幸な」，(C) assured「自信のある」，(D) convinced「確信に満ちた」。

PART 7

Questions 153-154 refer to the following article.
設問 153-154 は次の記事に関するものである。

Density-2000 Wins Again	Density-2000が再び勝利
Q153 Globe-biz.net has released its list of top-selling mobile phones for this month. According to the list, Q154 Density-2000 by Bensen is in first place for the third consecutive month. In second place is Hyuwa-90 by Hyuwa Electronics.	Globe-biz.netは今月最もよく売れている携帯電話のリストを発表した。そのリストによれば，Bensen社のDensity-2000が3カ月連続の1位を獲得している。2位はHyuwaエレクトロニクス社のHyuwa-90である。
It has been quite a year for Bensen, with its Density-2000 selling 35 million units worldwide. Bensen also overtook Hyuwa, becoming the biggest mobile phone manufacturer in January this year.	Density-2000の販売台数が全世界で3,500万台に上り，Bensen社にとってはなかなかの1年となった。Bensen社はまた，今年の1月にHyuwa社を追い越して最大の携帯電話メーカーになっている。
More details on Density-2000 are available on page 27 — Q153 find out if the features that attract thousands are suitable for you.	Density-2000に関する詳細は27ページに掲載されている。多くの人に人気の特色がご自身に満足のいくものかどうかを，ぜひ確認してほしい。

語句 □top-selling 最もよく売れている　□in first place 1位に
□for the third consecutive month 3カ月連続で　□overtake ～を追い越す

153. Where would the article most likely appear?
(A) In a technology magazine
(B) In a historical novel
(C) In a scholarly journal
(D) In a business report

記事はどこに掲載されていると思われるか。
(A) テクノロジー雑誌
(B) 歴史小説
(C) 学術雑誌
(D) 営業報告書

正解 **(A)**

解説 冒頭にGlobe-biz.net has released its list of top-selling mobile phones for this month.と書かれていることから，この記事が掲載されている媒体は「携帯電話の売り上げ」を扱うようなものだと分かる。最後の文でfind out if the features that attract thousands are suitable for you.とあり，読者が携帯電話を選ぶ際の指針にしてほしいと述べていることから，正解は(A)だ。

154. What is indicated in the article?
(A) Hyuwa-90 has sold more than Density-2000.
(B) Hyuwa is the largest mobile phone manufacturer.
(C) Density-2000 has been a best-selling product for 3 months.
(D) Bensen sold less than 35 million mobile phones last year.

記事にはどんなことが示されているか。
(A) Hyuwa-90はDensity-2000より売り上げが良かった。
(B) Hyuwaは最大の携帯電話メーカーである。
(C) Density-2000は3カ月間で一番よく売れた製品である。
(D) Bensen社は昨年，携帯電話の売り上げが3,500万台未満だった。

正解 **(C)**

解説 What is indicated ～？の問題は問題文を区切りの良いところまで読んだ上で解答するのがコツだが，この問題の正解の根拠は，記事の冒頭付近に登場している。Density-2000 by Bensen is in first place for the third consecutive month.とあるため，Density-2000は3カ月連続で最もよく売れている商品であることが分かる。よって，正解は(C)だ。

Questions 155-156 refer to the following advertisement.
設問 155-156 は次の広告に関するものである。

Get the Professional Look with MP Solutions!

How can MP Solutions improve your business? The way in which you present your material says a lot about your company. Create sophisticated, professional-looking documents by using our thermal binding system. We offer only the highest performance machines in the market.

We provide:
Fast delivery
The machines are normally delivered and are ready for use within 2-3 days from the time of your call.

Q156 User support
Customers will be provided with an exclusive phone number where an expert will answer any questions you may have.

Flexible lease terms
Q155 Our machines are available for short or long-term lease. At this time, items are not available for retail purchases.

MP Solutions社でプロの仕上がりを！

MP Solutions社があなたのビジネスを改善する方法とは？
資料の見せ方で会社の様子がよく分かります。わが社のサーマルバインド製本機を使って，洗練されたプロの仕上がりの文書を作成してください。わが社は市場でトップレベルの性能を誇る機材のみをお届けしています。

わが社は次のようなサービスを提供します。
迅速なお届け
お電話をいただいてから通常2，3日以内に機材をお届けし，使用可能な状態になります。

ユーザーサポート
お客さま専用電話をご用意し，専門家があらゆるご質問にお答えします。

自由なリース期間
わが社の機材は短期，または長期のリース契約となります。現時点で小売は行っておりません。

語句 □sophisticated 洗練された □thermal binding system サーマルバインド製本機
□exclusive 専用の

155. What type of service does MP Solutions offer?
(A) Document shipping service
(B) Equipment rental service
(C) Printer maintenance service
(D) Fashion consultation service

MP Solutions社はどんなタイプのサービスを提供しているか。
(A) 文書配送サービス
(B) 機器のレンタルサービス
(C) 印刷機のメンテナンスサービス
(D) ファッション関係のコンサルティングサービス

正解 **(B)**

解説 サービスを列挙している最後の項目にOur machines are available for short or long-term lease. とある。ここから機器の短期及び長期のリースを提供している会社だということが分かるため，正解は(B)だ。中盤のFast deliveryの項目にあるThe machines are normally deliveredから，機器を提供している会社だということは分かるが，決定的な正解の根拠は，最後の項目のleaseである。

156. What is suggested in the advertisement?
(A) Orders are delivered to destinations overnight.
(B) A support service is available to customers.
(C) Payment can be made in installments.
(D) Support is offered to users 24 hours a day.

広告でどんなことが分かるか。
(A) 注文品は一晩で送り先に配送される。
(B) 顧客はサポートサービスが受けられる。
(C) 分割払いが可能である。
(D) ユーザーサポートは24時間営業である。

正解 **(B)**

解説 User supportの項目にCustomers will be provided with an exclusive phone number where an expert will answer any questions you may have. と書かれている。ユーザーサポート体制が敷かれていることが分かるため，(B)が正解だ。(A)はovernightではなくwithin 2-3 days，(D)は24 hours a dayとは言及されていないので，いずれも不適切。

語句 □in installments 分割払いで

Questions 157-159 refer to the following Web page.

設問 157-159 は次のウェブページに関するものである。

Pinecone Entertainment	Pinecone Entertainment
Q158 Our entertainment division offers tailor-made packages to suit functions of up to 300 people. Our four DJs devote an enormous amount of time to music research and Q157 (D) meet with clients beforehand to discuss requests. Our goal is your satisfaction! Q157 (A) (C) With our lighting and audio-visual effects, we can create just the mood you are looking for!	わが社のエンターテインメント部門は300名までのイベントに対応して，ご要望にぴったりのパックプランをご用意します。わが社の4人のDJは音楽のリサーチに膨大な時間をかけており，リクエストの打ち合わせをするために，事前にお客さまとミーティングを行います。わが社はお客さまの満足を目指しています！　照明，音響や映像の効果で，お望みどおりの雰囲気を作り出します！
Mr. Enzo Rankin, Dacota Financial Institute, says,	Dacota Financial Institute，Enzo Rankin様より
"Thank you for your performance at our gala dinner. Judging from the fact that you were able to extend your services for a few hours and from the compliments we received from guests, I must say hiring you was a great idea. Q159 Our guests came from all walks of life and all of them were happy."	「われわれの祝賀ディナーでのパフォーマンスに感謝いたします。数時間のサービスの延長が可能だったことや，お客さまからいただいたお褒めの言葉から判断すると，貴社にお願いしたのは大成功でした。われわれのお客さまは各界にわたりましたが，どなたも満足していらっしゃいました」

語句　□tailor-made オーダーメードの　□devote A to B　AをBに充てる
□an enormous amount of ～ 膨大な～　□beforehand 事前に，前もって
□gala dinner 祝賀ディナー　□judging from ～ ～から判断すると
□from all walks of life あらゆる職業の

157. What is NOT provided by Pinecone Entertainment?
(A) Lighting adjustment
(B) Market research
(C) Audio-visual effects
(D) Pre-event meeting

Pinecone Entertainment が提供していないものは何か。
(A) 照明の調整
(B) 市場調査
(C) 視聴覚効果
(D) 事前ミーティング

正解 **(B)**
解説 (A), (C), (D) に関しては，それぞれ問題文中の前半に登場している。3つの選択肢の内容を問題文と照合できた時点で，残ったものを正解としてマークすればよい。music research と (B) の Market research を混同しないように注意したい。

158. What is indicated about Pinecone Entertainment's service?
(A) It is customized for each client.
(B) It guarantees 100 percent satisfaction.
(C) It is suitable for events of all sizes.
(D) It must be reserved one week in advance.

Pinecone Entertainment のサービスについてどんなことが示されているか。
(A) 顧客の注文に合わせる。
(B) 100%の満足を保証する。
(C) あらゆる規模のイベントに適している。
(D) 1週間前に予約しなくてはならない。

正解 **(A)**
解説 冒頭で Our entertainment division offers tailor-made packages と述べているため，この会社はオーダーメードの何かを提供していることが理解できる。これを customized と言い換えている (A) が正解だ。

159. What is mentioned in Mr. Rankin's comment?
(A) The event ended earlier than expected.
(B) The attendants were happy with the food quality.
(C) The guests came from a variety of backgrounds.
(D) The company had been recommended by a guest.

Rankin さんのコメントでは何が述べられているか。
(A) イベントは予定より早く終わった。
(B) 出席者は食事の質に満足した。
(C) 客はさまざまな経歴があった。
(D) 会社はある客によって推薦されていた。

正解 **(C)**
解説 問題文後半の Rankin さんのコメントを読むと，Our guests came from all walks of life と述べられている。from all walks of life は「あらゆる職業の」という意味なので正解は (C) だが，知らない場合は消去法を使うのもよいだろう。you were able to extend your services for a few hours からイベントは予定より延長されたことが分かるので (A) は不適切。

Questions 160-163 refer to the following e-mail.
設問 160-163 は次のEメールに関するものである。

From: Margaret Klimov [Mklimov@lonetech.com]
To: Jim Barros [Jbarros@lonetech.com]
Subject: Ice Hockey Event
Date: Wednesday, March 7

Hi Jim,

I wonder if you got the message I left on your desk on Monday. Q160 Q163 (A) Have you already reserved the bus to Yolanda Ice Hockey Stadium? If so, please notify me of the pick-up time and meeting point as I am making Q163 (B) the final copy of the itinerary of the event to distribute to staff members at tomorrow's meeting.

Incidentally, Q162 there are a few dozen sheets of name tag stickers in the storage room if you need them for the event. I thought there were some paper cups and napkins left over from last year's picnic but didn't find any. The storage room is usually open on weekdays, but if it's locked, you can get the key from Elena in the accounting department.

Q161 Q163 (D) I read in the newspaper that it will be nice weather on Friday. I hope you will all enjoy yourselves, and I look forward to hearing all about it when you return!

Margaret

送信者：Margaret Klimov [Mklimov@lonetech.com]
宛先：Jim Barros [Jbarros@lonetech.com]
件名：アイスホッケーのイベント
日付：3月7日 水曜日

こんにちは，Jim

月曜日にあなたのデスクに残したメッセージは受け取ってくれたでしょうか。Yolandaアイスホッケースタジアムへ行くバスはもう予約しましたか。もし予約したなら，明日のミーティングでスタッフに配るイベントの予定表の決定稿を作成しているので，迎えの時間と集合場所を知らせてください。

ちなみに，イベント用に名札ステッカーが必要なら倉庫に何十枚かあります。去年のピクニックで残った紙コップと紙ナプキンがあるはずだと思いましたが，見あたりませんでした。倉庫はいつも平日なら開いていますが，もし鍵が掛かっていたら，経理部のElenaから鍵をもらってください。

新聞を見ると，金曜日はお天気がいいようです。皆さん，楽しく過ごせるよう祈っています。帰ったら，いろいろ聞かせてもらうのを楽しみにしています！

Margaret

語句 □incidentally ちなみに

160. What is the purpose of the e-mail?
(A) To inform a colleague of an office clean-up
(B) To reserve a bus for a sports team
(C) To obtain missing information
(D) To ask about existing stocks

Eメールの目的は何か。
(A) 同僚にオフィスの清掃について知らせること
(B) スポーツチームのためにバスを予約すること
(C) 不足している情報を入手すること
(D) 現在の在庫について問い合わせること

正解 **(C)**

解説 文書の目的を問う頻出の問題だ。第1段落でHave you already reserved the bus to Yolanda Ice Hockey Stadium? If so, please notify me of the pick-up time and meeting pointと述

べているため，Eメールの送信者は迎えの時間と集合場所を知りたいということが分かる。これを抽象的に言い換えている(C)が正解だ。

161. When will the outing take place?
(A) Monday
(B) Wednesday
(C) Friday
(D) Sunday

小旅行はいつ行われるか。
(A) 月曜日
(B) 水曜日
(C) 金曜日
(D) 日曜日

正解 **(C)**

解説 Eメールの終わりの方にI read in the newspaper that it will be nice weather on Friday.と書かれている。話題はYolandaアイスホッケースタジアムに行くことなので，このイベントが開催されるのはFridayだと判断できる。よって正解は(C)だ。(A)のMondayはEメールの送信者がデスクにメッセージを残した日であり，(B)のWednesdayはEメールを送信した日だ。

162. What can be found in the storage room?
(A) Adhesive labels
(B) Disposable cups
(C) Picnic baskets
(D) Paper towels

倉庫には何があるか。
(A) 粘着ラベル
(B) 使い捨てのコップ
(C) ピクニック用のバスケット
(D) ペーパータオル

正解 **(A)**

解説 storage roomをキーワードとして問題文を読み進めていく。中盤にthere are a few dozen sheets of name tag stickers in the storage roomとあるため，倉庫にあるのは名札ステッカーだ。これを言い換えた(A)のAdhesive labelsが正解である。次の文にI thought there were some paper cups and napkins ... but didn't find any.とあるので，(B)のコップは存在が確認されておらず，(D)のペーパータオルについては言及がない。よって(B)と(D)は誤りだ。

語句 □adhesive label 粘着ラベル　□disposable 使い捨ての

163. What is probably NOT true about the event?
(A) Transportation will be arranged.
(B) Schedules will be handed out beforehand.
(C) All employees will participate.
(D) The weather is expected to be sunny.

イベントに関して，正しくないと考えられるのは何か。
(A) 移動手段が手配される。
(B) 予定表が事前に配られる。
(C) 従業員全員が参加する。
(D) 天気は良いと予想される。

正解 **(C)**

解説 (A)はバスが手配される予定とあり，(B)にあるschedulesは明日配布される予定となっている。(D)は新聞でnice weather on Fridayと予想されているため，残った(C)が正解だ。従業員全員が参加することになっているとはEメールのどこにも書かれておらず，最後の1文からEメールの送信者も参加しないことが分かる。

Questions 164-166 refer to the following e-mail.
設問 164-166 は次のEメールに関するものである。

From: Jimmy Chang [Jchang@ssf.com]
To: Colin Peters [Cpeters@osc.org]
Subject: GMT Technologies
Date: April 29

Dear Mr. Peters,

Following the near miss incident at the Abo factory last week, Q164 I was assigned to conduct an assessment of worker safety in twelve GMT factories. Upon careful inspection, I found all safety equipment at the factories in good working condition. However, twenty-five accidents and ten near misses were reported within GMT facilities last year. This year, there have so far been a total of five accident reports. The analysis of incidents shows that 40 percent of the injuries were caused by falling. This included falling from steps, chairs, stools and slipping on wet or uneven surfaces on the floor. Q165 Regrettably, many of the reported incidents could have been avoided if workers followed basic safety rules, such as using ladders to reach higher shelves, wiping any spills on the floor and not leaving unnecessary tools lying around. My conclusion is that the number of accidents can be significantly lowered by reinforcing workplace safety through Q166(D) rewarding workers who demonstrate safe behaviors, Q166(B) encouraging workers to participate in developing safety programs, and Q166(A) placing signs and guidelines in appropriate locations. My full report is attached to this e-mail for the review of the Oakland Safety Commission.

Jimmy Chang
SSF, Inc.

送信者：Jimmy Chang [Jchang@ssf.com]
宛先：Colin Peters [Cpeters@osc.org]
件名：GMT Technologies社
日付：4月29日

Peters様

先週のAbo工場におけるニアミス事故を受けまして，私は12あるGMT工場の作業員の安全性に関するアセスメント実施の担当者となりました。注意深く調査した結果，工場内の全ての安全装置は順調に作動していることが分かりました。しかしながら，GMTの施設内で，昨年中に25件の事故と10件のニアミス事故が報告されています。今年はこれまでのところ，合計で5件の事故の報告が届いています。事故を分析した結果，負傷の40パーセントは転倒によるものだということが分かりました。これには，階段，椅子，スツールからの転倒と，床のぬれた箇所や平らでない箇所でのスリップが含まれています。残念なことに，報告された事故の多くは，作業員が基本的な安全規則を守っていれば防ぎ得たものであり，その一例としては，高い棚に手を伸ばすときははしごを使う，床にこぼれたものは拭き取る，不要な道具を辺りに置きっ放しにしないなどが挙げられます。
結論として，安全な行動を取った作業員を表彰したり，作業員の安全プログラム作成への参加を促したり，適切な場所に標識やガイドラインを設置したりすることを通して，職場の安全を強化することにより，事故の件数は大きく減らせると思われます。Oakland安全委員会にご覧いただくため，私の詳細な報告書をこのEメールに添付しています。

Jimmy Chang
SSF社

語句
□near miss incident ニアミス事故，事故に至らなかった人為的ミス
□be assigned to do ～することを担当する　□uneven surface　平らではない箇所
□regrettably 残念なことに　□significantly 大きく，大いに
□reinforce ～を強化する，補強する

164. What was the content of Mr. Chang's assignment?
(A) To negotiate better working conditions
(B) To investigate the cause of a lone accident
(C) To evaluate the safety of working environments
(D) To implement a new security policy

Changさんの任務の内容は何か。
(A) より良い労働条件を交渉すること
(B) 単独事故の原因を調査すること
(C) 労働環境の安全性を評価すること
(D) 新しい安全対策を実行すること

正解 **(C)**

解説 Changさんの任務に関しては，メールの冒頭でI was assigned to conduct an assessment of worker safety in twelve GMT factories.と書かれている。作業員の安全性に関するアセスメントの実施を行うとのことなので，これを言い換えている(C)が正解だ。

165. What is indicated as the main reason for the incidents?
(A) A malfunction in the machinery
(B) Failure to follow regulations
(C) Lack of human resources
(D) Too much overtime work

事故の主要な原因としてどんなことが示されているか。
(A) 機械の誤作動
(B) 規則に従わないこと
(C) 人材不足
(D) 過剰な時間外労働

正解 **(B)**

解説 メールの中盤にRegrettably, many of the reported incidents could have been avoided if workers followed basic safety rulesとある。今までに起こった事故の多くは，作業員が基本的な安全規則を守っていれば防ぐことができたというのが調査の結果だ。これを端的にまとめた(B)のFailure to follow regulationsが正解となる。

166. What is NOT a suggestion made by Mr. Chang?
(A) Putting up signs on site
(B) Getting workers involved in some programs
(C) Making stricter rules to protect confidentiality
(D) Rewarding employees who act safely

Changさんの提案ではないものはどれか。
(A) 現場に標識を掲げる
(B) いくつかのプログラムに作業員を関与させる
(C) 機密性を守るためにより厳しい規則を作る
(D) 安全な行動を取る従業員を表彰する

正解 **(C)**

解説 Changさんの提案は，メールの終わりの方にまとめて書かれている。(C)のMaking stricter rules to protect confidentialityは機密保持について述べており，安全性を主題としているメールの内容とは関連がない。

語句 □put up ～ ～を掲げる　□confidentiality 機密性

Questions 167-168 refer to the following book review.
設問 167-168 は次の書評に関するものである。

Book of the Month Reviewed by Michael Gottenberg	今月の1冊 書評：Michael Gottenberg
Meals and Magic By Lorenzo Carreras Illustrated. 258 pages Don Juan Publishing. £19.99	*Meals and Magic* Lorenzo Carreras著 図版入り 258ページ Don Juan出版 19.99ポンド
Bookstores today are filled with stacks of books dedicated to helping you with creating great healthy dishes in no time. But have you ever wondered how those images of steaming home-cooked pasta or lamb curry that make your mouth water are taken?	書店は近頃，とても健康的な料理を瞬く間に作るのに役立つ目的で作られた数多くの本であふれかえっています。しかし，湯気の立った自家製パスタやラムカレーのよだれが出るような写真がどのようにして撮られたのだろうと考えたことはありますか。
Wonder no more — Lorenzo Carreras takes you behind the scenes in his new book *Meals and Magic*. Q167 A self-confessed food enthusiast, Carreras interviews chefs, photographers and editors to discover the secret behind creating magnificent food photographs.	もう考える必要はありません。Lorenzo Carrerasが彼の新刊*Meals and Magic*で，（撮影の）裏側へ連れて行ってくれます。美食家を自認するCarrerasは，素晴らしい料理写真の撮影の裏側にある秘密を解き明かすために，シェフや写真家，編集者にインタビューしています。
The book is filled with tricks experienced photographers use to make the dishes look fresh, such as brushing oil over finished food to add shine, and hiding hot towels behind the plate to create steam. Even if you are not a professional cook, Q168 it will be simple to apply the tips in the book to take amazing snapshots of your own culinary handiwork.	この本では，完成した料理につやを出すために油を塗ったり，湯気を作り出すために皿の背後に蒸しタオルを隠したりと，経験豊かな写真家たちが料理を出来たてに見せるために使うトリックがたくさん紹介されています。プロの料理人でなくても，あなたの手料理のすてきなスナップショットを撮るために，本にあるヒントを取り入れるのはいたって簡単でしょう。

語句 □stacks of ～ 大量の～ □dedicated to～ ～に打ち込んでいる □in no time すぐに
□home-cooked 自家製の □make one's mouth water よだれが出る
□wonder no more もう考える必要はありません □self-confessed 自認する
□enthusiast 熱心な人 □magnificent 素晴らしい，壮大な
□brush ～をはけで塗る，軽くかすめる □tip こつ，ヒント □culinary 料理の
□handiwork 手仕事

167. What is indicated about Mr. Carreras?
(A) He is a skilled photographer.
(B) He works with Michael Gottenberg.
(C) He is passionate about food.
(D) He cooks delicious meals.

Carrerasさんについてどんなことが示されているか。
(A) 熟練した写真家である。
(B) Michael Gottenbergと一緒に働いている。
(C) 食べ物が大好きである。
(D) おいしい料理を作る。

正解 **(C)**

解説 Carrerasさんの著作についてのレビューだが，第2段落で彼がどんな人間なのか説明されている。A self-confessed food enthusiastとあるため，Carrerasさんは美食家だと自認していることが分かる。これをpassionate about foodと言い換えた(C)が正解だ。

語句 □passionate 情熱的な，熱烈な

168. What is suggested about the photographic techniques described in the book?
(A) They were developed over many years.
(B) They determine the sales of a product.
(C) They require professional equipment.
(D) They can easily be adopted by amateurs.

本で説明されている写真技術についてどんなことが分かるか。
(A) 長年にわたって開発されてきた。
(B) 製品の売り上げを決定づける。
(C) プロが使う機材を必要とする。
(D) アマチュアでも簡単に取り入れることができる。

正解 **(D)**

解説 レビューの最後にit will be simple to apply the tips in the book to take amazing snapshots of your own culinary handiwork.とある。この本に書かれているヒントを取り入れるのは，プロでなくてもいたって簡単であるとのことなので，それをcan easily be adopted by amateursと言い換えた(D)が正解になる。

語句 □determine ～を決定する　□adopt ～を取り入れる

Questions 169-171 refer to the following article.

設問 169-171 は次の記事に関するものである。

Drought Affects Milk Production

The drought over much of the south-eastern region is putting pressure on dairy farmers. Over the last seven months, the region has experienced a 35 percent decrease in the production of crops such as corn and soybeans. Q169 This has resulted in the doubling of crop prices, which in turn has affected the price of animal feed.

Compared to last year, Q170 the cost of animal feed has increased by 20 percent and many farmers are being forced to use cheaper, less nutritious cattle feed. Not only has this lead to a drop in the total production of milk, but it is affecting the density and creaminess of the product.

Those who refuse to compromise on quality are driven to take on more debt, or to simply leave the field. Q171 Analysts say many of the small dairy farmers will be forced out of business while larger farms and corporate milking operations may manage to get through, but then, only just.

干ばつが生乳の生産に影響

南東部の大部分を襲っている干ばつは酪農農家を圧迫している。ここ7カ月間，この地域ではトウモロコシや大豆などの農作物の生産が35％落ち込んでいる。この結果，農作物の価格が2倍に跳ね上がり，それによって今度は家畜用飼料の価格に影響が出ている。

昨年と比べて，家畜用飼料のコストは20％増加し，多くの農家がより廉価で栄養価の低い家畜用飼料を使うことを余儀なくされている。これは生乳の総生産量の低下を招くだけでなく，製品の濃度やクリーミーさにも影響を及ぼしている。

品質の面で妥協したくない人々は，さらに負債を抱えたり，農場を手放すしかない状況に追い込まれている。小規模な酪農家の多くは廃業に追い込まれ，一方で大規模農場や会社組織の生乳生産業者はどうにか切り抜けるかもしれないが，それも辛うじてであるとアナリストは分析している。

語句
□drought 干ばつ　□dairy farmer 酪農家　□soybean 大豆
□be forced to do ～するのを余儀なくされる　□cattle feed 家畜用飼料
□compromise 妥協する　□milking operation 生乳生産業

169. How much did crop prices increase?
(A) 20 percent
(B) 35 percent
(C) 50 percent
(D) 100 percent

農作物の価格はどのくらい上昇したか。
(A) 20％
(B) 35％
(C) 50％
(D) 100％

正解 **(D)**

解説 農作物の価格がどのくらい上昇したかについては，記事の前半にThis has resulted in the doubling of crop pricesと書かれている。doubling，つまり農作物は倍の価格になったことが分かるので，正解は(D)だ。35 percentや20 percentという数字も記事内に出てくるが，数字がそのまま正解にならないことも多々ある。内容の理解を最優先とし，絶えず「正解は言い換えられているのでは？」という意識を持って解答していこう。

170. What is indicated about animal feed?
(A) It is mainly manufactured in the south-eastern region.
(B) It is in low supply across the world.
(C) It generally does not contain a lot of vitamins.
(D) It has gotten more expensive than before.

家畜の飼料についてどんなことが示されているか。
(A) 主に南東部で生産されている。
(B) 世界中で供給が少ない。
(C) 一般的にビタミン類をあまり多く含んでいない。
(D) 以前より高価になっている。

正解 **(D)**

解説 記事の中盤でthe cost of animal feed has increased by 20 percent and many farmers are being forced to use cheaper, less nutritious cattle feed.と述べられている。家畜用飼料は高価になってきていて，安くて栄養価の低い飼料で代用せざるを得ない現状である。よって，(D)が正解だ。

171. What is suggested by analysts?
(A) Larger corporations should help small farmers.
(B) Both small and large farmers will have a hard time.
(C) Small farmers will need to make more products.
(D) Large farms will be hit the hardest by the drought.

アナリストは何と述べているか。
(A) 大企業は小規模農家を援助すべきである。
(B) 小規模農家も大規模農家も苦難を経験することになる。
(C) 小規模農家はより多く生産することが必要になる。
(D) 大規模農家は干ばつによって最も激しく打撃を受けることになる。

正解 **(B)**

解説 アナリストの見解については，記事の最後の方に書かれている。Analysts say many of the small dairy farmers will be forced out of business while larger farms and corporate milking operations may manage to get throughとあり，小規模農家は廃業し，大規模農家だったら何とか切り抜けられるかもしれないという見解だ。これを簡潔にまとめた(B)が正解である。

Questions 172-175 refer to the following letter.
設問 172-175 は次の手紙に関するものである。

March 28

Mr. Jonathan Lee
767 Kensington Drive
Springfield, VT 05465

Dear Mr. Lee,

Q172 After house hunting for several months, I was delighted to discover your beautiful home located at 767 Kensington Drive. Since I enjoy hiking as a hobby, Q173 (B) the wooded surroundings near the house is perfect for me. It is rare to find such nature and calm so close from downtown Springfield, where incidentally my office is located. Moreover, Q173 (A) I was impressed by the consideration given to the floor layout. Q173 (C) The location of the two bedrooms on the upper floor gives a lot of privacy and shuts out noise from the living room on the first floor.

Q172 I have carefully considered my offering price and have decided to offer $139,000. Q174 My reason for not offering the asking price of $143,000 is because Q175 I noticed that the floorboards in several rooms need to be fixed, and the living room wall needs a new paint job. I think it is a fair offer compared to local housing prices. Q174 For example, a similar two-bedroom house just one block away on Dexter Avenue sold for $128,000.

Thank you for considering my offer. I look forward to hearing from you.

Sincerely,
Russ Taylor
Russ Taylor

3月28日

Jonathan Lee 様
Kensington Drive 767 番地
Springfield, VT 05465

Lee 様

数カ月間の家探しの末，Kensington Drive 767 番地にあるあなたの美しい家を見つけられて，うれしく思いました。趣味としてハイキングを楽しみますので，家が森に近いことは私にとって理想的です。Springfield の繁華街からごく近くに，このような自然と静けさのある場所はなかなか見つけられないものです。そこには，たまたま私の勤務先もあります。さらに，フロアレイアウトへの配慮にも感動しました。上の階の寝室2部屋の配置によってプライバシーがかなり守られ，1階の居間の騒音が遮断されます。

付け値について慎重に検討し，139,000 ドルを付けることに決めました。提示価格の 143,000 ドルを付けない理由は，いくつかの部屋の床板は修理する必要があり，居間の壁は新たに塗装する必要があることに気付いたためです。この地域の住宅価格を考えると，妥当な付け値だと思います。例えば，わずか 1 ブロック離れた Dexter Avenue にある同じような寝室 2 部屋の家は，128,000 ドルで売却されました。

私の申し出をご検討くださり，ありがとうございます。お返事をお待ちしております。

敬具
Russ Taylor（署名）
Russ Taylor

語句
- □house hunting 家探し
- □wooded 森のある
- □be rare to do なかなか～できない
- □upper floor 上の階
- □offering price 付け値
- □asking price（売り手の）提示価格

172. Who most likely wrote the letter?
(A) A property owner
(B) A real estate agent
(C) A home buyer
(D) A next-door neighbor

手紙を書いたのは誰だと考えられるか。
(A) 不動産の所有者
(B) 不動産業者
(C) 住宅の購入者
(D) 隣家の住人

正解 **(C)**

解説 手紙の書き手のRuss Taylorは，冒頭でAfter house hunting for several monthsと書いているが，これだけでは正解の根拠としての決め手に欠ける。第2段落にあるI have carefully considered my offering price and have decided to offer $139,000.まで読み進めてから解答すべき問題だ。この2つの情報をあわせて考えると，手紙の書き手は住宅を買おうとしていると判断できる。よって，正解は(C)だ。

173. What is NOT indicated about the house?
(A) It has a well thought-out layout.
(B) It is surrounded by woods.
(C) It has more than one floor.
(D) It has been soundproofed.

家について示されていないことはどれか。
(A) 考え抜かれたレイアウトである。
(B) 森に囲まれている。
(C) 2階以上ある。
(D) 防音装置が施されている。

正解 **(D)**

解説 家に関する情報は，最初の段落にまとめて書かれている。防音装置に関しては手紙のどこにも言及されていないので，正解は(D)だ。(C)のmore than oneという表現は「2つ以上ある」という意味である。

語句 □well thought-out 考え抜かれた　□soundproofed 防音装置が施された

174. What is suggested about the asking price of the house?
(A) It has been reduced.
(B) It is comparatively high.
(C) It is similar to others on the market.
(D) It is not negotiable.

家の提示価格についてどんなことが分かるか。
(A) 値下げされた。
(B) 比較的高い。
(C) 売りに出されている他の物件と同程度である。
(D) 交渉の余地がない。

正解 **(B)**

解説 家の提示価格に関する情報は，手紙の最後の部分に書かれている。Taylorさんは「提示価格の143,000ドルを付けない」と言ったり「わずか1ブロック離れたDexter Avenueにある同じような寝室2部屋の家は，128,000ドルで売却された」と言ったりしている。提示価格が「高い」ということの理由付けを述べているので，これを抽象化した(B)のIt is comparatively high.が正解だ。

175. What can be inferred about Mr. Taylor?
(A) He is retiring from his job.
(B) He plans to repair the house.
(C) He is a native of Springfield.
(D) He expects housing values to fall.

Taylorさんについて推測できることは何か。
(A) 退職する予定である。
(B) 家の修繕をする予定である。
(C) Springfield出身の人である。
(D) 家の価値が下がると思っている。

正解 **(B)**

解説 Taylorさんは第2段落で，I noticed that the floorboards in several rooms need to be fixed, and the living room wall needs a new paint job.と述べている。「修理を必要とする」ことを理解しつつ「購入したい」と言っているので，(B)のHe plans to repair the house.が正解となる。(C)のSpringfieldはTaylorさんの職場がある場所で，出身地ではない。

語句 □a native of ～ ～出身の人

Questions 176-180 refer to the following letter.

設問 176-180 は次の手紙に関するものである。

August 1	8月1日
Mr. Albert Shea 178 Orange Street Orlando, FL 36729	Albert Shea 様 Orange Street 178 番地 Orlando, FL 36729
Dear Mr. Shea,	Shea 様
Please be advised that Q176 the monthly magazine, *Boating Today*, will cease publication after the September issue. However, we are happy to announce that Q178 the magazine *Seamaster* has agreed to fulfill your subscription for the remaining term of six months.	月刊誌*Boating Today*は，9月号をもちまして廃刊になることをお知らせいたします。ただし，残りの6カ月間については*Seamaster*誌が購読の引き受けに同意したことをお伝えいたします。
Where *Boating Today* brought you insights into the world of cruisers and yachts, *Seamaster* brings you the same deep insights into the world of fishing. Q179 We are sure *Seamaster* will light the same passion in you for fishing that you have for boating.	*Boating Today*は，クルーザーやヨットの世界への洞察をあなたにもたらしましたが，*Seamaster*は釣りの世界に関して同様に深い洞察をもたらす雑誌です。*Seamaster*はあなたの舟遊びに対する情熱と同じように，釣りに対する情熱にも火を付けてくれるはずだと確信しています。
You will receive an issue of *Seamaster* for every remaining issue of *Boating Today* that you were entitled to receive. If you are already subscribed to *Seamaster*, your subscription will be extended for the term left on your original *Boating Today* subscription.	あなたが受け取ることになっていた*Boating Today*の残りの各号に対応する*Seamaster*をあなたにお送りすることになります。すでに*Seamaster*を購読されている場合は，*Boating Today*の元々の購読期間の残りの分だけ，購読期間が延長されることになります。
Q180 If you are not satisfied with this arrangement and wish to receive a refund, please contact the Subscription Department at 555-2790 before September 15.	もしこの対応にご満足いただけず，返金をご希望される場合は，9月15日までに購読部555-2790へご連絡ください。
Sincerely, Willie Boggs Willie Boggs Subscription Department	敬具 Willie Boggs（署名） Willie Boggs 購読部

語句 □please be advised that ～ ～をお知らせします　□cease ～を停止する，中止する
□insight into ～ ～への洞察　□be entitled to do ～する資格がある

176. What is the purpose of the letter?
(A) To advertise a newly inaugurated publication
(B) To inform a reader of a magazine discontinuance
(C) To subscribe to a daily newspaper
(D) To recommend an interesting article

手紙の目的は何か。
(A) 新規に創刊された出版物の宣伝をすること
(B) 読者に雑誌の廃刊を伝えること
(C) 日刊紙の購読をすること
(D) 興味深い記事を推奨すること

正解 **(B)**

解説 文書の目的は最初の方で述べられることが多い。the monthly magazine, *Boating Today*, will cease publication after the September issue. と書かれているため，雑誌の廃刊を伝える内容であると分かる。よって，正解は (B) だ。

語句 □newly inaugurated 新たに始まった　□magazine discontinuance 雑誌の廃刊

177. The word "fulfill" in paragraph 1, line 3, is closest in meaning to
(A) charge
(B) reward
(C) deliver
(D) compromise

第1段落・3行目のfulfillに最も近い意味の語は
(A) ～を請求する
(B) ～に報いる
(C) ～を果たす
(D) ～を妥協して解決する

正解 **(C)**

解説 the magazine *Seamaster* has agreed to fulfill your subscription for the remaining term of six months. において，fulfillは「（義務）を果たす，遂行する」という意味で使われていることが分かる。正解は (C) の deliver だ。

178. What is indicated about *Seamaster*?
(A) Its first edition is coming out in September.
(B) It contains articles on ships and boats.
(C) It will be sent in the place of *Boating Today*.
(D) It has the same theme as *Boating Today*.

*Seamaster*についてどんなことが示されているか。
(A) 創刊号が9月に発行される予定だ。
(B) 船やボートに関する記事を掲載している。
(C) *Boating Today*の代わりに送られてくる予定だ。
(D) *Boating Today*と同じテーマである。

正解 **(C)**

解説 最初の段落にthe magazine *Seamaster* has agreed to fulfill your subscription for the remaining term of six months. とあり，*Boating Today*の廃刊後6カ月間は*Seamaster*が代わりに送られてくるということが分かる。よって，正解は (C) だ。

語句 □in the place of ～ ～の代わりに

179. What is suggested in the letter?
(A) Boating and fishing are similar activities.
(B) Readers of *Boating Today* will also enjoy *Seamaster*.
(C) Both of the magazines are aimed at novice fishermen.
(D) Fishing is more enjoyable than boating.

手紙からどんなことが分かるか。
(A) 舟遊びと釣りは同じような活動である。
(B) *Boating Today*の読者は*Seamaster*も満喫するだろう。
(C) どちらの雑誌も釣りの初心者を対象としている。
(D) 釣りは舟遊びよりも楽しい。

正解 **(B)**

解説 第2段落に We are sure *Seamaster* will light the same passion in you for fishing that you have for boating.「*Seamaster* はあなたの舟遊びに対する情熱と同じように，釣りに対する情熱にも火を付けてくれるはずです」とあることから，この内容を端的にまとめている(B)が正解となる。

語句 □novice 初心者

180. According to the letter, who should contact the Subscription Department?

(A) People wishing to subscribe to *Boating Today*

(B) Clients who already have a subscription with *Seamaster*

(C) Customers wanting reimbursement of the subscription fee

(D) Subscribers who need to change the delivery address

手紙によると，購読部に連絡すべきなのは誰か。

(A) *Boating Today* の購読を希望する人

(B) すでに *Seamaster* の購読をしている顧客

(C) 購読料の返金を希望する顧客

(D) 送付先住所を変更する必要のある購読者

正解 **(C)**

解説 最後の段落に，If you are not satisfied with this arrangement and wish to receive a refund, please contact the Subscription Department at 555-2790 before September 15. と書かれている。返金を希望する人は購読部に電話をかけなくてはいけないということだ。wish to receive a refund を wanting reimbursement と言い換えた(C)が正解だ。

Questions 181-185 refer to the following notice and e-mail.
設問 181-185 は次の案内とEメールに関するものである。

Posted Date: May 7
KGK, Inc.
Now Hiring

Job Description: Q185 KGK, Inc. is a prominent independent oil and gas company based in Texas. We are seeking a manufacturing engineer whose primary responsibility will be to assist in the development and implementation of production techniques. Q182 The individual will need to coordinate with other engineers to achieve clearly defined goals.

Qualifications:
Bachelor's degree in engineering
3-5 years relative experience

Documents required:
Q184 Application letter
Comprehensive résumé with picture

Q183 Deadline of submission of required documents is May 15. A 3-hour written examination will be administered on the following day. Qualified persons can take the exam anytime between 10 A.M. and 5 P.M.

Clark Gold
CGold@kgk.com
Human Resources
KGK, Inc.

掲載日：5月7日
KGK社
従業員募集

職務内容：KGK社は，テキサス州に本拠地を置く著名な独立系石油ガス会社です。当社では，製造技師を募集しておりますが，その主要な責務は製造技術の開発と実施における補佐となります。明確に定められた目標を達成するために，他の技師たちと協力していただく必要があります。

資格：
工学の学士号
関連分野における3～5年の経験

必要書類：
応募用紙
詳細にわたる履歴書（写真付き）

必要書類の提出期限は5月15日です。翌日，3時間の筆記試験を行います。適格者は午前10時から午後5時の間ならいつでも試験を受けていただけます。

Clark Gold
CGold@kgk.com
人事部
KGK社

To: Clark Gold [CGold@kgk.com]
From: Edward Wise [ewise@zennifer.com]
Date: May 10
Subject: Manufacturing Engineer Position

Dear Mr. Gold,

I am writing in response to a notice posted on Jobwide.com.

宛先：Clark Gold [CGold@kgk.com]
送信者：Edward Wise [ewise@zennifer.com]
日付：5月10日
件名：製造技師職

Gold様

Jobwide.comに掲載された案内を見て，ご連絡させていただきます。

My name is Edward Wise and as you can see from my CV, I have graduated from Hopeton University with a degree in engineering. Q184 I received top marks in my classes as is shown on the attached transcript.

Q185 While I was a student, I interned at the oil plant of Thames Global in Singapore every summer. After graduation, I joined Blare Corporation, where I have been working as a manufacturing engineer for three years. I have a reputation of being reliable, hard-working and passionate about my work. Reference letters are available upon request. Also, please find my application letter attached to this e-mail.

Thank you for your consideration, and I look forward to hearing from you.

Sincerely,
Edward Wise

私はEdward Wiseと申しまして，履歴書からお分かりのとおり，Hopeton大学で工学の学位を取得して卒業しました。添付の成績証明書に示されていますが，各授業でトップの成績を取っています。

学生時代には，毎年夏にシンガポールにあるThames Globalの石油プラントで実習生として働きました。卒業後はBlare社に就職し，製造技師として3年間働いてきました。仕事については，信頼ができて，勤勉で，熱心だという評判をいただいています。ご要請があれば，推薦状もご用意できます。また，このEメールに添付した応募用紙もご覧ください。

ご検討いただきますよう，よろしくお願い申し上げます。お返事をお待ちしております。

敬具
Edward Wise

語句 □prominent 著名な　□primary 主要な　□assist in ～ ～を手伝う
□defined 明確に定めた　□bachelor's degree 学士号
□comprehensive 包括的な，総合的な　□administer ～を施行する
□CV（curriculum vitaeの略で）履歴書　□top marks トップの成績
□transcript 成績証明書

181. In the notice, the word "primary" in paragraph 1, line 2, is closest in meaning to
(A) basic
(B) leading
(C) peripheral
(D) social

案内の第1段落・2行目のprimaryに最も近い意味の語は
(A) 基本的な
(B) 一番の
(C) 周辺の
(D) 社会的な

正解 **(B)**

解説 We are seeking a manufacturing engineer whose primary responsibility will be to assist in the development and implementation of production techniques. の中では，primaryは「主要な，主な」という意味で使われている。選択肢の中で同じような意味を持っているのは，(B)のleadingだ。

182. What is suggested about the job?
(A) It is temporary.
(B) It involves team work.
(C) It offers a high salary.
(D) It requires traveling.

職務についてどんなことが示されているか。
(A) 一時的である。
(B) チームワークが必要とされる。
(C) 高い給料が支給される。
(D) 出張が要求される。

正解 (B)

解説 案内の最初の段落にThe individual will need to coordinate with other engineers to achieve clearly defined goals.とあるため，この仕事は他の技師たちと協力することを求められることが分かる。これを端的に表した，(B) のIt involves team work.が正解だ。

183. When will candidates take a written exam?
(A) May 7
(B) May 10
(C) May 15
(D) May 16

候補者はいつ筆記試験を受けるか。
(A) 5月7日
(B) 5月10日
(C) 5月15日
(D) 5月16日

正解 (D)

解説 案内の最後の段落にDeadline of submission of required documents is May 15. A 3-hour written examination will be administered on the following day.と書かれている。書類の締め切りが5月15日で，その翌日に筆記試験が実施されるのだから，(D)が正解となる。

184. What unrequired document is sent with the e-mail?
(A) An application letter
(B) A medical form
(C) Academic records
(D) A letter of reference

要求されていないどんな書類がEメールに添付して送られているか。
(A) 応募用紙
(B) 医師の診断書
(C) 学業成績
(D) 推薦状

正解 (C)

解説 両文書参照型の問題だ。案内のDocuments required: の項目からApplication letterとComprehensive résumé with pictureの2つが求められていることをまず押さえる。Wiseさんが書いたEメールの最初の方にI received top marks in my classes as is shown on the attached transcript.とあり，transcriptには「成績証明書」という意味がある。transcriptをAcademic recordsと言い換えた(C)が正解だ。transcriptの意味を知らなかったとしても，トップの成績を取ったことが記されていることから(C)を選べるだろう。

185. What can be inferred about Mr. Wise?
(A) He recently graduated from university.
(B) He does not have the appropriate experience.
(C) He is familiar with KGK, Inc.'s line of work.
(D) He read the notice in the newspaper.

Wiseさんについてどんなことが推測できるか。
(A) 最近大学を卒業した。
(B) 適切な経験がない。
(C) KGK社の業種についてよく知っている。
(D) 案内を新聞で読んだ。

正解 (C)

解説 両文書参照型の問題だ。案内にKGK, Inc. is a prominent independent oil and gas companyとあるため，KGK社は石油ガス会社だということが分かる。Eメールの中盤にWhile I was a student, I interned at the oil plant of Thames Global in Singapore every summer.と書かれていることから，Wiseさんは石油業界で働いた経験があることが分かる。つまり，彼は石油業界のことを知っていると判断できるので，正解は(C)だ。

語句 □line of work 業種，職種

Questions 186-190 refer to the following article and e-mail.
設問 186-190 は次の記事とEメールに関するものである。

New Grafton Community Center Opens	新Graftonコミュニティーセンターがオープン
Over a year after Miles Hall was damaged by a passing tornado, Q188 the town of Grafton opened the doors to its new community center on Thursday, October 6.	Miles Hallが竜巻の通過で被害を受けてから1年以上たち，Graftonの町は10月6日木曜日に新しいコミュニティーセンターの扉を開けた。
The cost of building the center was initially estimated to reach $1,200,000, which was over the town's already stretched budget of $920,000. The town then decided to use municipal employees to complete the project. Q186 Through using town labor, the total cost was held at $920,000.	このセンターの建設費用は，当初は120万ドルに及ぶと見込まれ，その額は，すでにぎりぎりだった92万ドルの町の予算を超えるものであった。そこで，町はこのプロジェクトを完了させるのに，町の職員を使うことに決めた。町の労働力を使ったことで，総費用は92万ドルに維持できた。
The new community center, housing a multi-purpose room, several program spaces, a fully-equipped kitchen and a children's learning center, was built on the south corner of Grafton Park.	多目的ルームやさまざまなプログラムに対応できるスペースがいくつかあり，全設備が装備されたキッチンや子どもの学習センターを有した新しいコミュニティーセンターは，Grafton公園の南角に建てられた。
Recently, there has been much debate about the fate of the original hall. The initial plan was to demolish it completely, but this has been met with strong opposition from the local community. Grafton Residents' Association member Carrie Houston says, "Miles Hall has been a part of the Grafton community for over 50 years. We hope to keep it that way for future generations."	最近，元のホールの運命については，多くの議論がなされている。当初の計画では完全に取り壊す予定であったが，これは地域の人々からの強い反対に遭った。Grafton町自治会のメンバーであるCarrie Houstonは，「Miles Hallは50年以上にもわたり，Grafton地域の一部であった。今後の世代でも，ホールはそのようにあり続けてほしいと願っている」と述べている。

To: Tim Watkins [twatkins@gpnews.com] From: Carrie Houston [Houston@teb.com] Date: December 20, 9:00 A.M. Subject: Follow-up	宛先：Tim Watkins [twatkins@gpnews.com] 送信者：Carrie Houston [Houston@teb.com] 日付：12月20日，午前9時00分 件名：フォローアップ
Dear Mr. Watkins,	Watkins様
Hello. Q188 You may remember me from the ribbon-cutting ceremony of the Grafton Community Center. Q189 I am writing with an update on Miles Hall, in case you would be interested in writing an article about it.	こんにちは。Graftonコミュニティーセンターでのリボンカットの記念式典にいましたから，私のことを覚えておられるのではないかと思います。Miles Hallについて記事を書くことにご興味があるのでしたらと思い，最新情報についてご連絡差し上げました。

Over the past few months, the Grafton Residents' Association has hosted several fundraising events to help preserve Miles Hall. Q190 We also repeatedly held discussions with town officials, and last week, they finally agreed to move the structure to its new home on 567 Haybale Avenue by the end of February next year. If you have any questions, please contact me at 555-2768.	ここ数カ月にわたって，Grafton町自治会はMiles Hall保存の助けになればと，資金集めのためのイベントをいくつか主催してまいりました。また，町当局と再三にわたり話し合いも行いましたが，ついに先週，この建物をHaybale Avenue 567番地にある新しい敷地に来年の2月末までに動かすことに合意していただけたのです。何かご質問があるようでしたら，555-2768までご連絡ください。
Carrie Houston	Carrie Houston

語句 □stretched budget ぎりぎりの予算 □municipal 町の，市の □house ～を収容する □multi-purpose 多目的の □fully-equipped kitchen 全設備が装備されたキッチン □fundraising 資金集め（の）

186. How was the town able to complete the building of the center without a proper budget?

町はどのようにして十分な予算がない中でセンター建設に成功したか。

(A) By changing contractors
(B) By using existing workers
(C) By applying for a grant
(D) By gathering volunteers

(A) 請負業者を変更する
(B) 今いる職員を使う
(C) 助成金を申請する
(D) ボランティアを集める

正解 **(B)**

解説 記事の第2段落にThrough using town labor, the total cost was held at $920,000. とある。センターの建設費用は120万ドルに及ぶと見込まれていたため，コストを節約するために町の職員を動員した。結果，（人件費を抑えることによって）費用を92万ドルにすることができたのだ。このことを簡潔に言い表している(B)が正解だ。

187. In the article, the word "held" in paragraph 2, line 4, is closest in meaning to

記事の第2段落・4行目のheldに最も近い意味の語は

(A) maintained
(B) approximated
(C) released
(D) compensated

(A) 維持された
(B) 見積もられた
(C) 解放された
(D) 補償された

正解 **(A)**

解説 Through using town labor, the total cost was held at $920,000. の中で，heldはwas heldの形で「維持された」という意味で使われている。選択肢にある単語で同じような意味で使うことができるのは，(A)のmaintainedだ。

188. What is indicated about Ms. Houston?
(A) She has been living in Grafton for 50 years.
(B) She attended an event on October 6.
(C) She is a member of the town council.
(D) She runs a children's learning center.

Houstonさんについてどのようなことが述べられているか。
(A) Graftonに50年住んでいる。
(B) 10月6日のイベントに出席した。
(C) 町議会のメンバーである。
(D) 子どもの学習センターを運営している。

正解 **(B)**

解説 両文書参照型の問題だ。Houstonさんは E メールの最初で，You may remember me from the ribbon-cutting ceremony of the Grafton Community Center. と書いている。記事の最初に the town of Grafton opened the doors to its new community center on Thursday, October 6. とあるため，Grafton コミュニティーセンターの記念式典が行われたのは10月6日だと判断することができる。以上から，(B) が正解となる。

189. Why did Ms. Houston send the e-mail to Mr. Watkins?
(A) To ask for some assistance
(B) To follow up on a job interview
(C) To inform him of a new development
(D) To inquire about an ongoing issue

HoustonさんはなぜWatkinsさんにEメールを送ったのか。
(A) 何らかの助けを求めるため
(B) 就職の面接についてさらに調べるため
(C) 新しい展開について彼に知らせるため
(D) 進行中の問題について尋ねるため

正解 **(C)**

解説 E メールの第1段落にある I am writing with an update on Miles Hall より，E メールの目的は Miles Hall の最新情報を知らせるためだと分かる。これを new development「新展開」と言い換えた (C) が正解。

語句 □follow up on～ ～についてさらに調べる　□development 進展，展開
□ongoing 進行中の

190. According to the e-mail, what will happen next year?
(A) Miles Hall will be renovated.
(B) A meeting will take place.
(C) A fundraiser will be organized.
(D) A building will be relocated.

Eメールによれば，来年何が起こるか。
(A) Miles Hallが改修される。
(B) 会議が開催される。
(C) 資金集めのイベントが企画される。
(D) 建物が移転される。

正解 **(D)**

解説 E メール後半に We also repeatedly held discussions with town officials, and last week, they finally agreed to move the structure to its new home on 567 Haybale Avenue by the end of February next year. とあるので，structure「建造物」が移転することが分かる。よって，正解は (D) だ。

語句 □fundraiser 資金集めのイベント

Questions 191-195 refer to the following e-mails.
設問 191-195 は次の２つのＥメールに関するものである。

To: Joanna Flore [jflore@lgar.com]
From: Erika Smith [SmithE@joosta.com]
Date: November 1, 10:25 A.M.
Subject: Introducing Joosta, Inc.

Dear Ms. Flore,

Hello! I am writing to introduce you to our company, Joosta, Inc. We are a German company which designs and produces top quality wooden toys. Our products have been widely enjoyed in Germany for over fifteen years. All our toys are made from safe, premium quality material and Q194 (B) each one is crafted by hand by an expert toymaker in Germany. Within the country, our products are sold in such reputable department stores as Axi and Rian Guus.

Q192 Currently, we are working to develop our clientele in the North American region. Q191 This is why we have prepared a sample package which you, as a retailer in North America, Q193 can receive for free by filling out the attached form and sending it back to us. It is important that you fill out all the entries on the form to ensure a swift delivery. Q194 (A) (B) Included in the package are a few of our most popular toys and some items from our brand-new children's apparel line. After you experience our products first-hand, you can then decide whether to place further orders with us.

We look forward to working with you.

Sincerely,
Q195 Erika Smith, Manager
Joosta, Inc.

宛先：Joanna Flore [jflore@lgar.com]
送信者：Erika Smith [SmithE@joosta.com]
日付：11月1日，午前10時25分
件名：Joosta 社のご紹介

Flore 様

こんにちは！ 私たちの会社，Joosta 社をご紹介するためにこのEメールを書いています。当社は最高品質の木製玩具のデザイン，および製造を行っているドイツの会社です。当社の製品は15年以上にわたり，ドイツで幅広くご愛顧いただいています。当社のおもちゃは全て安全で高品質な材料を使用しており，ドイツの専門職人が一つ一つ手作りしています。国内では，当社の製品はAxiやRian Guusといった一流百貨店で販売されています。

当社は現在，北米地域における顧客開拓に取り組んでいます。このようなわけで，北米の小売業者である貴店が添付の用紙に記入し，ご返送くだされば無料で受け取ることができるサンプルパッケージをご用意しております。迅速な配達をお約束するためには，用紙の全ての項目に必要事項を記入していただくことが重要です。パッケージには，当社の最も人気のあるおもちゃ数点と最新の子ども服を数点，同梱いたします。当社製品を直接ご体験いただいて，それから当社へ注文するか否かをお決めください。

貴店とのお取り引きを心待ちにしています。

敬具
Erika Smith, マネージャー
Joosta 社

To: Joanna Flore [jflore@lgar.com]
From: Adrian Appel [AppelA@joosta.com]
Date: November 7, 9:00 A.M.
Subject: Sample Pack

Dear Ms. Flore,

宛先：Joanna Flore [jflore@lgar.com]
送信者：Adrian Appel [AppelA@joosta.com]
日付：11月7日，午前9時00分
件名：サンプルパック

Flore 様

We are delighted to hear of your interest in our products. A sample package is on its way! Should you decide to place an order, simply fill out and Q194 (D) return the order sheet enclosed in the package.

In an effort to reduce our carbon footprint, we no longer provide printed literature with our sample packs. However, detailed product information and technical documentation can be downloaded from our Web site.

Q195 Regarding your question concerning high-volume order discount, the manager will get back to you with details in a separate e-mail which will be sent shortly.

Thank you.

Adrian Appel, Customer Representative
Joosta, Inc.

当社商品にご関心を持ってくださっていることで，うれしく思っております。サンプルパッケージは，ただ今お送りしているところです！　もしご注文をお決めになりましたら，パッケージに同梱した注文用紙にご記入の上，ご返送いただくだけで構いません。

二酸化炭素排出量削減のため，現在ではサンプルパックに印刷物を同梱しておりません。ただし，詳細な製品情報と技術文書は，当社ウェブサイトからダウンロードできます。

大量注文割引に関するご質問については，マネージャーが間もなくお送りする別のEメールで詳細をお伝えいたします。

よろしくお願いします。

Adrian Appel，顧客担当者
Joosta社

語句　□premium 上等な，高級な　□clientele 顧客　□swift 迅速な
□carbon footprint 二酸化炭素排出量　□printed literature 印刷物
□technical documentation 技術文書　□high-volume 大量の

191. Who most likely is Ms. Flore?
(A) A representative of a manufacturing company
(B) A customer of a department store
(C) A store owner in North America
(D) A wood supplier based in Germany

Floreさんとは誰だと考えられるか。
(A) 製造会社の代表者
(B) 百貨店の顧客
(C) 北米の店主
(D) ドイツを拠点とした木材供給業者

正解　**(C)**

解説　1つ目のEメール第2段落に，This is why we have prepared a sample package which you, as a retailer in North Americaと書かれているため，Floreさんは北米の小売業者だと分かる。よって，正解は(C)だ。

192. What can be inferred about Joosta, Inc.?
(A) It is a family-owned company.
(B) It is expanding its business.
(C) Its products are manufactured abroad.
(D) Its main customer base is in North America.

Joosta社について何が推測できるか。
(A) 家族経営企業である。
(B) 事業を拡大している。
(C) 商品は国外で製造されている。
(D) 主な顧客基盤は北米にある。

正解　**(B)**

解説　Joosta社は，1つ目のEメールの送信者であるSmithさんが勤務している会社だ。第2段落にCurrently, we are working to develop our clientele in the North American region. とあるので，この会社は現在，北米地域における顧客開拓に取り組んでいることが分かる。よって，正解

は(B)だ。北米で顧客基盤を開拓してはいるが，主な基盤になったとは書かれていないので(D)は不正解である。

193. What is Ms. Flore encouraged to do?
(A) Let customers try out Joosta, Inc. products
(B) Return a document to receive complimentary samples
(C) Complete and send a form to enter a contest
(D) Read customer reviews on Joosta, Inc.'s Web site

Floreさんは何をするよう勧められているか。
(A) 顧客にJoosta社の商品を試用させる
(B) 無料サンプルを受け取るために書類を返送する
(C) コンテストに参加するために用紙に記入して送る
(D) Joosta社のウェブサイトでカスタマーレビューを読む

正解 **(B)**

解説 191.の正解の根拠と同じ部分を含めた文に「添付の用紙に記入し，返送すれば無料で受け取ることができるサンプルパッケージを用意している」という内容が書かれている。これをまとめて表現した(B)のReturn a document to receive complimentary samplesが正解だ。

194. What is NOT included in the package?
(A) Some garments
(B) Handmade toys
(C) A product catalogue
(D) An order form

パッケージに含まれていないものは何か。
(A) 衣類
(B) 手作りのおもちゃ
(C) 商品カタログ
(D) 注文用紙

正解 **(C)**

解説 1つ目のEメールの終盤にIncluded in the package are a few of our most popular toys and some items from our brand-new children's apparel line.とあるため，(A)と(B)がパッケージに含まれていることが分かる。また，2つ目のEメールの最初の方にreturn the order sheet enclosed in the package.とあるので，(D)の注文用紙もパッケージに含まれていることが分かる。よって，正解は(C)。「印刷物は同梱していない」や「詳しい製品情報はウェブサイトからダウンロード」といった表現からも，商品カタログは入っていないと考えられる。

語句 □garment 衣類

195. What is indicated about high-volume orders?
(A) A separate price list will be sent.
(B) The toy designs do not allow for mass production.
(C) Joanna Flore will need to meet with the manager.
(D) Erika Smith will provide more information.

大量注文についてどんなことが示されているか。
(A) 別に価格表が送られる。
(B) おもちゃのデザインの都合上，大量生産は不可能である。
(C) Joanna Floreはマネージャーと会う必要がある。
(D) Erika Smithがさらに情報を提供する。

正解 **(D)**

解説 両文書参照型問題だ。2つ目の文書の終わりにRegarding your question concerning high-volume order discount, the manager will get back to you with details in a separate e-mailと書かれているため，大量注文に関するEメールをJoosta社のマネージャーが送ることになっていると分かる。また，1つ目のEメールの最後の部分からErika Smithはこの会社のマネージャーだと分かるため，正解は(D)だ。

語句 □mass production 大量生産

Questions 196-200 refer to the following article and letter.

設問 196-200 は次の記事と手紙に関するものである。

NEWPORT — Potential visitors to the Newport Flower Show are not the only ones hoping for better summer weather. As the unusually rainy summer forces many flower shows to be canceled, organizers hope the same won't happen to Q198 their show which brings in approximately 40,000 visitors to the town each year. The show, which is hosted by the Newport Horticultural Society and costs £300,000 to stage, is a big boost to Newport's economy.

Q196 "I don't think the event will be canceled totally, but I'm afraid it will be severely curtailed like the flower shows at Stony Shade or Templeton." said Rolf Kelly, a Newport business owner.

This year at the Newport Flower Show, Q197 on top of the usual display of various flowers and over 100 fantastic English-style gardens, a demonstration by the rescue dog team will take place. Also, a glass pavilion has once again been set up to house the many species of roses.

Bob Martin, President of the Newport Horticultural Society says, "We have prepared a stunning range of events with the help of the local community. For example, this is our first attempt to incorporate animals into our show, which we hope will be appreciated by people of all ages but especially by our younger guests."

ニューポート一夏の天気がもっと良くなることを期待しているのは，ニューポート・フラワーショーへの来場見込み客だけではない。いつになく雨の多い夏のため，多くのフラワーショーが中止に追い込まれており，毎年約4万人の来場者を町に動員するショーに同様の事態が起こらないことを，主催者は願っている。ニューポート園芸協会が主催し，実施に30万ポンドの費用がかかるショーは，ニューポート経済を大きく後押しするものなのだ。

「イベントが完全に中止になるとは思いませんが，Stony Shade や Templeton のフラワーショーのように大幅に短縮される可能性はありますね」と，ニューポート市で事業経営をしている Rolf Kelly さんは語った。

今年のニューポート・フラワーショーでは，さまざまな花や100以上の幻想的な英国風庭園といった通常の展示に加えて，救助犬チームによるデモンストレーションが行われる予定だ。また，多彩な種のバラを収容するためにガラスの展示館が再び建てられた。

ニューポート園芸協会の Bob Martin 会長は，「地域社会の助けを借りて驚くほど幅広いイベントを準備しました。例えば，ショーに動物を取り入れるのは今回が初めての試みで，これがあらゆる年齢の人々，特に若いお客さまに気に入っていただけることを願っています」と語った。

August 31

Mr. Bob Martin
Newport Horticultural Society
287 Bane Street
Newport, South Wales
NP18 6G5

Dear Mr. Martin,

I would like to congratulate you on the success of last week's flower show. I'm happy to hear

8月31日

Bob Martin 様
ニューポート園芸協会
Bane Street 287 番地
Newport, South Wales
NP18 6G5

Martin 様

先週のフラワーショーのご成功に，お祝いの言葉を述べさせていただきます。悪天候にも

that Q198 you had a turnout of around 40,000 visitors despite adverse weather conditions. I visited the show twice during its opening days myself. Q197 I loved the glass pavilion section last year and the roses were magnificent this year as well.	かかわらず，約4万人の来場客があったと聞き，うれしく思っております。私自身は開催期間中に2回，ショーを見に行きました。昨年はガラスの展示館のセクションをとても気に入ったのですが，バラは今年も壮大に咲いていました。
Q199 Q200 I deeply appreciate the kind suggestion by the Newport Horticultural Society of donating flowers and plants for the Newport Hospital playground. Unfortunately, however, at this time we do not have enough funds or manpower to plant and maintain them. Nevertheless, we thank you for thinking of us.	ニューポート病院の遊び場用に花や植物を寄付するというニューポート園芸協会による親切なご提案に深く感謝いたします。しかし残念なことに，現時点で当院には花や植物を植えて，維持できるほどの資金や人手がありません。とは言いましても，当院のことをお考えくださり，感謝いたします。
Sincerely, Jing Wong Jing Wong, Director	敬具 Jing Wong（署名） Jing Wong，理事長

語句 □boost to ～ ～への弾み □curtail ～を縮小する □on top of ～ ～に加えて
□stunning 素晴らしい，驚くほどの □incorporate A into B AをBに組み入れる
□turnout 人出 □adverse weather conditions 悪天候

196. Why is Mr. Kelly concerned?
(A) A major town event has been canceled.
(B) The water shortage has damaged plants.
(C) Business has been slow in Newport.
(D) Some other flower shows were cut short.

Kellyさんはなぜ心配しているか。
(A) 町の主要イベントが中止になったため。
(B) 水不足が植物に被害を与えたため。
(C) ニューポートの景気が停滞気味であるため。
(D) いくつかの他のフラワーショーが短縮されたため。

正解 **(D)**

解説 記事の第2段落に "I don't think the event will be canceled totally, but I'm afraid it will be severely curtailed like the flower shows at Stony Shade or Templeton." said Rolf Kelly とある。Kellyさんが心配しているのは，他のフラワーショーのようにイベントが短縮されてしまうことだ。be severely curtailed を were cut short と言い換えた(D)が正解だ。

語句 □be cut short 短縮される

197. What feature is new to this year's show?
(A) Glass pavilion
(B) English gardens
(C) Rescue dog demonstration
(D) Children's playground

今年のショーに新たに登場する呼び物は何か。
(A) ガラスの展示館
(B) 英国風庭園
(C) 救助犬のデモンストレーション
(D) 子ども用の遊び場

正解 **(C)**

解説 今年のショーの追加情報に関しては，記事の第3段落に書かれている。on top of the usual

display of various flowers and over 100 fantastic English-style gardens, a demonstration by the rescue dog team will take place. とあるので，救助犬のデモンストレーションが追加されることが分かる。よって，正解は(C)だ。(A)のglass pavilionは記事にhas once again been set upとあり，手紙の中盤にもI loved the glass pavilion section last yearとあることから，昨年もあったことが分かるので不正解。

198. What can be inferred about the turnout?
(A) It was poorer than expected.
(B) It was more than usual.
(C) It was less than last year.
(D) It was about the same as usual.

人出に関して推測できることは何か。
(A) 予想より少なかった。
(B) 例年より多かった。
(C) 昨年より少なかった。
(D) 例年と同程度だった。

正解 **(D)**

解説 記事の最初の段落にtheir show which brings in approximately 40,000 visitors to the town each year. とあることから，ショーには毎年約4万人の人出があることが分かる。また，手紙の最初の段落にyou had a turnout of around 40,000 visitorsと書かれているため，今年も例年通り約4万人がイベントを訪れたということが分かる。よって，正解は(D)だ。

199. What is the purpose of the letter?
(A) To congratulate an award winner
(B) To report on the outcome of an event
(C) To thank for a monetary donation
(D) To decline a proposed offer

手紙の目的は何か。
(A) 受賞者にお祝いを述べること
(B) イベントの成果について報告すること
(C) 義援金について感謝の意を述べること
(D) 提案された申し出を断ること

正解 **(D)**

解説 手紙の第2段落全体が，この手紙を書いた理由となっている。「ニューポート病院の遊び場用に花や植物を寄付するという親切なご提案に深く感謝いたします。しかし残念なことに，現時点で当院には花や植物を植えて，維持できるほどの資金や人手がありません」と，協会の申し出を断る内容だ。これを簡潔に言い換えた(D)のTo decline a proposed offerが正解となる。

200. What type of organization does Mr. Wong most likely work for?
(A) A regional committee
(B) A local school
(C) A health service
(D) A charity organization

Wongさんはどのような種類の組織で働いていると考えられるか。
(A) 地域の委員会
(B) 地元の学校
(C) 医療サービス
(D) 慈善組織

正解 **(C)**

解説 手紙を書いたのがWongさんである。199.と同じ部分がこの問題でも正解の根拠となる。ここでWongさんはニューポート病院への寄付の提案に謝辞を述べ，最後の1文でもwe thank you for thinking of us.と主語をweにして感謝している。以上から，このような内容を書くのはニューポート病院の関係者だと推測できるので，正解は(C)だ。

キリトリ

Training 解答用紙

Part 3

No.	ANSWER A B C D	No.	ANSWER A B C D
1	Ⓐ Ⓑ Ⓒ Ⓓ	11	Ⓐ Ⓑ Ⓒ Ⓓ
2	Ⓐ Ⓑ Ⓒ Ⓓ	12	Ⓐ Ⓑ Ⓒ Ⓓ
3	Ⓐ Ⓑ Ⓒ Ⓓ		
4	Ⓐ Ⓑ Ⓒ Ⓓ		
5	Ⓐ Ⓑ Ⓒ Ⓓ		
6	Ⓐ Ⓑ Ⓒ Ⓓ		
7	Ⓐ Ⓑ Ⓒ Ⓓ		
8	Ⓐ Ⓑ Ⓒ Ⓓ		
9	Ⓐ Ⓑ Ⓒ Ⓓ		
10	Ⓐ Ⓑ Ⓒ Ⓓ		

Part 4

No.	ANSWER A B C D	No.	ANSWER A B C D
1	Ⓐ Ⓑ Ⓒ Ⓓ	11	Ⓐ Ⓑ Ⓒ Ⓓ
2	Ⓐ Ⓑ Ⓒ Ⓓ	12	Ⓐ Ⓑ Ⓒ Ⓓ
3	Ⓐ Ⓑ Ⓒ Ⓓ		
4	Ⓐ Ⓑ Ⓒ Ⓓ		
5	Ⓐ Ⓑ Ⓒ Ⓓ		
6	Ⓐ Ⓑ Ⓒ Ⓓ		
7	Ⓐ Ⓑ Ⓒ Ⓓ		
8	Ⓐ Ⓑ Ⓒ Ⓓ		
9	Ⓐ Ⓑ Ⓒ Ⓓ		
10	Ⓐ Ⓑ Ⓒ Ⓓ		

Part 5

No.	ANSWER A B C D	No.	ANSWER A B C D	No.	ANSWER A B C D	No.	ANSWER A B C D
1	Ⓐ Ⓑ Ⓒ Ⓓ	11	Ⓐ Ⓑ Ⓒ Ⓓ	21	Ⓐ Ⓑ Ⓒ Ⓓ	31	Ⓐ Ⓑ Ⓒ Ⓓ
2	Ⓐ Ⓑ Ⓒ Ⓓ	12	Ⓐ Ⓑ Ⓒ Ⓓ	22	Ⓐ Ⓑ Ⓒ Ⓓ	32	Ⓐ Ⓑ Ⓒ Ⓓ
3	Ⓐ Ⓑ Ⓒ Ⓓ	13	Ⓐ Ⓑ Ⓒ Ⓓ	23	Ⓐ Ⓑ Ⓒ Ⓓ	33	Ⓐ Ⓑ Ⓒ Ⓓ
4	Ⓐ Ⓑ Ⓒ Ⓓ	14	Ⓐ Ⓑ Ⓒ Ⓓ	24	Ⓐ Ⓑ Ⓒ Ⓓ	34	Ⓐ Ⓑ Ⓒ Ⓓ
5	Ⓐ Ⓑ Ⓒ Ⓓ	15	Ⓐ Ⓑ Ⓒ Ⓓ	25	Ⓐ Ⓑ Ⓒ Ⓓ	35	Ⓐ Ⓑ Ⓒ Ⓓ
6	Ⓐ Ⓑ Ⓒ Ⓓ	16	Ⓐ Ⓑ Ⓒ Ⓓ	26	Ⓐ Ⓑ Ⓒ Ⓓ	36	Ⓐ Ⓑ Ⓒ Ⓓ
7	Ⓐ Ⓑ Ⓒ Ⓓ	17	Ⓐ Ⓑ Ⓒ Ⓓ	27	Ⓐ Ⓑ Ⓒ Ⓓ	37	Ⓐ Ⓑ Ⓒ Ⓓ
8	Ⓐ Ⓑ Ⓒ Ⓓ	18	Ⓐ Ⓑ Ⓒ Ⓓ	28	Ⓐ Ⓑ Ⓒ Ⓓ	38	Ⓐ Ⓑ Ⓒ Ⓓ
9	Ⓐ Ⓑ Ⓒ Ⓓ	19	Ⓐ Ⓑ Ⓒ Ⓓ	29	Ⓐ Ⓑ Ⓒ Ⓓ	39	Ⓐ Ⓑ Ⓒ Ⓓ
10	Ⓐ Ⓑ Ⓒ Ⓓ	20	Ⓐ Ⓑ Ⓒ Ⓓ	30	Ⓐ Ⓑ Ⓒ Ⓓ	40	Ⓐ Ⓑ Ⓒ Ⓓ

Part 5 Review of Training

No.	ANSWER A B C D	No.	ANSWER A B C D	No.	ANSWER A B C D	No.	ANSWER A B C D
1	Ⓐ Ⓑ Ⓒ Ⓓ	11	Ⓐ Ⓑ Ⓒ Ⓓ	21	Ⓐ Ⓑ Ⓒ Ⓓ	31	Ⓐ Ⓑ Ⓒ Ⓓ
2	Ⓐ Ⓑ Ⓒ Ⓓ	12	Ⓐ Ⓑ Ⓒ Ⓓ	22	Ⓐ Ⓑ Ⓒ Ⓓ	32	Ⓐ Ⓑ Ⓒ Ⓓ
3	Ⓐ Ⓑ Ⓒ Ⓓ	13	Ⓐ Ⓑ Ⓒ Ⓓ	23	Ⓐ Ⓑ Ⓒ Ⓓ	33	Ⓐ Ⓑ Ⓒ Ⓓ
4	Ⓐ Ⓑ Ⓒ Ⓓ	14	Ⓐ Ⓑ Ⓒ Ⓓ	24	Ⓐ Ⓑ Ⓒ Ⓓ	34	Ⓐ Ⓑ Ⓒ Ⓓ
5	Ⓐ Ⓑ Ⓒ Ⓓ	15	Ⓐ Ⓑ Ⓒ Ⓓ	25	Ⓐ Ⓑ Ⓒ Ⓓ	35	Ⓐ Ⓑ Ⓒ Ⓓ
6	Ⓐ Ⓑ Ⓒ Ⓓ	16	Ⓐ Ⓑ Ⓒ Ⓓ	26	Ⓐ Ⓑ Ⓒ Ⓓ	36	Ⓐ Ⓑ Ⓒ Ⓓ
7	Ⓐ Ⓑ Ⓒ Ⓓ	17	Ⓐ Ⓑ Ⓒ Ⓓ	27	Ⓐ Ⓑ Ⓒ Ⓓ	37	Ⓐ Ⓑ Ⓒ Ⓓ
8	Ⓐ Ⓑ Ⓒ Ⓓ	18	Ⓐ Ⓑ Ⓒ Ⓓ	28	Ⓐ Ⓑ Ⓒ Ⓓ	38	Ⓐ Ⓑ Ⓒ Ⓓ
9	Ⓐ Ⓑ Ⓒ Ⓓ	19	Ⓐ Ⓑ Ⓒ Ⓓ	29	Ⓐ Ⓑ Ⓒ Ⓓ	39	Ⓐ Ⓑ Ⓒ Ⓓ
10	Ⓐ Ⓑ Ⓒ Ⓓ	20	Ⓐ Ⓑ Ⓒ Ⓓ	30	Ⓐ Ⓑ Ⓒ Ⓓ	40	Ⓐ Ⓑ Ⓒ Ⓓ

Part 7

No.	ANSWER A B C D	No.	ANSWER A B C D	No.	ANSWER A B C D
1	Ⓐ Ⓑ Ⓒ Ⓓ	11	Ⓐ Ⓑ Ⓒ Ⓓ	21	Ⓐ Ⓑ Ⓒ Ⓓ
2	Ⓐ Ⓑ Ⓒ Ⓓ	12	Ⓐ Ⓑ Ⓒ Ⓓ	22	Ⓐ Ⓑ Ⓒ Ⓓ
3	Ⓐ Ⓑ Ⓒ Ⓓ	13	Ⓐ Ⓑ Ⓒ Ⓓ	23	Ⓐ Ⓑ Ⓒ Ⓓ
4	Ⓐ Ⓑ Ⓒ Ⓓ	14	Ⓐ Ⓑ Ⓒ Ⓓ	24	Ⓐ Ⓑ Ⓒ Ⓓ
5	Ⓐ Ⓑ Ⓒ Ⓓ	15	Ⓐ Ⓑ Ⓒ Ⓓ	25	Ⓐ Ⓑ Ⓒ Ⓓ
6	Ⓐ Ⓑ Ⓒ Ⓓ	16	Ⓐ Ⓑ Ⓒ Ⓓ	26	Ⓐ Ⓑ Ⓒ Ⓓ
7	Ⓐ Ⓑ Ⓒ Ⓓ	17	Ⓐ Ⓑ Ⓒ Ⓓ	27	Ⓐ Ⓑ Ⓒ Ⓓ
8	Ⓐ Ⓑ Ⓒ Ⓓ	18	Ⓐ Ⓑ Ⓒ Ⓓ		
9	Ⓐ Ⓑ Ⓒ Ⓓ	19	Ⓐ Ⓑ Ⓒ Ⓓ		
10	Ⓐ Ⓑ Ⓒ Ⓓ	20	Ⓐ Ⓑ Ⓒ Ⓓ		

Practice Test 解答用紙

	Part 1		Part 2						Part 3				Part 4			
	No.	ANSWER A B C D	No.	ANSWER A B C	No.	ANSWER A B C	No.	ANSWER A B C	No.	ANSWER A B C D	No.	ANSWER A B C D	No.	ANSWER A B C D	No.	ANSWER A B C D
LISTENING SECTION	1	Ⓐ Ⓑ Ⓒ Ⓓ	1	Ⓐ Ⓑ Ⓒ	11	Ⓐ Ⓑ Ⓒ	21	Ⓐ Ⓑ Ⓒ	1	Ⓐ Ⓑ Ⓒ Ⓓ	11	Ⓐ Ⓑ Ⓒ Ⓓ	1	Ⓐ Ⓑ Ⓒ Ⓓ	11	Ⓐ Ⓑ Ⓒ Ⓓ
	2	Ⓐ Ⓑ Ⓒ Ⓓ	2	Ⓐ Ⓑ Ⓒ	12	Ⓐ Ⓑ Ⓒ	22	Ⓐ Ⓑ Ⓒ	2	Ⓐ Ⓑ Ⓒ Ⓓ	12	Ⓐ Ⓑ Ⓒ Ⓓ	2	Ⓐ Ⓑ Ⓒ Ⓓ	12	Ⓐ Ⓑ Ⓒ Ⓓ
	3	Ⓐ Ⓑ Ⓒ Ⓓ	3	Ⓐ Ⓑ Ⓒ	13	Ⓐ Ⓑ Ⓒ	23	Ⓐ Ⓑ Ⓒ	3	Ⓐ Ⓑ Ⓒ Ⓓ	13	Ⓐ Ⓑ Ⓒ Ⓓ	3	Ⓐ Ⓑ Ⓒ Ⓓ	13	Ⓐ Ⓑ Ⓒ Ⓓ
	4	Ⓐ Ⓑ Ⓒ Ⓓ	4	Ⓐ Ⓑ Ⓒ	14	Ⓐ Ⓑ Ⓒ	24	Ⓐ Ⓑ Ⓒ	4	Ⓐ Ⓑ Ⓒ Ⓓ	14	Ⓐ Ⓑ Ⓒ Ⓓ	4	Ⓐ Ⓑ Ⓒ Ⓓ	14	Ⓐ Ⓑ Ⓒ Ⓓ
	5	Ⓐ Ⓑ Ⓒ Ⓓ	5	Ⓐ Ⓑ Ⓒ	15	Ⓐ Ⓑ Ⓒ	25	Ⓐ Ⓑ Ⓒ	5	Ⓐ Ⓑ Ⓒ Ⓓ	15	Ⓐ Ⓑ Ⓒ Ⓓ	5	Ⓐ Ⓑ Ⓒ Ⓓ	15	Ⓐ Ⓑ Ⓒ Ⓓ
	6	Ⓐ Ⓑ Ⓒ Ⓓ	6	Ⓐ Ⓑ Ⓒ	16	Ⓐ Ⓑ Ⓒ	26	Ⓐ Ⓑ Ⓒ	6	Ⓐ Ⓑ Ⓒ Ⓓ			6	Ⓐ Ⓑ Ⓒ Ⓓ		
	7	Ⓐ Ⓑ Ⓒ Ⓓ	7	Ⓐ Ⓑ Ⓒ	17	Ⓐ Ⓑ Ⓒ	27	Ⓐ Ⓑ Ⓒ	7	Ⓐ Ⓑ Ⓒ Ⓓ			7	Ⓐ Ⓑ Ⓒ Ⓓ		
	8	Ⓐ Ⓑ Ⓒ Ⓓ	8	Ⓐ Ⓑ Ⓒ	18	Ⓐ Ⓑ Ⓒ	28	Ⓐ Ⓑ Ⓒ	8	Ⓐ Ⓑ Ⓒ Ⓓ			8	Ⓐ Ⓑ Ⓒ Ⓓ		
	9	Ⓐ Ⓑ Ⓒ Ⓓ	9	Ⓐ Ⓑ Ⓒ	19	Ⓐ Ⓑ Ⓒ	29	Ⓐ Ⓑ Ⓒ	9	Ⓐ Ⓑ Ⓒ Ⓓ			9	Ⓐ Ⓑ Ⓒ Ⓓ		
	10	Ⓐ Ⓑ Ⓒ Ⓓ	10	Ⓐ Ⓑ Ⓒ	20	Ⓐ Ⓑ Ⓒ	30	Ⓐ Ⓑ Ⓒ	10	Ⓐ Ⓑ Ⓒ Ⓓ			10	Ⓐ Ⓑ Ⓒ Ⓓ		

	Part 5								Part 6				Part 7					
	No.	ANSWER A B C D	No.	ANSWER A B C D	No.	ANSWER A B C D	No.	ANSWER A B C D	No.	ANSWER A B C D	No.	ANSWER A B C D	No.	ANSWER A B C D	No.	ANSWER A B C D	No.	ANSWER A B C D
READING SECTION	1	Ⓐ Ⓑ Ⓒ Ⓓ	11	Ⓐ Ⓑ Ⓒ Ⓓ	21	Ⓐ Ⓑ Ⓒ Ⓓ	31	Ⓐ Ⓑ Ⓒ Ⓓ	1	Ⓐ Ⓑ Ⓒ Ⓓ	11	Ⓐ Ⓑ Ⓒ Ⓓ	1	Ⓐ Ⓑ Ⓒ Ⓓ	11	Ⓐ Ⓑ Ⓒ Ⓓ	21	Ⓐ Ⓑ Ⓒ Ⓓ
	2	Ⓐ Ⓑ Ⓒ Ⓓ	12	Ⓐ Ⓑ Ⓒ Ⓓ	22	Ⓐ Ⓑ Ⓒ Ⓓ	32	Ⓐ Ⓑ Ⓒ Ⓓ	2	Ⓐ Ⓑ Ⓒ Ⓓ	12	Ⓐ Ⓑ Ⓒ Ⓓ	2	Ⓐ Ⓑ Ⓒ Ⓓ	12	Ⓐ Ⓑ Ⓒ Ⓓ	22	Ⓐ Ⓑ Ⓒ Ⓓ
	3	Ⓐ Ⓑ Ⓒ Ⓓ	13	Ⓐ Ⓑ Ⓒ Ⓓ	23	Ⓐ Ⓑ Ⓒ Ⓓ	33	Ⓐ Ⓑ Ⓒ Ⓓ	3	Ⓐ Ⓑ Ⓒ Ⓓ			3	Ⓐ Ⓑ Ⓒ Ⓓ	13	Ⓐ Ⓑ Ⓒ Ⓓ	23	Ⓐ Ⓑ Ⓒ Ⓓ
	4	Ⓐ Ⓑ Ⓒ Ⓓ	14	Ⓐ Ⓑ Ⓒ Ⓓ	24	Ⓐ Ⓑ Ⓒ Ⓓ	34	Ⓐ Ⓑ Ⓒ Ⓓ	4	Ⓐ Ⓑ Ⓒ Ⓓ			4	Ⓐ Ⓑ Ⓒ Ⓓ	14	Ⓐ Ⓑ Ⓒ Ⓓ	24	Ⓐ Ⓑ Ⓒ Ⓓ
	5	Ⓐ Ⓑ Ⓒ Ⓓ	15	Ⓐ Ⓑ Ⓒ Ⓓ	25	Ⓐ Ⓑ Ⓒ Ⓓ	35	Ⓐ Ⓑ Ⓒ Ⓓ	5	Ⓐ Ⓑ Ⓒ Ⓓ			5	Ⓐ Ⓑ Ⓒ Ⓓ	15	Ⓐ Ⓑ Ⓒ Ⓓ	25	Ⓐ Ⓑ Ⓒ Ⓓ
	6	Ⓐ Ⓑ Ⓒ Ⓓ	16	Ⓐ Ⓑ Ⓒ Ⓓ	26	Ⓐ Ⓑ Ⓒ Ⓓ	36	Ⓐ Ⓑ Ⓒ Ⓓ	6	Ⓐ Ⓑ Ⓒ Ⓓ			6	Ⓐ Ⓑ Ⓒ Ⓓ	16	Ⓐ Ⓑ Ⓒ Ⓓ	26	Ⓐ Ⓑ Ⓒ Ⓓ
	7	Ⓐ Ⓑ Ⓒ Ⓓ	17	Ⓐ Ⓑ Ⓒ Ⓓ	27	Ⓐ Ⓑ Ⓒ Ⓓ	37	Ⓐ Ⓑ Ⓒ Ⓓ	7	Ⓐ Ⓑ Ⓒ Ⓓ			7	Ⓐ Ⓑ Ⓒ Ⓓ	17	Ⓐ Ⓑ Ⓒ Ⓓ		
	8	Ⓐ Ⓑ Ⓒ Ⓓ	18	Ⓐ Ⓑ Ⓒ Ⓓ	28	Ⓐ Ⓑ Ⓒ Ⓓ	38	Ⓐ Ⓑ Ⓒ Ⓓ	8	Ⓐ Ⓑ Ⓒ Ⓓ			8	Ⓐ Ⓑ Ⓒ Ⓓ	18	Ⓐ Ⓑ Ⓒ Ⓓ		
	9	Ⓐ Ⓑ Ⓒ Ⓓ	19	Ⓐ Ⓑ Ⓒ Ⓓ	29	Ⓐ Ⓑ Ⓒ Ⓓ	39	Ⓐ Ⓑ Ⓒ Ⓓ	9	Ⓐ Ⓑ Ⓒ Ⓓ			9	Ⓐ Ⓑ Ⓒ Ⓓ	19	Ⓐ Ⓑ Ⓒ Ⓓ		
	10	Ⓐ Ⓑ Ⓒ Ⓓ	20	Ⓐ Ⓑ Ⓒ Ⓓ	30	Ⓐ Ⓑ Ⓒ Ⓓ	40	Ⓐ Ⓑ Ⓒ Ⓓ	10	Ⓐ Ⓑ Ⓒ Ⓓ			10	Ⓐ Ⓑ Ⓒ Ⓓ	20	Ⓐ Ⓑ Ⓒ Ⓓ		

キリトリ

キリトリ

Final Test 解答用紙

LISTENING SECTION

Part 1		Part 2						Part 3						Part 4					
No.	ANSWER A B C D	No.	ANSWER A B C	No.	ANSWER A B C	No.	ANSWER A B C	No.	ANSWER A B C D	No.	ANSWER A B C D	No.	ANSWER A B C D	No.	ANSWER A B C D	No.	ANSWER A B C D	No.	ANSWER A B C D
1	Ⓐ Ⓑ Ⓒ Ⓓ	11	Ⓐ Ⓑ Ⓒ	21	Ⓐ Ⓑ Ⓒ	31	Ⓐ Ⓑ Ⓒ	41	Ⓐ Ⓑ Ⓒ Ⓓ	51	Ⓐ Ⓑ Ⓒ Ⓓ	61	Ⓐ Ⓑ Ⓒ Ⓓ	71	Ⓐ Ⓑ Ⓒ Ⓓ	81	Ⓐ Ⓑ Ⓒ Ⓓ	91	Ⓐ Ⓑ Ⓒ Ⓓ
2	Ⓐ Ⓑ Ⓒ Ⓓ	12	Ⓐ Ⓑ Ⓒ	22	Ⓐ Ⓑ Ⓒ	32	Ⓐ Ⓑ Ⓒ	42	Ⓐ Ⓑ Ⓒ Ⓓ	52	Ⓐ Ⓑ Ⓒ Ⓓ	62	Ⓐ Ⓑ Ⓒ Ⓓ	72	Ⓐ Ⓑ Ⓒ Ⓓ	82	Ⓐ Ⓑ Ⓒ Ⓓ	92	Ⓐ Ⓑ Ⓒ Ⓓ
3	Ⓐ Ⓑ Ⓒ Ⓓ	13	Ⓐ Ⓑ Ⓒ	23	Ⓐ Ⓑ Ⓒ	33	Ⓐ Ⓑ Ⓒ	43	Ⓐ Ⓑ Ⓒ Ⓓ	53	Ⓐ Ⓑ Ⓒ Ⓓ	63	Ⓐ Ⓑ Ⓒ Ⓓ	73	Ⓐ Ⓑ Ⓒ Ⓓ	83	Ⓐ Ⓑ Ⓒ Ⓓ	93	Ⓐ Ⓑ Ⓒ Ⓓ
4	Ⓐ Ⓑ Ⓒ Ⓓ	14	Ⓐ Ⓑ Ⓒ	24	Ⓐ Ⓑ Ⓒ	34	Ⓐ Ⓑ Ⓒ	44	Ⓐ Ⓑ Ⓒ Ⓓ	54	Ⓐ Ⓑ Ⓒ Ⓓ	64	Ⓐ Ⓑ Ⓒ Ⓓ	74	Ⓐ Ⓑ Ⓒ Ⓓ	84	Ⓐ Ⓑ Ⓒ Ⓓ	94	Ⓐ Ⓑ Ⓒ Ⓓ
5	Ⓐ Ⓑ Ⓒ Ⓓ	15	Ⓐ Ⓑ Ⓒ	25	Ⓐ Ⓑ Ⓒ	35	Ⓐ Ⓑ Ⓒ	45	Ⓐ Ⓑ Ⓒ Ⓓ	55	Ⓐ Ⓑ Ⓒ Ⓓ	65	Ⓐ Ⓑ Ⓒ Ⓓ	75	Ⓐ Ⓑ Ⓒ Ⓓ	85	Ⓐ Ⓑ Ⓒ Ⓓ	95	Ⓐ Ⓑ Ⓒ Ⓓ
6	Ⓐ Ⓑ Ⓒ Ⓓ	16	Ⓐ Ⓑ Ⓒ	26	Ⓐ Ⓑ Ⓒ	36	Ⓐ Ⓑ Ⓒ	46	Ⓐ Ⓑ Ⓒ Ⓓ	56	Ⓐ Ⓑ Ⓒ Ⓓ	66	Ⓐ Ⓑ Ⓒ Ⓓ	76	Ⓐ Ⓑ Ⓒ Ⓓ	86	Ⓐ Ⓑ Ⓒ Ⓓ	96	Ⓐ Ⓑ Ⓒ Ⓓ
7	Ⓐ Ⓑ Ⓒ Ⓓ	17	Ⓐ Ⓑ Ⓒ	27	Ⓐ Ⓑ Ⓒ	37	Ⓐ Ⓑ Ⓒ	47	Ⓐ Ⓑ Ⓒ Ⓓ	57	Ⓐ Ⓑ Ⓒ Ⓓ	67	Ⓐ Ⓑ Ⓒ Ⓓ	77	Ⓐ Ⓑ Ⓒ Ⓓ	87	Ⓐ Ⓑ Ⓒ Ⓓ	97	Ⓐ Ⓑ Ⓒ Ⓓ
8	Ⓐ Ⓑ Ⓒ Ⓓ	18	Ⓐ Ⓑ Ⓒ	28	Ⓐ Ⓑ Ⓒ	38	Ⓐ Ⓑ Ⓒ	48	Ⓐ Ⓑ Ⓒ Ⓓ	58	Ⓐ Ⓑ Ⓒ Ⓓ	68	Ⓐ Ⓑ Ⓒ Ⓓ	78	Ⓐ Ⓑ Ⓒ Ⓓ	88	Ⓐ Ⓑ Ⓒ Ⓓ	98	Ⓐ Ⓑ Ⓒ Ⓓ
9	Ⓐ Ⓑ Ⓒ Ⓓ	19	Ⓐ Ⓑ Ⓒ	29	Ⓐ Ⓑ Ⓒ	39	Ⓐ Ⓑ Ⓒ	49	Ⓐ Ⓑ Ⓒ Ⓓ	59	Ⓐ Ⓑ Ⓒ Ⓓ	69	Ⓐ Ⓑ Ⓒ Ⓓ	79	Ⓐ Ⓑ Ⓒ Ⓓ	89	Ⓐ Ⓑ Ⓒ Ⓓ	99	Ⓐ Ⓑ Ⓒ Ⓓ
10	Ⓐ Ⓑ Ⓒ Ⓓ	20	Ⓐ Ⓑ Ⓒ	30	Ⓐ Ⓑ Ⓒ	40	Ⓐ Ⓑ Ⓒ	50	Ⓐ Ⓑ Ⓒ Ⓓ	60	Ⓐ Ⓑ Ⓒ Ⓓ	70	Ⓐ Ⓑ Ⓒ Ⓓ	80	Ⓐ Ⓑ Ⓒ Ⓓ	90	Ⓐ Ⓑ Ⓒ Ⓓ	100	Ⓐ Ⓑ Ⓒ Ⓓ

READING SECTION

Part 5								Part 6				Part 7							
No.	ANSWER A B C D	No.	ANSWER A B C D	No.	ANSWER A B C D	No.	ANSWER A B C D	No.	ANSWER A B C D	No.	ANSWER A B C D	No.	ANSWER A B C D	No.	ANSWER A B C D	No.	ANSWER A B C D	No.	ANSWER A B C D
101	Ⓐ Ⓑ Ⓒ Ⓓ	111	Ⓐ Ⓑ Ⓒ Ⓓ	121	Ⓐ Ⓑ Ⓒ Ⓓ	131	Ⓐ Ⓑ Ⓒ Ⓓ	141	Ⓐ Ⓑ Ⓒ Ⓓ	151	Ⓐ Ⓑ Ⓒ Ⓓ	161	Ⓐ Ⓑ Ⓒ Ⓓ	171	Ⓐ Ⓑ Ⓒ Ⓓ	181	Ⓐ Ⓑ Ⓒ Ⓓ	191	Ⓐ Ⓑ Ⓒ Ⓓ
102	Ⓐ Ⓑ Ⓒ Ⓓ	112	Ⓐ Ⓑ Ⓒ Ⓓ	122	Ⓐ Ⓑ Ⓒ Ⓓ	132	Ⓐ Ⓑ Ⓒ Ⓓ	142	Ⓐ Ⓑ Ⓒ Ⓓ	152	Ⓐ Ⓑ Ⓒ Ⓓ	162	Ⓐ Ⓑ Ⓒ Ⓓ	172	Ⓐ Ⓑ Ⓒ Ⓓ	182	Ⓐ Ⓑ Ⓒ Ⓓ	192	Ⓐ Ⓑ Ⓒ Ⓓ
103	Ⓐ Ⓑ Ⓒ Ⓓ	113	Ⓐ Ⓑ Ⓒ Ⓓ	123	Ⓐ Ⓑ Ⓒ Ⓓ	133	Ⓐ Ⓑ Ⓒ Ⓓ	143	Ⓐ Ⓑ Ⓒ Ⓓ	153	Ⓐ Ⓑ Ⓒ Ⓓ	163	Ⓐ Ⓑ Ⓒ Ⓓ	173	Ⓐ Ⓑ Ⓒ Ⓓ	183	Ⓐ Ⓑ Ⓒ Ⓓ	193	Ⓐ Ⓑ Ⓒ Ⓓ
104	Ⓐ Ⓑ Ⓒ Ⓓ	114	Ⓐ Ⓑ Ⓒ Ⓓ	124	Ⓐ Ⓑ Ⓒ Ⓓ	134	Ⓐ Ⓑ Ⓒ Ⓓ	144	Ⓐ Ⓑ Ⓒ Ⓓ	154	Ⓐ Ⓑ Ⓒ Ⓓ	164	Ⓐ Ⓑ Ⓒ Ⓓ	174	Ⓐ Ⓑ Ⓒ Ⓓ	184	Ⓐ Ⓑ Ⓒ Ⓓ	194	Ⓐ Ⓑ Ⓒ Ⓓ
105	Ⓐ Ⓑ Ⓒ Ⓓ	115	Ⓐ Ⓑ Ⓒ Ⓓ	125	Ⓐ Ⓑ Ⓒ Ⓓ	135	Ⓐ Ⓑ Ⓒ Ⓓ	145	Ⓐ Ⓑ Ⓒ Ⓓ	155	Ⓐ Ⓑ Ⓒ Ⓓ	165	Ⓐ Ⓑ Ⓒ Ⓓ	175	Ⓐ Ⓑ Ⓒ Ⓓ	185	Ⓐ Ⓑ Ⓒ Ⓓ	195	Ⓐ Ⓑ Ⓒ Ⓓ
106	Ⓐ Ⓑ Ⓒ Ⓓ	116	Ⓐ Ⓑ Ⓒ Ⓓ	126	Ⓐ Ⓑ Ⓒ Ⓓ	136	Ⓐ Ⓑ Ⓒ Ⓓ	146	Ⓐ Ⓑ Ⓒ Ⓓ	156	Ⓐ Ⓑ Ⓒ Ⓓ	166	Ⓐ Ⓑ Ⓒ Ⓓ	176	Ⓐ Ⓑ Ⓒ Ⓓ	186	Ⓐ Ⓑ Ⓒ Ⓓ	196	Ⓐ Ⓑ Ⓒ Ⓓ
107	Ⓐ Ⓑ Ⓒ Ⓓ	117	Ⓐ Ⓑ Ⓒ Ⓓ	127	Ⓐ Ⓑ Ⓒ Ⓓ	137	Ⓐ Ⓑ Ⓒ Ⓓ	147	Ⓐ Ⓑ Ⓒ Ⓓ	157	Ⓐ Ⓑ Ⓒ Ⓓ	167	Ⓐ Ⓑ Ⓒ Ⓓ	177	Ⓐ Ⓑ Ⓒ Ⓓ	187	Ⓐ Ⓑ Ⓒ Ⓓ	197	Ⓐ Ⓑ Ⓒ Ⓓ
108	Ⓐ Ⓑ Ⓒ Ⓓ	118	Ⓐ Ⓑ Ⓒ Ⓓ	128	Ⓐ Ⓑ Ⓒ Ⓓ	138	Ⓐ Ⓑ Ⓒ Ⓓ	148	Ⓐ Ⓑ Ⓒ Ⓓ	158	Ⓐ Ⓑ Ⓒ Ⓓ	168	Ⓐ Ⓑ Ⓒ Ⓓ	178	Ⓐ Ⓑ Ⓒ Ⓓ	188	Ⓐ Ⓑ Ⓒ Ⓓ	198	Ⓐ Ⓑ Ⓒ Ⓓ
109	Ⓐ Ⓑ Ⓒ Ⓓ	119	Ⓐ Ⓑ Ⓒ Ⓓ	129	Ⓐ Ⓑ Ⓒ Ⓓ	139	Ⓐ Ⓑ Ⓒ Ⓓ	149	Ⓐ Ⓑ Ⓒ Ⓓ	159	Ⓐ Ⓑ Ⓒ Ⓓ	169	Ⓐ Ⓑ Ⓒ Ⓓ	179	Ⓐ Ⓑ Ⓒ Ⓓ	189	Ⓐ Ⓑ Ⓒ Ⓓ	199	Ⓐ Ⓑ Ⓒ Ⓓ
110	Ⓐ Ⓑ Ⓒ Ⓓ	120	Ⓐ Ⓑ Ⓒ Ⓓ	130	Ⓐ Ⓑ Ⓒ Ⓓ	140	Ⓐ Ⓑ Ⓒ Ⓓ	150	Ⓐ Ⓑ Ⓒ Ⓓ	160	Ⓐ Ⓑ Ⓒ Ⓓ	170	Ⓐ Ⓑ Ⓒ Ⓓ	180	Ⓐ Ⓑ Ⓒ Ⓓ	190	Ⓐ Ⓑ Ⓒ Ⓓ	200	Ⓐ Ⓑ Ⓒ Ⓓ

掲載写真クレジット一覧

《本冊》

p.12 例 1 © iStockphoto.com/apixel
例 2 © YuliaB - Fotolia.com
p.14 © Olcha - Fotolia.com

Training

p.16 1 © iStockphoto.com/Gautier Willaume
2 © aigarsr - Fotolia.com
3 © Tomoyuki Hosoda
4 © Tomoyuki Hosoda
5 © Alliance - Fotolia.com
6 © simon gurney - Fotolia.com
7 © iStockphoto.com/Britta Kasholm-Tengve
8 © xy - Fotolia.com
9 © frog-travel - Fotolia.com
10 © Tomoyuki Hosoda
11 © picsfive - Fotolia.com
12 © Tomoyuki Hosoda
13 © Tomoyuki Hosoda
14 © Tomoyuki Hosoda
15 © Frédéric Prochasson - Fotolia.com
p.17 16 © iStockphoto.com/NicoElNino
17 © iStockphoto.com/Anne Clark
18 © WavebreakmediaMicro - Fotolia.com
19 © AVAVA - Fotolia.com
20 © Kasia Bialasiewicz - Fotolia.com
21 © auremar - Fotolia.com
22 © auremar - Fotolia.com
23 © Tupungato - Fotolia.com
24 © jedi-master - Fotolia.com
25 © Kyoko Hasegawa
26 © iStockphoto.com/photogl
27 © Tomoyuki Hosoda
28 © Jose Ignacio Soto - Fotolia.com
29 © Tomoyuki Hosoda
30 © pr2is - Fotolia.com
31 © Galyna Andrushko - Fotolia.com
32 © Tomoyuki Hosoda
33 © iStockphoto.com/Ruvan Boshoff
p.18 34 © vvoe - Fotolia.com
35 © iStockphoto.com/kali9
36 © kazoka303030 - Fotolia.com
37 © iStockphoto.com/Christopher Hudson
38 © Kasia Bialasiewicz - Fotolia.com
39 © Tomoyuki Hosoda
40 © Tomoyuki Hosoda
41 © Tomoyuki Hosoda
42 © moonrise - Fotolia.com
43 © iStockphoto.com/ahmet naim danışoğlu
44 © iStockphoto.com/Izabela Habur
45 © WavebreakmediaMicro - Fotolia.com
46 © Dmitry Vereshchagin - Fotolia.com
47 © Gabi Moisa - Fotolia.com
48 © WavebreakMediaMicro - Fotolia.com
49 © Oleg Kulakov - Fotolia.com
50 © Piano107 - Fotolia.com

Practice Test

p.23 1 © grthirteen - Fotolia.com
2 © endostock - Fotolia.com
p.24 3 © Kyoko Hasegawa
4 © Carson Liu - Fotolia.com
p.25 5 © maexchensfotos - Fotolia.com
6 © nikomi - Fotolia.com
p.26 7 © Piotr Wawrzyniuk - Fotolia.com
8 © iStockphoto.com/AVAVA
p.27 9 © iStockphoto.com/mediaphotos
10 © iStockphoto.com/Darren Mower

《別冊》

Final Test

p.3 1 © Alex Ishchenko - Fotolia.com
2 © Cyril Comtat - Fotolia.com
p.4 3 © bertys30 - Fotolia.com
4 © Kadmy - Fotolia.com
p.5 5 © Aaron Kohr - Fotolia.com
6 © poco_bw - Fotolia.com
p.6 7 © blickwinkel2511 - Fotolia.com
8 © Mariano Pozo Ruiz - Fotolia.com
p.7 9 © juniart - Fotolia.com
10 © Robert Kneschke - Fotolia.com

新TOEIC®テスト 990点攻略

別冊

Obunsh